Brilliant

Adobe®
Flash® Professional CS5

Steve Johnson

Perspection, Inc.

D1143633

Prentice Hall
is an imprint of

PEARSON

Harlow, England • London • New York • Boston • San F
Sydney • Tokyo • Singapore • Hong Kong • Seoul • T
Cape Town • Madrid • Mexico City • Amsterdam • Mur

Pearson Education Limited

Edinburgh Gate

Harlow

Essex CM20 2JE

England

and Associated Companies throughout the world

Visit us on the World Wide Web at:

www.pearsoned.co.uk

Original edition, entitled ADOBE® FLASH® PROFESSIONAL CS5 ON DEMAND, 1st edition, 0789744430 by JOHNSON, STEVE; PERSPECTION, INC., published by Pearson Education, Inc., publishing as Que/Sams, Copyright © 2010 Perspection, Inc.

ISBN: 978-0-273-74063-6

British Library Cataloguing-in-Publication Data

A catalogue record for this book is available from the British Library

10 9 8 7 6 5 4 3 2 1

14 13 12 11 10

Printed and bound in the United States of America

Brilliant Guides

What you need to know and how to do it

When you're working on your computer and come up against a problem that you're unsure how to solve, or want to accomplish something in an application that you aren't sure how to do, where do you look?? Manuals and traditional training guides are usually too big and unwieldy and are intended to be used as an end-to-end training resource, making it hard to get to the info you need right away without having to wade through pages of background information that you just don't need at that moment – and helplines are rarely that helpful!

Brilliant guides have been developed to allow you to find the info you need easily and without fuss and guide you through the task using a highly visual, step-by-step approach – providing exactly what you need to know when you need it!!

Brilliant guides provide the quick easy-to-access information that you need, using a detailed index and troubleshooting guide to help you find exactly what you need to know, and then presenting each task on one or two pages. Numbered steps then guide you through each task or problem, using numerous screenshots to illustrate each step. Added features include "See Also…" boxes that point you to related tasks and information in the book, whilst "Did you know?…" sections alert you to relevant expert tips, tricks and advice to further expand your skills and knowledge.

In addition to covering all major office applications, and related computing subjects, the *Brilliant* series also contains titles that will help you in every aspect of your working life, such as writing the perfect CV, answering the toughest interview questions and moving on in your career.

Brilliant guides are the light at the end of the tunnel when you are faced with any minor or major task!

Acknowledgements

Perspection, Inc.

Brilliant Adobe Flash Professional CS5 has been created by the professional trainers and writers at Perspection, Inc. to the standards you've come to expect from Que publishing. Together, we are pleased to present this training book.

Perspection, Inc. is a software training company committed to providing information and training to help people use software more effectively in order to communicate, make decisions, and solve problems. Perspection writes and produces software training books, and develops multimedia and Web-based training. Since 1991, we have written more than 100 computer books, with several bestsellers to our credit, and sold over 5 million books.

This book incorporates Perspection's training expertise to ensure that you'll receive the maximum return on your time. You'll focus on the tasks and skills that increase productivity while working at your own pace and convenience.

We invite you to visit the Perspection web site at:

www.perspection.com

Acknowledgements

The task of creating any book requires the talents of many hard-working people pulling together to meet impossible deadlines and untold stresses. We'd like to thank the outstanding team responsible for making this book possible: the writer, Steve Johnson; the editor, Adrian Hyde; the production editors, James Teyler and Beth Teyler; proofreader, Adrian Hyde; and the indexer, Katherine Stimson.

At Que publishing, we'd like to thank Greg Wiegand and Laura Norman for the opportunity to undertake this project, Cindy Teeters for administrative support, and Sandra Schroeder for your production expertise and support.

Perspection

About The Author

Steve Johnson has written more than 50 books on a variety of computer software, including Adobe Photoshop CS4, Adobe Flash CS4, Adobe Dreamweaver CS4, Adobe InDesign CS4, Adobe Illustrator CS4, Microsoft Windows 7, Microsoft Office 2007, Microsoft Office 2008 for the Macintosh, and Apple Mac OS X Snow Leopard. In 1991, after working for Apple Computer and Microsoft, Steve founded Perspection, Inc., which writes and produces software training. When he is not staying up late writing, he enjoys playing golf, gardening, and spending time with his wife, Holly, and three children, JP, Brett, and Hannah. Steve and his family live in Pleasanton, California, but can also be found visiting family all over the western United States.

Contents

Introduction

Welcome to *Brilliant Adobe Flash Professional CS5*, a visual quick reference book that shows you how to work efficiently with Flash CS5. This book provides complete coverage of basic to advanced Flash skills.

How This Book Works

You don't have to read this book in any particular order. We've designed the book so that you can jump in, get the information you need, and jump out. However, the book does follow a logical progression from simple tasks to more complex ones. Each task is presented on no more than two facing pages, which lets you focus on a single task without having to turn the page. To find the information that you need, just look up the task in the table of contents or index, and turn to the page listed. Read the task introduction, follow the step-by-step instructions in the left column along with screen illustrations in the right column, and you're done.

What's New

If you're searching for what's new in Flash CS5, just look for the icon: **New!**. The new icon appears in the table of contents and throughout this book so you can quickly and easily identify a new or improved feature in Flash. A complete description of each new feature appears in the New Features guide in the back of this book.

Keyboard Shortcuts

Most menu commands have a keyboard equivalent, such as Ctrl+P (Win) or ⌘+P (Mac), as a quicker alternative to using the mouse. A complete list of keyboard shortcuts is available on the Web at *www.perspection.com*.

How You'll Learn

How This Book Works

What's New

Keyboard Shortcuts

Step-by-Step Instructions

Real World Examples

Workshops

Adobe Certified Expert

Get More on the Web

Step-by-Step Instructions

This book provides concise step-by-step instructions that show you "how" to accomplish a task. Each set of instructions includes illustrations that directly correspond to the easy-to-read steps. Also included in the text are time-savers, tables, and sidebars to help you work more efficiently or to teach you more in-depth information. A "Did You Know?" provides tips and techniques to help you work smarter, while a "See Also" leads you to other parts of the book containing related information about the task.

Easy-to-follow introductions focus on a single concept.

Illustrations match the numbered steps.

Numbered steps guide you through each task.

See Also points you to related information in the book.

Did You Know? alerts you to tips, techniques and related information.

Real World Examples

This book uses real world example files to give you a context in which to use the task. By using the example files, you won't waste time looking for or creating sample files. You get a start file and a result file, so you can compare your work. Not every topic needs an example file, such as changing options, so we provide a complete list of the example files used throughout the book. The example files that you need for project tasks along with a complete file list are available on the Web at *www.perspection.com.*

Real world examples help you apply what you've learned to other tasks.

Workshops

This book shows you how to put together the individual step-by-step tasks into in-depth projects with the Workshop. You start each project with a sample file, work through the steps, and then compare your results with a project results file at the end. The Workshop projects and associated files are available on the Web at *www.perspection.com.*

Workshops

Introduction

The Workshop is all about being creative and thinking outside of the box. These workshops will help your right-brain soar, while making your left-brain happy, by explaining why things work the way they do. Exploring Flash's possibilities is great fun; however, always stay grounded with knowledge of how things work. Knowledge is power.

Getting and Using the Project Files

Each project in the Workshop includes a start file to help you get started with the project, and a final file to provide you with the results of the project so you can see how well you accomplished the task.

Before you can use the project files, you need to download them from the Web. You can access the files at *www.perspection.com* in the software downloads area. After you download the files from the Web, uncompress the files into a folder on your hard drive to which you have easy access from Flash.

Project 1: Creating and Customizing Scrollable Text

Skills and Tools: Flash component and ActionScripting

Flash comes with a set of built-in components—Button, CheckBox, Label, RadioButton, and UIScrollBar—that make it easy to add elements and controls to a Flash document. The components are available in the Components panel. There is a set of components for use with Flash documents (ActionScript 2.0) and another one for use with Flash documents (ActionScript 3.0). However, each set contains many of the same components. Some of the components include a skin, or look and feel, which you can customize to suit your own artistic nature.

The Project

In this project, you'll learn how to create scrollable text using the UIScrollBar component, and then customize the component.

The Process

1 Open Flash CS5, create a new document (3.0), and then save it as scroll_text_component.fla.

*The **Workshops** walk you through in-depth projects to help you put Flash to work.*

Adobe Certified Expert

This book prepares you fully for the Adobe Certified Expert (ACE) exam for Adobe Flash CS5. Each Adobe Certified Expert certification level has a set of objectives, which are organized into broader skill sets. To prepare for the certification exam, you should review and perform each task identified with an ACE objective to confirm that you can meet the requirements for the exam. Information about the ACE program is available in the back of this book. The Adobe Certified Expert objectives and the specific pages that cover them are available on the Web at *www.perspection.com.*

Adobe Certified Expert

About the Adobe Certified Expert (ACE) Program

The Adobe Certified Expert (ACE) program is for graphic designers, Web designers, systems integrators, value-added resellers, developers, and business professionals seeking official recognition of their expertise on Adobe products.

What Is an ACE?

An Adobe Certified Expert is an individual who has passed an Adobe Product Proficiency Exam for a specific Adobe software product. Adobe Certified Experts are eligible to promote themselves to clients or employers as highly skilled, expert-level users of Adobe software. ACE certification is a recognized worldwide standard for excellence in Adobe software knowledge. There are three levels of ACE certification: Single product certification, Specialist certification, and Master certification. To become an ACE, you must pass one or more product-specific proficiency exams and sign the ACE program agreement. When you become an ACE, you enjoy these special benefits:

+ Professional recognition
+ An ACE program certificate
+ Use of the Adobe Certified Expert program logo

What Does This Logo Mean?

It means this book will prepare you fully for the Adobe Certified Expert exam for Adobe Flash Professional CS5. The certification exam has a set of objectives, which are organized into broader skill sets. The Adobe Certified Expert objectives and the specific pages throughout this book that cover the objectives are available on the Web at *www.perspection.com.*

 FL CS5

529

Get More on the Web

In addition to the information in this book, you can also get more information on the Web to help you get up-to-speed faster with Flash CS5. Some of the information includes:

Transition Helpers

◆ **Only New Features.** Download and print the new feature tasks as a quick and easy guide.

Productivity Tools

◆ **Keyboard Shortcuts.** Download a list of keyboard shortcuts to learn faster ways to get the job done.

More Content

◆ **Photographs.** Download photographs and other graphics to use in your Flash documents.

◆ **More Content.** Download new content developed after publication.

You can access these additional resources on the Web at *www.queondemand.com* or *www.perspection.com*.

Keyboard Shortcuts

Adobe Flash CS5

If a command on a menu includes a keyboard reference, known as a keyboard short-cut, to the right of the command name, you can perform the action by pressing and holding the first key, and then pressing the second key to perform the command quickly. In some cases, a keyboard shortcut uses three keys. Simply press and hold the first two keys, and then press the third key. Keyboard shortcuts provide an alternative to using the mouse and make it easy to perform repetitive commands.

If you're searching for new keyboard shortcuts in Adobe Flash CS5, just look for the letter: N. The N appears in the Keyboard Shortcuts table so you can quickly and easily identify new or changed shortcuts.

Keyboard Shortcuts		
Operation/Tool	Windows	Macintosh
3D Rotation Tool (select in Toolbox)	W	W
3D Translation Tool (select in Toolbox)	G	G
Add Anchor Point Tool	=	=
Arrow/Selection tool (select in Toolbox)	V	V
Subselection tool	A	A
Arrow/Selection tool (temporary access)	Ctrl	⌘
Bone tool (select in Toolbox)	X	X
Bind tool (select in Toolbox)	Z	Z
Brush tool (select in Toolbox)	B	B
Constrain (ovals to circles, rectangles to squares, lines and rotation to 45-degree angles)	Shift+drag	Shift+drag
Convert corner point to curve point (Subselection tool)	Alt+drag	Option+drag
Convert Anchor Point Tool	C	C
Create new corner point (Arrow tool)	Alt+drag a line	Option+drag a line
Deco tool (select in Toolbox)	U	U
Delete Anchor Point Tool	-	-

Additional content is available on the Web.

Working Together with Adobe Programs

Introduction

Adobe programs are designed to work together so you can focus on what you need to do, rather than on how to do it. In fact, the Adobe programs share tools and features for your most common tasks so you can work uninterrupted and move seamlessly from one program to another. Adobe Creative Suite is an integrated collection of programs that work together to help you create designs in print, on the Web, or on mobile devices. When you install Adobe Creative Suite or a stand-alone Adobe program, you also get additional Adobe programs—Bridge, CS Live, ConnectNow, Device Central, Extension Manager, and ExtendScript Toolkit—to help you perform specific jobs, such as locating, downloading, and modifying images for projects, managing files and program extensions and testing files for different mobile devices.

Adobe Bridge is a program that lets you view, open, modify, and manage images located on your computer from any Adobe Creative Suite program. Adobe Bridge is literally the glue that binds Adobe Creative Suite programs together into one cohesive unit with shared tools. Bridge allows you to search, sort, filter, manage, and process image files one at a time or in batches. You can also use Bridge or Mini Bridge to do the following: create new folders; rename, move, delete and group files; edit metadata; rotate images; create web galleries and contact sheets; and run batch commands. You can also import files from your digital camera and view file information and metadata.

What You'll Do

Explore Adobe Programs

Explore Adobe Bridge

Get Started with Adobe Bridge

Get Photos from a Digital Camera

Work with Raw Images from a Digital Camera

Work with Images Using Adobe Bridge

Set Preferences in Adobe Bridge

Automate Tasks in Adobe Bridge

Use Mini Bridge

Explore CS Live Services

Share My Screen

Review CS Documents

Explore Adobe Device Central

Check Content Using Adobe Device Central

Use Adobe Extension Manager

Additional content is available on the Web.

Getting Started with Flash CS5

Introduction

Flash is an application for developing rich content, user interfaces, and Web applications. Adobe Flash Professional CS5 allows designers and developers to integrate video, text, audio, and graphics into rich experiences that deliver superior results for interactive marketing and presentations, e-learning, and application user interfaces. Most major commercial Web sites have implemented Flash content because of its cross-platform consistency, rich graphics capabilities, and small file sizes.

After you create and fine-tune multimedia content in Flash, you can deliver it on the Web within a browser using the Flash Player. Flash Player is a software product developed by Adobe for browsers on the Macintosh and Windows. Flash is the world's most pervasive software platform, used by millions of professionals and reaching more than 97% of Web-enabled desktops worldwide, as well as a wide range of consumer electronic devices, such as PDAs and mobile phones. You can also deliver Flash content as a separate application using AIR or an application on an Apple iPhone.

Flash operates virtually the same on both Macintosh and Windows versions, except for a few keyboard commands that have equivalent functions. You use the [Ctrl] and [Alt] keys in Windows, and the ⌘ and [Option] keys on a Macintosh computer. Also, the term *popup* on the Macintosh and *list arrow* in Windows refer to the same type of option.

What You'll Do

Prepare to Install Flash

Install and Start Flash

View the Flash Window

Create a Project Plan

Build a Flash Project

Create a New Document

Create a New Document from a Template

Open an Existing Document

Change Document Properties

Work with Document Windows

Save a Document

Save a Document in Different Formats

Get Help While You Work

Get Online Updates and Support

Finish Up

Preparing to Install Flash

System Requirements

Before you can install Flash Professional CS5 and development content, you need to make sure your computer meets the minimum system requirements. You can create Flash content on Windows and Macintosh computers. As a Flash developer, you also need to be aware of the system requirements for viewers of your Flash movies in a browser using the Adobe Flash Player. Web users need to download and install the player in order to view and interact with Flash content. The Flash Player is free and widely distributed over the Web at *www.adobe.com*.

Some Flash CS5 features require the latest version of QuickTime. During the installation, use the *Recommended* installation type to install the required components. You can obtain the latest version of QuickTime at *www.quicktime.com*.

For Windows Computers

You need to have a computer with the following minimum configuration:

- Intel Pentium 4, Centrino, Xeon, or Core Duo processor or equivalent.

- 1 GB of RAM (2 GB recommended).

- 2.5 GB available disk space.

- 16-bit (thousands of colors), 1024 x 768 resolution.

- Microsoft Windows XP with Service Pack 3 or higher; Windows Vista with Service Pack 1, Windows 7.

- Internet or phone connection required for activation.

- QuickTime 7.x or higher; DirectX version 9.0c or higher.

For Macintosh Computers

You need to have a computer with the following minimum configuration:

- Multicore Intel-based Macintosh.

- 1 GB of RAM (2 GB recommended).

- 2.5 GB available disk space.

- 16-bit (thousands of colors), 1024 x 768 resolution.

- Mac OS X 10.5.x, or later.

- Internet or phone connection required for activation.

- QuickTime 7.x or higher.

For Viewers in a Browser

Your visitors need to have a computer with the Flash Player and the following minimum configuration:

- **For Windows 98/Me.** Internet Explorer 5.5, Netscape 7.x, Mozilla 1.x, Firefox 1.x, AOL 9, or Opera 7.11.

- **For Windows 2000.** Internet Explorer 5.x, Netscape 7.x, Mozilla 1.x, Firefox 1.x, CompuServe 7, AOL 9, or Opera 7.11.

- **For Windows 7/Vista/XP/Windows 2003 Server.** Internet Explorer 6.0, Netscape 7.x, Mozilla 1.x, CompuServe 7, Firefox 1.x, AOL 9, or Opera 7.11.

- **For Macintosh OS X 10.1.x - Mac X 10.4.x.** Safari 2.x, Internet Explorer 5.2, Netscape 7.x, Mozilla 1.x, Firefox 1.x, AOL for OS X, Opera 6, or Safari 1.x.

Installing Flash

To perform a standard application install, insert the Adobe Flash Professional CS5 installation disc into the drive on your computer, and then follow the on-screen instructions. Because the setup process is different for Macintosh OS X and Windows platforms, general steps are provided to help you get started, and the on-screen instructions will guide you through the rest. Make sure to have your serial number handy because you'll be asked to enter it during the installation process. If you're updating from a previous version of Flash, you'll be required to verify the older version with your serial number for the previous version. The Flash installation includes all the components you need, including the Flash Player 10, to develop Flash content. The Flash Player is software installed on a user's computer that allows them to view published Flash movies (SWFs) in a Web page or through the player.

Install Flash Professional CS5

1. Insert the Flash Professional CS5 DVD into your DVD ROM drive, or download the software online to your hard disk.

2. If necessary, double-click the DVD icon or open the folder with the downloaded software, and then double-click the setup icon.

3. Follow the on-screen instructions to install the product; the installer asks you to read and accept a licensing agreement, enter a serial number, indicate the language you want, enter or create an Adobe ID or skip the step, and specify where you want to install the software.

Did You Know?

Most Adobe applications can be downloaded. It's all very simple, you go to *www.adobe.com*, click the Products menu item, and then select the application you want to purchase. You will need a credit card (of course), and a lot of bandwidth.

Starting Flash

You can start Flash in several ways, depending on the platform you are using. When you start Flash, the computer displays a splash screen and then the Flash window. When you start a new Flash session or close all documents, a Welcome screen appears in the Document window, providing easy access links to open a document, open a recent item, create new documents, create new documents from template, and display online video tutorials to help you get started. You can also use links to access many Flash related Adobe Web sites, including Adobe CS Live Online Services (**New!**) and Adobe Flash Exchange, where you can download additional applications and information.

Start Flash in Windows

1 Click **Start** on the taskbar.

2 Point to **All Programs** (which changes to Back).

3 Point to an Adobe Collection CS5 menu, if needed.

4 Click **Adobe Flash Professional CS5**.

5 If you're starting Flash Professional CS5 for the first time, you might be prompted to specify the following:

◆ Enter or create an Adobe ID to register the product, click **Submit**, and then click **Done**.

The Flash Professional CS5 window opens, displaying the Welcome screen.

Did You Know?

You can hide the Welcome screen. On the Welcome screen, select the Don't Show Again check box.

You can set launch preferences to customize how Flash starts. Click the Flash (Mac) or Edit (Win) menu, click Preferences, click the General category, select an option from the On Launch list arrow, and then click OK.

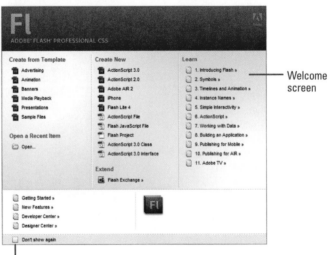

Welcome screen

Don't Show Again check box

Start Flash in Macintosh

1. Open the Applications folder (located on the main hard drive).

2. Double-click the **Adobe Flash CS5** folder.

3. Double-click the **Adobe Flash CS5** application icon.

4. If you're starting Flash CS5 for the first time, you might be prompted to specify the following:

    ◆ Enter or create an Adobe ID to register the product, click **Submit**, and then click **Done**.

    The Flash Professional CS5 window opens, displaying the Welcome screen.

Did You Know?

You can create a shortcut on the Macintosh. Drag and drop the Flash application to the bottom of the monitor screen, and then add it to the dock.

You can work in other programs as Flash starts up. When you start Flash, the Welcome screen no longer stays in front, so you can work in other programs (**New!**).

Shortcut for Adobe Flash CS5

For Your Information

Launching Flash and Opening a Document

You can also start Flash and open a Flash document at the same time. Double-click the Flash file icon in Windows Explorer (Win) or in a Macintosh folder (Mac). You can identify a Flash document by the file icon or FLA file extension. A file extension is a three-letter suffix at the end of a filename that identifies the file type for the operating system. The Macintosh doesn't need to use file extensions, but added the feature to promote cross platform use. In the Mac Operating System (OS) 10 or later, you have the option to show or hide file extensions. When you are working on both platforms, using file extensions on the Macintosh allows Windows and Flash to recognize and open the files.

Viewing the Flash Window

Panel Windows
Gives you access to authoring tools
and attribute settings for elements.

Welcome screen
Provides easy access links to create and open Flash documents.

Tools Panel
Contains drawing and other related tools to create and manipulate graphics.

Property Inspector
Displays information about the properties and attributes of tools and graphic elements.

Document Window
Displays open Flash
documents, which include an
Edit bar, Timeline and Stage.

Edit Bar
Displays what editing mode you
are working in and allows you to
switch scenes.

Timeline
Gives you a visual representation of every frame, layer and
scene in the document.

Stage
Provides a place to compose the
content for individual frames,
which includes drawing artwork
or arranging imported graphics.

Creating a Project Plan

Before you begin to create a movie in Flash, it's important to develop a project plan first. The project plan provides a **site map** for you to follow as you build your project in Flash. Without a project plan, you'll inevitably hit road blocks, which will cause you to waste time redesigning all of or portions of the movie. Planning a movie project involves determining its purpose, identifying the audience, logically developing the content, organizing the structure of the content, developing the layout and design, and identifying the delivery computer system. With a project plan in place, you'll be ready to create a movie in Flash.

Plan a Movie

Creating a movie can take a long time; it's worth the effort to plan carefully. The tendency for most first-time Flash developers is to start creating a movie without carefully planning the project. Before you begin, you need to develop and follow a plan. Otherwise, you might end up spending a lot of time fixing or completely changing parts of the movie, which you could have avoided from the beginning. You need to figure out the goal of the project, the look and feel of your production, its length and size, how it will interact with the viewer, and how and for whom it will be distributed.

When planning a movie, it's important to accomplish the following:

Determine the purpose

Is it for training? Sales? Entertainment? Informing? The answer will determine the types of features you may want to include or exclude in the movie. If the purpose is to create a training site, you might want to include simple navigation, easy-to-use instructional material, and a help system. On the other hand, if the purpose is to create a sales promotion, you might want to include eye-catching graphics, videos, and audio to get users' attention and draw them into the presentation.

Identify the audience

How you create your movie will depend on how you classify the intended audience. If the intended audience consists of novice computer users, you will have to concentrate on making the navigational controls and layout as simple to use as possible. If the users are experienced computer users, you can include more advanced features and interactions.

Develop the content and organize the structure

The most beneficial planning tools for the multimedia developer are the script and schematic flowchart. The script tells the story of your movie production in text form. Just like in the movies, a script is used to describe each section, to list audio or video, and to provide a basis for the text that will appear onscreen. Schematic flowcharts are the best way to sketch the navigational structure of a movie and make sure that each of the sections is properly connected. After you have the script and schematic flowchart mapped out on paper, you will quickly see the correlation between what you have developed and what you will begin to set up in Flash.

Develop the layout and design of the movie

The storyboard tells the story of your movie in visual form. It helps you design the layout of each screen in your movie. The storyboard follows the script and develops visual frames of the movie's main transitional points, which help you develop the Flash media elements you will use to create your movie. A storyboard can take a long time to develop, but the media elements you assemble and create in the process will shorten the overall development time. As you develop your layout and design, be sure to keep:

- ◆ Navigation easy to understand and consistent from page to page, such as navigation bars or drop-down menus
- ◆ Text easy to read
- ◆ Sound and animation limited
- ◆ Movie file sizes as small as possible for fast downloads. Break up large files into small ones for easy management
- ◆ Color consistent and appropriate for the audience
- ◆ Content accessible to users with visual or auditory impairments

Identify the delivery computer system and browser to be used for playback

Some computers are more up-to-date than others. You need to determine the minimum computer hardware and software requirements in which your movie will be delivered. The hardware and software requirements will determine what types of media you can use and how the movie will play back.

Some hardware requirements you need to consider for the delivery computer system are (1) CPU (central processing unit), which determines the speed with which your computer can compute data; (2) RAM (system memory), which determines how fast files load and how smoothly they run; (3) Sound cards, which determine if you can use sound files; (4) Video cards, which determine the quality and speed of the graphic and video display, and (5) Monitor resolution, which determines the color display (number of available colors), size (1024 x 768 is typical, while 1440 x 900 is becoming more and more available), and overall look of your movie.

Some software requirements you need to consider are the operating system version and supported browser type and version. See "Preparing to Install Flash" on page 2 for specific details about these requirements.

Sample script

Sample flowchart

Building a Flash Project

After you develop a project plan, you can use Flash to create a movie according to the plan. Creating a movie involves six main steps: setting up movie properties, assembling media elements, positioning the media elements on the Stage and sequencing them in the Timeline, adding custom functionality and interactive elements, previewing and testing the movie, and finally publishing or exporting the movie for distribution.

Build a Movie with Flash

Before you start creating a movie using Flash based on your project plan, it's important to understand the process of developing Flash software. The basic steps for developing interactive multimedia software with Flash are listed below.

Step 1: Set up document properties

Before you start a Flash project, you need to create a new document and set up initial document properties, such as the user's viewable screen size, for how your movie looks and operates. It is important to specify document property settings that affect the entire movie at the beginning of the project, such as how colors are defined and the size and location of the Stage, so you don't have to redesign the movie later.

Step 2: Create or import media elements

Media elements include graphics, images, buttons, videos, sounds, and text. You can create new media elements in Flash or import ones that have already been developed. Flash provides several tools for creating media elements, including shape and paint tools, and text creation tools. You can also add media elements from the Library, a media storage area. Media elements are either static or dynamic. **Static** media is an element, such as

text or graphics, created or imported into a movie that doesn't change unless the author makes the change and republishes the movie. **Dynamic** media is an element, such as data, MP3 sound, a JPEG image, or Flash Live Video (FLV) video, stored outside of the published movie and loaded when needed or changed by scripting, which makes updating easy, keeps file sizes down, and provides personalized information to the user.

Step 3: Position the elements on the Stage and sequence them in the Timeline

The Stage is the viewing area you use to display where media elements appear in a movie, and the Timeline is the area you use to organize what you want to occur at the time and duration you specify. You use the Stage to create the look and feel for your production; you use the Stage and Timeline together to arrange the media elements in space and time. The Stage represents the media elements' position in space (where) and the Timeline represents the media elements' position in time (when).

Step 4: Add navigational components, interactive behaviors, and motion effects

Scripting allows you to add custom functionality to your movie, such as moving objects on the Stage, formatting text, storing and managing information, performing mathematical operations, and controlling the movie in response to specific conditions and events, such as a mouse click. In Flash, scripts are written in ActionScript, a Flash-specific programming language. To help you get started scripting and save you some time, Flash comes with built-in components, and scripts called **behaviors**. **Components** are elements you can use to quickly create a user interface. For example, components can include buttons, arrows, or other navigation elements that move the viewer to different parts of a movie or to different locations on the Web. After you add a component, you can use behaviors to add functionality to the component to make it do what you want. In addition to behaviors, you can use built-in Timeline effects to add motion to elements. As you build in movie navigation and organization, it's good design to break up large projects into smaller movies, which can be quickly accessed from a main movie. This keeps Internet download times to a minimum, and it makes projects easier to update, and more manageable for a team to produce.

Step 5: Preview and test the movie

After you create your project, you use one of the Test Movie commands to preview and test the movie to make sure it runs the way you want it to. It's important to test the functionality of your movie early and often during the development process to catch problems while they are still minor.

Step 6: Publish the document as a movie file for use over the Internet

When the movie runs the way you want it to, you can publish your production as a Flash movie that viewers can play on a Web page, using a browser with the Flash Player. Flash publishes the movie file (.swf) and creates an HTML file with information to display the movie file. Viewers can't change the movies in the SWF format; they can only play them.

Step 3: Position the elements on the Stage and sequence them in the Timeline

Step 4: Add navigational components, interactive behaviors, and motion effects

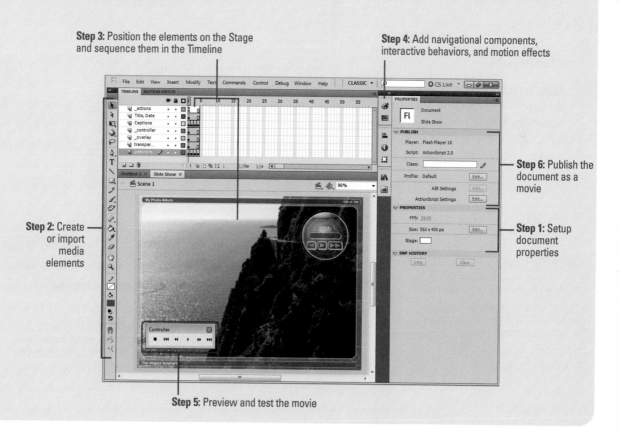

Step 2: Create or import media elements

Step 6: Publish the document as a movie

Step 1: Setup document properties

Step 5: Preview and test the movie

Creating a New Document

A file in Flash is called a **document**. Flash documents, which have the FLA filename extension, contain all the information required to develop, design, and test interactive content. Flash documents are not the same as the movies you play with the Flash Player. Instead, you publish your Flash documents as Flash movies, which have the SWF filename extension and contain only the information needed to display the movie. A new Flash document is based on the scripting language you want to use, either ActionScript 2.0 or ActionScript 3.0. You can create new documents in several ways including using the New command on the File menu and the New Document task pane. When you open a new Flash document, it's blank, ready for you to create or insert text, graphics, and other media content. By default, the first Flash document is titled Untitled1. Flash numbers new documents consecutively. You can open and work on as many new documents as you have memory (RAM) for.

Create a New Blank Document

1. Click the **File** menu, and then click **New**.

   TIMESAVER *Click Flash Document on the Welcome screen to create a new blank document.*

2. Click the **General** tab.

3. Click **ActionScript 3.0** or **ActionScript 2.0**.

   IMPORTANT *ActionScript 2.0 and ActionScript 3.0 are not compatible with each other. ActionScript 3.0 is recommended.*

   ◆ If you want to create a specific type of document, click the type you want.

4. Click **OK**.

Documents with the FLA extension

Document with other extensions

Did You Know?

You can open a new window with a copy of the current document. Create or open the Flash document you want to open in a new window, click the Window menu, and then click Duplicate Window.

For Your Information

Creating New Documents for Other Purposes

In addition to creating FLA documents in ActionScript 2.0 or 3.0 for the Flash Player, you can also create FLA documents to publish applications for **Adobe AIR 2.0** (for Mac, Windows, and Linux), **iPhone OS** (for iPhone, iTouch, and iPad devices) (**New!**), **Flash Lite 4** (a Flash player for less power and memory-constraint devices), and **Adobe Device Central** (for mobile devices).

Creating a New Document from a Template

Flash makes it easy to create many common documents based on a template. A **template** opens a Flash document (such as an animation or set of menus) with predefined formatting and placeholder text, graphics, and actionscripts. The templates make it easy to create common types of Flash projects. Flash comes with a set of templates, which includes the following categories (**New!**): Advertising, Animation, Banners, Media Playback, Presentations, and Sample Files. When you select a template category, a list of templates appears. Select a template to display a brief description. If you can't find the template you want, you can check the Adobe Flash Support Center Online Web site for more.

Create a New Document from a Template

1. Click the **File** menu, and then click **New**.

   TIMESAVER *Click a template category on the Welcome screen to open the New From Template dialog box, where you can select a template.*

2. Click the **Templates** tab.

3. Click a template category.

4. Click the template you want to use.

5. View the templates in the Preview box and read the description.

6. Click **OK**.

See Also

See "Saving a Document in Different Formats" on page 22 for information on saving a document as a template.

Opening an Existing Document

You can open an existing document file and the Flash program at one time, or you can open the file from within Flash. In Flash, you can use the Welcome screen, Open commands on the File menu, or Adobe Bridge CS5 (a stand-alone file management program that comes with Flash CS5) to open Flash documents, scripts, and movies in several formats. The default file format for Flash is FLA. However, the internal format of an FLA file is XFL (eXtensible Form Language) (**New!**). XFL allows you to exchange file content between programs, such as Adobe InDesign and Adobe After Effects. You can also open an XFL file as you would an FLA file. When you open a document, a tab appears across the top of the Document window, which you can click to display it.

Open a Flash Document

1. Click the **File** menu, and then click **Open**.

    TIMESAVER *Click Open or a recently opened Flash document name on the Welcome screen to open a document.*

2. To open a specific type of Flash file, click the **File as type** list arrow (Win), or the **File type** popup (Mac), and then select the file format you want.

3. Navigate to the drive or folder where the file is located.

4. Click the document file you want to open.

5. Click **Open**.

Did You Know?

You can view what is inside of an XFL file. An XFL file is essentially a ZIP package containing the XML and the assets for a FLA file. To view the actual XML and assets of the FLA file, change the .XFL file extension to .ZIP and unzip the folder.

Other Dynamics

Format	Description
ActionScript (.as)	A file to store ActionScript code for a Flash document.
XFL (.xfl, .xml)	A packaged XML representation of a FLA file along with the assets for that file.
Communications (.asc)	A file to store ActionScript code on a computer with Flash Communication Server.
FLA Document (.fla)	A Flash document you create and save in Flash authoring environment.
JavaScript (.jsfl)	A separate file with JavaScript code to add new functionality to Flash.
Flash Movie (.swf)	A compressed movie file you publish in the Flash authoring environment.

Open a Recently Opened Document

1. Click the **File** menu, and then point to **Open Recent**.

2. Click the document you want to open.

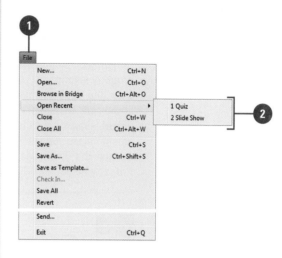

Browse Documents in Adobe Bridge

1. Click the **File** menu, and then click **Browse in Bridge**.

   Adobe Bridge CS5 opens, displaying files and folder on your computer.

2. Select a workspace display to view your files the way you want.

3. Navigate to the drive or folder where the Flash file is located.

4. To open a Flash file, double-click the file icon.

5. When you're done, click the **File** menu, and then click **Return to Adobe Flash**.

   TIMESAVER *Press ⌘+Option (Mac) or Ctrl+Alt+O (Win).*

Changing Document Properties

When you create a new Flash document or open an existing one, you need to set up or change the document properties. You set document properties at the beginning of the project to make basic decisions about how your movie looks and operates. You use the Document Properties dialog box or the Property Inspector to specify document property settings that affect the entire movie, such as the background color, the size and location of the Stage, the **frame rate**—the number of frames per second in which the computer plays an animation, and the unit of measure for rulers. These settings apply only to the current document unless you set Flash defaults to apply to every document. You can use the Properties command on the Window menu to display the Property Inspector, which appears vertically on the screen.

View Document Properties

1. Click the **Selection** tool on the Tools panel.

2. Click the **Window** menu, and then click **Properties** to open the Property Inspector.

   TIMESAVER *Press* ⌘+F3 *(Mac) or Ctrl+F3 (Win).*

3. View the document properties at the top of the Property Inspector:

   ◆ **Stage Size.** The current size appears in the button label.

   ◆ **Background Color.** The color of the Stage background.

   ◆ **Frame Rate.** The speed at which the movie runs.

Document name

Did You Know?

You can change the background color quickly in the Property Inspector. Open the Property Inspector, click the Background color box, and then select a color from the panel.

You can change the frame rate quickly in the Property Inspector. Open the Property Inspector, and then enter the number of animation frames to be displayed every second in the Frame Rate box.

Change Document Properties

1 Create or open a document.

2 Click the **Modify** menu, and then click **Document**.

TIMESAVER Click the Size button in the Property Inspector or double-click the frame-rate box in the Status bar on the Timeline.

3 To set the Stage dimensions, do one of the following:

◆ **Specify size in pixels.** Enter values in the Width and Height boxes. The default size is 550 x 400 pixels.

◆ **Set size to an equal space around content.** Click Contents.

◆ **Set size to the maximum print area.** Click Printer.

◆ **Set size to default setting.** Click Default.

4 Click the **Background Color** box, and then select a color.

5 Enter a frame rate. For most computers playing from the Web, 8 fps (frames per second) to 24 fps is adequate. The default is 24 fps.

6 To specify the unit of measure for rulers, click the **Ruler Units** popup, and then select an option.

7 To set properties for all new documents, click **Make Default**.

8 Click **OK**.

See Also

See "Displaying Rulers" on page 89 for information on using rulers.

See "Displaying Rulers" on page 89 for information on using rulers.

For Your Information

Improving Searchability by Internet Search Engines

When you add a title and description to Flash document properties, you're making it easier for Internet search engines to categorize the content in your Flash movie file (.swf). The title and description boxes are metadata properties for the SWF file format. The Internet uses metadata as a standard format for gathering and transferring data. When you enter a title and description, use descriptive keywords that reflect the type of user you want to attract to your Web site.

Working with Document Windows

When you open multiple documents, you can use the Window menu or tabs at the top of the Document window to switch between them. You can click a tab name to switch and activate the document. By default, tabs are displayed in the order in which you open or create documents. When you want to move or copy information between documents, it's easier to display several Document windows on the screen at the same time and move them around. However, you must make the window active to work in it. Each tab also includes a Close button to quickly close a document. If the document view is too small or large, you can change it to suite your needs.

Switch Between Multiple Documents

1. Open more than one document.

2. Click a tab name to switch to the document.

   TIMESAVER *Press Ctrl+Tab or Ctrl+Shift+Tab to cycle to the tab you want.*

   ◆ You can also click the **Window** menu, and then click a document name at the bottom of the menu.

Change the Document View

① Open more than one document.

② Click the **View Size** list arrow in the Edit bar, and then select a view size: **Fit in Window**, **Show Frame**, **Show All**, or a percentage.

◆ You can also enter a custom percentage in the View Size box, and then press Enter (Win) or Return (Mac).

③ To display the document window in the full screen, click the **Window** menu, and then click **Hide Panels**.

◆ To show panels, click the **Window** menu, and then click **Show Panels**.

TIMESAVER *Press F4 to toggle between Hide/Show Panels.*

panels hidden

Move Document Windows Around

① Open more than one document.

② Do either of the following:

◆ **Rearrange the order of tabbed documents.** Drag a windows' tab to a new location.

◆ **Dock or undock a document window.** Drag the window's tab out of the group or into the group.

② Undocked document window

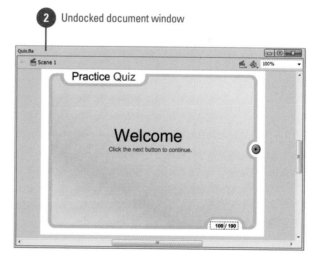

Saving a Document

When you save a Flash CS5 document within the authoring environment, the document is saved in the FLA format. If you want to display a document in the Adobe Flash Player, you need to publish or export the document in the SWF format. When you save a new document, you give it a name and specify the location in which to save the file. Name your documents clearly so you can easily locate them later. An unsaved Flash file displays an asterisk (*) after the name in the document name tab. To retain older versions of a document as you update it, use the Save As command and give each new version a new number with the old name, such as project1, project2 and so forth. In addition to saving files in the FLA format, you can also save flash content in the XFL (eXtensible Form Language) format (**New!**) as an uncompressed Flash document for use in other programs, such as Adobe InDesign and Adobe After Effects.

Save a Document in the Flash Format

1 Click the **File** menu, and then click **Save**.

If you are saving a document for the first time, continue. Otherwise, Flash saves the current document.

◆ To save a file with a different name, click the **File menu**, and then click **Save As**.

2 Type the new file name.

3 Navigate to the drive or folder location where you want to save the document.

4 Click **Save**.

5 If the file was created in Flash CS4, click **Save** or **Cancel** to convert it to Flash CS5.

Did You Know?

You can revert to the last saved version of a document. Click the File menu, and then click Revert.

You can save more than one document at a time. Click the File menu, and then click Save All.

Save a Document in the Flash CS5 Uncompressed Format

1. Click the **File** menu, and then click **Save As**.

2. Click the **Format** popup (Mac) or **Save As Type** list arrow (Win), and then click **Flash CS5 Uncompressed Document (*.xfl)**.

3. Type the new file name.

4. Navigate to the drive or folder location where you want to save the document.

5. Click **Save**.

   A folder with the Flash document file name is created in the specified location containing the XML (Extensible Markup Language) and the assets for the FLA file (**New!**).

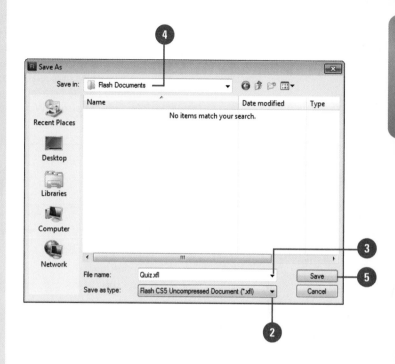

Did You Know?

You can move or copy a file quickly in a dialog box (Win). In the Open or Save As dialog box, right-click the file you want to move or copy, click Cut or Copy, open the folder where you want to paste the file, right-click a blank area, and then click Paste.

There is a difference between Save and Save As. When you save an existing document using the Save command, Flash performs a quick save, which appends new content to the existing file. When you save a new document using the Save As command, Flash performs a complete save, which saves and compacts the content into a small file.

For Your Information

Using an XFL Flash Uncompressed Document

In Flash CS5, you can save a Flash document (FLA) as a Flash uncompressed document (XFL) (**New!**). An XFL file is essentially a folder containing separate files, including XML files and other asset files for the FLA file. The XML (Extensible Markup Language) file contains the document information for your Flash project. XML uses a standard set of rules for encoding information so other programs can use it. You can use a Flash uncompressed document in the XFL format in other programs, such as Adobe InDesign and Adobe After Effects. If you use other development programs like Flypaper, you can use the XFL format to work on the document in both programs. To view the actual XML and assets of the FLA file, open the folder in Windows Explorer (Win) or Finder (Mac). Since all the assets for a FLA file are in a folder, you can also edit the individual files, such as an XML document, or a graphic file, in other programs, such a word-processing or graphics program. With live update (**New!**) with XFL files, you can edit any asset from an uncompressed XFL document while the document is open in Flash. When you finish editing and save an asset, the changes are automatically updated in Flash.

Saving a Document in Different Formats

A file type specifies the document format (for example, a template) as well as the program and version in which the file was created (for example, Flash CS5). You might want to change the type if you're creating a custom template or sharing files with someone who has an earlier version of Flash, such as Flash CS4. You use the Save As dialog box to change the file type for a document. The Format popup (Mac) or Save As Type list arrow (Win) displays a list of the available formats for Flash.

Save a Document in the Flash CS4 Format

1 Click the **File** menu, and then click **Save As**.

2 Click the **Format** popup (Mac) or **Save As Type** list arrow (Win), and then click **Flash CS4 Document (*.fla)**.

3 Type the new file name.

4 Navigate to the drive or folder location where you want to save the document.

5 Click **Save**.

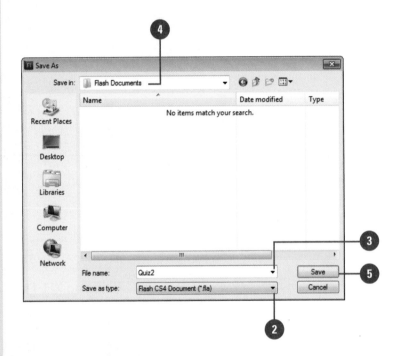

Did You Know?

You can delete a file in a dialog box (Win). In the Open or Save As dialog box, right click the file you want to delete, and then click Delete.

Save a Document as a Template

1 Click the **File** menu, and then click **Save as Template**.

2 If a warning dialog box appears, click **Save As Template**.

3 Type a name for the new template.

4 Click the **Category** list arrow, and then click a category template.

5 Type a description for the new template.

6 Click **Save**.

7 If the file was created in Flash CS4, click **Save** or **Cancel** to convert it to Flash CS5.

See Also

See "Creating a New Document from a Template" on page 13 for information on creating a new document from a Flash template.

Getting Help While You Work

At some time, everyone has a question or two about using a program. When you start Flash Help, the Adobe Community Help window opens (**New!**), displaying help categories and topics. You can search product help from Local Help, Community Help, or Adobe.com by using keywords or phrases or browsing through a list of categories and topics to locate specific information. Local Help accesses product help on your local computer, Community Help accesses product help online, and Adobe.com accesses related help information on Adobe.com. When you perform a search using keywords or phrases, a list of possible answers is shown from the search location with the most likely responses at the top. Along with help text, some help topics include links to text and video tutorials. In addition, comments and ratings from users are available to help guide you to an answer. You can add feedback and suggestions by signing in to Adobe.com using an Adobe ID.

Get Help Information

1. Click the **Help** menu, and then click **Flash Help**.

   TIMESAVER *Press F1 (Win) or* ⌘+/ *(Mac).*

   The Adobe Community Help window opens, displaying product help information.

2. If you want help with ActionScript, Flash Development, or other support resources, click the appropriate link.

3. Click Help categories (plus sign icons) until you display the topic you want.

   ◆ What's New. Click **What's new in Adobe Flash Professional CS5** under Using Flash Professional CS5.

4. Click the topic you want.

5. Read the topic, and if you want, click any links to get information on related topics or definitions.

6. When you're done, click the **Close** button (Win) or click the **Adobe Help** menu (Mac), and then click **Quit Adobe Help**.

Click to open help in a PDF

Click to collapse/expand panel

Search for Help Information

1 In Flash, on the Application bar, type one or more keywords in the Search box, and then press Enter (Win) or Return (Mac).

◆ You can also click the **Help** menu, and then click **Flash Help** to open Help and use the Search box.

The Adobe Community Help window opens, displaying a list of topics that match the keywords you entered in the Search box.

2 To search another CS product, click the **Select Product** list arrow, and then select a CS product.

3 To refine a search, click **Search Options** to expand it, and then select any of the following options:

◆ **Search Location.** Select Local Help, Community Help, or Adobe.com.

◆ **Filter Results.** For Adobe.com, select a filter option.

4 Click the link to the topic you want from the search list of results.

5 Click a link or scroll to display a topic, and then read the topic. If you want, click any links to get information on related topics or definitions.

◆ **Next and Previous Topics.** Click the **Previous** or **Next** button on the right side of the Help web page.

6 When you're done, click the **Close** button (Win) or click the **Adobe Help** menu (Mac), and then click **Quit Adobe Help**.

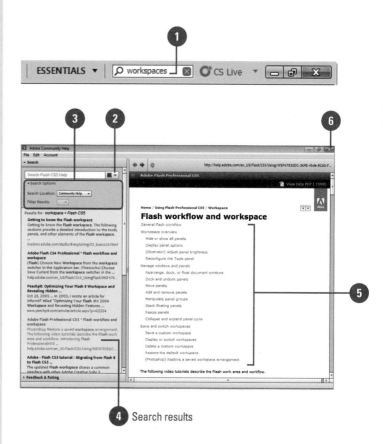

Search results

Flash Help Commands

Help Commands	Description
Flash Help	Access Flash Help window
Flash Support Center	Access Flash support on the Web
Adobe Product Improvement Program	Participate in the direction of future versions of Adobe products
Flash Exchange	Access Flash downloadable applications
Omniture	Access information about the Omniture company on the Web
Manage Extensions	Access Flash extension information
Adobe Online Forums	Access user conversations on the Web

Getting Online Updates and Support

Adobe offers a quick and easy way to update Flash CS5 and other CS5 related programs with any new software downloads directly from Flash using the Help menu. Adobe can notify you of updates in the menu bar (**New!**). If you need more detailed information about a Flash task or feature, you can find out the latest information on the Web from the Adobe Flash Support Center and Flash Exchange Web sites. The Adobe Flash Support Center provides technical notes, documentation updates, and links to additional resources in the Flash community, while the Adobe Flash Exchange allows you to download additional applications and commands that other Flash users have developed and posted to extend the functionality of Flash. Some of the posted items are free while other charge a fee. You can access the Flash Support Center and the Flash Exchange from within Flash using commands on the Help menu.

Get Product Updates Online

1. Click the **Help** menu, and then click **Updates**.

   Flash checks your software with the latest available version and automatically updates it.

2. To manually check, click the **Check For New Updates** button.

3. To change preferences, click **Preferences**, select the update options you want, and then click **Done**.

4. Click **Quit**.

Did You Know?

You can register to receive notices about upgrades and new products. If you haven't already registered during installation, click the Help menu, click Product Registration, and then follow the online instructions.

You can deactivate and activate Flash using the Help menu. If you have Flash installed on two computers, yet only have one license, you can use the Deactivate and Activate commands on the Help menu to go between the computers.

Get Online Support Information

1 Click the **Help** menu, and then click **Flash Support Center**.

Your Web browser opens, displaying the Adobe support Web site.

2 Search on the Web site for the help information you need.

3 When you're done, close your Web browser.

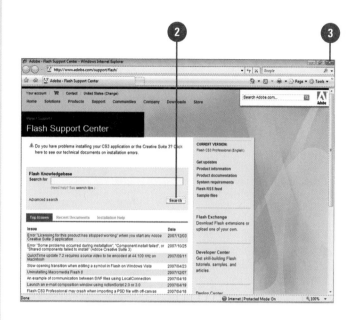

Get Resources from the Flash Exchange

1 Click the **Help** menu, and then click **Flash Exchange**.

Your Web browser opens, displaying the Adobe support Web site.

2 Search on the Web site for the help information you need, or click the **Product** popup, and then select a product to display the resource types you need.

3 Scroll through the list, and then follow the on-screen instructions to download and purchase (if necessary) the resources you want.

4 When you're done, close your Web browser.

Finishing Up

After you work on a document, you can close the document by closing the document or by exiting Flash. You should save the document before closing it. Exiting Flash closes the current document and the Flash program and returns you to the desktop. You can use the Exit command on the File menu (Win) or Quit Flash command on the Flash menu (Mac) to close a document and exit Flash, or you can use the Close button on the Flash Document tab. If you try to close a document without saving your final changes, a dialog box opens, asking if you want to do so.

Close a Document

1. Click the **Close** button on the Document tab, or click the **File** menu, and then click **Close**.

   TIMESAVER *Press ⌘+W (Mac) or Ctrl+W (Win) to close a document. Click the File menu, and then click Close All to close all open documents.*

2. If necessary, click **Yes** to save any changes you made to your open documents before the program quits.

Document tab Close button

Exit Flash

1. Choose one of the following:

   ◆ Click the **Flash** menu, and then click **Quit Flash** (Mac).

   ◆ Click the **Close** button, or click the **File** menu, and then click **Exit** (Win).

2. If necessary, click **Yes** to save any changes you made to your open documents before the program quits.

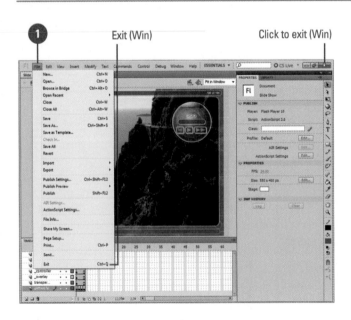

Exit (Win)

Click to exit (Win)

Working Within the Flash Environment

Introduction

Getting to know the Flash authoring environment makes you more effective and efficient as you create movies. You'll get to know the parts of the Flash window, which include the Timeline, Stage, panels, and Property Inspector.

The Tools panel, also known as the Toolbox, contains tools that you can use to draw, paint, select, and modify artwork. The Timeline represents the overall structure of a Flash document and controls the content. The Timeline consists of layers, frames, and scenes that make up a Flash document. Layers are like transparent sheets stacked on top of one another. Each layer can contain different images that appear on the Stage. A frame displays content at a specific moment on the Stage. The order in which frames appear in the Timeline determines the order in which they appear in the document. As you play a document, the playhead moves through the Timeline displaying the current frame with each layer on the Stage. If a project requires many animation sequences with hundreds of frames, you can organize the animations into scenes to make them easier to work with and manage. Below the Timeline is the Stage, which provides a place to compose the content for individual frames. Panels are windows that allow you to view, organize, and change elements and related options in a document. The Property Inspector is a specialized panel that allows you to change object-specific attributes and options.

Flash uses built-in keyboard shortcuts designed specifically for Flash. The built-in keyboard shortcuts are organized into sets, which you can duplicate and customize to create your own personalized set. Flash allows to you set preferences to customize the way you work in the program. As you design and develop a movie, you can print frames to review your work.

What You'll Do

Examine the Flash Window

Use the Timeline

Work with Layers

View and Organize Layers

Change Layer Properties

Use Guide Layers

Work with Frames

Work with Scenes

Use the Edit Bar and Main Toolbar

Resize Panels

Use the Tools Panel

Work with Panels

Dock and Undock Panels

Group and Ungroup Panels

Create a Workspace

Create Keyboard Shortcuts

Set Flash Preferences

Work with Page Setup

Print a Document

Examining the Flash Window

When you start Flash, the program window displays several windows of varying sizes you can use to create a movie. These windows include the Timeline/Stage, various panels, and the Property Inspector. Depending on your installation and previous program usage, not all of these windows may appear, or additional ones may be visible. You'll do the bulk of your work in Flash with these windows.

In Flash, windows appear in the work-space with a title bar, such as the Timeline window, or in a panel. A **panel** is a window you can collapse, expand, and group with other panels, known as a panel group, to improve accessibility and workflow. A panel appears with a shaded header bar, which includes the window title and additional options. A panel group consists of either individual panels stacked one on top of the other

Document Window
Displays open Flash documents, which includes a Timeline, Edit bar, and Stage.

Timeline
Gives you a visual representation of every frame, layer and scene in the document.

Search Box
Allows you to search Adobe Community Help online.

Tools Panel
Contains drawing and other related tools to create and manipulate graphics.

Panel Windows
Gives you access to authoring tools and attribute settings for elements.

Stage
Provides a place to compose the content for individual frames, which includes drawing artwork or arranging imported graphics.

Main Toolbar
Contains buttons for commonly used commands. Point to a button to display a Tooltip.

Property Inspector
Displays information about the properties and attributes of tools and graphic elements.

or related panels organized together with tabs, such as the Components panel, to navigate from one panel to another. The Flash window displays the menu bar at the top. The menu bar also contains a Workspace menu, Search box, CS Live menu, Close button, and resizing buttons.

A **menu** is a list of commands that you use to accomplish specific tasks. A **command** is a directive that accesses a feature of a program. Flash has its own set of menus, which are located on the menu bar along the top of the Flash window. On a menu, a check mark identifies a feature that is currently selected (that is, the feature is enabled or on). To disable (turn off) the feature, you click the command again to remove the check mark. A menu can contain several check-marked features. A bullet (Win) or diamond (Mac) also indicates that an option is enabled, but a menu can contain only one bullet-or diamond-marked feature per menu section. To disable a command with a bullet or diamond next to it, you must select a different option in the section on the menu.

When you perform a command frequently, it's faster, and sometimes more convenient, to use a shortcut key, which is a keyboard alternative to using the mouse. When a shortcut key is available, it is listed beside the command on the menu, such as ⌘+F3 (Mac) or Ctrl+F3 (Win) for the Properties command on the Window menu.

Flash (for Windows) also includes a Main toolbar. The **Main toolbar** contains buttons for the most frequently used commands. Clicking a button on a toolbar is often faster than clicking a menu and then clicking a command. When you position the pointer over a button, a tooltip appears, displaying the button name.

The **Tools panel** contains a set of tools you can use to create shapes, such as lines, rec-

tangles, rounded rectangles, and ellipses. You can fill shapes with a color, pattern, or custom tile. The shapes and buttons you create in Flash are saved as media elements in the layers.

The **Document window** displays open Flash documents, which include a Timeline, Edit bar, and Stage. Flash (for Windows) also includes tabs to make it easier to switch back and forth between documents. At the top of the Document window is the Edit bar. The Edit bar displays what editing mode you are working in, and allows you to switch scenes.

The **Timeline** organizes and controls media elements over a linear timeline in rows called channels and in columns called frames. The Timeline displays a movie's Timeline and monitors the playback frame-by-frame. A frame represents a single point in a movie. The Timeline includes layers that control different parts of the movie.

The **Stage** is the visible portion of a movie, on which you determine where your media elements appear. The Stage is the rectangle area below the Timeline where you place graphic content, including vector art, text boxes, buttons, imported bitmap graphics, or audio and video clips. You can define the properties of your Stage, such as its size and color.

The **Property Inspector** provides a convenient way to view and change attributes of any selected object or multiple objects on the Stage in your movie. After you select an object, relevant commands and associated fields for it appear in the Property Inspector. You can apply filters, such as gradient controls to text, buttons, and movie clips. In addition, you can display the Property Inspector horizontally (like previous versions of Flash) or vertically.

Using the Timeline

The Timeline represents the overall structure of a Flash document and controls the content. The Timeline consists of layers, frames, and scenes that make up a Flash document. Layers appear on the left side of the Timeline and frames contained in each layer appear in a row to the right of the layer. The Timeline header above the frames displays the frame numbers. At the bottom of the Timeline, a Status bar appears, displaying the current frame indicator, the current rate indicator, and the elapsed time indicator. Sometimes it is hard to work with frames in a small view in the Timeline. You can change the size of frames and display frames with tinted cells. In addition, you can display thumbnail previews of frame content, which is useful for viewing animations.

Change the Timeline Display

- To lengthen or shorten layer name fields, drag the bar separating the layer names and the frames in the Timeline.

- To heighten or shorten the Timeline, drag the bar separating the Timeline and the Stage.

- To hide or show the Timeline panel, click the gray bar to the right of the Timeline tab.

Drag edge to change height of Timeline.

Drag to change length of layer name fields.

Resize the Timeline Display

① Do one of the following:

- If the Timeline is docked to the program window, drag the bar separating the Timeline from the program window.

- If the Timeline is not docked to the program window, drag the size box in the lower right corner.

Drag to resize Timeline.

Change the Display of Frames in the Timeline

1. Click the **Frame View** button in the Timeline.

2. Select one of the following options from the list:

   ◆ To change the width of frame cells, click **Tiny**, **Small**, **Normal**, **Medium**, or **Large**.

   ◆ To display thumbnails of the content of each frame scaled to fit the Timeline frames, click **Preview**.

   ◆ To display thumbnails of each full frame, click **Preview In Context**.

   This is useful for viewing animation movement within their frames.

   ◆ To decrease the height of frame cell rows, click **Short**.

   ◆ To turn frame sequence tinting on and off, click **Tinted Frames**.

   ◆ To disregard audio in the Timeline, click **Scrub Audio** (**New!**).

   ◆ To close the current tab, click **Close**. To close all the tabs, click **Close Group**.

Preview in frame view

See Also

See "Working with Panels" on page 52 for information on using the Timeline panel.

Working with Layers

Layers are like transparent sheets stacked on top of one another. Each layer can contain different images that appear on the Stage. You can draw and edit objects on one layer without affecting objects on another layer. Layers in a document are listed in the left column of the Timeline. Before you can work with a layer, you need to select it, or make it active. A pencil icon next to a layer or layer folder indicates it is active. Only one layer can be active at a time, even though you can select more than one layer. A new document comes with one layer, but you can add more to organize content on the Stage. As you create multiple layers of related content, you can create layer folders to make it easier to manage the layers.

Create a New Layer

1. Click the layer or folder above which you want to insert a layer.

2. Click the **New Layer** button at the bottom of the Timeline.

   The new layer appears above the selected layer.

Did You Know?

Flash names layers in order based on the highest number. If you add Layers 2 and 3, and then delete Layer 2. The next time you add a layer, Flash names it Layer 4.

New layer   Active layer

Create a New Layer Folder

1. Click the layer or folder above which you want to insert a layer folder.

2. Click the **New Folder** button at the bottom of the Timeline.

   The new layer folder appears above the selected layer.

New layer folder

Rename a Layer or Folder

1. Double-click the name of a layer or folder.

2. Type a name.

3. Press Return (Mac) or Enter (Win).

Delete a Layer or Folder

1. Select the layer or folder you want to delete.

2. Click the **Delete** button at the bottom of the Timeline.

Did You Know?

There are several ways to select a layer. You can click the name of a layer or folder in the Timeline, click a frame in the Timeline of the layer you want to select, or select an object on the Stage that is located on the layer you want to select.

You can select multiple layers. To select contiguous layers or folders, click the first layer or folder, and then Shift+click the last layer or folder. To select noncontiguous layers or folders, ⌘+click (Mac) or Ctrl+click (Win) the layers or folders you want to select.

Viewing Layers

Flash includes controls (Eye, Lock, and Outline icons) in the layers section of the Timeline that allow you to quickly hide, show, lock, or unlock layers and layer folders, and display objects on a layer as colored outlines. Using colored outlines makes it easier to distinguish in which layer an object appears. When you hide a layer or folder with the Eye icon, a red X appears next to the name. When you lock a layer or folder with the Lock icon, a padlock appears next to the name. When you display layers as colored outlines with the Outline icon, a frame appears next to the name. When you change a folder, the controls affect all layers within a folder.

Show or Hide a Layer or Folder

1 Do one of the following:

◆ Click the Eye column to the right of the layer or folder to show or hide it.

◆ Click the **Eye** icon to show or hide all layers or folders.

◆ Option+click (Mac) or Alt+click (Win) in the Eye column to the right of a layer or folder to show or hide all other layers or folders.

Eye icon

Lock or Unlock Layers or Folders

1 Do one of the following:

◆ Click in the Lock column to the right of the layer or folder to lock or unlock it.

◆ Click the **Lock** icon to lock or unlock all layers or folders.

◆ Option+click (Mac) or Alt+click (Win) in the Lock column to the right of a layer or folder to lock or unlock all other layers or folders.

Lock icon

View the Contents of a Layer as Outlines

1 Do one of the following:

- ◆ Click the Outline column to the right of the layer's name to display its objects as outlines.

- ◆ Click the **Outline** icon to display objects on all layers as outlines.

- ◆ Option+click (Mac) or Alt+click (Win) in the Outline column to the right of a layer to display objects on all other layers as outlines.

Did You Know?

Hidden layers are visible when you publish a document. When you publish a Flash document as a SWF movie, hidden layers are visible in the Flash movie file.

See Also

See "Changing Layer Properties" on page 40 for information on changing the outline color.

View contents as outline

Outline icon

View contents not as outline

Outline column icon

Organizing Layers

In much the same way you organize files on your computer, you can use similar concepts to organize layers and layer folders in a document. You can expand or collapse a layer folder to show or hide its contents. You can also move a layer or folder into a layer folder or to another place in the layers list. Layer folders can contain layers and other layer folders. In addition, you can copy a layer or copy the contents of a layer folder.

Expand or Collapse a Layer Folder

1 Do one of the following:

◆ Click the triangle to the left of the folder name to expand or collapse the folder.

◆ Control+click (Mac) or right-click (Win) any layer, and then click **Expand All Folders** or **Collapse All Folders**.

1 Collapsed layer folder

Move a Layer or Layer Folder

◆ To move a layer or folder into a layer folder, drag the layer or folder to the destination layer folder name in the Timeline.

◆ To move a layer or folder to another location, drag the layer or folder to a new position in the Timeline.

Drag Controls layer to the Behind Scenes folder

Layers in the folder

Copy a Layer

1. Click the layer you want to select.
2. Click the **Edit** menu, point to **Timeline**, and then click **Copy Frames**.
3. Click the **New Layer** button.
4. Click the new layer to select it.
5. Click the **Edit** menu, point to **Timeline**, and then click **Paste Frames**.

Copy the Contents of a Layer Folder

1. If necessary, click the triangle to the left of the folder name to collapse it.
2. Click the folder layer to select the entire folder.
3. Click the **Edit** menu, point to **Timeline**, and then click **Copy Frames**.
4. Select the layer below where you want to copy the layer folder.
5. Click the **New Folder** button.
6. Click the new layer folder to select it.
7. Click the **Edit** menu, point to **Timeline**, and then click **Paste Frames**.

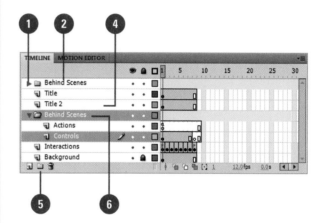

Changing Layer Properties

The Layer Properties dialog box makes it easy to changes several layer options at once. You can change a layer name, show or lock a layer, change a layer type or outline color, and modify the layer height to show more information in the Timeline. Setting layer properties of a folder automatically sets the properties for all the layers within that folder.

Change Layer Properties

1. Select the layer in the Timeline.

2. Click the **Modify** menu, point to **Timeline**, and then click **Layer Properties**.

3. Select from the following options:

   ◆ **Name.** Enter a new name.

   ◆ **Show.** Select this check box to show the layer.

   ◆ **Lock.** Select this check box to lock the layer or clear it to unlock the layer.

   ◆ **Type.** Select a layer option: Normal, Mask, Masked, Folder, or Guide.

   ◆ **Outline Color.** Click the Color box, and then select a color.

   ◆ **View Layer As Outlines.** Select this check box to view the layer as outlines.

   ◆ **Layer Height.** Click the list arrow, and then select a percentage to display more information in the Timeline.

4. Click **OK**.

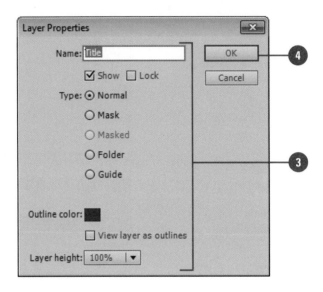

Layer Types

Layer	Description
Normal	The default layer type.
Mask	Mask layers hide and reveal portions of linked layers that lie directly beneath the mask layer.
Masked	Masked layers contain elements that can be hidden or revealed by a mask layer.
Folder	Folder layers allow you to organize layers.
Guide	There are two types of guide layers: guides and motion guides. Guides help you place and align objects on the Stage, motion guides designate a path that an animated object follows. Guided layers contain objects that follow an animation path. You need to link the guided layer to the motion guide.

Using Guide Layers

Guide layers help you draw and align objects on layers that appear on the Stage. After you create a guide layer, you can align objects on other layers to objects you create on the guide layer. You can make any layer a guide layer. You can also create a motion guide layer to control the movement of objects in a motion tweened animation.

Create a Guide Layer

1. Click the layer you want to convert to a guide layer.

2. Control+click (Mac) or right-click (Win) the selected layer, and then click **Guide**.

Did You Know?

You can change a guide layer back to a normal layer. Control (Mac) or right-click (Win) the selected layer, and then click Guide.

You can convert a guide layer to a motion guide layer. Drag a normal layer onto a guide layer.

See Also

See "Using Snap Align" on page 94 for information on snapping items you draw or drag to snap to lines or shapes.

Aligning objects using the guide layer.

Working with Frames

A **frame** displays content at a specific moment on the Stage. The order in which frames appear in the Timeline determines the order in which they appear in the document. The Timeline displays each frame in sequential order from 1 to the end of the document. As you play a document, the **playhead** moves through the Timeline displaying the current frame with each layer on the Stage. When you work with frames, you can select, insert, delete, and move frames in the Timeline. When you move frames in the Timeline, you can place them on the same layer or a different layer. If you want to display a specific frame in a document, you can move the playhead to the frame in the Timeline to display the frame content on the Stage. Another type of frame is called a keyframe. A keyframe defines a change in an animation or uses actions to modify a document.

Select One or More Frames

◆ To select one frame, click on the frame.

> **IMPORTANT** *If the Span Based Selection preference is turned on, clicking a frame selects the entire frame sequence between two keyframes.*

◆ To select multiple contiguous frames, click the first frame in the sequence, hold down Shift, and then click the last frame in the sequence.

◆ To select multiple noncontiguous frames, ⌘+click (Mac) or Ctrl+click (Win) the frames you want to select.

Did You Know?

You can center the Timeline on the current frame. Click the Center Frame button at the bottom of the Timeline.

See Also

See "Using the Timeline" on page 32 for information on changing the view size of frames in the Timeline.

Playhead   Select one frame

Select multiple contiguous frames

Select multiple noncontiguous frames

Insert a Frame

1 Click the frame's location in the Timeline header, or drag the playhead to the frame where you want to insert a frame.

2 Click the **Insert** menu, point to **Timeline**, and then click **Frame**.

Did You Know?

You can add labels to frames to reference in ActionScripts. In the Timeline, select the frame you want. In the Property Inspector, enter a name in the Name box under Label.

Delete Frames

1 Select the frame, keyframe, or sequence you want to delete.

2 Click the **Edit** menu, point to **Timeline**, and then click **Remove Frames**.

Did You Know?

You can move a frame sequence or keyframe. Drag the frame sequence or keyframe to another location in the Timeline.

You can copy a frame sequence or keyframe. Option+drag (Mac) or Alt+drag (Win) the frame sequence or keyframe to another location in the Timeline.

Working with Scenes

If a project requires a lot of animations with hundreds of frames, you can organize the animations into scenes to make them easier to work with and manage. The Scene panel makes it easy to display the number of scenes in the document, select current scenes for editing, create new scenes, duplicate scenes, delete scenes, and reorder them. You can also use the Edit bar to select a scene to edit. When you select a scene, Flash displays it on the Stage. When you publish a document as a movie, the scenes play in order unless you add interactivity to play them differently. Be aware that scenes are treated like self-contained movies, so transitions between scenes with interactivity may not be seamless.

Open the Scene Panel and Select a Scene

1. Click the **Window** menu, point to **Other Panels**, and then click **Scene**.

    TIMESAVER *Press Shift+F2.*

    A list of scenes appears in order in the panel. In a new document, the Scene panel displays only the default Scene 1.

2. Click the scene you want to display.

Add a Scene

1. If necessary, open the Scene panel.

2. Click the **Add Scene** button in the Scene panel.

New scene

Did You Know?

Flash names scenes in order based on the highest number. If you add Scenes 2 and 3, and then delete Scene 2, the next time you add a scene, Flash names it Scene 4.

Rename a Scene

1. If necessary, open the Scene panel.

2. Double-click the scene you want to rename.

3. Type a new name.

4. Press Return (Mac) or Enter (Win).

Delete a Scene

1. If necessary, open the Scene panel.

2. Click the scene you want to delete.

3. Click the **Delete Scene** button in the Scene panel.

4. Click **OK** to confirm the deletion.

> **TIMESAVER** *If you don't want to display the Confirmation dialog box, press ⌘+click (Mac) or Ctrl+click (Win) the Delete Scene button.*

Did You Know?

You can undo the deletion of a scene. If you mistakenly delete a scene, you can undo; press ⌘+Z (Mac) or Ctrl+Z (Win).

You can reorder scenes in the Scene panel. In the Scene panel, drag a selected scene up or down in the list.

For Your Information

Playing and Testing Scenes

After you finish creating and working with scenes in a Flash document, you can quickly playback all the scenes in Flash or test a scene in a browser with commands on the Control menu. To playback all scenes in the order in which they appear in the Scenes panel, click the Control menu, and then click Play All Scenes. To test the active scene, click the Control menu, and then click Test Scene. To change the settings for the SWF file created using the Test Scene command, use the Publish Settings command on the File menu.

Using the Edit Bar

The Edit bar contains controls and information for editing scenes and symbols, and for changing the view size of the Stage. The Edit bar lets you know what editing mode you are working in and allows you to switch scenes. The Scene button allows you to edit a scene in document-editing mode, while the Symbol button allows you to edit symbols in the symbol-editing mode. The Back button on the Edit bar returns you to document-editing mode.

Show and Hide the Edit Bar

◆ To display the Edit bar, click the **Window** menu, point to **Toolbars**, and then click **Edit Bar** to select the check mark.

◆ To hide the Edit bar, click the **Window** menu, point to **Toolbars**, and then click **Edit Bar** to deselect the check mark.

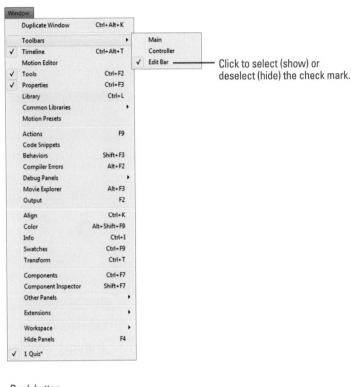

Click to select (show) or deselect (hide) the check mark.

Back button

Current scene or symbol being edited

Edit bar

Change View Size of the Stage

1. Click the **View Size** list arrow in the Edit bar, and then select a view size percentage or an option:

   - ◆ **Fit To Window**
   - ◆ **Show Frame**
   - ◆ **Show All**

Did You Know?

You can use the Hand tool to move the Stage to change the view. Click the Hand tool (H) on the Tools panel, and then drag the Stage to change the view.

Select a Scene or Symbol to Edit

- ◆ To select a scene, click the **Edit Scene** button in the Edit bar, and then select a scene from the list.

- ◆ To select a symbol, click the **Edit Symbol** button in the Edit bar, and then select a symbol from the list.

Select and type a view percentage

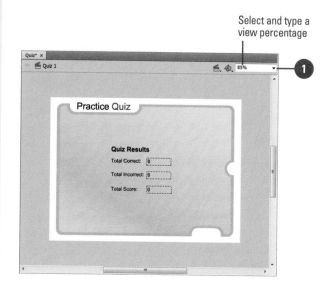

Edit Scene button   Edit Symbol button

Using the Main Toolbar

If you use Windows, you can display and use the Main toolbar above the Document menu window to quickly access common document and object-related commands, such as New, Open, Save, Print, Cut, Copy, Paste, Redo, Undo, Snap To Objects, Smooth, Straighten, Rotate And Skew, Scale, and Align. When you're finished working with the Main toolbar, you can hide it to create more workspace.

Show and Hide the Main Toolbar in Windows

◆ To display the Main toolbar, click the **Window** menu, point to **Toolbars**, and then click **Main** to select the check mark.

◆ To hide the Main toolbar, click the **Window** menu, point to **Toolbars**, and then click **Main** to deselect the check mark.

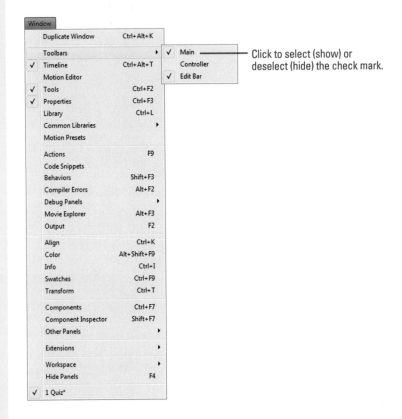

Click to select (show) or deselect (hide) the check mark.

Did You Know?

You can use Undo and Redo commands on the menu bar. The Undo and Redo commands on the Edit menu undo (returns you to a previous point) and redo (re-performs commands you undid) actions you've taken in a document. The names of the Undo and Redo commands change to reflect the current action.

Flash supports 100 undo and redo levels. To change the number of undo levels, click the Edit (Win) or Flash (Mac) menu, click the General tab, specify a number in the Undo Levels box, and then click OK. The lower the number of levels, the less amount of memory the program needs to run.

Main toolbar

Resizing Panels

If you need more workspace, you can use the double-arrow button (at the top of a panel group) to quickly minimize a panel group, such as the Tools panel or Property Inspector. When you click the double-arrow button, the panel group collapses to icons, which increases the size of the workspace. You can click the icons to display the panel. When you click the double-arrow button again, the panel group reopens. If you need to increase or decrease the size of a docking panel, you can drag the resize bar at the top-left side of the panel group to resize it as you would any window.

Minimize and Maximize Panels

1 To minimize or maximize a docking channel, click the **Double-arrow** button at the top of the panel group.

The double-arrow direction indicates whether the panel minimizes or maximizes.

For example, if the double-arrow points to the left of the Tools panel that means when you click it the Tools panel minimizes. If the double-arrow points to the right that means when you click it the Tools panel maximizes.

Double-arrow button; maximized panel

Drag to resize panel

Double-arrow button; minimized panel

Using the Tools Panel

The **Tools panel**, also known as the Toolbox, contains tools that you can use to draw, paint, select, and modify artwork. The Tools panel is divided into 4 main sections: (1) the first section at the top contains selection and transform tools; (2) the next section contains tools for drawing, painting, and adding text; (3) the next selection contains tools for changing, modifying, drawing and painting; and (4) the last section contains additional tool options for zooming and panning in the program window, changing stroke and fill colors, and selecting other options. You can show or hide the Tools panel as necessary and customize the Tools panel to display the tools you use most often. You can now expand and collapse the Tools panel to switch between one and two columns of tools. When you customize the Tools panel, you can display more than one tool in a location. The top tool in the group appears with an arrow in the lower right corner of its icon. When you click and hold the pointer on the top tool, the other tools in the group appear in a pop-up menu. When you select a tool from the group, it appears in the Tools panel as the top tool.

Show and Hide the Tools Panel

◆ To display the Tools panel, click the **Window** menu, and then click **Tools** to select the check mark.

◆ To hide the Tools panel, click the **Window** menu, and then click **Tools** to deselect the check mark.

◆ To collapse and expand the Tools panel between one and two columns, click the double-arrows at the top of the Tools panel.

Did You Know?

You can move the Tools panel. Drag the title bar or textured area at the top of the Tools panel to the desired location.

Click to select (show) or deselect (hide) the check mark.

Click to expand and collapse Tools panel

Tools panel

Customize the Tools Panel

1. Click the **Flash** (Mac) or **Edit** menu (Win), and then click **Customize Tools Panel**.

2. Click a tool in the Tools panel graphic.

3. To add a tool, select the tool in the Available Tools list, and then click **Add**.

   TIMESAVER *You can add more than one tool to a location.*

4. To remove a tool, select the tool in the Current Selection list, and then click **Remove**.

5. Click **OK**.

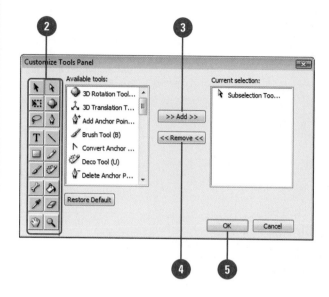

Did You Know?

You can restore the Tools panel to the default layout. Click the Flash (Mac) or Edit menu (Win), click Customize Tools Panel, click Restore Defaults, and then click OK.

You can identify keyboard shortcuts for the Tools panel. In the Customize Tools Panel dialog box, the letter in parenthesis indicates the keyboard shortcut.

For Your Information

Creating Tools

Flash lets you design your own Tools, using the JSFL language. In addition you can download tools created by other authors at the Adobe Exchange at http://www.adobe.com/cfusion/exchange/index.cfm. Although Adobe has yet to properly document the JSFL language, point your browser to *http://www.dynamicflash.co.uk/jsfl/* for a look at how JSFL is implemented in the Flash environment.

Working with Panels

Panels are windows that allow you to view, organize, and change elements and related options in a document. In Flash, you work with several panel windows at one time. Instead of continually moving, resizing, or opening and closing windows, you can collapse or expand individual panels within a window with a single click to save space. A panel appears with a header, which includes the tab titles and three accessibility options: the Minimize/Maximize button, the Close button, and an Options menu. The entire set of panels includes a double arrow you can use the collapse and expand the entire panel between icons with text and full panels. You use the Minimize/Maximize button to collapse or expand panels. The Options menu provides you with panel specific commands, including group, rename, maximize, close a panel, and use the Help system.

Open and Close a Panel

1 Click the **Window** menu.

2 Do one of the following:

◆ Click a panel name, such as Properties, Timeline, Tools, and Library.

◆ Point to a panel category, such as Other Panels, and then click a panel name.

TIMESAVER *To close a panel, click the Close button on the panel or the tab you want.*

Panels on Window menu

More panels on Window submenu

Collapse and Expand a Panel

1 To collapse or expand an open panel, click the header bar or double-click the title tab on the header bar of the panel.

TIMESAVER *To hide and show all panels, click the Window menu, and then click Hide Panels.*

TIMESAVER *To Auto-Collapse Icon Panels or Auto-Show Hidden Panels, right-click (Win) or option-click (Mac), and then select a command.*

Expanded panel

Collapsed panels

Collapse and Expand the Panel Set Between Icons and Panels

- ◆ To collapse the panel set to icons with text, click the double arrow pointing right (Collapse to Icons) at the top of the panels.

- ◆ To expand the panel set from icons with text to full panels, click the double arrow pointing left (Expand Dock) at the top of the panels.

- ◆ To have an expanded panel icon automatically collapse or hide when you click away, right-click (Win) or control-click (Mac) a panel, and then click **Auto-Collapse Icon Panels** or **Auto-Show Hidden Panels**.

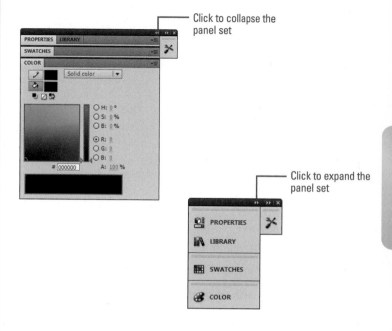

Click to collapse the panel set

Click to expand the panel set

Use the Panel Options Menu

1. Open or expand a panel.

2. Click the **Options** button on the right side of the panel header bar.

3. Click a command from the list (commands vary). Common commands include:

   - ◆ **Help.** Accesses Flash Help.

   - ◆ **Close.** Closes the currently displayed tab in the panel.

   - ◆ **Close Group.** Closes all the tabs in the panel.

Docking and Undocking Panels

You can dock and undock, or temporarily attach and detach, panels or panel groups. You can display panels using the Window menu, and then drag them around the program window to dock or undock them to other panels. You can even drag the Property Inspector panel to display it horizontally or vertically. However, document panels and the Stage cannot be docked. When you drag a panel over a dockable area, an outline around the target dock appears. When you release the mouse button, the panel snaps to the dockable area and stays there until you move it. You can even drag a panel tab to a new position. If you attempt to dock a panel over an undockable area, no outline appears.

Dock a Panel

1. Position the pointer on the panel tab or panel set header bar.

2. Drag the window away from the panel to a panel.

   ◆ **Add to Panel.** Drag to a panel until a blue rectangle appears around the panel.

   ◆ **Append to Panel.** Drag to a panel until a blue line appears along the side of the panel.

Undock a Panel

1. Position the pointer on the panel tab or panel set header bar.

2. Drag the window away from the panel to an empty area of the Flash window.

Grouping and Ungrouping Panels

You can group panels together to improve organization and workflow. When you group panels together, you can stack one on top of the other, or group related panels together as a tabbed panel group, such as the Component Inspector panel. You can add a panel to an existing panel group or you can create a new panel group. If you no longer need panels grouped together, you can ungroup them. You can use the panel tab to group or ungroup as well as dock or undock panel windows.

Group Panels Together

1. Position the pointer on the panel tab or panel set header bar.

2. Drag the window away from the panel to another panel window.

   ◆ **Add to Panel.** Drag to a panel until a blue rectangle appears around the panel.

   ◆ **Append to Panel.** Drag to a panel until a blue line appears along the side of the panel.

Ungroup Panels

1. Position the pointer on the panel tab or panel set header bar.

2. Drag the window away from the panel to an empty area of the Flash window.

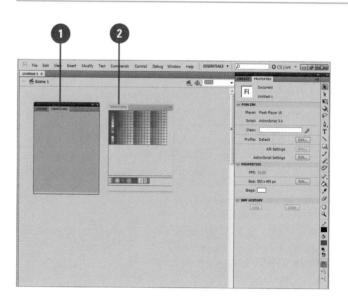

Creating a Workspace

As you work with Flash, you'll open, close, and move around windows and panels to meet your individual needs. After you customize the Flash workspace, you can save the location of windows and panels as a workspace, or custom panel set, which you can display by using the Workspace menu on the Applications bar or the Workspaces submenu on the Window menu. You can create custom workspaces, or use a workspace provided by Flash, which are designed for space and work-flow efficiency. The built-in workspaces include Classic, Debug, Designer, Developer, or Essentials. If you no longer use a custom work-space, you can remove it at any time. You can also rename a custom workspace to improve recognition.

Create a Workspace

1. Open and position the panels you want to include in a panel set.

2. Click the **Workspace** menu (the menu name displays the current workspace), and then click **New Workspace**.

    ◆ You can also click the **Window** menu, point to **Workspace**, and then click **New Workspace**.

    The New Workspace dialog box opens.

3. Type a name in the Name box.

4. Click **OK**.

    The panel set is now saved.

Display a Workspace

1. Click the **Workspace** menu (the menu name displays the current workspace), and then select a panel option:

    ◆ **Custom panel name.** Displays a custom panel layout that you created.

    ◆ Animator, **Classic**, **Debug**, **Designer**, **Developer**, **Essentials**, or **Small Screen**. Displays panel layouts created by Adobe for specific purposes in Flash.

Workspace menu

Custom panel

Delete a Workspace

1. Click the **Window** menu, point to **Workspace**, and then click **Manage Workspaces**.

   The Manage Workspaces dialog box opens.

2. Select the panel set you want to delete.

3. Click **Delete**.

4. Click **Yes** to confirm the deletion.

5. Click **OK**.

   The panel set is now deleted.

Did You Know?

You can hide all panels. Click the Window menu, and then click Hide Panels to select the check mark.

Rename a Workspace

1. Click the **Window** menu, point to **Workspace**, and then click **Manage Workspaces**.

   The Manage Workspaces dialog box opens.

2. Select the panel set you want to rename.

3. Click **Rename**.

4. Type a new name, and then click **OK**.

   The panel set is now renamed.

5. Click **OK**.

Creating Keyboard Shortcuts

Flash uses built-in keyboard shortcuts designed specifically for Flash. A complete list of the keyboard shortcuts is available in the back of this book. The built-in keyboard shortcuts are organized into sets, which you can duplicate and customize to create your own personalized set. If you use other programs, such as Adobe Illustrator or Adobe Photoshop, and you are more comfortable using their keyboard shortcuts for common commands, you can select a built-in keyboard shortcut set from any of the graphics programs to use in Flash.

Create a Keyboard Shortcut Set

1. Click the **Flash** (Mac) or **Edit** (Win) menu, and then click **Keyboard Shortcuts**.

2. Click the **Current Set** popup, and then select a set.

3. Click the **Duplicate Set** button.

4. Type a name for the new shortcut set.

5. Click **OK**.

Delete button

Did You Know?

You can delete a custom keyboard shortcut set. Click the Flash (Mac) or Edit (Win) menu, click Keyboard Shortcuts, select a shortcut set from the Current Set popup, and then click the Delete button. You cannot delete a built-in keyboard shortcut set that comes with Flash.

You can rename a custom keyboard shortcut set. Click the Flash (Mac) or Edit (Win) menu, click Keyboard Shortcuts, select a shortcut set from the Current Set popup, click the Rename Set button, enter a new name, and then click OK. You cannot rename a built-in keyboard shortcut set that comes with Flash.

Add or Remove a Keyboard Shortcut

1 Click the **Flash** (Mac) or **Edit** (Win) menu, and then click **Keyboard Shortcuts**.

2 Click the **Current Set** popup, and then select the set in which you want to change.

3 Click the **Commands** popup, and then select a shortcut category, such as Drawing Menu Commands, Drawing Tools, Test Movie Menu Commands, and Workplace Accessibility Commands.

4 Select the command for which you want to add or remove a shortcut in the Commands list.

5 Do the following:

◆ To add a shortcut, click the **Add Shortcut** (+) button, and then press the key combination to enter the new shortcut key in the Press Key box.

◆ To remove a shortcut, click the **Remove Shortcut** (-) button.

6 Click **Change**.

7 To add or remove additional shortcuts, repeat Steps 2-6.

8 Click **OK**.

Keyboard shortcut

For Your Information

Export keyboard shortcuts as HTML

You can now export Flash keyboard shortcuts as an HTML file that you can view and print using a standard Web browser. To export the keyboard shortcuts, click the Flash (Mac) or Edit (Win) menu, click Keyboard Shortcuts, click the Current Set list arrow, select the set you want, click the Export Set As HTML button, enter a file name, specify a location, and then click Save.

Setting General Preferences

Flash allows you to set general preferences to customize the way you work in the program. You can specify what you want to display or open when you launch Flash. Some of the preferences allow you to specify the number of undo levels, enable multiple selection, show tooltips, open documents and test movies in tabs, enable span-based selection in the Timeline, make the first frame of each scene in a document a named anchor, and select a specific selection highlight color for different element types, such as drawings, groups, and symbols. You can also set Project preferences for closing and saving project files. In Flash, the Preferences dialog box is reorganized with new categories and options for ease of use, such as having have Flash open a new document tab instead of opening in its own window.

Set General Preferences

1. Click the **Flash** (Mac) or **Edit** (Win) menu, and then click **Preferences**.

2. Click the **General** category.

3. Select from the following options:

   ◆ **On Launch.** Select an option to specify which document opens when you start the program.

      ◆ **Welcome Screen.**

      ◆ **New Document.**

      ◆ **Last Documents Open.**

      ◆ **No Document.**

   ◆ **Undo Levels.** Select Document or Object-level Undo, and then enter a value from 2 to 300 to set the number of undo/redo levels. The default level is 100.

   ◆ **Open Test Movie In Tabs.** Select this check box to have Flash open a test movie in document tab.

   ◆ **Auto-Collapse Icon Panels.** Select this check box to automatically collapse the panel set to Icons only.

   ◆ **Shift Select.** Select or deselect this check box to control the selection of multiple elements.

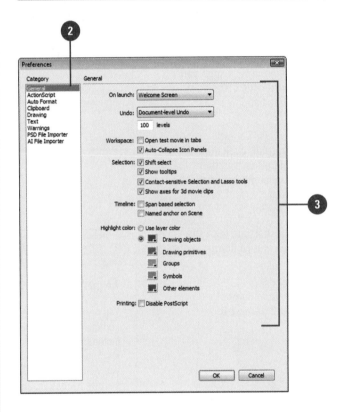

- **Show Tooltips**. Select to display tooltips when the pointer points to a button or control.

- **Contact-Sensitive Selection and Lasso Tools.** For the object drawing model, select to select objects when any part of the marquee touches it. Clear it to select objects that are completely enclosed by the marquee. Points within the selection will be selected.

- **Show Axes For 3D Movie Clips.** Select to show axes for 3d movie clips.

- **Span Based Selection.** Select to use span-based selection instead of frame-based selection.

- **Named Anchor On Scene.** Select to make the first frame of each scene in a document a named anchor.

- **Highlight Color.** Select the Use Layer Color option to use the current layer's outline color, or select the option, and then select a color for Drawing objects, Drawing primitives, groups, symbols, and other elements.

- **Printing (Win).** Select the Disable PostScript check box if you have problems printing to a postscript printer.

4 Click **OK**.

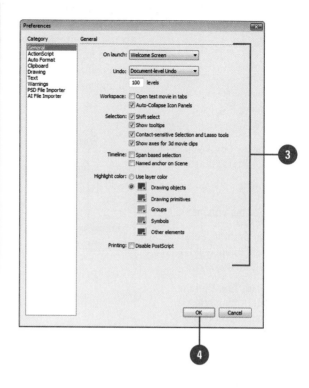

For Your Information

Setting Drawing Model Options

You can draw shapes in Flash using two main drawing models: Merge Drawing and Object Drawing. **Merge Drawing** model automatically merges shapes that you draw when you overlap them. If you select a shape that has been merged with another, and move it, the shape below it is moved too. For example, if you draw a square and overlay a circle on top of it, and then select the circle and move it, the portion of the square that overlaid the circle is removed. **Object Drawing** model allows you to draw shapes as separate objects that do not automatically merge together when overlaid. This lets you overlap shapes without altering their appearance should you choose to move them apart, or rearrange their appearance. Flash creates each shape as a separate object that you can individually manipulate. When you select a shape created using the Object Drawing model, Flash surrounds the shape with a rectangular bounding box. You can use the Pointer tool to move the object by clicking the bounding box and dragging the shape anywhere you'd like to position it on the Stage. You can now extend the Object Drawing mode by creating primitive rectangles and ovals in **Primitive mode**, which allows you to edit properties in the Property Inspector and specify the corner radius of rectangles and inner radius of ovals. This makes it easy to create pie wedges, round off corners, and other shapes.

Setting Text Preferences

When you edit or work with text in a Flash document, you can specify text related preferences. You can select a font to use when substituting missing fonts, or select text orientation options, which is useful when using English (horizontal) or Asian (vertical) language fonts. In addition, you can select a language as an input method.

Set Text Preferences

1. Click the **Flash** (Mac) or **Edit** (Win) menu, and then click **Preferences**.

2. Click the **Text** category.

3. Select from the following options:

   ◆ **Show Asian Text Options.** Select to show Asian text options in the Property Inspector (**New!**).

   ◆ **Show Right-To-Left Text Options.** Select to show Direction options in the Property Inspector (**New!**).

   ◆ **Font Mapping Default.** Click the list arrow, and then select a font to use when substituting missing fonts. Click the **Style** list arrow, and then select a font style.

   ◆ **Show For Missing Fonts.** Select to show the Font Mapping dialog box.

   ◆ **Vertical Text options.**

      ◆ **Default Text Orientation.** Select to make default orientation vertical, which is useful for Asian fonts.

      ◆ **Right To Left Text Flow.** Select to reverse the default text direction.

      ◆ **No Kerning.** Select to turn off kerning for vertical text.

   ◆ **Input Method.** Select the Text Input Window check box (Mac) or language option to select a language type.

   ◆ **Font Menus.** Select check boxes and option to show fonts in menus.

4. Click **OK**.

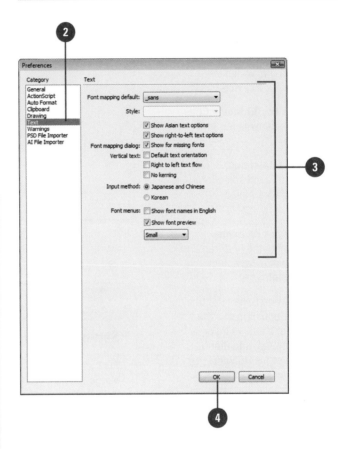

Setting Clipboard Preferences

When you copy or cut graphics to the Clipboard, you can set preferences to determine how you want to paste the graphic into a Flash document. The preference options give you control over the size and quality of the graphics you insert in a document. If you are using Windows, the Clipboard preferences include options for bitmaps and gradients in the Windows Metafile format. If you are using a Macintosh, the Clipboard preferences include options for the PICT format.

Set Clipboard Preferences

1. Click the **Flash** (Mac) or **Edit** (Win) menu, and then click **Preferences**.

2. Click the **Clipboard** category.

3. Select from the following options:

   ◆ **Bitmaps (Win).** Select options for Color Depth and Resolution to specify these parameters for bitmaps copied to the Clipboard. Select Smooth to apply anti-aliasing. Enter a value in the Size Limit box to specify the amount of RAM that is used when placing a bitmap on the Clipboard.

   ◆ **PICT Settings (Mac).** Select Objects to preserve data copied to the Clipboard as a vector graphic, or select one of the bitmap formats to convert the image. Enter a value for Resolution. Select the Include Postscript check box to include Postscript data. For gradients, select an option to specify quality in the PICT.

   ◆ **Gradient quality.** Select an option to specify the quality of gradient fills placed in the Windows Metafile.

4. Click **OK**.

② Macintosh options

Windows options

Setting Warning Preferences

Flash provides warning messages when you perform actions that might create problems for your document or lose important data. The warnings help you avoid compatibility problems with Flash CS4 and character corruption from encoding, which lets you know about missing fonts, URL changes, and symbol conversion. Additional warnings let you know when importing audio and video content inserts frames and when motion frames or target objects contain ActionScript.

Set Warning Preferences

1. Click the **Flash** (Mac) or **Edit** (Win) menu, and then click **Preferences**.

2. Click the **Warnings** category.

3. Select from the following options:

   ◆ **Warn On Save For Adobe Flash CS4 Compatibility.** When you save documents with content features specific to Flash CS5.

   ◆ **Warn On URL Changes In Launch And Edit.** If the URL for a document has changed.

   ◆ **Warn On Inserting Frames When Importing Content.** When Flash inserts frames while you import audio or video files.

   ◆ **Warn On Encoding Conflicts When Exporting ActionScript Files.** When you create a document with different language characters for export.

   ◆ **Warn On Conversion Of Effect Graphic Objects.** When you attempt to edit a symbol with effects applied to it.

   ◆ **Warn on sites with overlapped root folder.** When you create a site in which the local root folder overlaps another site.

   ◆ **Warn On Behavior Symbol Conversion.** When you convert a symbol with a behavior attached to a symbol of a different type.

   ◆ **Warn On Symbol Conversion.** When you convert a symbol to a symbol of a different type.

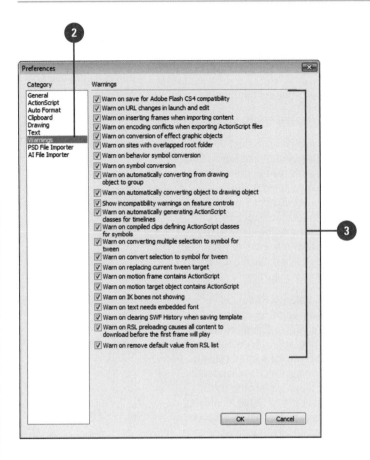

- **Warn On Automatically Converting From Drawing Object To Group.** When you convert an object drawn in Object Drawing mode to a group.

- **Warn On Automatically Converting Objects To Drawing Objects.**

- **Show Incompatibility Warnings On Feature Controls.** When controls are not supported by the Flash Player version specified in Publish Settings.

- **Warn On Automatically Generating ActionScript Classes For Timelines.** When you don't create a class, Flash does.

- **Warn On Compiled Clips Defining ActionScript Classes For Symbols.** When you try to create ActionScript classes for symbols.

- **Warn On Converting Multiple Selection To Symbol For Tween.** When you don't have a symbol to create a tween.

- **Warn On Replacing Current Tween Target.** When you try to replace the current tween target

- **Warn On Motion Frame Contains ActionScript.**

- **Warn On Motion Target Object Contains ActionScript.**

- **Warn On IK Bones Not Showing.**

- **Warn On Text Needs Embedded Font.** When a font is not available on your computer (**New!**).

- **Warn On Clearing SWF History When Saving Template (New!).**

- **Warn On RSL Preloading Causes All Content To Download Before The First Frame Will Play (New!).**

- **Warn On Remove Default Value From RSL List (New!).**

4 Click **OK**.

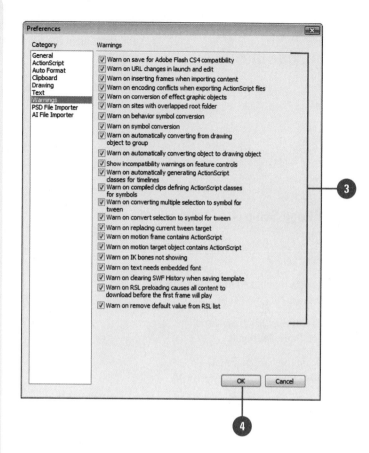

Working with Page Setup in Macintosh

You can use the Page Setup dialog box in Macintosh to select the size and location in the printer of the paper you want to use. You can also select the page orientation (portrait or landscape) that best fits the entire document or any selection. **Portrait** orients the page vertically (taller than it is wide) and **landscape** orients the page horizontally (wider than it is tall). When you shift between the two, the margin settings automatically change. **Margins** are the blank spaces between the edges of a page and the image. The printer only prints within these margins. You can use the Print Margins dialog box to change margins and layout. The layout options allow you to specify the frames you want to print, and the frame size and display on the page.

Work with Page Setup in Macintosh

1. Open a document.

2. Click the **File** menu, and then click **Page Setup**.

3. Click the **Settings** list arrow, and then click **Page Attributes**.

4. Select from the various Page Attributes options:

   ◆ **Format For.** Click the Format For list arrow, and then select a printer. If your printer is not accessible from the list, click the Edit Printer List, and then add your printer (you may need the printer disc, or access to the Internet, to load the latest drivers).

   ◆ **Paper Size.** Click the Paper Size list arrow, and then select from the available options. The default printer will determine the available paper sizes.

   ◆ **Orientation.** Click the Portrait, Landscape Left, or Landscape Right button.

   ◆ **Scale.** Enter a percentage value to increase (over 100) or decrease (under 100) the size of the printed document.

5. Click **OK**.

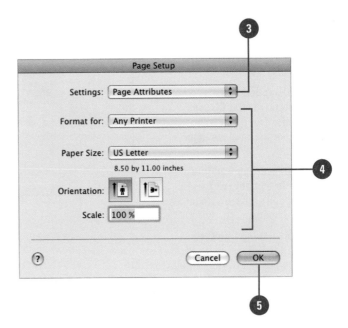

Change Print Margins and Layout in Macintosh

1. Open a document.

2. Click the **File** menu, and then click **Print Margins**.

3. Enter Left, Right, Top, and Bottom page margins, and then select the Center check boxes to center material on the page.

4. Select from the Layout options:

   - Frames. Click the **Frames** list arrow, and then click **First Frame Only** or **All Frames**.

   - Layout. Click the **Layout** list arrow, and then select a layout option: **Actual Size**, **Fit On One Page**, or one of the Storyboard options.

   - Scale. Enter a scale percentage value.

5. Click **OK**.

Working with Page Setup in Windows

You can use the Page Setup dialog box in Windows to select the size and location in the printer of the paper you want to use. You can also select the page orientation (portrait or landscape) that best fits the entire document or any selection. When you shift between the two, the margin settings automatically change. Margins are the blank spaces between the edges of a page and the image. You can also change page layout options, which allow you to specify the frames you want to print, and the frame size and display on the page. The printer only prints within these margins. Different printer models support different options and features; the available options depend on your printer and printer drivers.

Work with Page Setup in Windows

1. Open a document.

2. Click the **File** menu, and then click **Page Setup**.

3. Select from the various Page Setup options:

   ◆ **Margins.** Enter Left, Right, Top, and Bottom page margins, and then select the check boxes to center material on the page.

   ◆ **Size.** Click the Size list arrow, and then select from the available options.

   ◆ **Source.** Click the Source list arrow, and then select from the available options.

   ◆ **Orientation.** Click the Portrait or Landscape option.

4. Select from the Layout options:

   ◆ **Frames.** Click the Frames list arrow, and then click First Frame Only or All Frames.

   ◆ **Layout.** Click the Layout list arrow, and then select a layout option.

   ◆ **Scale.** Enter a scale percentage value.

5. Click **OK**.

Set Printer Properties in Page Setup

1 Open a document.

2 Click the **File** menu, and then click **Print**.

TIMESAVER *Press ⌘+P (Mac) or Ctrl+P (Win).*

3 Click the **Name** list arrow, and then select the printer you want to use.

4 Click **Properties**.

5 Select the printer options you want; each printer displays different options.

6 Click **OK** to close the Properties dialog box.

7 Click **OK** to close the Print dialog box.

Printing a Document in Macintosh

The Print command is probably the most used of all Flash's print options. In addition to normal printing functions, such as Copies and Pages, the Print command gives you other menus that let you control specific printing functions, such as output ink and color management. Understand that the options available for the Print command will be partially determined by the default printer. For example, if your default printer uses more than one paper tray, you will see options for selecting a specific tray for the current print job. In spite of the differences, there are some universal options to all print jobs, and these are covered here.

Print a Document in Macintosh

1. Open a document.

2. Click the **File** menu, and then click **Print**.

3. Click the **Printer** popup, and then select from the available printer descriptions.

   IMPORTANT *Changes made here override any changes made in the Page Setup dialog box.*

4. Click the **Presets** popup, and then select from the available preset options.

5. Select the various Copies & Pages options: **Number Of Copies**, **Collated**, **Print All** or **Range Of Pages**.

6. Click the **Print Options** popup, click **Layout**, and then select the various options: Pages Per Sheet, Layout Direction, and if you want a Border.

7. Click the **Print Options** popup, click **Color Matching**, and then select the option you want to match color using ColorSync (on your computer) or the printer.

8 Click the **Print Options** popup, click **Paper Handling**, and then select your options.

9 Click the **Print Options** popup, click **Scheduler**, and then select the option you want to specify when you want to print the document.

10 Click the **Print Options** popup, click **Summary**, and then view the summary of settings.

11 Click the following options to finalize your print:

◆ **PDF.** Displays a menu to save a Flash document as a PDF with the option you want. The options include Fax PDF, Mail PDF, and Compress PDF.

◆ **Preview.** Displays a preview of the printed document

◆ **Supplies.** Displays an Apple Store Web site for printer supplies.

◆ **Cancel.** Stops a print job.

◆ **Print.** Prints the current document.

12 If you need additional help along the way, click the **Help** button.

Printing a Document in Windows

Printing a paper copy is the most common way to preview and share your documents. You can use the Print dialog box to set how many copies to print, specify a range of pages to print, and print your document. Understand that the options available for the Print command will be determined by the default printer, and operating system. Different printers will display different options; there are some options that are fairly universal, and these options are covered here.

Print a Document in Windows

1. Open a document.

2. Click the **File** menu, and then click **Print**.

   TIMESAVER *Press* ⌘*+P (Mac) or Ctrl+P (Win).*

3. If necessary, click the **Name** list arrow, and then click the printer you want.

4. Type the number of copies you want to print.

5. Specify the pages to print:

   ◆ **All**. Prints the entire document.

   ◆ **Pages**. Prints the specified pages.

   ◆ **Selection**. Prints the selected item.

6. Click **OK**.

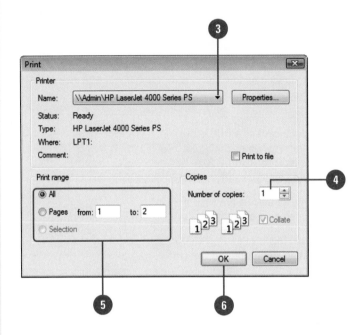

Creating Graphics

Introduction

Flash offers a full suite of tools for creating and editing graphics. When you draw in Flash, you create vector art. **Vectors** are mathematical descriptions of lines and points that, when connected, form shapes and objects. Vector-defined art is not limited by resolution like bitmaps are, so they can be scaled to any size without a loss in quality or increase in file size. This is the basis of Flash; and the main reason Flash files are so small and why they can be deployed on so many platforms. Vector graphics are also fully editable after they are created so you can continue to adjust their properties. Included in Flash are many of the drawing tools and procedures familiar to the seasoned user of vector drawing programs. It is also a good place for the beginner to learn. Sketch naturally with the Pencil and Brush tools or use vector-based objects, such as the Rectangle or Oval tools or the Polystar tool. Use the Pen tool to create lines and shapes with Bézier curves. Whatever is drawn can be edited and modified with a variety of tools and palettes. When you select an object or graphic on the Stage, the Property Inspector displays the attributes of that object that are modifiable, such as fill and stroke color, position, and scale.

You can draw shapes in Flash using two drawing models: Merge Drawing and Object Drawing. The **Merge Drawing** model, the default (like previous versions of Flash), automatically merges shapes that you draw when you overlap them. If you select a shape that has been merged with another, and move it, the shape below it is moved too. The **Object Drawing** model allows you to draw shapes as separate objects that do not automatically merge together when you overlap them. You can now extend the Object Drawing mode by creating primitive rectangles and ovals in **Primitive mode**, which allows you to edit properties in the Property Inspector and specify the corner radius of rectangles and inner radius of ovals. This makes it easy to create pie wedges, round off corners, and other curved shapes.

What You'll Do

Work with Object Drawing

Draw Lines and Shapes

Use the Selection Tools

Zoom In and Out

Move Around with the Hand Tool

Use Rulers, Grids, and Guides

Modify Grid and Guide Settings

Use Snap Align

Change Stroke and Fill Colors

Create Custom Colors

Add Colors Using the Kuler Panel

Edit Strokes with the Ink Bottle

Edit Fills with the Paint Bucket

Use the Spray Brush and Deco Tools

Edit Strokes and Fills with the Eyedropper

Create Gradients

Use the Fill Lock

Use Paint Brush Modes

Draw with the Pen Tool

Modify Shapes

Use the Free Transform Tool

Use Transform Options for Shapes

Change Drawing Settings

Working With Object Drawing

Previously in Flash, all shapes in the same layer on the Stage could change other overlapping shapes, known as Merge Drawing. In Flash, you can create shapes directly on the Stage that do not affect other overlapping shapes, known as Object Drawing. By default, Flash uses Merge Drawing. To draw shapes using Object Drawing, you use the Object Drawing button on the Tools panel. When you select a shape created using Object Drawing, Flash selects the shape with a rectangular bounding box, which you can use with the Pointer tool to move the shape on the Stage. You can use General preferences to set selection options for contact-sensitivity when selecting shapes created using Object Drawing.

Enable and Use Object Drawing

1. Select a drawing tool on the Tools panel that supports Object Drawing (Pencil, Line, Pen, Brush, Oval, Rectangle, and Polygon).

2. Select the **Object Drawing** button on the Tools panel.

    TIMESAVER *Press the J key to toggle between Merge and Object Drawing.*

3. With the **Pointer** tool, click to select an object, and then drag the bounding box to move it.

4. To switch back Merge Drawing, click the **Object Drawing** button again.

Did You Know?

You can convert a Merge Drawing shape to an Object Drawing shape. Select the shape on the Stage, click the Modify menu, point to Combine Objects, and then click Union.

See Also

See "Setting General Preferences" on page 60 for information on options for contact-sensitivity when selecting shapes created using Object Drawing.

Bounding box ③

Objects created with Object Drawing

Drawing with the Line Tool

The Line tool draws perfectly straight lines in any direction you drag your mouse. In Flash, a line is called a stroke and there is a variety of thicknesses (0-200 pixels), styles, colors, and gradient fills that can be applied to it. You can also create your own line style for specific types of dashed, dotted or artistic lines. You can constrain the path a line draws to 45-degree angles or create closed shapes by intersecting the lines you draw. In Merge Drawing when a line overlaps another line on the same layer, it essentially cuts it into two pieces that can be edited as separate objects. You can also specify a line cap and join type. A **join** is the place where two strokes meet (Miter, Round, or Bevel). A **cap** is the end point of a stroke that does not join with another stroke. Select Stroke hinting to make stroke intersections easier to view.

Use the Line Tool

① Click the **Line** tool on the Tools panel.

The pointer becomes a crosshair that you can drag on the Stage.

TIMESAVER *Press N to select the Line tool.*

② Click and drag on the Stage, and then release the mouse when the line is the length you need.

TIMESAVER *Hold down the Shift key, and then drag to draw a 45, 90, or 180 degree line.*

③ To change line properties, click to select the stroke, and then specify the options (Color, Weight (0-200), Style, Width and Height, Cap, Join, or Miter) you want in the Property Inspector.

TROUBLE? *To display the Property Inspector, click the Window menu, and then click Properties.*

See Also

See "Changing Stroke and Fill Colors" on page 96 for information on using color.

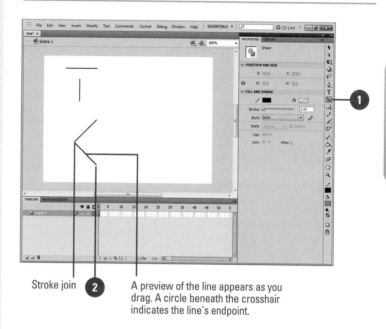

Stroke join

A preview of the line appears as you drag. A circle beneath the crosshair indicates the line's endpoint.

Stroke width and height

Stroke Color — Fill Color

Stroke Weight and Style

Cap and Join options

Stroke Scale and Hinting

Drawing with the Pencil Tool

Use the Pencil tool for freeform drawing. When you draw with the Pencil tool you are creating strokes. It works the same way as a real pencil with options for smoothing and straightening. Depending upon which mode you choose, Flash makes corrections to the drawn line. Smooth mode softens the curve of the line you draw while Straighten mode transforms the line into a series of straight-line segments and standard curves. If you are using the Pencil or Brush tools with Smooth mode, you can specify the degree of smoothness. Additionally, Flash performs shape recognition to the lines you draw so that if it detects something approximating a simple geometric shape such as a rectangle, oval, or triangle, it converts your drawing into whichever shape it detects. To bypass these modifications, select Ink mode. This mode allows for the most freeform drawing with minimal correction by Flash.

Use the Pencil Tool in Straighten Mode

1 Click the **Pencil** tool on the Tools panel.

The pointer becomes a pencil. The Pencil tool options appear at the bottom of the Tools panel. The default mode is Straighten.

TIMESAVER *Press Y to select the Pencil tool.*

2 Draw on the Stage with the Pencil, and then release the mouse.

A rough preview of the line appears as you draw. In Straighten mode, Flash transforms the line into a series of straight-line segments and standard curves.

3 To change the straighten rate, select the object, click the **Modify** menu, point to **Shape**, click **Advanced Straighten**, enter a value, and then click **OK**.

Did You Know?

Flash converts rough shapes into clean, geometric shapes. Set the tolerance level of shape recognition in the Drawing preferences.

Flash straightens the drawn line.

Pencil mode is set to straighten by default.

Flash applies shape recognition in Straighten mode.

Use the Pencil Tool in Smooth Mode

① Click the **Pencil** tool on the Tools panel.

The pointer becomes a pencil. The Pencil tool options appear at the bottom of the Tools panel.

② Click the **Pencil mode** list arrow in the Options area of the Tools panel, and then click **Smooth**.

③ In the Property Inspector, click the **Smoothing** list arrow, and then click a value from 1 to 100.

The default value is set to 50. The greater the smoothing value, the smoother the resulting line.

TROUBLE? *To display the Property Inspector, click the Window menu, and then click Properties.*

④ Draw on the Stage with the Pencil, and then release the mouse.

A rough preview of the line appears as you draw. In Smooth mode, Flash smoothes the line you draw into curved line segments.

⑤ To change the smooth rate and angles (above and below), select the object, click the **Modify** menu, point to **Shape**, click **Advanced Smooth**, enter a value, and then click **OK**.

Flash smoothes the drawn line.

Use Ink mode for more freeform drawing.

Select to display a live preview of your changes

Did You Know?

You can disable straightening and smoothing. Click the Pencil mode list arrow in the Options area of the Tools panel, and then click Ink mode to yield a line closest to the line you've drawn with minimal corrections performed by Flash.

For Your Information

Smoothing Curves Another Way

You can also smooth curves by optimizing the shape. Optimizing a shape refines curved lines and fill outlines by reducing the number of curves used to define the shape. To optimize a shape, click it, click the Modify menu, point to Shape, click Optimize, specify a smoothing level, select additional options (select Use Multiple Passes to repeat the smoothing process until you can't anymore, and select Show Totals Message to display an alert when smoothing is complete), and then click OK.

Drawing Shapes with the Rectangle and Oval Tools

The Flash Tools panel includes several tools for quickly creating simple geometric vector shapes. They are easy to use; you just click and drag on the Stage to create the shapes. The Rectangle tool creates rectangles with square or rounded corners. The Oval tool creates circular shapes such as ovals and circles. These shapes can be comprised of Strokes, which are lines that surround and define the shape, Fills, which are a color or texture inside the shape, or both. You can create two types of shapes: Drawing or Primitive. Drawing, or standard, shapes are self contained; the stroke and fill of a shape are not separate elements, while for Primitive shapes they are separate elements.

Draw with the Oval Tool

1. Click the **Oval** or **Oval Primitive** tool on the Tools panel.

   TIMESAVER *Press O to select an Oval tool.*

2. Select a **Stroke** and **Fill Color** from the Colors area of the Tools panel.

3. Click and drag on the Stage, and then release the mouse.

   TIMESAVER *Press and hold Shift while you drag to create a circle.*

4. In the Properties Inspector, change the values you want.

Draw with the Rectangle Tool

1. Click the **Rectangle** or **Rectangle Primitive** tool on the Tools panel.

   TIMESAVER *Press R to select a Rectangle tool.*

2. Select a **Stroke** and **Fill** color from the Colors area of the Tools panel.

3. Click and drag on the Stage, and then release the mouse.

   TIMESAVER *Press and hold Shift while you drag to create a square.*

4. In the Properties Inspector, change the values you want.

Draw a Rounded Rectangle

1 Click the **Rectangle** or **Rectangle Primitive** tool on the Tools panel.

2 Enter a value for the corner radius in the Properties Inspector.

3 To create an exact size rectangle shape, select the shape, enter the width and height values in the Properties Inspector.

4 Click and drag on the Stage, and then release the mouse.

Did You Know?

You can enter values ranging from 0 to 100 points in the Rectangle Settings dialog box. A value of zero gives you a straight-sided-square. Higher numbers produce squares with more rounded sides.

You can hold down the Shift key while dragging to produce a perfect square with equal sides or a perfect circle. If you want to draw an oval or a rectangle without a stroke or fill, you can set either of these options to No Fill in the Colors area of the Tools panel or in the Color panel.

You can draw shapes without a stroke or a fill. Set either of these properties to No Fill in the Colors section of the Tools panel or in the Color panel.

You can set specific sizes with a dialog box. Alt+click (Win) or Option+click (Mac) a rectangle or oval, set the values you want, and then click OK.

See Also

See "Changing Stroke and Fill Colors" on page 96 for information on changing shapes.

5 points   20 points   35 points

For Your Information

Creating Primitive Rectangles and Ovals

In addition to creating standard rectangles and ovals, you can now create Primitive rectangles and ovals. A Primitive shape allows you to change its attributes in the Property Inspector. The Primitive shape tools allow you to specify the corner radius of rectangles, and the start and end angle and the inner radius of ovals using controls in the Property Inspector, which makes it easy to create pie wedges, rounded corners, and other curved shapes. When either of the Primitive shape tools is selected, the Property Inspector retains the values of the last primitive object that you edited.

Using the Polystar Tool

Working in much the same way as the Oval and Rectangle tools, the new Polystar tool allows you to easily create complex vector shapes. You can use this tool to create polygons and stars with up to 32 sides. Choose between creating a polygon or a star. Both styles have characteristics that can be adjusted in the Property Inspector before you draw the shape. Both the polygon and star style can have up to 32 sides, with the star style having an additional star point size that can be set. Experiment with several options to get the kind of shape you want.

Draw a Polygon or Star Shape

1. Click and hold the **Rectangle** tool on the Tools panel, and then point to **PolyStar Tool**.

    The pointer becomes a crosshair that you can drag anywhere on the Stage.

2. Click **Options** in the Property Inspector.

    TIMESAVER *Press ⌘+F3 (Mac) or Ctrl+3 (Win) to open the Property Inspector.*

3. Click the **Style** list arrow, and then select **Polygon** or **Star**.

4. Enter a value for the number of sides. You can create an object with up to 32 sides.

5. For the Star style, you can specify an additional option for your point size. You can enter a value ranging from .10 to 1.0 points.

6. Click **OK**.

7. Click and drag on the Stage, and then release the mouse.

See Also

See "Editing Strokes with the Ink Bottle" on page 102 for information on editing an object.

Polystar shape

Understanding Selections

When you create vector graphics in Flash, they are comprised of distinct elements that can be selected separately or as a whole with a variety of selection tools. The type of editing you need to perform determines which tool you use. For example, a simple rectangle drawn is comprised of four line segments that surround the contour of the shape and one fill in the center. Each of these five parts can be selected in tandem or individually with the Selection tool. Likewise, any stroke that intersects another stroke or fill splits them into distinct elements that can be selected separately.

In Normal selection mode, holding down the Shift key adds to the selection any additional elements you click on. You can change this option in the General tab of the Preferences window so that it isn't necessary to use the Shift key to perform this function. Double-click any stroke to select other strokes connected to it or double-click a fill to select it and any strokes that touch or intersect it. To select an entire shape (strokes and fills) or just a portion of it, you can drag a selection rectangle with the Selection tool or draw a freeform selection area with the Lasso tool. These methods work best for very complex shapes with many intersecting strokes and fills, or if there is only a portion of the shape you need to edit.

The Sub-Selection and Pen tools allow you to select the entire shape (strokes and fills) simultaneously, making its anchor points and Bézier handles visible for editing. Use this method when you need to edit the contours of the shape with precision.

For information on making selections using the Object Drawing model, see "Working with Object Drawing", on page 74.

Selection Examples

Each element (4 lines and a fill) can be selected separately.

Shift-select to add elements to the selection.

Single line segment.

When two line segments intersect, four new line segments are created that can be selected separately.

Double-click a fill to select it and any connected strokes.

Double-click a stroke to select all connected strokes.

Click and drag to select a portion of the shape.

Only a portion of the fill and strokes is selected.

Selecting Strokes with the Selection Tool

There are several ways to select objects in Flash. You can select an object's stroke or fill or both. You can use the Selection tool to select parts of the object or drag over a portion of it to create a selection rectangle. The Property Inspector displays the properties of what is selected including Stroke line weight and style, Fill color, pixel dimensions, and X and Y coordinates. When a stroke or fill is selected, a dotted pattern appears over it indicating it has been selected. This makes editing and modifying graphics simple and illustrates the versatility of the vector-based graphics model used in Flash.

Select a Stroke with the Selection Tool

1. Click the **Selection** tool on the Tools panel.

   The pointer becomes an arrow.

   TIMESAVER *Press V to select the Selection tool.*

2. Position the arrow on the edge of the shape.

   Notice that Flash displays a small curved line icon when you position the arrow over a Curve point and a corner line icon when over a Corner point.

3. Click on any part of the stroke.

   Flash only selects a portion of it. This is because what appears to be one whole shape is actually a series of lines connected by points and each can be selected separately.

Curve point detected

Corner point detected

See Also

See "Working with Object Drawing" on page 74 for information on selecting overlapping objects on the same layer.

Select Multiple Stroke Segments

1 Click the **Selection** tool on the Tools panel.

The pointer becomes an arrow.

TIMESAVER *Press V to select the Selection tool. You can temporarily switch to the Selection tool from any other tool by pressing* ⌘ *(Mac) or Ctrl (Win).*

2 Click on any part of the stroke to select one segment.

3 Hold down the Shift key, and then click other strokes to add them to the selection.

Did You Know?

You can turn off the Shift-select feature in the General tab of the Preferences dialog box. When this feature is disabled, you can add to the selected segments by clicking them without the need to hold down the Shift key. In this mode, holding the Shift key and clicking a selected stroke segment deselects that segment.

Shift-select to add stroke segments to the selection.

Select Connected Stroke Segments

1 Click the **Selection** tool on the Tools panel.

The pointer becomes an arrow.

2 Double-click any part of the segment or stroke to select all connected strokes.

All connected stroke segments selected.

Selecting Strokes and Fills with the Selection Tool

The Selection tool provides the most simple and versatile procedures for selecting objects in Flash. The Selection tool selects anything you click on (provided it isn't on a locked layer). Double-clicking shapes with the Selection tool selects all fills and strokes that are connected. Shift-selecting allows you to add to the selection only what you need. Alternately, dragging a selection rectangle on the Stage with the Selection tool creates a bounding box that selects anything you drag it over. This bounding box method is the most reliable technique for selecting very complex objects with many intersecting strokes and fills.

Select Fills with the Selection Tool

① Click the **Selection** tool on the Tools panel.

The pointer becomes an arrow.

② Position the arrow in the Fill area or the center of the shape and click.

The fill becomes highlighted with a dotted pattern to indicate it has been selected. Hold down the Shift key to add other strokes and fills to the selection.

Double-clicking the shape selects both the fill and the stroke.

Selected fill

Select with a Selection Rectangle

① Click the **Selection** tool on the Tools panel.

The pointer becomes an arrow.

② Click on the Stage above and to the left of the shape you want to select and drag to create a Selection Rectangle, and then release the mouse when the bounding box fully encloses the shape.

Both fill and strokes are selected.

Making Selections with the Lasso Tool

Use the Lasso tool when you want to select shapes that are too close to shapes you don't want to select. This tool allows you to draw around the shape, selecting everything contained in the shape you draw. In the default mode, you can draw a freeform lasso around the object you want to select. You can also choose the Polygon mode for defining the selected area with a series of straight-line segments.

Select with the Lasso Tool

1. Click the **Lasso** tool on the Tools panel.

   TIMESAVER *Press L to select the Lasso tool.*

2. Draw around the shapes you want to select.

3. To complete the selection, return to the point where you started.

Did You Know?

You can select single or multiple objects. Holding the Shift key adds line segments and fills them. Shift-clicking selected items deselects them.

Select with the Lasso Tool in Polygon Mode

1. Click the **Lasso** tool on the Tools panel.

2. Click the **Polygon Mode** button in the Options area of the Tools panel.

3. Click near the area you want to select. Move the pointer and click again. Keep clicking until the object or portion you want to select is surrounded.

4. Double-click to complete the selection.

Selected shape

Flash draws a preview of the selection lasso as you draw.

Selected shape

Zooming In and Out with the Magnifying Glass

Because the Stage and Work Area in Flash share the same space with a variety of panels, palettes and windows, it is often necessary to change the magnification level. You can use the Magnifying Glass to zoom out and see the entire piece or zoom in to do more detailed work on a small portion. The tool is made up of two modifiers: a plus (+) symbol in the circle indicates enlargement of the Stage and a minus (-) indicates reduction. Flash allows magnification levels from 8 percent to 2000 percent.

Zoom In

1. Click the **Zoom** tool on the Tools panel.

2. Click the **Enlarge** button in the Options area of the Tools panel.

   The pointer becomes a magnifying glass with a plus (+) symbol in it.

3. Click on the area of the Stage you want to zoom into.

   TIMESAVER *Press Z to select the Zoom tool. To temporarily toggle between the Enlarge and Reduce Modifiers buttons in the Options area of the Tools panel, press Option (Mac) or Alt (Win).*

Zoom Out

1. Click the **Zoom** tool on the Tools panel.

2. Click the **Reduce** button in the Options area of the Tools panel.

   The pointer becomes a magnifying glass with a minus (-) symbol in it.

3. Click on the area of the Stage you want to zoom out from.

Zoom Into a Specific Area by Dragging on the Stage

1️⃣ Click the **Zoom** tool on the Tools panel.

2️⃣ Click the **Reduce** or **Enlarge** button in the Options area of the Tools panel.

3️⃣ Click on the area of the Stage you want to magnify and drag the pointer.

Did You Know?

You can change the magnification level in several places. The Zoom Control field in the top right hand corner of the Stage allows you to enter a value or access a list arrow with various magnification levels. You can also change the magnification submenu in the View menu or use the keyboard shortcuts ⌘+ - (Mac) or Ctrl+ - (Win) to zoom out, and ⌘+ + (Mac) or Ctrl+ + (Win) to zoom in. Quickly switch to 100 percent magnification by pressing ⌘+1 (Mac) or Ctrl+1 (Win).

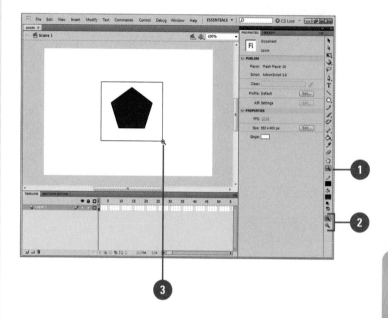

Moving Around with the Hand Tool

At certain magnifications, parts of the Stage may not be viewable. Use the Hand tool to quickly move to different parts of the Stage without having to change the magnification level. The Stage is the active area of your movie, the only area that will be visible in the exported Flash movie. The gray area around the Stage is the work area called the **pasteboard**, which you can use to store artwork and other objects without having them be visible in the published movie. The objects might not be visible on the Stage, but they contribute to the overall file size. It is a good idea to clean up your files before exporting the final movie. The Hand tool allows you to easily access objects contained on the pasteboard if you are doing detailed work at high magnification.

Move the Stage View

1. Click the **Hand** tool on the Tools panel.

   The pointer becomes a small hand that moves the entire Stage revealing other parts of the Stage as you drag.

   TIMESAVER *Pressing the space bar temporarily changes the active tool to the Hand tool. Continue holding as you drag.*

2. Click and drag the Stage to move the view.

Did You Know?

You can turn off the visibility of the Work Area (the gray space around the Stage) and quickly change the View scale to 100 percent. Toggle the Work Area option in the View menu or use the keyboard shortcut ⌘+Shift+W (Mac) or Ctrl+Shift+W (Win). This is a great way to temporarily see what is viewable in the exported Flash SWF file when you are working with large images that extend past the Stage boundaries.

For Your Information

Using the Info Pane

The Info pane display information about objects on the Stage. Click the Window menu, and then click Info. The Info pane displays width (W), height (H), object position (X, Y), mouse position (X, Y), and color info Red, Green, Blue, and Alpha (R, G, B, A). The W and H values display live info (**New!**) while you draw or resize an object. The X and Y values display live info (**New!**) while you move an object. The RGBA values display when you move the pointer over a symbol (**New!**).

Displaying Rulers

Ruler bars are located on the top and left sides of the Stage and serve several purposes. They let you measure the width and height of Flash elements and they let you place guides on the screen to control placement of objects on the Stage. In all, Rulers serve a very important role. When you display rulers, you can use guides to help you correctly align objects with other objects. By using guides, you have access to precise alignment systems. To use the guides, the ruler bars must first be visible. When you no longer need the rulers, you can hide the rulers to free up more workspace.

Show and Hide Rulers

1 Click the **View** menu, and then click **Rulers**.

A check mark next to the option means its visibility is enabled.

2 To hide rulers, click the **View** menu, and then click **Rulers** to remove the check mark and hide the rulers.

TIMESAVER *Press
⌘+Option+Shift+R (Mac) or
Ctrl+Alt+Shift+R (Win) to turn
the ruler on and off.*

Horizontal ruler

Vertical ruler

Did You Know?

You can change the unit of measure displayed on the Rulers. Click the Modify menu, click Document, click the Ruler Units list arrow, select a unit of measure, and then click OK.

For Your Information

Using the Pasteboard Work Area

You can use the work area (called the **Pasteboard**) around the Stage to store artwork and other objects, such as components, without having them be visible in the published movie. The objects might not be visible on the Stage, but they contribute to the overall file size. It is a good idea to clean up your files before exporting the final movie. You can clean up by removing any artwork outside the boundaries of the Stage or by putting them on a guide layer.

Using Grids and Guides

Flash comes with guides, grids, and rulers to help you lay out artwork and objects with precision. A grid is a series of crisscrossed lines that aid in aligning objects to each other on the Stage. Guides and grids are modifiable. You can change their visibility, position, color, and frequency. These items are invisible by default, but they can be easily turned on and adjusted. Though you see them in the Flash development environment, they are invisible on export. Use guides to align art and objects to each other on vertical or horizontal paths, or turn on the grid for use in designing a layout that is proportional and balanced.

Show and Hide Grids

1. Click the **View** menu, point to **Grid**, and then click **Show Grid**.

   ◆ You can also right-click (Win) or control-click (Mac) the **Stage**, point to **Grid**, and then click **Show Grid**.

   A check mark next to the option means its visibility is enabled.

2. To hide the grid, click the **View** menu, point to **Grid**, and then click **Show Grid** to remove the check mark and hide the grid.

   TIMESAVER *Press* ⌘+*apostrophe (') (Mac) or Ctrl+apostrophe (') (Win) to toggle Grid visibility on and off.

See Also

See "Modifying Grid and Guide Settings" on page 92 for information on changing settings.

Grid when visible

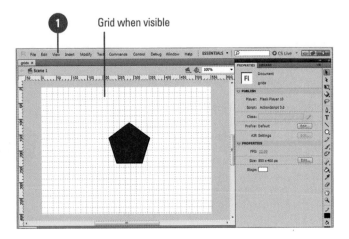

Create Guides

1 Click the **View** menu, and then click **Rulers** to display rulers.

2 Click on the vertical ruler on the left side of the work area with the Arrow pointer and drag to the right, and then release the mouse where you want to place the vertical guide.

   A small directional triangle and line appears next to the pointer as you drag indicating that you are dragging the guide.

3 Click on the horizontal ruler at the top of the work area with the Arrow pointer and drag down, and then release the mouse where you want to place the horizontal guide.

4 Reposition the guides by selecting them with the pointer.

Did You Know?

You can turn guide visibility on and off, lock guides, and enable or disable snapping to guides. Click the View menu, and then click Guides to access these options or use the following keyboard shortcuts: ⌘+; (Mac) or Ctrl+; (Win) toggles between showing and hiding guides. Option+⌘+; (Mac) or Ctrl+Alt+; (Win) locks and unlocks guides. Shift+⌘+; (Mac) or Ctrl+ Shift+; (Win) turns Snapping on and off.

See Also

See "Displaying Rulers" on page 89 for information on showing and hiding rulers.

Modifying Grid and Guide Settings

The need for grids and guides varies depending upon the type of document you are working on. They are useful for aligning text and graphics to interface elements and are an invaluable tool for creating a well composed and proportioned layout. Every project is different and has different requirements, so Flash allows the display, behavior, and characteristics of guides and grids to be altered to fit your needs. They are only visible in the Flash development environment, and are not exported in the Flash movie.

Modify Grid

1 Click the **View** menu, point to **Grid**, and then click **Edit Grid**.

> **TIMESAVER** *Press Option+⌘+G (Mac) or Ctrl+Alt+G (Win) to quickly access the Grid dialog box.*

2 Click the **Color** list arrow, and then click a grid line color.

3 Select or clear the **Show Grid** check box to show or hide the grid.

4 Select or clear the **Show Over Objects** check box to show or hide the grid over objects.

5 Select or clear the **Snap To Grid** check box to enable or disable snapping.

6 Enter values for horizontal and vertical dimensions for the grid lines.

7 Click the **Snap Accuracy** list arrow, and then select a level of sensitivity for snapping to the grid. Select from Must Be Close, Normal, Can Be Distant, and Always Snap.

8 To make the current grid settings the default for new Flash files, click the **Save Default** button.

9 Click **OK**.

Modify Guides

1. Click the **View** menu, point to **Guides**, and then click **Edit Guides**.

   TIMESAVER *Press Option+Shift+⌘+G (Mac) or Ctrl+Alt+Shift+G (Win) to quickly access the Guides dialog box.*

2. Click the **Color** list arrow, and then click a guide line color.

3. Select or clear the **Show Guides** check box to show or hide guides.

4. Select or clear the **Snap To Guides** check box to enable or disable snapping.

5. Select or clear the **Lock Guides** check box to enable or disable movement of guides.

6. Click the **Snap Accuracy** list arrow, and then select a level of sensitivity for snapping to the guides. Select from Must Be Close, Normal, Can Be Distant.

7. To remove all guides from the active scene, click **Clear All**.

8. To make the current guides the default guides for new Flash files, click **Save Default**.

9. Click **OK**.

   TIMESAVER *Press ⌘+; (Mac) or Ctrl+; (Win) to toggle between showing and hiding guides; press Option+⌘+; (Mac) or Ctrl+Alt+; (Win) to lock and unlock guides; or press Shift+⌘+; (Mac) or Ctrl+Shift+; (Win) to turn Snapping on and off.*

Using Snap Align

Snap Align is a new feature that enables dynamic alignment of art and objects on the Stage. Simply drag an object on the Stage and dashed lines appear that aid you in aligning to the edge or center vertices of other objects on the Stage. In the Edit Snapping dialog box you can enable and disable snap options, set the distance objects are to be from the movie borders and from each other before they snap, and save the settings as default. Additionally, you can choose to snap objects to edges or vertical and horizontal centers. Using the Snap Align feature enables you to lay out artwork more precisely and dynamically.

Enable Snap Align

1. Click the **View** menu, point to **Snapping**, and then click **Snap Align**.

   A check mark appears next to the menu item when Snap Align is enabled.

2. Drag an object on the Stage.

   Depending on the behaviors set in the Snap Align Settings dialog box, gray dashed lines appear when the edges or center vertices of objects move to within a certain pixel distance.

Snap Align to other items: Grid, Guides, Pixels, and Objects.

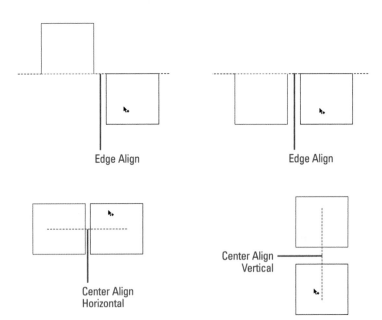

Edge Align

Edge Align

Center Align Horizontal

Center Align Vertical

Configure Snap Align and Save Defaults

① Click the **View** menu, point to **Snapping**, and then click **Edit Snapping**.

② Select the snap check box options you want to turn on.

③ Click **Advanced**.

④ Select from the following options:

◆ **Snap align settings.** Enter a value for the distance an object needs to be before it will snap to the boundaries of the stage movie (in pixels).

◆ **Object spacing.** Enter a value for horizontal and vertical edge tolerance (in pixels).

◆ **Center alignment.** Select the check boxes to center alignment on horizontal or vertical vertices or both.

⑤ To make the snap align setting the default for future use, click **Save Default**.

⑥ Click **OK**.

For Your Information

Snapping to an Object

You can use the Snap to Object command in the View menu or use the Snap option for the Selection tool on the Tools panel. If the Snap option is enabled, a small black ring appears under the pointer when you drag an object. The small ring changes to a larger ring when the object is within snapping distance of another object.

Changing Stroke and Fill Colors

Artwork created in Flash can have strokes and fills. Strokes and fills behave differently and are edited in different ways. A stroke is an outline. It describes the edges of a shape or it can be a simple line. You can create strokes with the Line tool or the Pencil tool. A fill is a solid shape, often contained or surrounded by a stroke. It is the surface area of a shape and can be a color, gradient, texture, or bitmap. Fills can be created with the Paintbrush tool and the Paint Bucket tool. The Oval, Rectangle, and Pen tool can create shapes with either a stroke or a fill, or both. You can edit the characteristics of strokes and fills, such as color, in several ways. If the shape is selected on the Stage, a color change to a stroke or fill can be made in any of the color palettes. Because Flash uses vectors to describe shapes, you can change their properties as much as you want without any loss in quality. It is important to grasp the concept behind them because they are the basis for drawing in Flash.

Change the Stroke Color

1. Click the **Selection** tool on the Tools panel.

2. Select the stroke of the shape by double-clicking it.

3. Click the **Stroke** color box on the Tools panel or Property Inspector.

4. Select a new color from the palette.

Active color

No stroke color

Click to access the Color Picker.

Did You Know?

You can change the stroke color in three other places. Stroke color boxes are also located in the Property Inspector, the Color panel, and the Swatches panel. In all cases, select the stroke you want to change and choose a new color from any of the palettes.

You can change the line width and style of a stroke or set the stroke color to None in the Property Inspector. Click the stroke you want to change to select it, and then select any of the options in the Property Inspector. Setting the stroke color to None removes the stroke from the shape.

Change the Fill Color

① Click the **Selection** tool on the Tools panel.

The pointer becomes an arrow.

② Click the fill of the shape to select it.

This is the area inside the stroke.

③ Click the **Fill** color box on the Tools panel or Property Inspector.

④ Select a new color from the palette.

Did You Know?

You can change the fill color in three other places. Fill color boxes are also located in the Property Inspector, the Color panel, and the Swatches panel. Just select the fill and choose a new color from one of the palettes by clicking on a new color box.

See Also

See "Editing Fills with the Paint Bucket" on page 103 for information on changing the fill color.

No fill color

Color Picker

Gradients

Creating Custom Colors

Each Flash document has its own color palette. The color palette displays as swatches when you access a color box or panel. The default color palette is the Web-safe palette of 216 colors. Flash allows you to edit and create new colors for strokes and fills in several ways in the Color panel. You can alter a color's RGB values (assigning it different levels of Red, Green or Blue), HSB values (**New!**) (assigning it different Hue, Saturation, Brightness), and Alpha (transparency). You can accomplish this by using sliders, dragging on a color-space, or entering a numeric value that corresponds to a specific color. In each case, you can save your color into the palette for easy access.

Create a Custom Color by Specifying a Value

1 Open the **Color** panel.

◆ To open the Color panel, click the **Window** menu, and then click **Color**.

TIMESAVER *Press Alt+Shift +F9 (Win) or Option+Shift+F9 (Mac).*

2 Click an RGB or HSB option, and then adjust the color RGB value between 0 and 255 or HSB percentage between 0 and 100.

3 Enter an alpha value between 0 and 100.

4 Click the **Options** button in the panel, and then click **Add Swatch**.

Options button
Color window

Did You Know?

You can alter the RGB or HSB values with the sliders located in the numeric entry boxes. Point to an entry box, and then drag the slider. Additionally, you can drag the cursor over the Color space bar at the bottom of the Color panel to change the color interactively.

You can also specify a color using a hexadecimal number in the Color panel. A hexadecimal number is an internal computer numbering scheme that is used to identify colors in a color palette.

Create a Custom Color with the Color Picker

1. Click a **Stroke** or **Fill** color box on the Tools panel or the Property Inspector.

2. Click the **Color Wheel** button to the far right of the palette.

3. Click a color from one of the available pickers (Mac) or from the Color window (Win).

4. Click **OK**.

No fill color

For Your Information

Working with Color Palettes

Each Flash file stores its own color palette, Web safe 216 by default. If you change colors in the default color palette, you can save the new palette as the default or change back to the Web safe 216 default. To view the color palette, click the Window menu, and then click Color Swatches. To load or save the default palette, click the Options button in the Color Swatches panel, and then click Load Default Colors or Save As Default. To reload the Web-safe color palette, click the Options button, and then click Web 216.

Adding Colors Using the Kuler Panel

The Kuler panel is an extension to Flash that allows you to use groups of color, or themes in your projects. You can use the panel to browse thousands of color themes, create your own using the complementary harmony rules, and share them with others in the Kuler community. After you find or create the theme you want, you can add it to the Swatches panel for use in your project. You can access the Kuler panel by using the Extensions submenu on the Window menu. The Kuler panel is also available in the CS5 version of Photoshop, InDesign, Illustrator, and Fireworks.

Browse Themes and Add to the Swatches Panel

1. Click the **Window** menu, point to **Extensions**, and then click **Kuler**.

2. Click the **Browse** tab.

3. To search for a theme, click in the Search box, enter the name of the theme, a tag, or a creator, and then press Enter (Win) or Return (Mac).

   IMPORTANT *In a search, use only alphanumerical characters (Aa-Zz, 0-9).*

4. To narrow down the browse list, click the popups, and then select the filter options you want. Some include Highest Rated, Most Popular, Newest.

   ◆ To save a search, click the first list arrow, click **Custom**, enter your search criteria, and then click **Save**.

5. To browse for a theme, click the **View previous set of themes** or **View next set of themes** button.

6. Select a theme in the panel.

7. To add the theme to the Swatches panel, click the **Add Selected Theme To Swatches** button.

Create or Edit a Theme

1. Click the **Window** menu, point to **Extensions**, and then click **Kuler**.

2. To create or edit a theme, do either of the following:

   ◆ **Create a theme.** Click the **Create** tab.

   ◆ **Edit a theme.** Click the **Browse** tab, select the theme you want to edit, and then click **Edit Theme in Create Panel.**

3. Click the **Select Rule** list arrow, and then select a harmony rule or **Custom**.

   The harmony rule uses the base color as the basis for generating the colors in the color group, so you can create a theme with complementary colors.

4. Select a color box, and then use the sliders and the color wheel to display the color you want.

5. Use the buttons below the color boxes to add/remove the theme color, add the current stroke/fill color as the base color, or adjust the other colors.

   ◆ Double-click a color box to set the active color in Flash.

6. Upon completion, do any of the following:

   ◆ **Save theme.** Click **Save Theme**, name the theme, and then click **Save** to create a new one.

   ◆ **Add to Swatches Panel.** Click the **Add This Theme to Swatches** button.

   ◆ **Upload to Kuler.** Click the **Upload Theme to Kuler** button.

Colors added from Kuler panel

Editing Strokes with the Ink Bottle

There are a number of ways to change the stroke of an object. You can select the stroke and change its characteristics in the Property Inspector, the Swatch palettes, and the Color panel. If you need to apply the stroke properties of one object to that of another, use the Ink Bottle tool. The Ink Bottle tool holds the properties you've set for strokes in any of the palettes. You can click any object on the Stage to change the properties of its stroke (color, line weight and style) or add a stroke to an object that doesn't have one.

Use the Ink Bottle

1. Select a stroke on the Stage, and then change Stroke attributes in the Property Inspector.

2. Click the **Ink Bottle** tool on the Tools panel.

    The pointer becomes a small ink bottle.

    TIMESAVER *Press S to select the Ink Bottle tool.*

3. Click on the stroke of the shape to update it with the new attributes.

    The stroke updates to the new color.

Did You Know?

You can click anywhere on the shape with the Ink Bottle to change the stroke. If the object on the Stage is selected (stroke and fill), click down with the Ink Bottle tool to update its stroke.

Stroke Color

Stroke Weight

Stroke Style

Built-in Stroke styles

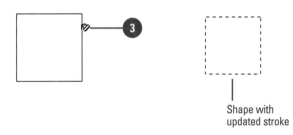

Shape with updated stroke

Editing Fills with the Paint Bucket

You can change the fill of an object with the Paint Bucket tool. The Paint Bucket stores the fill color you've set on the Tools panel or in the Property Inspector. You can change the fill color of any existing shape on the Stage by touching down on the shape with this tool. You can also add a fill to any shape that has a closed stroke. After you select the Paint Bucket tool, you can select Paint Bucket sensitivity options located at the bottom of the Tools panel.

Use the Paint Bucket

1. Change the **Fill** color box in either the Property Inspector, the Colors area of the Tools panel, or the Color panel.

2. Click the **Paint Bucket** tool on the Tools panel.

   The pointer becomes a small paint bucket.

   TIMESAVER *Press K to select the Paint Bucket tool.*

3. Click in the fill of a shape on the Stage.

   The fill updates to the new color.

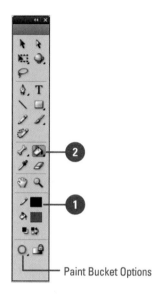

Paint Bucket Options

Did You Know?

You can set the sensitivity of the Paint Bucket tool in the Options areas of the Toolbox. These settings allow the Paint Bucket tool to close gaps in a shape (such as a break in the stroke line) and adjust how large or small a gap needs to be before Flash will close it.

Paint Bucket sensitivity

Shape with updated fill

Editing Strokes and Fills with the Eyedropper

The Eyedropper tool allows you to select the attributes of a shape such as fill and stroke color, and line weight and style, and then transfer them to other shapes. This tool detects whether you are selecting a stroke or a fill, and then changes into the Ink Bottle (when selecting strokes) or the Paint Bucket (when selecting fills). Instead of taking several steps to copy attributes from one shape to another, the Eyedropper provides a quick means for storing and transferring attributes between editable shapes.

Use the Eyedropper Tool to Edit Strokes and Fills

1. Click the **Eyedropper** tool on the Tools panel.

   The pointer becomes an eyedropper.

   TIMESAVER *Press I to select the Eyedropper tool.*

2. Position the eyedropper over the stroke or fill of a shape on the Stage.

   ◆ **Strokes.** When you are positioned over a stroke, a tiny pencil appears next to the tool. When you click on the stroke the Eyedropper becomes an Ink Bottle.

   ◆ **Fills.** When you are positioned over a fill, a tiny paint brush appears next to the tool. When you click on the fill the Eyedropper becomes a Paint Bucket.

3. Click on another shape's stroke or fill to transfer the selected attributes.

   The stroke or fill updates to the new color.

Tiny Pencil appears indicating eyedropper is positioned over a stroke.

Ink Bottle appears when you click on a stroke.

Tiny Paint brush appears indicating eyedropper is positioned over a fill.

Paint Bucket appears when you click on a fill.

Creating Gradients

Flash can create a number of paint effects in addition to solid colors. Gradients are made up of two or more colors that gradually fade into each other. They can be used to give depth to an object or create realistic shadows. Two gradient modes are available: linear and radial. Linear gradients are made up of parallel bands of color. Radial gradients radiate from a center focal point. Both can be edited for color, alpha, and position within a fill or stroke. You can add up to 16 colors to a gradient, precisely control the location of the gradient focal point, and apply other parameters. A gradient behaves like any other fill or stroke. It can be saved to the palette as a swatch using the Color panel Options button, and added to other shapes with the Paint Bucket tool.

Create a Multi-Color Gradient

1. With the **Selection** tool, select the fill or stroke of a shape on the Stage.

2. In the Color panel, click the **Fill Style Type** list arrow, and then click **Linear** Gradient or **Radial Gradient**.

3. To select the gradient display style (**New!**), click a Flow button: **Extend Color**, **Reflect Color**, or **Repeat Color**.

4. Position the pointer on the Color Picker box to display a circle pointer (**New!**).

5. Click in the Gradient bar to create a color proxy indicated by a little box with a triangle on top.

   TIMESAVER *To remove a proxy color indicator, drag it down.*

6. Click one of the color proxy indicators to select it.

7. Click a new color from the Color Picker box above.

8. Drag the color proxy indicator along the Gradient bar to adjust the color placement.

9. Repeat steps 4-8 to add up to 15 more gradient colors.

Example: 3-Color Linear Gradient

Using the Fill Lock

As you increase the complexity and number of shapes in your movie, it can become tricky to edit each object separately. When using gradient fills on several objects you can choose to span a gradient across several of these objects or give each object its own discreet gradient. The Lock Fill feature allows you to control how a fill is applied, essentially locking its position so that depending on where the shapes are positioned relative to the gradient, the one gradient spans all of the shapes. If you apply the same gradient to multiple shapes with the Fill Lock off, the gradient is applied to each shape independently.

Lock Gradients

1. Create two simple shapes using the **Rectangle** or **Oval** tool.

2. Select the first shape on the Stage with the Selection tool.

3. Click the **Paint Bucket** tool on the Tools panel.

   TIMESAVER *Press K to select the Paint Bucket tool.*

4. Click the **Lock Fill** button in the Options area of the Tools panel.

5. Select a Gradient from the Colors area of the Tools panel or use the Color panel or Property Inspector.

6. Click the **Eyedropper** tool on the Tools panel, and then click on the gradient fill in the first shape.

7. Click down on the second shape to add the gradient fill.

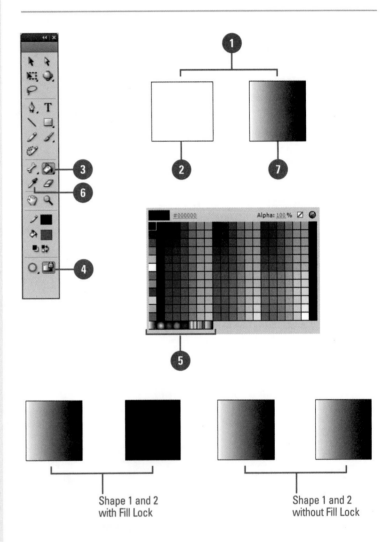

Shape 1 and 2 with Fill Lock

Shape 1 and 2 without Fill Lock

Did You Know?

You can quickly add a gradient that spans all of your shapes. Select all of the objects you want to fill, and then choose a gradient. Click the Paint Bucket tool and make sure Fill Lock is not selected. With your shapes still selected, click them with the Paint Bucket.

Using Paint Brush Modes

In addition to size, shape, and color settings for the Paint Brush tool, you can control how the brush behaves when painting on existing shapes and objects on the Stage. Paint Brush modes can restrict the area affected by the tool to fills or selections, empty areas of the Stage or specific shapes. When the Paint Brush tool is selected, a list arrow menu appears on the Tools panel. Select from the following modes: Paint Normal, Paint Fills, Paint Behind, Paint Selection, and Paint Inside. Each performs a specific operation providing you with varying levels of control as you paint. Flash previews your paint path as you paint, but it only affects the areas you've specified in the Paint modes. When you release the mouse, these previews disappear.

Use Paint Brush Modes

1. Click the **Brush** tool on the Tools panel.

2. Click the **Brush Mode** list arrow in the Options area on the Tools panel, and then select from the following:

   ◆ **Paint Normal.** The brush paints over everything including strokes and other fills.

   ◆ **Paint Fills.** Painting only affects existing fills and empty areas of the Stage. Strokes are ignored.

   ◆ **Paint Behind.** The Paint Brush only affects empty areas of the Stage keeping existing lines and fills intact.

   ◆ **Paint Selection.** Painting only affects the selected areas you define with any of the selection tools.

   ◆ **Paint Inside.** The Paint Brush only affects the fill of the shape you started in, ignoring other shapes and empty areas on the Stage.

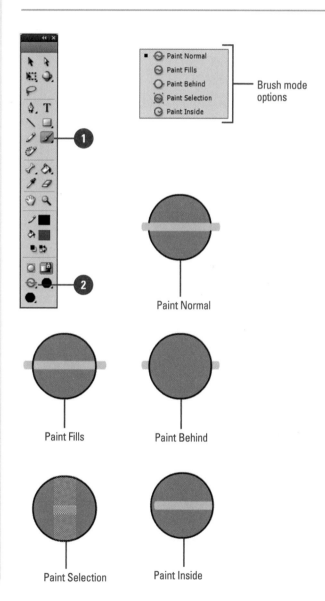

Brush mode options

Paint Normal

Paint Fills

Paint Behind

Paint Selection

Paint Inside

Using the Spray Brush Tool

The Spray Brush tool allows you to spray particles onto the Stage using the current fill color. If you want to create a more complex pattern, you can also use a movie clip or graphic symbol from the library as a particle. You can adjust the spray pattern by selecting Symbol and Brush options in the Property Inspector. The Symbol options include Scale, Random scaling, Rotate symbol, and Random rotation, while the Brush options include Width, Height, and Brush angle.

Use the Spray Brush Tool

① Click the **Spray Brush** tool on the Tools panel.

② Select a fill color for the default spray of dots and other options in the Property Inspector.

◆ **Color Selector.** Select a fill color for the default spray particle.

◆ **Edit.** Select a custom symbol from the library. You can use any movie clip or graphic symbol in the library as the spray particle.

◆ **Scale.** Scale the width and height of a symbol used as a spray particle.

◆ **Random Scaling.** Randomly spray particles on the Stage with different sizes.

◆ **Rotate Symbol.** Rotates the symbol spray particle around a center point.

◆ **Random Rotation.** Randomly rotate spray particles on the Stage.

◆ **Width and Height.** Specifies the brush width and height.

◆ **Brush Angle.** Specifies the spray angle of the particles.

③ Click or drag on the Stage where you want the pattern to appear.

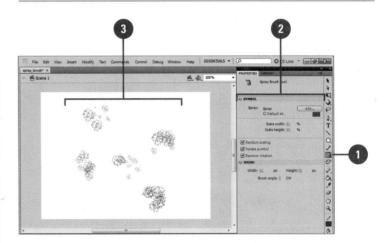

Using the Deco Tool

The Deco tool allows you to apply a kaleidoscopic drawing effect to the Stage or a selected object on the Stage. You can apply several effects (**New!**): Vine Fill, Grid Fill, Symmetry Brush, 3D Brush, Building Brush, Decorated, Fire Animation, Flame Brush, Flower Brush, Lightning Brush, or Tree Brush. The Vine effect fills the Stage, symbol, object, or closed area with a vine pattern. You can also use your own artwork (symbols) for the leaves and flowers.The Grid effect fills the Stage, symbol, object, or closed area with a symbol from the library. You can create grid patterns, such as a tiled background or checkerboard. The Symmetry effect arranges symbols symmetrically around a central point, which you can control with a set of handles. You can create circular elements, such as a planet. The default symbol for the Symmetry effect is a 25 x 25 pixel black rectangle with no stroke. You can use other brushes (**New!**) to draw buildings, flames, lightning, trees, and other effects to add fire and smoke animations (**New!**) or a particle system (**New!**).

Use the Deco Tool

1. Click the **Deco** tool on the Tools panel.

2. In the Property Inspector, click the **Drawing Effect** list arrow, and then select a drawing effect.

3. For the Vine Fill, Grid Fill, or Particle System effect, select a fill color for the default shape, or select a symbol.

   ◆ **Color Selector.** Select a fill color for the default pattern.

   ◆ **Edit.** Select a custom symbol from the library. You can use any movie clip or graphic symbol in the library as the pattern.

4. Specify the advanced options you want for the different effects; options vary depending on the selected effect.

5. Click the Stage or within the shape or symbol (Vine Fill, Grid Fill, and Particle System) where you want the pattern to appear.

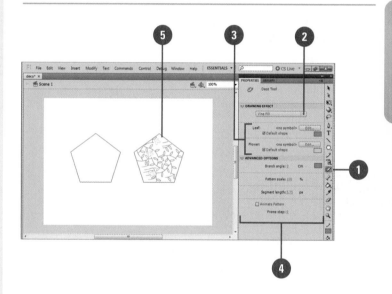

Drawing with the Pen Tool

The Pen tool is the basis for vector drawing. The Pen tool now behaves similarly to the Illustrator Pen tool to provide consistency across Adobe software. Flash provides a number of ways to draw and edit objects that are unique to Flash, but the Pen tool utilizes procedures that will be familiar to those who have used other vector drawing programs. The Pen tool utilizes anchor points and Bézier handles to create lines and shapes and behaves in a way that is familiar to those who have used other programs such as Adobe Illustrator and Adobe FreeHand. You can use the Pen tool arrow to select a different pen to add, delete, or convert anchor points. You can edit the anchor points and vectors to create the drawings you want.

Use the Pen Tool to Create an Open Path

1. Click the **Pen** tool on the Tools panel.

   TIMESAVER *Press P to quickly select the Pen tool.*

2. Click on the Stage.

   An anchor point is created.

3. Move your pointer to another position, and then click again.

   Flash connects the two anchor points.

4. Double-click to end the path.

   TIMESAVER *Ctrl+click (Win) or Command+click a blank area to leave the path open.*

Did You Know?

You can end an open path using a keyboard shortcut. Press ⌘+click (Mac) or Ctrl+click (Win).

See Also

See "Modifying Shapes with the Sub-Selection Tool" on page 116 for information on using tools.

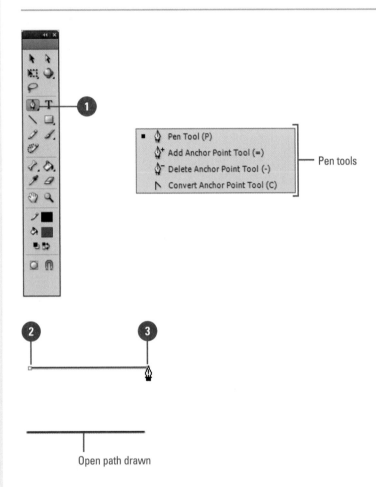

Pen Tool (P)
Add Anchor Point Tool (=)
Delete Anchor Point Tool (-)
Convert Anchor Point Tool (C)

Pen tools

Open path drawn

Use the Pen Tool to Create a Closed Path

① Click the **Pen** tool on the Tools panel.

   TIMESAVER *Press P to quickly select the Pen tool.*

② Click on the Stage.

   An anchor point is created.

③ Move your pointer to another position, and then click again.

   Flash connects the two anchor points.

④ Move the pointer to a third position, and then click again.

   Flash connects the second and third anchor points.

⑤ Move the pointer back to the first anchor point.

   A small circle appears next to the pen pointer indicating you can close the path of the shape.

⑥ Click to close the shape.

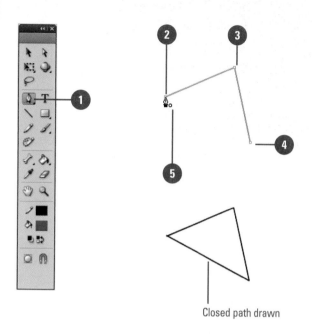

Closed path drawn

Did You Know?

You can delete an anchor point with the Pen tool. Click the Pen tool arrow, click Delete Anchor Point tool, and then click the point you want to delete.

You can add an anchor point with the Pen tool. Click the Pen tool arrow, click Add Anchor Point tool, and then click where you want to add a point.

You can create horizontal, vertical, and 45 degree lines while you draw. Hold the Shift key while you draw to constrain a line to horizontal, vertical, and 45 degree angles.

Understanding Pen Pointers

Pointer	Description
Initial Anchor Point ♙ₓ	First pointer to create the beginning of a new path.
Sequential Anchor Point ♙	Creates an anchor point with a line connecting the previous anchor point.
Add Anchor Point ♙₊	Adds an anchor point to existing path.
Delete Anchor Point ♙₋	Deletes an anchor point within a path.
Continue Path ♙	Extends a new path from an existing anchor point.
Close Path ♙ₒ	Closes the path of a drawing on the starting anchor point.
Join Paths ♙ₒ	Closes the path except not over the starting anchor point.
Retract Bézier Handle ♙	Displays Bézier handles when you point to an anchor. Click to retract the handles and revert to straight segments.
Convert Anchor Point ⼂	Converts a corner point without direction lines to a corner point with independent direction lines. Use Shift+C modifier keys to toggle the pen.

Drawing Curves with the Pen Tool

The Pen tool can be used to draw precise and complex curves by simply clicking and dragging it on the Stage. These curves can be modified with precision by adjusting the Bézier handles that extend from the anchor points, or you can move the anchor points themselves. In this way, you can create any number of shape variations. For best results, make the grid visible so aligning anchor points isn't such a mystery.

Create Curved Line Segments

1. Click the **Pen** tool on the Tools panel.

2. Click on the Stage without releasing the mouse, drag up, and then release the mouse.

3. Position the pointer to the right of the original point, drag in the opposite direction of the curve, and then release the mouse when the curve is where you want it.

4. Continue adding points as needed. To end the path, double-click or point to the last anchor point drawn and click on it.

Curved line segment drawn

Create S-Curves

1. Click the **Pen** tool on the Tools panel.

2. Click on the Stage without releasing the mouse, drag down, and then release the mouse.

3. Position the pointer to the right of the original point, drag in the same direction as the first drag, and then release the mouse when the curve is where you want it.

4. Continue adding points as needed. To end the path, double-click or return to the last anchor point drawn and click on it.

S-Curve drawn

Modifying Shapes with the Selection Tool

In Flash, unlike other vector drawing programs, you can edit shapes and lines in a unique, freeform way by simply dragging with the Arrow Selection tool. You can quickly adjust the curve or corner of a shape or line without having to select anchor points or use any other tools. This way of editing shapes is also useful for creating shape tweens where amorphous, organic movement is desired. This is what sets Flash apart from other animation tools and gives it its distinctive style. Additionally, you can convert curved line segments into corner points with this simple drag technique.

Use the Selection Tool to Modify a Shape

① Click the **Oval** tool on the Tools panel and then create a simple oval shape.

② Click the **Selection** tool on the Tools panel.

The pointer becomes an arrow.

③ Make sure the shape you want to modify is not selected.

④ Position the pointer on the edge of the shape, and then drag to modify the shape.

You can pull the curve to any position.

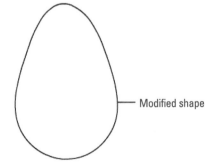

Modified shape

Convert Line Segments with the Selection Tool

1. Create a simple oval shape using the **Oval** tool.

2. Click the **Selection** tool on the Tools panel.

   The pointer becomes an arrow.

3. Make sure the shape you want to modify is not selected.

4. Position the pointer on the edge of the shape.

5. Press Option+drag (Mac) or Alt+drag (Win) to create a corner point.

Modified shape

More corners added

Modifying Shapes with the Sub-Selection Tool

Vector shapes are made up of anchor points connected by line segments. There are two types of anchor points: corner points and curve points. Corner points connect two line segments in a sharp angle such as the corner of a square. Curve points define a curve or positions along a straight line and can be modified with Bézier handles. These handles extend out from the curve point and allow for very precise modification of the shape of the curve. The Sub-Selection tool works hand-in-hand with the Pen tool to create and modify shapes and lines in this way.

Use the Sub-Selection Tool to Modify a Shape

1. Create a simple oval shape using the **Oval** tool.

2. Click the **Sub-Selection** tool on the Tools panel.

   The pointer becomes an empty (or white) arrow.

3. Click on the edge of the shape to reveal the anchor points, and then click on an anchor point to select it or drag a selection rectangle to select multiple anchor points.

   The anchor points are the little white squares around the edge of the shape. When selected, Bézier handles appear on either side of the anchor point.

4. Grab one of the handles or the anchor points themselves and drag it, and then release the mouse.

Did You Know?

You can also use the arrow keys on the keyboard to move selected anchor points. Select one or more anchor points with the Sub-Selection tool, and then press the arrow keys to move the anchor point and its connected lines in the direction of the key you press.

Convert Corner Points to Curve Points

① Create a simple rectangle shape using the **Rectangle** tool.

② Click the **Sub-Selection** tool on the Tools panel.

The pointer becomes an empty (or white) arrow.

③ Click on the edge of the shape to select it and then click on one of the corner points to select it.

④ Press Option+drag (Mac) or Alt+drag (Win) the point to convert it to a curve point and create Bézier handles.

Convert Curve Points to Corner Points

① Create a simple oval shape using the **Oval** tool.

② Click the **Pen** tool on the Tools panel.

The pointer becomes a small pen.

③ Click on the edge of the shape to reveal the anchor points.

④ Position the pointer over one of the curve points.

A small corner icon appears.

⑤ Click on the point to convert it to a corner point.

All anchor points converted to corner points.

Using the Free Transform Tool

There are a number of ways to change the scale or size of graphics in Flash. The Free Transform tool on Tools panel allows you to interactively scale and rotate any selected object or shape on the Stage. Nearly every object in Flash can be transformed with these two functions of the Free Transform tool including groups, symbols, text, bitmaps, and editable shapes. The Free Transform tool allows you to select an object on the Stage and then interactively change its size or rotate it freely. Both options are available at once depending on where you place your mouse on the bounding box that appears.

Change the Scale of an Object

1. Select the object by clicking on it or by dragging a selection marquee around it with the **Selection** tool.

2. Click the **Free Transform** tool on the Tools panel.

   TIMESAVER *Press Q to select the Free Transform tool.*

3. Click the **Scale Modifier** button in the Options area of the Tools panel.

4. Drag any of the small handles on the bounding box to change the size of the shape. The corner handles resize proportionally while the handles along the sides resize either horizontally or vertically.

5. To change the transformation point, drag the circle handle.

For Your Information

Working with the Transformation Point

When you transform an object, a transformation point appears at the center of the object. The point is initially placed in the center of the object, but you can move it at any time. To move the transformation point during a transformation, drag the point. To set it back to the center, double-click the point. To switch the point of origin for a scale or skew, Alt+drag (Win) or Option+drag (Mac) the point. To monitor the location of the transformation point (X and Y positions), click the center square in the grid in the Info panel (available on the Windows menu).

Rotate and Skew an Object

① Select the object by clicking on it or by dragging a selection marquee around it.

② Click the **Free Transform** tool on the Tools panel.

TIMESAVER *Press Q to select the Free Transform tool.*

③ Click the **Rotate/Skew Modifier** button in the Options area of the Tools panel.

④ Drag any of the corner handles on the bounding box to rotate the shape. Drag the handles along the side to skew the object.

⑤ To change the transformation point, drag the circle handle.

Did You Know?

You can hold down the Shift key to constrain the rotation scale proportionally. When rotating, it constrains the rotation to 45-degree turns.

For Your Information

Working with Scale and Rotate

In the Default mode, both Scale and Rotate are enabled. Move the pointer to any of the four corner handles in the bounding box to enable the Rotate function. Scale and Rotate work relative to a center transformation point on the shape, which becomes visible when the shape is selected with the Free Transform tool. Move this point if you want to scale or rotate a shape from a different part of the shape. This is especially important when tweening and animating. You can change the scale and rotate objects by entering values in the Transform panel or in the Property Inspector. You can also access all of the Transform modes and some additional effects, such as Flip Horizontal and Vertical from the Transform submenu in the Modify menu.

Using Transform Options for Shapes

In addition to the scale and rotation changes that can be applied to groups, symbols, bitmaps, text and editable shapes, there are two additional transforms available only to editable shapes. Distort and Envelope are two modes available in the Free Transform tool options that enable you to transform the vectors of editable shapes to varying degrees. Distort transformations work on adjoining edges, tapering them down to vanishing points, similar to perspective. Envelope transformations allow you to warp the edges of a shape by splitting it up into smaller portions each controlled by their own vectors and anchor points.

Distort a Shape

1. Select the object.

2. Click the **Free Transform** tool on the Tools panel.

   TIMESAVER *Press Q to select the Free Transform tool.*

3. Click the **Distort Modifier** button in the Options area of the Tools panel.

4. Drag any of the corner handles on the bounding box to distort the shape.

5. Drag any of the side handles on the bounding box to skew or stretch the shape.

Change the Envelope of a Shape

1. Select the object.

2. Click the **Free Transform** tool on the Tools panel.

   TIMESAVER *Press Q to select the Free Transform tool.*

3. Click the **Envelope Modifier** button in the Options area of the Tools panel.

4. Drag any of the handles on the bounding box to pull the shape in any direction or use the Bézier handles to fine tune the curves.

Transforming Gradient Fills

After you create a gradient fill, you can transform it by adjusting the size, rotation, width, or center of the fill with the Gradient Transform tool (formerly called the Fill Transform tool). For a radial gradient, you can now adjust the focal point (center) of a gradient fill applied to an object. You can also use the Gradient Transform tool to modify a bitmap fill.

Adjust a Gradient Fill

1. Click the **Gradient Transform** tool on the Tools panel.

2. Click the gradient fill to select it.

   A bounding box appears around it.

3. Position the pointer over an editing handle on the bounding box to identify its function.

   ◆ **Center point.** Four-way arrow.

   ◆ **Focal point.** Inverted triangle.

   ◆ **Size.** Circle with an arrow.

   ◆ **Rotation.** Four arrows in the shape of a circle.

   ◆ **Width.** Double-ended arrow.

4. Click and drag an editing handle to adjust the gradient fill.

> ### See Also
>
> See "Modifying a Bitmap Fill" on page 212 for information on using the Gradient Transform tool with bitmaps.

Linear gradient

Use Color panel to change color gradient settings

Radial gradient

Moving and Rotating Objects in 3D Space

In Flash, you can add 3D perspective effects to a movie clip by moving and rotating it in 3D space on the Stage. When you move or rotate a movie clip by the z axis, it becomes a 3D movie clip. Moving an object in 3D space is called **translation**, and rotating an object in 3D space is called **transformation**. Flash provides two different 3D space: global and local. Global 3D space is the Stage space, while local 3D space is the movie clip space. The default mode is global. You can move a movie clip in 3D space with the 3D Translation tool. When you do, three axes appear in the 3D object: the x axis is read, the y axis is green, and the z axis is blue. In addition, you can rotate a movie clip in 3D space with the 3D Transformation tool. When you do, you can rotate around an individual axis or use the orange free rotate control to rotate around the x and y axes at the same time. If you want to change the effect of the rotation, move the center point. When you select a 3D object, it appears with a 3D axis overlay.

Move Objects in 3D Space

1. Click the **3D Translation** tool on the Tools panel.

   TIMESAVER *Press G to select the 3D Translation tool.*

2. Click the **Global Transform** button on the Tools panel to select it for global mode or deselect it for local mode. The default is global.

   TIMESAVER *Press D to toggle between global and local mode.*

3. Select one or more movie clip objects.

   ◆ When you select multiple movie clips, and move one of them, the others move in the same way. Shift double-click one of the selected objects to move the axis controls to that object.

4. Drag the arrow tips (x- and y-axis) in the direction of the arrow or the black dot (z-axis) up or down.

   ◆ You can also move the object manually by using the Property Inspector.

Rotate Objects in 3D Space

1. Click the **3D Rotation** tool on the Tools panel.

   TIMESAVER *Press W to select the 3D Rotation tool.*

2. Click the **Global Transform** button on the Tools panel to select it for global mode or deselect it for local mode. The default is global.

3. Select one or more movie clip objects.

   ◆ When you select multiple movie clips, and move one of them, the others move in the same way. Shift double-click one of the selected objects to move the axis controls to that object.

4. Drag one of the four axis controls to rotate around that axis, or the free rotate control to rotate x and y axis at the same time.

5. To move the rotation control center point relative to the movie clip, drag the center point.

   ◆ Double-click the center point to move it back to the center of the movie clip.

Did You Know?

You can turn the overlay on and off. Click the Edit (Win) or Flash (Mac), click Preferences, click General, select or clear the Show axes for 3d movie clips check box, and then click OK.

Changing the Perspective Angle in 3D Space

The Perspective Angle affects the size and view of 3D movie clips on the Stage. It's like zooming in and out with a camera lens, which changes the angle of view through the lens. When you increase the angle, 3D objects appear closer to the viewer. When you decrease the angle, 3D objects appear further away. The default angle is 55 degrees of view, which is like a normal camera lens. You can adjust the value from 1 degree to 180 degrees. You can control only one viewpoint, or camera. Each Flash file has only one Perspective Angle.

Change Perspective Angle in 3D Space

1. Select the 3D movie clip instance on the Stage that you want to change.

2. Click the **Window** menu, and then click **Properties** to open the Property Inspector.

3. Enter a new value in the Perspective Angle box or drag the hot text to change the value in the Property Inspector.

Did You Know?

You can automatically change the appearance 3D objects when you change the size of the Stage. Click the Modify menu, click Document, select or clear the Adjust 3D Perspective Angle to preserve current stage projection check box, and then click OK.

Adjusting the Vanishing Point in 3D Space

Vanishing Point gives you the ability to move 3D movie clips and still maintain the same visual perspective of the original. Vanishing Point controls the orientation of the z-axis of 3D movie clips on the Stage. As you move the z-axis, 3D movie clips recede towards the Vanishing Point, which you can adjust to create the appearance you want. Each Flash file has only one Vanishing Point. If you move the Vanishing Point back to the default position in center of the Stage, you can use the Reset button in the Property Inspector.

Adjust the Vanishing Point in 3D Space

1. Select the 3D movie clip instance on the Stage that you want to change.

2. Click the **Window** menu, and then click **Properties** to open the Property Inspector.

3. Enter an x- and y-axis value in the Vanishing Point boxes or drag the hot text to change the value in the Property Inspector.

   As you drag the hot text, guides indicating the location of the Vanishing Point appears on the Stage.

4. To move the Vanishing Point back to the center of the Stage, click the **Reset** button in the Property Inspector.

Cutting and Pasting Graphics Between Layers

Unless you lock or hide layers, or lock objects, the graphics on all layers are available for editing. You can select objects on one or more layers, cut or copy them, and then paste them all into a single layer. Flash can have only one layer active at a time. When you create and paste graphics, Flash places them on the active layer of a document. You can paste objects in two different ways: Paste In Center and Paste In Place. Paste In Center puts objects in the center of the open Flash window, which might not be the Stage. If you want to paste to the center of the Stage, you need to center the Stage in the open window. Paste In Place puts objects at the same location it had been when you cut or copied it.

Paste Objects Between Layers

1. Create or open a document with several layers.

2. Select one or more objects on the Stage.

   Flash selects the object's layer in the Timeline.

3. Click the **Edit** menu, and then click **Cut** or **Copy**.

4. Select a destination layer in the Timeline.

5. Click the **Edit** menu, and then click **Paste In Center**.

   Flash pastes the objects on the Stage in the middle of the active layer.

Did You Know?

You can use the area around the Stage to store graphics and other objects. Flash allows you to use the area around the Stage, called the Pasteboard, to store items for use later without having them appear on the Stage when you play the movie (SWF) file.

Shape pasted on layer 2 in the center.

Use the Paste In Place Command Between Layers

1. Create or open a document with several layers.

2. Select one or more objects on the Stage.

   Flash selects the object's layer in the Timeline.

3. Click the **Edit** menu, and then click **Cut** or **Copy**.

4. Select a destination layer in the Timeline.

5. Click the **Edit** menu, and then click **Paste In Place**.

   Flash pastes the objects into their original locations on the Stage.

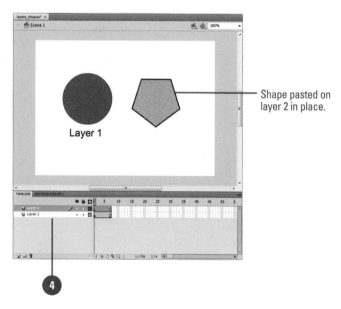

Shape pasted on layer 2 in place.

Working with Graphics on Different Layers

When you select an object on the Stage, Flash selects the object's layer in the Timeline. The reverse is also true. When you select a layer in the Timeline, Flash selects all the objects for that layer on the Stage. As you work with objects on different layers, it helps to know how selections work. Unless you lock or hide layers, or lock objects, the objects on all layers, either active or inactive, are available for editing. You can activate a layer and edit objects on inactive layers.

Edit Object on Inactive Layers

1. Create or open a document with several layers.

2. Click the **Selection** tool on the Tools panel.

3. Select an object on the Stage.

   Flash selects the object's layer in the Timeline.

4. Click a blank area of the Stage.

   Flash deselects the object but keeps the active layer.

5. Make changes to another object in another layer (inactive layer) without actually selecting the object. You can do any of the following:

   ◆ Drag an object's outline to reshape it.

   ◆ Select a tool on the Tools panel, such as the Paint Bucket tool, and use it to modify the object.

   Flash modifies the object in the inactive layer. The active layer didn't change. Flash changes active layers only if you select an object.

Layer 1 active

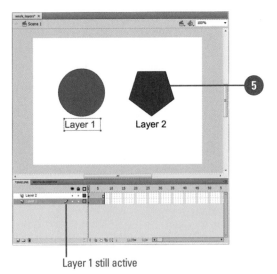

Layer 1 still active

Distributing Graphics to Layers

If you have several objects on a single layer, and need to move them onto separate layers, you can use Cut and Paste in place for each object or you can save time by using the Distribute to Layers command. The Distribute to Layers commands puts each object (shapes, groups, and symbols) in a selection on a separate layer; any unselected objects remain on their original layer. This command comes in handy when you want to create a motion tweening animation, which requires objects to be on individual layers.

Place Selected Objects on Separate Layers

① Create or open a document with several objects on a single layer.

② Select all the objects on a single layer you want to distribute to separate layers.

   TIMESAVER *Click the Edit menu, and then click Select All or press ⌘+A (Mac) or Ctrl+A (Win).*

③ Click the **Modify** menu, point to **Timeline**, and then click **Distribute To Layers**.

   TIMESAVER *Press ⌘+Shift+D (Mac) or Ctrl+Shift+D (Win) to distribute to layers.*

   Flash creates a layer for each object. New layers appear at the bottom of the Timeline in the order in which you originally placed them on the Stage. Each object is placed in the same location on the Stage (like the Paste In Place command).

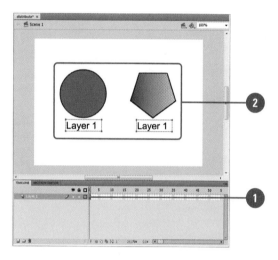

See Also

See Chapter 8, *"Animating with Motion Tweening"* on page 237 for information on using motion tweening.

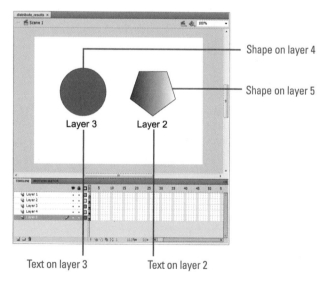

Shape on layer 4

Shape on layer 5

Text on layer 3

Text on layer 2

Changing Drawing Settings

The Drawing category on the Preferences dialog box contains a number of drawing settings that control the sensitivity and behavior of Flash's drawing tools. Make changes to the tolerance levels for smoothing or straightening, set the sensitivity for line and shape recognition, or fine-tune snapping. You can exercise greater control over your drawing or allow Flash to perform corrections and adjustments as you draw. You can customize the way you use Pen tools, draw connecting lines and smooth curves, and recognize lines and shapes.

Change the Drawing Settings

1. Click the **Flash** (Mac) or **Edit** (Win) menu, and then click **Preferences**.

2. Click the **Drawing** category.

3. Specify the drawing option you want:

   ◆ **Pen Tool options.** Select check boxes to show pen preview, solid points, and precise cursors.

   ◆ **Connect Lines.** Determines how close the ends of any two lines need to be before Flash connects them. It controls when a line is converted into a perfectly straight line.

   ◆ **Smooth Curves.** Determines the amount of smoothing applied to a drawn line. The lower the smoothing applied, the closer the line appears to what you have drawn.

   ◆ **Recognize Lines.** Defines how straight a line drawn with the Pencil tool must be before it's converted into a perfectly straight line.

   ◆ **Recognize Shapes.** Sets how precise simple geometric shapes must be drawn before they are detected as shapes.

   ◆ **Click Accuracy.** Determines how near to a shape the pointer must be before it's recognized.

   ◆ **IK Bone Tool.** Automatically sets the transformation point.

4. Click **OK**.

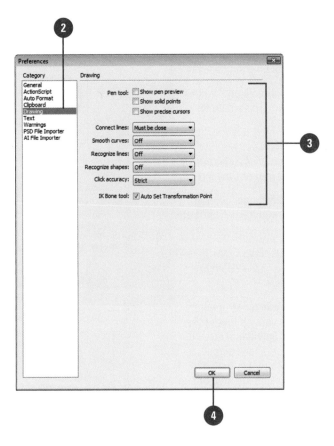

Working with Groups, Symbols, and Instances

4

Introduction

All vector objects are editable. As the complexity of your document increases, you can protect artwork from being inadvertently changed by storing it in special modes called groups and symbols. Groups provide a quick way to seal a shape by storing it in a bounding box that can only be edited by entering a group editing mode. Groups are created on the Stage and are not stored anywhere else. For items that are more global to your movie, you can convert them into symbols. The basis for interactivity and animation in Flash resides in its use of these reusable objects.

You can create artwork and then save that artwork as a symbol that is stored in the Library of your Flash document. Symbols are an efficient way to build your movies because you can reuse these assets as instances on the Timeline, and Flash will only store it in your file once. Apply ActionScript to control a movie clip symbol instance and to add interactivity, place art inside of button symbols to create hit states, or apply a variety of transparency and color effects to instances on the Stage. The Library stores all of the reusable art and objects in your movie including symbols, sounds, video clips, bitmaps, and components. It can be organized and sorted for easy access to your movie's assets. A Library can also be shared with other Flash documents.

Creating Groups

When you group artwork on the Stage, you prevent it from interacting with other artwork on the same layer. **Grouping** essentially stores the artwork in a bounding box that can only be edited by entering a special group editing mode, which you can easily do by double-clicking the group. For example, if you draw a shape over another shape on the same layer, the strokes and fills of the second shape will cut through or replace the strokes and fills of the shape directly beneath it. Grouping your artwork prevents this from happening. You can also use grouping to combine several shapes into one group so you can manipulate them simultaneously. You can ungroup artwork or objects that have been grouped by using the ungroup option or by breaking them apart. Doing so removes the bounding box and the artwork can be freely edited.

Group Artwork on the Same Layer

1. Select the artwork on the Stage that you want to group with any of Flash's selection tools or methods.

2. Click the **Modify** menu, and then click **Group**.

   TIMESAVER Press ⌘+G (Mac) or Ctrl+G (Win) to quickly group selected objects or artwork.

Selected ungrouped artwork

Selected grouped artwork in bounding box

Ungroup Artwork

1. Select the artwork on the Stage that you want to ungroup.

2. Click the **Modify** menu, and then click **Ungroup**.

   TIMESAVER Press Shift+⌘+G (Mac) or Shift+Ctrl+G (Win) to quickly ungroup selected objects or artwork.

Selected grouped artwork

Artwork ungrouped or broken apart

See Also

See "Breaking Symbols Apart" on page 155 for information on taking apart elements.

Arranging Multiple Groups

When objects are grouped they appear on top of shapes that aren't grouped on the same layer. Each subsequent group that is created will appear on top of the last. This is called the stacking order. Flash allows you to change this order with the Arrange command. You can send a group or symbol to the bottom of this stack or bring one at the bottom to the top. Additionally, you can change the order incrementally.

Change the Stacking Order

1. Select the group whose stacking order you want to change.

2. Click the **Modify** menu, point to **Arrange**, and then click:

   ◆ **Bring To Front**. The selected object is brought to the top of the stack.

   TIMESAVER *Press Option+Shift+Up (Mac) or Ctrl+Shift+Up (Win).*

   ◆ **Bring Forward**. The selected object is brought up one level in the stacking order.

   TIMESAVER *Press ⌘+Up (Mac) or Ctrl+Up (Win).*

   ◆ **Send Backward**. The selected object is brought down one level in the stacking order.

   TIMESAVER *Press ⌘+Down (Mac) or Ctrl+Down (Win).*

   ◆ **Send To Back**. The selected object is brought to the bottom of the stack.

   TIMESAVER *Press Option+Shift+Down (Mac) or Ctrl+Shift+Down (Win).*

1

2 Bring To Front

Opening the Library Panel

The **Library** panel is where all of the reusable assets in your Flash movie are stored. An **asset** is any artwork or object you have made into symbols, such as fonts, graphic symbols, movie clips, and buttons. Flash also stores bitmaps, sounds, video clips, and components in the Library. You can also open libraries from other Flash files to quickly transfer assets from one project to another. In Flash, you can use a single Library panel to view the library items of multiple Flash files at the same time.

Open the Library

1. Click the **Window** menu, and then click **Library**.

   TIMESAVER *Press ⌘+L (Mac) or Ctrl+L (Win) to open the Library panel.*

2. Click the **Document** list arrow, and then select a library from a currently opened document.

3. If you want one library selected regardless of what document is active, simply select the library from the Document list arrow menu, and click the **Pin** button.

Open Other Libraries

① Click the **File** menu, point to **Import**, and then click **Open External Library**.

> **TIMESAVER** *Press ⌘+Shift+O (Mac) or Ctrl+Shift+O (Win) to open the Open As Library dialog box.*

② Navigate to the drive or folder where the Flash movie containing the Library is located.

③ Select the library file.

④ Click **Open**.

The Library appears docked underneath the Library of the active project.

Did You Know?

You can use sample common libraries included with Flash and create your own. To use a common library, click the Window menu, point to Common Libraries, select the library type you want from the submenu, and then drag items from the library to your document. To create a common library, create a Flash file (.fla) with a library containing the symbols you want, and then save the file to the Libraries folder located in the Flash application folder on your hard disk.

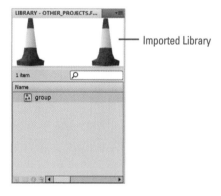

Imported Library

Working with the Library Panel

You can organize your Library assets into folders, sort the items, duplicate symbols or change their behavior. You can sort items by name, type, date, use count, or ActionScript linkage identifier. If you have a long list of items in your Library, you can search for the ones you want. The improved Library panel also allows you to set properties on most multiple Library items at once.

Organize Items in the Library Panel

1. Click the **Window** menu, and then click **Library**.

2. Use any of the following options to organize items in the Library panel:

   ◆ **Search.** Click in the Search box, start to type the name of the item you want to find. As you type, the list of Library items narrows to display the items that match what you typed.

   Click **X** in the Search box to display all the items in the Library panel.

   ◆ **Sort.** Click the name header to sort the Library items from A-Z or Z-A.

   ◆ **New Folder.** Click the **New Folder** button, type a name, and then press Enter (Win) or Return (Mac).

   ◆ **Use Folders.** Select a Library item from the list and drag it to the folder where you want to store it. Click the triangle to expand/collapse the folder.

   ◆ **Delete Item.** Select the items you want to delete, and then click the **Delete** button.

   ◆ **Rename Item.** Double-click the item you want to rename, type a new name, and then press Enter (Win) or Return (Mac).

Search box

Options menu

New Library Panel

Preview controller

Click the column header to sort items.

Delete button

New Folder button

Create New Symbol button

Access Library Options

1. Click the **Options** menu on the Library panel.

   A menu of options for adding, deleting, organizing, and configuring Library items appears, such as:

   ◆ **New Font.** Create a font symbol to embed a font in a movie.

   ◆ **New Symbol.** Create a symbol.

   ◆ **Duplicate.** Make a copy of the selected items.

   ◆ **Edit or Edit With.** Edit items in a library. Select the item first.

   ◆ **Linkage.** Define properties to share library assets for runtime or author development time.

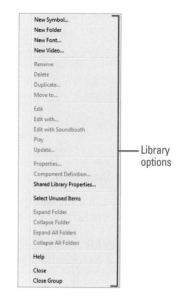

Library options

Change Library Item Properties

1. Click the **Window** menu, and then click **Library**.

2. Select the Library items you want to change.

   To select multiple items, hold down Ctrl (Win) or ⌘ (Win), and the click the items you want to select.

3. Click the **Properties** button.

4. Make the changes you want for the Library items.

5. Click **OK**.

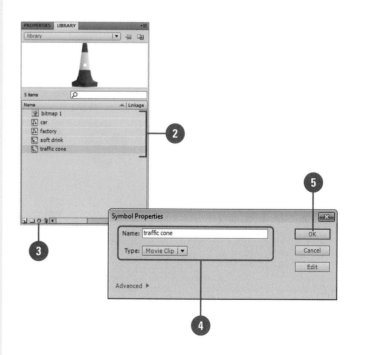

Creating Symbols

Using symbols is an efficient way to add artwork or elements to your Flash movie. When you create a symbol, it is stored in the Library where it can be reused as an instance in the Timeline. You can turn graphics or animations you've made into symbols or create a new one from scratch. There are three default symbol types you can choose from: graphic, movie clips, and buttons. How you use the symbol will determine which of these three types to use. Symbols have their own discrete Timelines. Think of a symbol as a package containing artwork that you can open and close. You enter a symbol editing mode to make changes and when you leave this mode the artwork is protected.

Create New Symbols

1. Click the **Insert** menu, and then click **New Symbol**.

   TIMESAVER Press ⌘+F8 (Mac) or Ctrl+F8 (Win) to create a new symbol.

2. Type a name for the symbol.

3. Select a symbol type option.

4. Click **OK**.

   Flash enters a special Symbol editing mode.

5. Create or insert a symbol item, and then click the **Back** button.

Click to set ActionScript options

Symbol editing mode indicator

Convert Existing Artwork into Symbols

1. Select the artwork on the Stage you want to make into a symbol.

2. Click the **Modify** menu, and then click **Convert To Symbol**.

   TIMESAVER Press F8 to convert the artwork into a symbol.

3. Type a name for the symbol.

4. Select a symbol type option.

5. Select a registration point.

6. Click **OK**.

   Symbol appears in the Library.

Convert Animations into Symbols

1. In the Timeline, select every frame in the animation that you want to make into a symbol.

2. Click the **Edit** menu, point to **Timeline**, and then click **Copy Frames**.

   TIMESAVER *Press Option+⌘+C (Mac) or Ctrl+Alt+C (Win) to copy frames.*

3. Click the **Insert** menu, and then click **New Symbol**.

4. Type a name for the symbol.

5. Select a movie clip or graphic symbol.

6. Click **OK**.

   Flash enters a special symbol editing mode.

7. Select the first frame of the Timeline.

8. Click the **Edit** menu, point to **Timeline**, and then click **Paste Frames**.

   TIMESAVER *Press Option+⌘+V (Mac) or Ctrl+Alt+V (Win) to paste frames.*

See Also

See "Editing in Symbol Mode" on page 140 for information on editing symbols in symbol editing mode.

New symbol's Timeline

For Your Information

Selecting a Registration Point

In the Convert to Symbol dialog box, there is a registration grid. The grid represents the symbol's bounding box. It displays a small black square to indicate the registration point for the graphic. A **registration point** is the axis from which a symbol rotates or aligns to other objects. You can view the registration point for a symbol by selecting it, and then opening the Property Inspector or the Info panel.

Editing in Symbol Mode

When you need to change or modify a symbol, you must enter a special symbol editing mode. Entering this mode allows you to view and edit the symbol's Timeline. Any changes you make are stored in the Library, and all other instances of the symbol are updated with these changes. You can choose to enter the symbol mode, entirely replacing the view of the main Timeline, or view the symbol in context to the main Timeline. Additionally, you can open the symbol mode in a new window.

Enter Symbol Editing Mode

1 Select the symbol you want to modify.

2 Click the **Edit** menu, and then click **Edit Symbols**.

Selecting Edit Symbols centers the symbol based on its registration point in the symbol editing work area. The Timeline is not visible.

TIMESAVER *Double-click the symbol, or press ⌘+E (Mac) or Ctrl+E (Win) to enter symbol editing mode.*

3 Modify the symbol or its Timeline.

Symbol editing mode

Edit Symbols button

Did You Know?

You can use the Edit Symbols button to access any symbol stored in the Library. When you click the Edit Symbols button in the Edit bar, a list of symbols stored in the Library appears from which you can select.

For Your Information

Entering and Viewing a Symbol's Editing Mode

There are two additional modes for viewing a symbol's editing mode: Edit In Place and Edit In New Window. You can access these options from the Edit menu or from the context-sensitive menus by Control-clicking (Mac) or right-clicking (Win) the instance on the Stage.

Edit In Place. Preserves the view of the symbol's position in the main Timeline, dimming everything else in the main Timeline. This feature is useful when you need to see a symbol's placement relative to other elements in the main Timeline as you edit it. To quickly Edit in Place, double-click the instance on the Stage.

Edit In New Window. Opens the symbol's Timeline in a new window.

Additionally, you can select the symbol from the Edit Symbol list arrow on the right side of the Information bar above the Timeline.

Exit Symbol Editing Mode

1 When you are finished making changes to a symbol, you can return to the main Timeline in several ways:

◆ Click the **Back** button or the **Scene name** on the Edit bar to return to the parent scene.

◆ Click the **Edit Scene** button on the Edit bar, and then click another Scene name.

◆ Click the **Edit** menu, and then click **Edit Document** to return to the main Timeline.

◆ Press ⌘+E (Mac) or Ctrl+E (Win).

Back button and Scene name   Edit Scene button

Edit bar with options for leaving symbol editing mode.

Return to main Timeline

Creating Instances

An **instance** is a copy of a symbol. When you use a symbol in your Timeline you are using an instance of it. You can animate an instance of a symbol and apply a variety of effects to it without affecting the original symbol in the Library. You can also use multiple instances of the same symbol. When you change the properties of an instance in the Timeline, you are only applying these changes to that copy, or instance, of the symbol. In this way, you keep the file size down because Flash only keeps track of the changes you've made while preserving the symbol in the form you created. If you have several instances of a symbol in your movie and you want to edit the artwork, you can make changes to the master symbol. When you do this, all of the instances of that symbol will be updated with these changes.

Place Instances on the Stage

① Open or expand the Library panel.

TIMESAVER *Press F11 or ⌘+L (Mac) or Ctrl+L (Win) to quickly open and close the Library panel.*

② Select the symbol from the list of assets and drag it to the Stage to create an instance of that symbol.

TIMESAVER *Drag the preview image of a symbol selected in the Library item list to create an instance of that symbol on the Stage.*

Instance of the symbol on the Stage ①

Filled keyframe indicates instance is placed on the Stage.

Edit Master Symbols

1. Double-click any instance of a symbol you want to edit.

2. Make changes to the symbol artwork or animation.

3. Click the **Back** button or **Scene name** on the Edit bar to return to the main Timeline.

   All of the instances reflect these changes.

All other instances update with new changes.

Changing Symbol and Instance Type

Symbols have three specific types that are set when you first create the symbol: graphic, movie clip, and button. You can change these types for a symbol's instance by selecting it and then selecting a new type option in the Property Inspector. Do this when you need the instance to display a behavior different than its parent symbol. Alternately, you can change the behavior of the parent symbol itself in the Library. All subsequent instances that you create from this symbol will exhibit the new behavior.

Change a Symbol's Behavior

1. Open or expand the Library panel.

2. Select the symbol from the list.

3. Click the **Properties** button at the bottom of the Library window to open the Symbol Properties dialog box.

4. Select a different symbol type option.

5. Click **OK**.

    The symbol displays a new behavior. All subsequent instances will default to this behavior.

Symbol begins as a movie clip.

Did You Know?

If you are already using instances of a symbol in your movie, they will not be affected by a change in behavior. Flash allows you to change the types of instances separately from your symbol's default behavior. To update the instance to a new symbol, select it on the Stage, and then change the type in the Property Inspector.

See Also

See "Breaking Symbols Apart" on page 155 for information on taking apart elements.

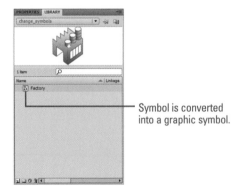

Symbol is converted into a graphic symbol.

Change the Symbol Behavior of an Instance

1. If necessary, open the Property Inspector.

2. Select the instance on the Stage.

3. Click the **Symbol** list arrow in the Property Inspector, and then select another behavior: **Movie Clip**, **Button**, or **Graphic**.

Did You Know?

You can use a method to change the symbol behavior of any instance. Select from any of the three options: graphic symbol, button, or movie clip. In this way, you can get graphic symbols to behave as movie clips, movie clips to behave like buttons, etc.

Symbol options for instances

Swapping Symbol Instances

Symbols are used in the Timeline as instances. If you apply motion or color effects to an instance, you only affect that instance, not its parent symbol. If you would like to swap the parent symbol for another symbol, while retaining any effects and/or animation that have been applied to the instance, you can use the Swap Symbol feature. All of the effects are preserved but are instead applied to and referencing the new chosen symbol. Alternately, if you are using several instances of a symbol and want to change the content (the master symbol itself) of one of these instances without affecting the other instances, you can duplicate and swap that symbol in the Swap dialog box. Essentially you create a new master symbol linked to your instance that is no longer related to the original master symbol and all its instances.

Swap Instances

1. If necessary, open the Property Inspector.

2. Select the instance on the Stage.

3. Click **Swap** in the Property Inspector to open the Swap Symbol dialog box.

   TIMESAVER *Control+click (Mac) or right-click (Win) the instance on the Stage, and then click Swap Symbol.*

4. Click a symbol from the list.

5. Click **OK**.

   The instance is now linked to a new symbol.

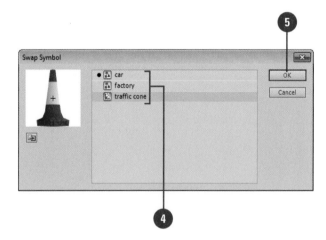

Duplicate Symbols During Swap

1. Select the instance on the Stage.

2. Click **Swap** in the Property Inspector.

3. Click the **Duplicate Symbol** icon in the bottom left-hand corner of the dialog box.

4. Enter a new name.

5. Click **OK**.

   The instance is now linked to a new symbol, copied from the original master symbol.

6. Click **OK**.

See Also

See "Breaking Symbols Apart" on page 155 for information on breaking symbols apart in symbol editing mode.

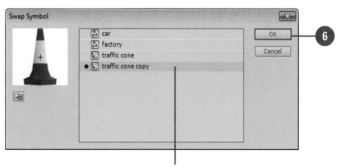

New master symbol created

Using Graphic Symbols

Graphic symbols can be used for static images and for animations that are in sync with the main Timeline. There are three instance options available to them: Loop, Play Once, and Single Frame. Set the instance to Loop if you want the symbol's Timeline to play continuously. Play Once plays the Timeline of a graphic symbol once and then stops. Single frame sets the instance to display as a single frame contained in the graphic symbol's Timeline. Unlike movie clip symbols, an animation contained in a graphic symbol can be seen in the main Timeline without having to export the Flash movie. However, any ActionScript and sounds that have been included in a graphic symbol's Timeline will not work.

Create a Graphic Symbol

1. Click the **Insert** menu, and then click **New Symbol**.

   TIMESAVER Press ⌘+F8 (Mac) or Ctrl+F8 (Win) to create a new symbol.

2. Type in a name for the symbol.

3. Click the **Type** list arrow, and then click **Graphic**.

4. Click **OK**.

   Flash enters a symbol editing mode that contains an empty Timeline for that symbol.

Did You Know?

Graphic symbol animations are synced up to the main Timeline. For example, if the animation in the graphic symbol spans 10 frames, the instance in the main Timeline must also span 10 frames if the entire animation is to be seen.

Change the Options for Graphic Symbol Instances

1. Select a graphic symbol instance on the Stage.

2. Click the list arrow in the Property Inspector, and then select from the following graphic options:

   - **Loop.** The Timeline in the graphic symbol will loop continuously.

   - **Play Once**. The Timeline in the graphic symbol will play once and stop. If there is no animation in the symbol or if there is only artwork on one frame, it will be treated as a static graphic.

   - **Single Frame**. Sets the instance to a single frame in the Timeline of the master symbol. When this is selected, the graphic symbol is treated as a static graphic.

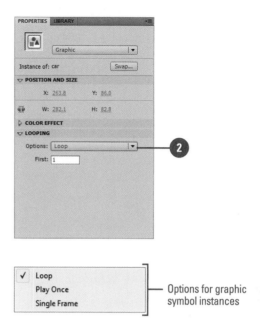

Options for graphic symbol instances

For Your Information

Converting a Graphic to a Symbol

In addition to creating a new symbol and adding a graphic, you can also convert an existing graphic to a symbol. Select the vector graphic on the Stage, click the Modify menu, and then click Convert To Symbol. In the Convert to Symbol dialog box, enter a name (that you'll refer to in an ActionScript), and then click the Graphic option as the type. The registration grid within the symbol bounding box displays a small black square to indicate the registration point for the graphic.

Using Button Symbols

Use buttons to add interactivity to your movie. Button symbols have their own four-frame Timeline. The first three frames define the states of the button: up, over, and down. The first frame is the Up state, which is the appearance of the button when in its normal, non-active state. The second frame is the Over state, which is triggered when the user places their mouse over the button. The third frame is the Down state, which appears when the user presses the button with their mouse. The fourth frame—which is invisible outside of the symbol editing mode—defines the active area. This is the area that the user must place their mouse over to activate the other states of the button. You can assign actions, such as sound or animation, to instances of buttons that tell Flash what to do when the button is clicked.

Create a Button

1. Click the **Insert** menu, and then click **New Symbol**.

    TIMESAVER *Press ⌘+F8 (Mac) or Ctrl+F8 (Win) to create a new symbol.*

2. Type in a name for the symbol.

3. Click the **Type** list arrow, and then click **Button**.

4. Click **OK**.

5. Place artwork in the keyframe of the first frame.

    This represents the button's Up state, its normal, inactive state.

6. Click the **Insert** menu, point to **Timeline**, and then click **Keyframe** to add a keyframe in the second frame (the Over state).

    TIMESAVER *Press F6 to quickly add a keyframe and press F7 to add a blank keyframe.*

7 Change the artwork or add new artwork in this frame.

8 Click the **Insert** menu, point to **Timeline**, and then click **Keyframe** to add a keyframe in the third frame (the Down state).

9 Alter the artwork or add new artwork in this frame.

10 Click the **Insert** menu, point to **Timeline**, and then click **Keyframe** to add a keyframe in the fourth frame (the active area).

11 Add a simple graphic (a rectangle or oval, for example) to define the active area.

12 To assign a sound to a state of the button, select the state's frame in the Timeline, open the Property Inspector, and then:

◆ Select a sound from the Sound list arrow menu.

◆ Select an event from the Synchronization list arrow menu.

13 Click the **Control** menu, point to **Test Movie**, and then click **Test**.

TIMESAVER *Press ⌘+Return (Mac) or Ctrl+Enter (Win) to test it.*

See Also

See "Enabling and Disabling Buttons" on page 152 for information on turning buttons on and off.

For Your Information

Adding Animation to a Button

There are several ways to add animation to a button. First, you can place an instance of the button symbol on the Stage and assign actions to it, not to frames in the button's Timeline. Another way is to create a button using a movie clip symbol or a button component. You can create more complex animation with the movie clip button. The downside is that file size increases. The button component provides more pre-built button types, such as PushButton and RadioButton, and customizable features. See Chapter 18, "Adding and Modifying Components" on page 427 for information on components and using button components.

Enabling and Disabling Buttons

Flash allows you to test your buttons within the development environment without having to export the movie. You can test the behavior of simple buttons by toggling the Enable Simple Buttons feature on and off. When buttons are enabled, you can't select them or enter their symbol editing mode normally. Disable this feature if you need to enter the symbol mode. You can quickly see how the different states of your button behave without having to export the whole flash movie. Any ActionScript applied to the button will be ignored.

Enable and Disable Buttons

① Place a button on the Stage.

② Click the **Control** menu, and then click **Enable Simple Buttons** to enable the button.

> **TIMESAVER** *Press Ctrl+Alt+B (Win) or Option+⌘+B (Mac) to toggle the enabling and disabling of simple buttons.*

③ Place the mouse over the button to test the Over state.

④ Press down on the button to test the Down state.

⑤ To disable the button, click the **Control** menu, and then click **Disable Simple Buttons**.

Did You Know?

Regardless of whether buttons are enabled or disabled, they will be functional when you export your movie. The Enable Simple Buttons command is only relevant to the Flash development environment.

See Also

See "Using Button Symbols" on page 150-151 for information on creating a button.

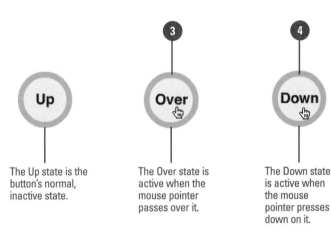

The Up state is the button's normal, inactive state.

The Over state is active when the mouse pointer passes over it.

The Down state is active when the mouse pointer presses down on it.

Creating Invisible Buttons

Buttons do not require graphics to be placed in the hit state frames (the first three frames). As long as the active area contains a shape, the button will be invisible but will be functional and ActionScript can be applied to it. The active area is the fourth frame in the button symbol Timeline. An instance of an invisible button appears as a transparent blue shape in the main Timeline, but it will not be visible in the exported movie.

Create an Invisible Button

1. Click the **Insert** menu, and then click **New Symbol**.

   TIMESAVER *Press ⌘+F8 (Mac) or Ctrl+F8 (Win) to create a new symbol.*

2. Click the **Type** list arrow, and then click **Button**.

3. Click **OK**.

4. Click the **Insert** menu, point to **Timeline**, and then click **Keyframe** to add a keyframe in the fourth frame (the active area).

   TIMESAVER *Press F6 to create a keyframe.*

5. Add a simple graphic (a rectangle or oval, for example) to define the active area.

6. Make sure the first three frames remain empty.

7. Return to the main Timeline.

8. Drag the invisible button from the Library to the Stage.

   Invisible buttons appear as transparent blue shapes but are invisible in the final export.

The first three frames of the button remain empty.

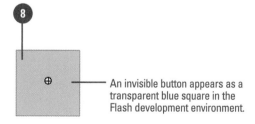

An invisible button appears as a transparent blue square in the Flash development environment.

Using Movie Clip Symbols

Movie clip symbols operate independently on the main Timeline. When you want an animation to loop on a single frame in the Timeline, you can store this animation in the Timeline of a movie clip that will sit on this frame. Movie clip instances can have actions applied to them and can be controlled from anywhere in the Flash movie through ActionScript. They can contain animations, interactive controls, sounds, and even other movie clips. Unlike graphic symbols, you can only see the first frame of the movie clip in the main Timeline. Export your movie to see the movie clip play.

Create and View Movie Clips Symbols

1. Click the **Insert** menu, and then click **New Symbol**.

2. Click the **Type** list arrow, and then click **Movie Clip**.

3. Click **OK**.

4. Add your content to the Movie Clip Timeline.

5. Return to the main Timeline by clicking the **Back** button or the **Scene name** on the Edit bar.

6. Drag the movie clip symbol to the Stage from the Library.

7. To change movie clip properties, select the clip on the Stage, and then change options in the Property Inspector.

   ◆ **Symbol.** Movie Clip, Graphic, or Button

   ◆ **X** and **Y position**

   ◆ **Width** and **Height**

   ◆ **Color.** Brightness, Tint, Alpha, and Advanced

8. Click the **Control** menu, point to **Test Movie**, and then click **Test**.

   TIMESAVER *Press ⌘+Return (Mac) or Ctrl+Enter (Win) to test it.*

Movie clip

Breaking Symbols Apart

Sometimes you'll need to break a symbol instance so that it is no longer linked to the master symbol. You might do this if you want to add something to the symbol without affecting the other instances. In this way, the content inside the symbol will become a simple graphic that you can adjust without affecting the master symbol you made it from or any of its instances.

Break an Instance

1. Select an instance on the Stage you would like to break.

2. Click the **Modify** menu, and then click **Break Apart**.

    TIMESAVER *Press ⌘+B (Mac) or Ctrl+B (Win) to quickly break apart a symbol.*

See Also

See "Swapping Symbol Instances" on page 146 for information on swapping symbol instances.

Symbol broken apart into an editable shape.

Modifying Instance Properties

You can alter the properties of an instance of a symbol without affecting the master symbol. Any transform applied to an instance can be animated with motion tweening. Flash will gradually draw the frames in between one transform to another. This is how you create movement in Flash. Change the scale of an instance or rotate and skew it. You can perform these functions interactively with the Free Transform tool. You can also add values in the Transform panel, or access additional Transform options in the program's Modify menu. Distort and Envelope cannot be applied to instances and are disabled on the Tools panel options when the Free Transform tool is selected.

Modify the Scale or Rotation

① Select the instance on the Stage.

② Click the **Free Transform** tool on the Tools panel.

> **TIMESAVER** *Press Q to quickly select the Free Transform tool.*

③ Click the **Scale** or **Rotate and Skew** button in the Options section of the Toolbar.

④ Drag the small handles around the bounding box to change the size of the instance or rotate it.

⑤ To use the Transform panel, click the **Window** menu, and then click **Transform**.

> **TIMESAVER** *Press Ctrl+T (Win) or ⌘+T (Mac) to open the Transform panel.*

The Transform panel allows you to enter values for various transforms.

Did You Know?

You can select multiple instances and change their properties simultaneously. Press Shift+select each instance you would like to alter in tandem. A bounding box will appear around all selected instances.

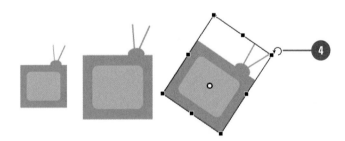

Use Additional Transform Commands

1. Select the instance on the Stage.
2. Click the **Modify** menu, point to **Transform**, and then click one of the following:

   - **Free Transform.** Transforms the object freely.

   - **Scale.** Constrains the transform to scale.

   - **Rotate And Skew.** Constrains the transform to rotate and skew.

   - **Scale And Rotate.** Constrains the transform to scale and rotation changes.

   - **Rotate 90° CW.** Rotates the selected object 90° clockwise.

   - **Rotate 90° CCW.** Rotates the selected object 90° counter-clockwise.

   - **Flip Vertical.** Flips the object along a vertical axis.

   - **Flip Horizontal.** Flips the object along a horizontal axis.

   - **Remove Transform.** Removes any transform effects applied to the selected instance.

Transforms objects freely

Constrain transforms

Rotate commands

Flip commands

Removes all applied Transform effects

Did You Know?

Changing the scale or rotation of an instance can also be done in the Transform panel. Simply select the instance, and then access the Transform panel. Click the Window menu, and then click Transform. The Modify menu includes additional trans-form commands not available any-where else.

Modifying Instance Color Styles and Blends

You can change the tint, brightness, or transparency of an instance in the Color list arrow located in the Property Inspector. This feature appears whenever an instance is selected on the Stage. If you would like to add a color to the instance, you can do so by selecting the Tint color style. Choose a color and then choose the amount of color that will be applied. You can adjust the Brightness (that is, how much white or black will be added) of an instance by choosing the Brightness color style. An instance can also be made transparent by altering the Alpha color style. An Alpha of zero will make the instance invisible, though it can still be selected and animated. This is useful when you want an object to fade on or off the Stage. You can also create unique composite image effects by varying color and transparency and applying a blend to two or more overlapping movie clips instances.

Modify the Brightness

1. Select the instance on the Stage.

2. Click the **Style** list arrow in the Property Inspector, and then click **Brightness**.

3. Enter a value between -100 and 100 (-100= no brightness, black; 100= maximum brightness, white).

    TIMESAVER *You can use the slider to the right of the field to interactively change the level of Brightness applied.*

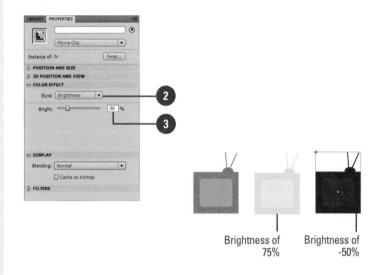

Brightness of 75%   Brightness of -50%

Modify the Tint Color

1. Select the instance on the Stage.

2. Click the **Color** list arrow in the Property Inspector, and then click **Tint**.

3. Click a color from the color box list arrow or enter an RGB value in the fields.

4. Enter a value between 0 and 100 (0= no color, 100= maximum saturation).

Tint of 50%   Tint of 100%

Modify the Transparency

① Select the instance on the Stage.

② Click the **Style** list arrow in the Property Inspector, and then click **Alpha**.

③ Enter a value between 0 and 100 (0= invisible, 100= fully visible).

TIMESAVER *You can use the slider to the right of the field to interactively change the level of Alpha applied.*

If you need to apply a color style with alpha you must use the Advanced option.

Alpha of 50%

Alpha of 25%

Modify the Blend

① Select the movie instance on the Stage.

② Click the **Style** list arrow and adjust the color and transparency.

③ Click the **Blending** list arrow, and then select a blend.

④ Position the movie clip with the blend over another symbol.

To achieve the effect you want, you will need to experiment with the color and transparency of the movie clip and blend mode.

Did You Know?

A blending mode contains different elements. It contains a blend color, opacity (degree of transparency), base color (pixel colors under blend), and result color.

Blend result color

Hard Light blend

Subtract blend

Difference blend

Using Advanced Color Options

An instance can have only one color style (Brightness, Tint, or Alpha) applied. To apply multiple color styles, you must use the Advanced feature in the Property Inspector's Color list arrow menu. This option allows you to change the percentage of Red, Green, or Blue (0% -100%) added or subtracted as well as the constant values of RGB (-255 to +255). Additionally, there is an Alpha scale that can be applied to each of these options. Apply a color, brightness, or alpha style to an instance and then access the Advanced options to make adjustments. The applied color style is preserved. Experiment with this features until you get the effects that you need.

Modify the Color and Transparency Simultaneously

1. Select the instance on the Stage.

2. Click the **Style** list arrow in the Property Inspector, and then click **Tint**, **Brightness** or **Alpha** and apply an effect.

3. Click the **Style** list arrow again, and then click **Advanced**.

4. Add or subtract percentages or values of RGB and Alpha.

Did You Know?

You can go directly to the Advanced panel to add color effects without having applied any Brightness, Tint, or Alpha. If you have already chosen one of these options and then enter the Advanced settings, your previous applied effect will be preserved and the sliders in the Advanced Settings window will reflect this change. For example, if you have added a tint of red to your instance, the sliders in the Advanced setting will show that red has been added.

Reduce the color values or alpha by a percentage.

Increase or decrease the constant color or alpha values.

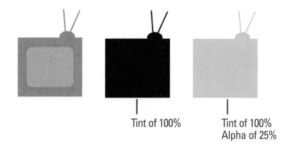

Tint of 100%

Tint of 100% Alpha of 25%

Using 9-Slice Scaling on a Movie Clip Symbol

In previous versions, Flash scales movie clips equally in height and width. For many rectangular movie clips, this method of scaling doesn't work very well at the corners. In Flash, a method called **9-slice scaling** is used. A movie clip is visually divided into nine areas, or slices, with a grid overlay (dotted lines called slide guides). Each area of the grid is scaled separately, except the corners, which provides more accurate results. The slide guides are set at 25% of the symbol's height and width by default. Before you can scale a movie clip, you need to enable 9-slice scaling. To edit a movie clip, you need to use symbol-editing mode.

Enable 9-Slice Scaling

1 Select the movie clip symbol you want in the Library panel.

2 Click the **Options** menu, and then click **Properties**.

3 Click **Advanced**.

4 Select the **Enable guides for 9-slice scaling** check box.

5 Click **OK**.

Scale a Movie Clip Symbol

1 Double-click the movie clip symbol in the Library to enter symbol-editing mode.

2 To see the scaling on the Stage, click the **Control** menu, and then click **Enable Live Preview**.

3 Drag the horizontal or vertical guides to scale the symbol.

The new position of the guides provides the new scaling.

3 Drag any guide 2

Setting Highlight Color Preferences

Flash allows you to set general preferences to customize the highlight, or selection, color of elements in Flash to make them easier to see. In the General category of the Preferences dialog box, you can select different colors for different types of elements, including drawing objects, drawing primitives, groups, symbols, and all other elements. If you don't want to set individual colors, you can use the layer color for all elements.

Set Highlight Color Preferences

1. Click the **Flash** (Mac) or **Edit** (Win) menu, and then click **Preferences**.

2. Click the **General** category.

3. Select the **Use Layer Color** option to use the current layer's outline color, or select the option, and then select the color you want for the following elements:

   ◆ **Drawing Objects.**

   ◆ **Drawing Primitives.**

   ◆ **Groups.**

   ◆ **Symbols.**

   ◆ **Other Elements.**

4. Click **OK**.

Working with Text

Introduction

In Flash, you can create two types of text: TLF (Text Layout Framework) or Classic. **TLF** provides advanced text capabilities (**New!**) for text in Flash targeted for Flash Player 10 and ActionScript 3.0 or later, while **Classic** provides the standard capabilities available in previous versions of Flash.

There are three types of Classic text: static, dynamic, and input. **Static** is text that doesn't change. **Dynamic** is text that updates, such as stock quotes, weather reports, or sports scores. **Input** is text entered by a user in forms or surveys. You can create editable text boxes for use as static display text or to implement dynamic text objects with the Text tool.

In the program's text menu, as well as the Property Inspector, there are a number of attributes to choose from such as Font type, style, size, color, indentation, orientation, and direction. Also included are familiar letter form formatting procedures for kerning, tracking, and anti-aliasing. Because text boxes are editable, you can change any text attribute—as well as the content in the text box—after it is created.

Use the Break Apart command to break editable text boxes into shapes and edit them with any of the selection tools or pen modifiers. This is especially useful for creating new font forms, and it also allows you to implement shape tweening. Create dynamic text boxes that can be updated from a text file on a server or some other source using ActionScript. In Flash, you can now configure the Find and Replace feature to target text contained in specific elements in your Flash document and swap these out with new entries from the built-in Adobe dictionaries or from a personal dictionary you create. Other features include the implementation of Cascading Style Sheets for consistent HTML text formatting and the built-in Spell Checker for enhanced productivity.

What You'll Do

Create Classic Static or TLF Text

Link Text Together

Change Font Type, Style, Size, and Color

Modify Tracking and Kerning

Change Text Alignment

Create Text Columns

Change Text Direction and Orientation

Change Advanced Text Options

Use Break Apart to Modify Characters

Use Anti-Alias Text

Use Font Mapping

Set Device Fonts Versus Embedded Fonts

Create Classic Dynamic Text and Input Text

Check Spelling

Use Find and Replace

Use Cascading Style Sheets with HTML Text

Creating Classic Static Text

Classic static text refers to any classic text box that isn't dynamic or input text. The Text tool creates an editable text box wherever you touch down on the Stage. Flash will keep the text on a single line until you press Enter (Win) or Return (Mac). If you need a text box with a predefined width, you can create a text box before you start typing. The entered text will automatically wrap relative to the boundaries of the box and any formatting settings you've applied. To re-enter an existing text box to change the text, simply double-click any character in the Text box or click it with the Text tool to activate it and make it ready to edit.

Create Classic Static Text

1. Click the **Text** tool on the Tools panel.

   The pointer becomes a crosshair with a small "T" in the corner.

   TIMESAVER *Press T to quickly select the Text tool.*

2. Click the **Text Engine** list arrow in the Property Inspector, and then click **Classic Text**.

3. Click the **Text Type** list arrow in the Property Inspector, and then click **Static Text**.

4. Click the Stage where you want to create a single line text box or drag to create a text box the size you want that automatically wraps.

5. Begin typing in the box that appears.

6. Click anywhere on the Stage outside the text box to deselect it.

7. To reselect a text box, click to select it.

   A black bounding box with square handles appears around a text box when it's selected.

8. To resize a text box, drag any of the black resize handles, the white small circle (single line) or white square (text block) to resize.

   The text in the box wraps to accommodate to the new size..

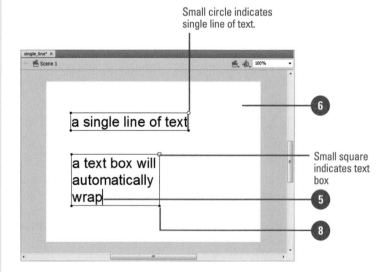

Small circle indicates single line of text.

Small square indicates text box

Creating TLF Text

TLF (Text Layout Framework) text (**New!**) provides advanced text capabilities in Flash documents targeted for Flash Player 10 and ActionScript 3.0 or later. You can create columns, rotate text, indent text, change text direction and orientation, change text case, adjust the text baseline, and apply text blending and color effects in the Property Inspector. TLF text created in Flash is read-only by default, however, you can change it to selectable or editable. If you need a text box with a predefined width, you can create a text box before you start typing. The entered text will automatically wrap relative to the boundaries of the box and any formatting settings you've applied. To re-enter an existing text box to change the text, simply double-click any character in the text box or click it with the Text tool to make it ready to edit.

Create TLF Text

1 Click the **Text** tool on the Tools panel.

The pointer becomes a crosshair with a small "T" in the corner.

TIMESAVER *Press T to quickly select the Text tool.*

2 Click the **Text Engine** list arrow in the Property Inspector, and then click **TLF Text**.

3 Click the Stage where you want your text box to begin or drag until the box is the size you need.

4 Begin typing in the box that appears.

5 Click anywhere on the Stage outside the text box to deselect it.

6 To reselect a text box, click to select it.

A black bounding box with square handles appears around a text box when it's selected.

7 To resize a text box, drag any of the black resize handles, the white small circle (single line) or white square (text block) to resize.

The text in the box wraps to accommodate to the new size..

a single line of text

a text box will automatically wrap

Small square indicates text box

Linking Text Together

If you type, paste, or import more text than a TLF text box can hold, an Overflow icon (a tiny red plus sign in a square) appears on the edge of the text box (**New!**). You can reshape the text box to display the text or create a thread (link) to another text box. You can thread overflow text from one text box to a new or existing text box (**New!**). You can think of the linked text boxes as one, however, each text box still retains it's own properties. If you no longer want to thread two or more text boxes, you can unthread or disconnect them. When you unthread text boxes, the text in the text box remains in the first text box (it may still overflow). When you disconnect text frames, the text in the text frames remains where it is.

Link Text Boxes Together

1. Click the **Text** tool on the Tools panel.

   The pointer becomes a crosshair with a small "T" in the corner.

   TIMESAVER *Press T to quickly select the Text tool.*

2. Click the **Text Engine** list arrow in the Property Inspector, and then click **TLF Text**.

3. Click the Stage where you want your text box to begin and drag until the box is the size you need.

4. Begin typing in the box that appears or paste in text from the Clipboard until it fills the entire text box.

5. Click the **Overflow** icon on the selected text box.

   The pointer changes to the Loaded Text cursor.

6. To create a new text box for the overflow text, click a blank area or drag to create a text box.

   To use an existing text box, click in an existing text box.

   Overflow text from the first text box threads to the second text box.

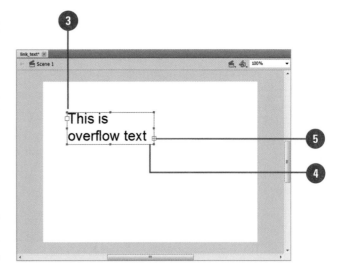

Unthread Text Boxes

1 Select the **Selection** tool or the **Text** tool on the Tools panel.

2 Select a threaded text box with the Selection tool or click in the threaded text box with the Text tool.

3 Double-click the **In Port** or **Out Port** icon on the selected object.

Did You Know?

You can delete a linked text box.
Select the text box with the Selection tool, and then press Delete. The text in the deleted text box is moved back to the remaining text box thread.

Change the Thread Between Text Boxes

1 Select the **Selection** tool or the **Text** tool on the Tools panel.

2 Select a threaded text box with the Selection tool or click in the threaded text box with the Text tool.

3 Click the **In Port** or **Out Port** icon on the selected object.

4 To create a new text frame for the overflow text, click a blank area or drag to create a text box.

To use an existing text box, click in an existing text box.

In Port   Out Port

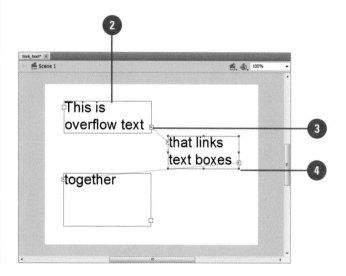

Changing Font Type, Style, Size, and Color

Flash includes a number of text properties to choose from. These include a font type, style, size, and color. You can set these attributes before you create a text box or alter them on existing text. To make changes to the entire text box, select it with the Selection tool without entering the box (or making it active). If you only want to change a portion of the box, enter the text box and select only those characters or words you want to change. Attributes such as font type, style, size, and color as well as more advanced text properties can be easily accessed in the Property Inspector. When the Text tool or any text box is selected, the Property Inspector displays all of the available attributes.

Change the Font Type, Style, and Size

1 Select the text box you want to change with the **Selection** tool or select text within the text box with the **Text** tool.

2 Click the **Family** list arrow in the Property Inspector, and then select a font name.

The Family menu displays the font name and sample text for each font style to make it easier to decide what font you want to use.

3 Click the **Style** list arrow in the Property Inspector, and then select a font style: **Regular**, **Italic**, **Bold**, or **Bold Italic**.

4 Click the current point value in the Property Inspector, and then enter another point value in the Size entry box.

5 Click any of the following format buttons in the Property Inspector:

- **Subscript** or **Superscript**.
- **Underline (TLF). (New!)**
- **Strikethrough (TLF). (New!)**

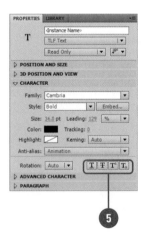

The Property Inspector displays text attributes whenever any text box is selected on the Stage.

Change the Font or Highlight Color

1. Select the text box you want to change with the **Selection** tool, or select text within the text box with the **Text** tool.

2. Click the **Color** box in the Property Inspector, and then select a fill color or click the **Color Wheel** icon to create or select a custom color.

3. Click the **Highlight** box (TLF) (**New!**) in the Property Inspector, and then select a fill color or click the **Color Wheel** icon to create or select a custom color.

Did You Know?

You can change the text color in any of the color palettes. Change the fill color of any selected text box by clicking on any of the color palettes. They are located in the Tools panel, the Color Mixer panel, and the Color Swatches panel.

You can change the font type, size, and style in the Text menu. Click the Text menu, point to Font, Size, or Style, and then select an option.

You can quickly select all text in a text box. If you are inside an active text box, press ⌘+A (Mac) or Ctrl+A (Win) to select all of the text.

See Also

See "Setting Text Preferences" on page 62 for information on setting options for showing font previews on font menus.

Modifying Tracking and Kerning

Sometimes the space between text characters can appear awkward or where increasing the space is a creative solution. Flash provides methods for adjusting these spaces, called kerning and tracking. **Tracking** is the space between characters and words on a single line and adjusting tracking affects the entire line. **Kerning** deals with the space between any two characters and adjusting it will only affect that space. Many Fonts contain built-in information about problematic character pairs. Flash makes use of this information when you turn on Auto Kern in the Property Inspector.

Adjust Tracking

1. Select the text in a text box you want to track or you can select the text box with the **Selection** tool.

2. Click the **Text** menu, point to **Letter Spacing**, and then click **Increase** or **Decrease**.

   The Tracking increases or decreases in 0.5-point (Classic) or 10 in 1000ths of an em (TLF) increments.

   TIMESAVER *You can adjust tracking in the Property Inspector with the Letter Spacing (Classic) or Tracking (TLF)* (**New!**) *entry box or slider.*

Did You Know?

You can quickly adjust kerning or tracking using the keyboard. Select the text or text box (to track) or place the cursor between two characters, and then press Option+⌘+right arrow (Mac) or Ctrl+Alt+right arrow (Win) to increase the space or Option+⌘+left arrow (Mac) or Ctrl+Alt+left arrow (Win) to decrease the space. Holding down the Shift key with this keyboard shortcut adjusts the space in larger increments.

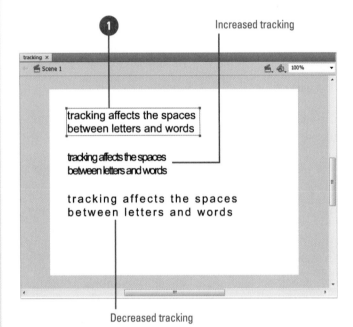

Increased tracking

tracking affects the spaces between letters and words

tracking affects the spaces between letters and words

tracking affects the spaces between letters and words

Decreased tracking

Letter Spacing Entry

Adjust Kerning

① Enter a text box on the Stage by double-clicking on it.

② Place the cursor between the two characters you want to kern.

③ Click the **Text** menu, point to **Letter Spacing**, and then click **Increase** or **Decrease**.

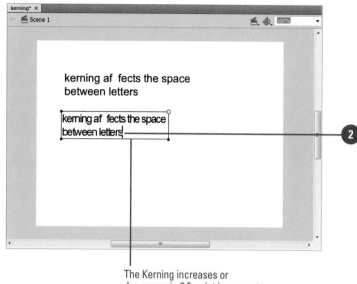

The Kerning increases or decreases in 0.5-point increments.

Set Auto Kerning

① Select the text box you want to change with the **Selection** tool.

② Select the **Auto Kern** check box (Classic) in the Property Inspector or click the **Kerning** list arrow (TLF), and then click **Auto (New!)**.

Auto kern is enabled for that text box.

Auto Kerning can correct problematic character combinations.

② Classic text

② TLF text

Changing Text Alignment

Similar to other text editing tools or word processing programs, Flash includes features for formatting paragraphs with alignment, margins, and indentation (**New!**). These features can be accessed through the Text menu and in the Property Inspector whenever any text box is selected on the Stage. Each text box can have its own individual properties assigned to it. Alignment governs the position of the text in a text box, margins are the space between the left and right side of the text and the boundaries of the text box, and indentation sets the amount of character spaces before the first line of text in a paragraph begins.

Align Paragraph Text

1. Select the text box you want to change with the **Selection** tool or select text within the text box with the **Text** tool.

2. In the Property Inspector in the Paragraph section, click one of the following:

   ◆ **Align Left**. Aligns text to the left margin.

   ◆ **Align Center.** Text is centered between the boundaries of the text box.

   ◆ **Align Right.** Aligns text to the right margin.

   ◆ **Justify.** Each line of text fills the width of the text box boundary. The last line aligned to the left.

      ◆ **Justify Center (TLF).** Justify with the last line aligned center (**New!**).

      ◆ **Justify Right (TLF).** Justify with the last line aligned right (**New!**).

      ◆ **Justify All (TLF).** Justify all the lines (**New!**).

   ◆ **Text Justify (TLF).** Distributes justification between letters or words (**New!**). Click the **Text Justify** list arrow, and then click **Word spacing** or **Letter spacing**.

Classic text

2 TLF text

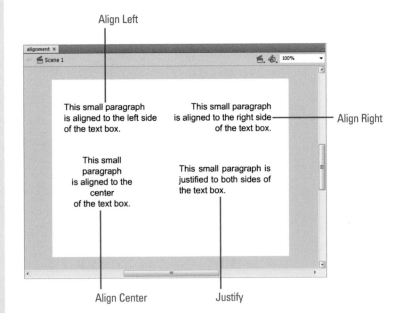

Align Left

Align Right

Align Center

Justify

This small paragraph is aligned to the left side of the text box.

This small paragraph is aligned to the right side of the text box.

This small paragraph is aligned to the center of the text box.

This small paragraph is justified to both sides of the text box.

Set Paragraph Text Margins, Indents, and Line Spacing

1. Select the text box you want to change with the **Selection** tool.

2. In the Property Inspector in the Paragraph section, enter values for any of the following:

   TROUBLE? *Options differ depending on the orientation of the text box.*

   ◆ **Indent**. Indents the first line of the paragraph.

   ◆ **Line Spacing (Classic) or Leading (TLF)**. Adjusts the space between lines of text.

   ◆ **Left Margin (Classic) or Start Margin (TLF)**. Adjusts the amount of space between the left barrier of the text box and the left side of the paragraph.

   ◆ **Right Margin (Classic) or End Margin (TLF)**. Adjusts the amount of space between the right barrier of the text box and the right side of the paragraph.

   ◆ **Space Before Paragraph (TLF)**. Adjusts the amount of space before a paragraph (**New!**).

   ◆ **Space After Paragraph (TLF)**. Adjusts the amount of space after a paragraph (**New!**).

   ◆ **Behavior**. Specifies the line type: Single Line, Multiline, or Multiline No Wrap.

2 Classic text

2 TLF text

Indentation space affects the first line of text.

Line Spacing is the space between the lines.

Left margin

Right margin

Did You Know?

You can transform text just like other objects. You can scale, rotate, skew, and flip text boxes to create unique effects.

Creating Text Columns

If you want to create columns for a more newspaper style for your text, you can create columns in a TLF text box (**New!**). In the Property Inspector for text, you can use the Container and Flow section to specify the number of columns, the gutter size between the columns, the padding size between the text and the border edge, the maximum number of characters, and the alignment to display the text the way you want. In addition, you can select a border and background fill color. If you want to offset the first line of text, you can specify the distance you want.

Create Text Columns

1. Select the TLF text box you want to change with the **Selection** tool or select text within the TLF text box with the **Text** tool.

2. Click the **Columns box** in the Property Inspector in the Container and Flow section, specify the number of columns you want.

3. In the Property Inspector in the Container and Flow section (**New!**), specify any of the following:

   ◆ **Alignment.** Click the **Align Top**, **Align Center**, **Align Bottom**, or **Justify** button.

   ◆ **Max Chars.** Specify the maximum number of characters allowed in the text box.

   ◆ **Gutter.** Specify a gutter width in pixels.

   ◆ **Padding.** Specify a **Left**, **Right**, **Top**, and **Bottom** padding width in pixels.

   ◆ **Border and Background Color.** Click the **Border** or **Background** color swatch, and then select a color.

   ◆ **1st Line Offset.** Click the **1st Line Offset** list arrow, and then select an option: **pt** (specify a height in points), **Auto** (default), **Ascent**, or **Line Height**.

Changing Text Direction

If you work with different languages that read from left to right across the screen, such as Arabic, instead of right to left, such as English, you can change the direction of text to display the language the way it's supposed to appear (**New!**). In the Property Inspector for text, you can use the Direction option to display text from left to right or right to left. If the Direction option is not available, you need to select the Show Right-to-Left Options on the Options menu in the Property Inspector or in Text Preferences.

Change Text Direction

1. Select the TLF text box you want to change with the **Selection** tool or select text within the TLF text box with the **Text** tool.

2. To show language related options (**New!**), click the **Options** button, and then click **Show Right-to-Left Options** to select it with a check mark.

3. To change the direction (**New!**), click the **Direction** list arrow, and then click **Left to Right** or **Right to Left**.

Did You Know?

You can always show right-to-left options. Select the Show Right-To-Left Text Options check box in the Text Preferences dialog box.

You can make right to left text flow the default. Select the Right To Left Text Flow check box in the Text Preferences dialog box.

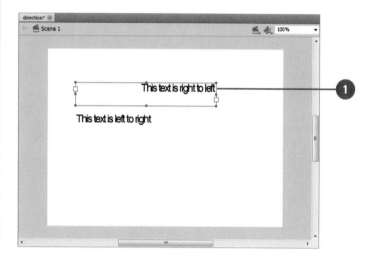

Changing Text Orientation

If you work with different languages that read vertically down the screen, such as Japanese, you can change the orientation of text to display the language the way it's supposed to appear (**New!**). In the Property Inspector for text, you can use the Orientation option to display text horizontally or vertically. If you need the text to rotate and follow the orientation of the line, you can set it to rotate automatically. If you're working with Asian text, you can use the Advanced Paragraph section in the Property Inspector to select options for Mojikumi, Kinsoku Shori Type, and Leading Model.

Change Text Orientation

1. Select the TLF text box you want to change with the **Selection** tool or select text within the TLF text box with the **Text** tool.

2. To change the orientation, click the **Orientation** button in the Property Inspector, and then click **Horizontal** or **Vertical**.

3. To show language related options, click the **Options** button, and then click **Show Asian Options** to select it with a check mark.

4. To change Asian text options, specify any of the following in the Advanced Paragraph section:

   ◆ **Mojikumi.** Select **Auto**, **Space**, or **East Asian**.

   ◆ **Kinsoku Shori Type.** Select **Auto**, **Prioritize Least Adjustment**, **Push In Kinsoku**, or **Push Out Only**.

   ◆ **Leading Model.** Select **Auto**, **Roman Up, Ideographic Top Up**, **Center Up, Top Down, Center Down**, or **Ascent Descent Up**.

Did You Know?

You can always show right-to-left options. Select the Show Asian Text Options check box in the Text Preferences dialog box.

Create a Vertical Text Block

1. Select the Classic text box you want to change with the **Selection** tool or select text within the Classic text box with the **Text** tool.

2. Click the **Change Orientation** button in the Property Inspector, and then click **Vertical**, or **Vertical, Left To Right**.

3. When you're finished, click anywhere on the Stage outside the text box.

Did You Know?

You can make vertical text the default orientation. Select the Default Text Orientation check box in the Text Preferences dialog box. This can be useful when working in some Asian languages.

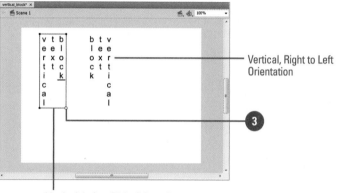

Vertical, Right to Left Orientation

Vertical, Left to Right Orientation

Rotate Characters in a Text Box

1. Select a character or word in a text box or select the text box with the **Selection** tool.

2. In the Property Inspector, click the **Rotate Text** button (Classic), enabled only for vertical text boxes, or click the **Rotation** list arrow (TLF) (**New!**), and then click **Auto**, **0°**, or **270°**.

Did You Know?

You can also rotate a text box with the Free Transform tool. Click the Free Transform tool, point to the outside edge of a corner (pointer changes to an arced arrow), and then drag.

Text rotates 90 degrees

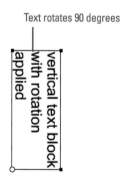

Changing Advanced Text Options

The Properties Inspector provides advanced options for TLF text (**New!**). In the Advanced Character section, you can change the text case (such as upper or lower case), specify a baseline for multi-language text or baseline shift (such as superscript or subscript), apply line breaks, and select the user's language and region. Similar to a feature in Adobe Photoshop, you can apply blending modes (**New!**) and color effects (**New!**) to a text box in front of another element, such as a graphic, to create a new look from the mix of color pixels.

Change Advanced Character Options

1 Select the TLF text box you want to change with the **Selection** tool or select text within the TLF text box with the **Text** tool.

2 In the Advanced Character section of the Property Inspector (**New!**), specify any of the following:

- ◆ Case. Changes the text to upper or lower case, or caps.

- ◆ Digit Case. Changes the text to settings specified by the font designer.

- ◆ Digit Width. Changes the text to proportional or tabular widths.

- ◆ Dominant Baseline. Changes the multiple language text to a common baseline.

- ◆ Alignment Baseline. Changes the baseline alignment for multiple language text.

- ◆ Ligatures. Changes the running together of letters, such as "Th."

- ◆ Break. Specifies the use of line breaks.

- ◆ Baseline Shift. Specifies the shift in the baseline in points (pt) or percentage (%). You can also select **Superscript** or **Subscript** for standard shifts.

- ◆ Locale. Specifies the user's language and region.

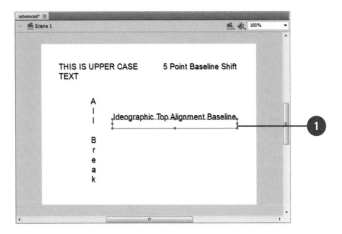

Add Display and Color Effects

① Select the TLF text box you want to change with the **Selection** tool.

② In the Display and Color Effect sections of the Property Inspector (**New!**), specify any of the following:

◆ **Display.** Click the **Blending** list arrow, and then select a blending effect.

  ◆ **Normal.** Removes the current blending effect.

With that in mind, the modes that produce the most stunning results are Multiply, Screen, Hard Light, and Difference.

◆ **Color Effect.** Click the **Style** list arrow, and then select a color effect.

  ◆ **None.** Removes the current color effect.

  ◆ **Brightness.** Specifies the lightness/darkness of the text.

  ◆ **Tint.** Specifies the blending of a color and white (which increases lightness) for the text.

  ◆ **Advanced.** Specifies the blending of a color and an alpha blend for the text.

  ◆ **Alpha.** Specifies the blending of two colors (allowing for transparency) for the text.

For Your Information

Loading an External Text File

If you have a body of text that may change over time, you can use the ActionScript command LoadVars to load a text file (.txt). To load the text file headlines.txt (which contains headlines="sample text") into the headlines dynamic text box (instance is *headlines_text* and var is n*ews_lv*) using the LoadVars object, you can use a similar script:

```
var news_lv:LoadVars = new LoadVars();
news_lv.load("c:/yourfolderlocation/headlines.txt");
news_lv.onLoad = function () {
        headlines_txt.text = news_lv.headlines;
}
```

Using Break Apart to Modify Characters

When a line of text is created in Flash, it appears in a bounding box that is editable. Sometimes you might need to adjust the characters separately or you might want to modify the shape of the characters themselves to create new character styles. The Break Apart command allows you to do this. There are two levels of breaking that you can utilize. The first break will separate the text box into singular, editable characters. This is useful if you want to reposition or align the letters of a word independently. The second break severs the text from its font reference: in essence it becomes a shape that you can edit with any of the drawing tools or pen modifiers.

Break a Text Box into Single Characters

1 Select the text box you want to change with the **Selection** tool.

2 Click the **Modify** menu, and then click **Break Apart**.

Each character appears in its own editable box.

TIMESAVER *Press ⌘+B (Mac) or Ctrl+B (Win) to use the Break Apart command.*

Text fields can be broken. — **1**

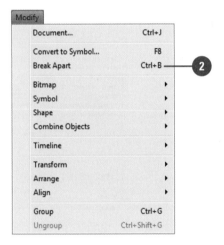

Text fields can be broken. — Broken text box

The text box is broken into separate text boxes that can be moved and edited separately.

Break a Text Box into Shapes

① Select the text box you want to change with the **Selection** tool.

② Click the **Modify** menu, and then click **Break Apart**.

The characters become individual text boxes.

③ Click the **Modify** menu again, and then click **Break Apart**.

The characters become simple shapes that you can adjust with Flash's drawing tools.

TIMESAVER *Press ⌘+B (Mac) or Ctrl+B (Win) twice to break text into editable shapes.*

See Also

See "Using the Free Transform Tool" on page 118 for information on transforming objects.

Text fields can be broken. ①

Text fields can be broken. — Characters become individual text boxes.

Text boxes become editable shapes.

For Your Information

Transforming Text

You can use the Free Transform tool or the options on the Modify menu under Transform to transform text boxes in the same ways you transform other objects. You can scale, rotate, skew and flip text boxes, but the text might become hard to read. However, you can still edit it. Important: when you scale a text box as an object, the point size in the Property Inspector may not be accurate. To restore a transformed object, select the object, click the Modify menu, point to Transform, and then click Remove Transform.

Using Anti-Alias Text

Anti-aliasing affects the pixels on the edge of a shape by allowing them to blend in with the background. It is a crucial feature when working with some text as it makes it appear smoother and more integrated. Flash includes FlashType, a new text rendering feature that improves anti-aliasing and readability for fonts. FlashType is enabled whenever Flash Player 7 or later is the selected player, and anti-aliasing is set to anti-aliasing for readability or custom. The drawback with anti-aliasing is that at smaller font sizes the text can appear blurry. To avoid this problem, use sans serif text, such as Helvetica or Arial, and don't use bold and italic. You can use anti-aliasing with static, dynamic, and input text. You apply anti-aliasing to text boxes instead of characters.

Set a Text Box to Anti-Alias Text

1. Select the text box you want to change with the **Selection** tool.

2. In the Character section of the Property Inspector (**New!**), click the **Anti-Alias** list arrow, and then select one of the following:

   ◆ **Use Device Fonts**. The SWF file uses fonts installed on the local computer to display fonts.

   ◆ **Bitmap Text (No Anti-Alias) (Classic)**. No text smoothing.

   ◆ **Anti-Alias for Animation (Classic)** or **Animation (TLF)**. Smooths out animation.

   ◆ **Anti-Alias for Readability (Classic)** or **Readability (TLF)**. Smooths out text.

   ◆ **Custom Anti-Alias (Classic)**. Modify font properties.

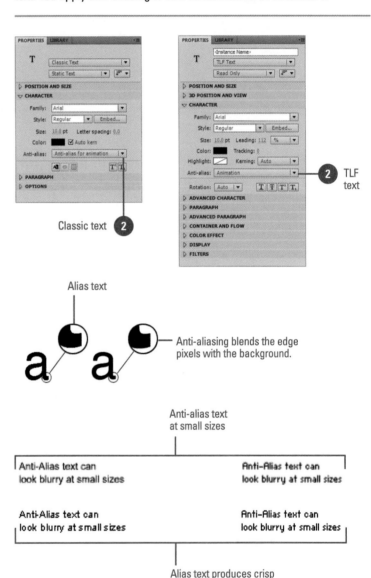

Classic text ②

② TLF text

Alias text

Anti-aliasing blends the edge pixels with the background.

Anti-alias text at small sizes

Anti-Alias text can look blurry at small sizes

Anti-Alias text can look blurry at small sizes

Anti-Alias text can look blurry at small sizes

Anti-Alias text can look blurry at small sizes

Alias text produces crisp fonts at small sizes.

Using Font Mapping

Select Substitute Fonts

1. Open the document with the fonts you want to map.

   ◆ To view all the font mappings saved on your computer, close all documents.

2. Click the **Flash** (Mac) or **Edit** (Win) menu, and then click **Font Mapping**.

3. Click a font in the Missing Fonts column.

   TIMESAVER *Press Shift+click to select multiple missing fonts to map to the same substitute font.*

4. Click the **Substitute Font** list arrow, and then click a font, or click **System Default**.

5. Click **OK**.

Did You Know?

You can delete the font mapping. Close all documents, click the Flash (Mac) or Edit (Win) menu, click Font Mapping, select a font mapping, click Delete, and then click OK.

You can turn off the Missing Font alert. Click the Flash (Mac) or Edit (Win) menu, click Font Mapping, select the Don't Show Again For This Document, Always Use Substitute Fonts check box, and then click OK.

If you open a document with a missing font on a computer, a Missing Font alert appears, asking you to choose a substitute font. You can open and use the Font Mapping dialog box to map a substitute font to the missing font, view the mapped fonts in the document, and delete a font mapping. After you select a substitute font, text appears with the correct font (if available) or the substitute font (if missing). When you use a substitute font, the text box or attributes might need to be adjusted.

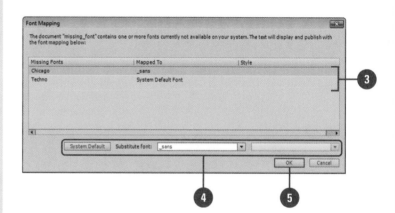

Setting Device Fonts Versus Embedded Fonts

When you include a font in your Flash document that is installed on your computer, you can include the font into the exported Flash movie. This is called an **embedded font** and it ensures that your fonts will look consistent when displayed on other computers. This adds to the file size, as each character from the selected font family has to be included in the final SWF. If file size is an issue, and the exact character matching is not important, you can choose to use device fonts. The Font Embedding dialog allows you to add or remove the fonts (all or part) you want to embed in the Flash document (**New!**). You can view a list of all your embedded fonts in one place. When a font is set to device, Flash will not embed the font information in the exported file. Instead the Flash Player will substitute the closest resembling font by name on the computer playing the Flash movie. The drawback is that you won't be able to predict how the fonts will display on every computer. To combat this uncertainty, Flash includes three device fonts. Each is designed with characteristics of typical fonts usually found by default on most computers. You can also choose device fonts when using small font sizes because they are not anti-alias and display clearly.

Embed Fonts

1. Select the text box with the fonts you want to embed with the **Selection** tool.

2. Click the **Embed** button in the Property Inspector.

3. Click the **Options** tab, and then specify a font name, family, style, and character ranges you want.

4. To add or delete an embedded font, do either of the following:

   ◆ Add New Font. Click **Add New Font** button, and then specify the font information in the Options tab.

   ◆ Delete Font. Select a font from the Font list, click the **Delete Selected Font** button, and then click **OK**.

5. Click the **ActionScript** tab, and then select options to export font information for ActionScript or to share font information for runtime sharing.

6. Click **OK**.

Embedded fonts

Set a Text Box to Device Font

1. Select the text box you want to set to the device font with the **Selection** tool.

2. Click the **Anti-Alias** list arrow in the Property Inspector, and then click **Use Device Fonts**.

Did You Know?

You can test for missing fonts. If there is incomplete font information on your computer, fonts may appear in the Font list in Flash but will not embed in the final movie. To test whether a font is complete, click the View menu, point to Preview Mode, and then click Antialias Text. If the text appears jagged, this means the font outlines are missing from the system.

Choose a Built-In Flash Device Font

1. Select the text box you want to set to the device font with the **Selection** tool.

2. Click the **Family** list arrow in the Property Inspector or click the **Text** menu, point to **Font**, and then select one of the following fonts:

   ◆ **_sans**. Matches up with a sansserif font, such as Helvetica or Arial.

   ◆ **_serif**. Matches up with a serif font, such as Times or Garamond.

   ◆ **_typewriter**. Matches up with a typewritten-looking font, such as Courier.

Creating Classic Dynamic Text and Input Text

When you create Classic text boxes in Flash, they default to static boxes. A static box is for display only and is hard-coded in the .swf. One cannot be changed unless you return to the Flash development environment, edit it, and re-export the file. If you need your text to be updatable from an outside source, such as a text document on a server or if you need the user to input text for you to retrieve and process with ActionScript, you can set your text box to enable this functionality. Setting your text box to dynamic text turns it into an ActionScript object that can be given an instance name or turned into a variable that can be populated from some other source outside of the .swf. This is great when you need to update content on the fly and would rather not have to deal directly with Flash for each update. If you require the user to enter a string of text, such as in a form, you can set a text box to input text. This enables the user to enter information in the text box that can be retrieved and processed.

Set a Classic Text Box to be Dynamic

1 Select the Classic text box you want to be a dynamic box with the **Selection** tool.

2 Click the **Text Type** list arrow in the Property Inspector, and then click **Dynamic Text**.

3 Select from the following properties:

- **Instance Name**. Gives the text box an instance name so it can be controlled with ActionScript.

- **Embed Options**. Allows you to choose which characters you want to embed in the text.

- **Letter Spacing**. Changes character position on a line.

- **Render Text As HTML**. Preserves Rich Text Formatting, allowing you to include hyperlinks and HTML tags.

- **Show Border**. Displays a border around the text box in the exported movie.

- **Variable Name**. Gives the text box a variable name for use with ActionScript.

dynamic text   dynamic text

1

Dynamic text boxes display in a dashed bounding box.

3

Instance Name

Embed Options

Letter Spacing

Show Border, Render Text As HTML

2

Line Type

Variable Name

Set a Classic Text Box to be an Input Box

1. Select the Classic text box you want to be an input box with the **Selection** tool.

2. Click the **Text Type** list arrow in the Property Inspector, and then click **Input Text**.

3. Select from the following properties:

   ◆ **Instance Name**. Gives the text box an instance name so it can be controlled with ActionScript.

   ◆ **Embed Options**. Allows you to choose which characters you want to embed in the text.

   ◆ **Letter Spacing**. Changes character position on a line.

   ◆ **Line Type**. Choose from Single Line and Multi-Line with or without Wrap, and Password (available only for Input text).

   ◆ **Selectability**. Allows or denies the user the ability to select the text in the exported movie.

   ◆ **Show Border**. Displays a border around the text box in the exported movie.

   ◆ **Variable Name**. Gives the text box a variable name for use with ActionScript.

   ◆ **Maximum Characters**. Limit the amount of characters a user can enter into the box.

Input text boxes display in a dashed bounding box.

Instance Name

Embed Options

Letter spacing

Show Border, Render Text As HTML

Line Type

Maximum Characters

Variable Name

Did You Know?

You can create scrolling text. Shift-double-click the handle of dynamic and input text to create text boxes that don't expand when you enter text on the Stage.

For Your Information

Using Multiple Languages in a Document

When you're working with Classic text in a Flash document, don't forget the global community. Flash supports multi-language authoring. You could create a document that displays text in Spanish and English, using a variety of methods: The text can be written within an external file and called using the #include ActionScript within a dynamic or text input box, or the text can be inserted into the document at runtime using an external XML (Extensible Markup Language) file. This allows you to insert different languages that automatically appear to the visitor. When you're working with multi-language Flash documents, click the Window menu, point to Other Panels, and then click Strings. The Strings panel lets you streamline the process of localizing content into multiple languages, because it collects and tracks all character strings throughout the development process in a central place. In the Strings panel, you can select a language and assign each text string, either a dynamic or input text box, in the document with a unique ID. The Strings panel has been improved to include multi-line support in the String box and the language XML file.

Checking Spelling

Flash includes a global spell-checker that is fully configurable. Search the entire Flash document or isolate specific elements to search in the Spelling Setup dialog box. You can choose from a variety of built-in dictionaries as sources including a personal dictionary you can edit. Additionally, you can choose which text characteristics to ignore, such as words with numbers and internet addresses, as well as choose what type of alternative suggestions you want Flash to provide.

Set Up Spell Checking

1. Click the **Text** menu, and then click **Spelling Setup**.

2. Select from the following options:

   ◆ **Document Options**. Specify which elements in the Flash document you want to spell check. You can also specify whether you want to live-edit the document during the Check Spelling process.

   ◆ **Dictionaries**. Select a built-in dictionary as a source. At least one dictionary must be selected to activate Check Spelling.

   ◆ **Personal Dictionary**. Specify an option to use a dictionary created and edited by you. Navigate to a text document on your hard drive or edit the default one included by clicking the Edit Personal Dictionary button. Each new entry in the personal dictionary must be on a separate line.

   ◆ **Checking Options**. Set word-level behaviors. You can have Internet addresses ignored, find duplicate words, or specify the types of suggestions you want displayed in the Check Spelling window.

3. Click **OK**.

Allow or deny on-the-fly editing during Spell Check

Set locations to Spell Check

Built-in Dictionaries

Set new location for Personal Dictionary

Set parameters for Spell Check

Use Spell Checking

1 Click the **Text** menu, and then click **Check Spelling**.

2 If Flash finds suspect words, the Check Spelling dialog box opens. Otherwise, Flash displays a message that the Spell Check is complete.

Word not found (*element*):

This identifies the suspect word and what type of element it was found in parenthesis.

3 Do one of the following:

- ◆ **Add To Personal.** Click to add the word to your personal dictionary.

- ◆ **Ignore.** Click the Ignore and Ignore All buttons to not flag this word again in this Check Spelling session.

- ◆ **Change.** Click Change or Change All. In the Change To and Suggestions boxes, Flash displays the closest alternatives to the suspect word.

- ◆ **Delete.** Click to delete the word from the box that contains it.

4 Continue until Flash produces a message that Check Spelling is complete or click **Close** to stop the Check Spelling process before it is completed.

Did You Know?

You must access the Spelling Setup once to activate Check Spelling. You need to activate Check Spelling to select a dictionary. Click the Text menu, and then click Spelling Setup.

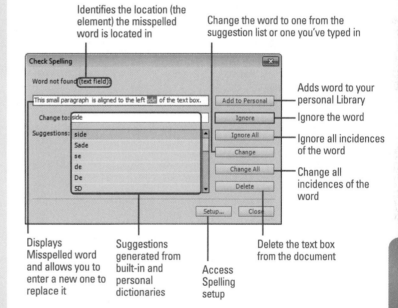

Identifies the location (the element) the misspelled word is located in

Change the word to one from the suggestion list or one you've typed in

Adds word to your personal Library

Ignore the word

Ignore all incidences of the word

Change all incidences of the word

Displays Misspelled word and allows you to enter a new one to replace it

Suggestions generated from built-in and personal dictionaries

Access Spelling setup

Delete the text box from the document

Using Find and Replace

Use Find and Replace to locate specific elements in your Flash document. You can specify where to look, what to look for, and what to replace it with. Choose to search the entire Flash document or the currently active scene. Each element you search for has its own configurable settings and options. Included is a log that shows the exact locations of the found element.

Locate Items with Find and Replace

1. Click the **Edit** menu, and then click **Find And Replace**.

   TIMESAVER *Press* ⌘+F *(Mac) or Ctrl+F (Win) to quickly open the Find and Replace window.*

2. Select where you want to search from the **Search In** list arrow menu.

3. Select which element from the **For** list arrow menu you want to search for in Flash:

   ◆ Text

   ◆ Font

   ◆ Color

   ◆ Symbol

   ◆ Sound

   ◆ Video

   ◆ Bitmap

4. Enter and/or select the parameters you want for your search.

5. To find the element with the characteristics you've entered, click **Find Next** or **Find All**.

6. To update the found element with the new characteristics, click **Replace** or **Replace All**.

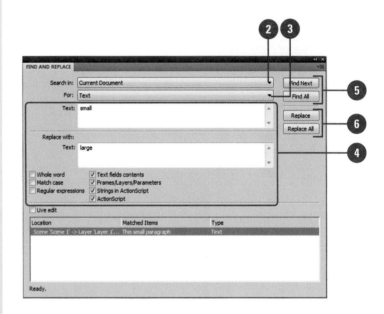

Using Cascading Style Sheets with HTML Text

Cascading Style Sheets (CSS) contain sets of formatting rules for HTML and XML text. CSS allow you to define certain text attributes and give them a style name. This style name, called a selector, can be applied to any implemented text. Each time you need to implement the defined style, you can refer back to the CSS. This allows for more control over the text displayed on your Web page. Load styles from an external CSS or create them within Flash using the Style Sheet Object. The ActionScript class for CSS is described as: TextField.StyleSheet. This is a new functionality and it is only available to SWFs in the Flash 7 Player or later.

Load an external CSS

In any text or HTML editor, place the following code:

```
// External CSS File: styles.css
headline {
        font-family: Arial, Helvetica, sans-serif;
     font-size: 12 px;
}
bodyText {
        font-family: Arial, Helvetica, sans-serif;
     font-size: 10 px;
}
```

This code is typically found in a CSS. This example defines two styles, one for a sans-serif headline at 12 pixels, the other a sans-serif body text at 10 pixels.

Select the first frame of your Flash movie. Place the following code in the Actions panel:

```
var css_styles = new TextField.StyleSheet();
css_styles.load("styles.css");
css_styles.onLoad = function(ok) {
  if(ok) {
    // display style names
    trace(this.getStyleNames());
  } else {
    trace("Error loading CSS file.");
  }
}
```

The CSS you created, "styles.css" is loaded into this object. A loader is created to ensure the CSS is loaded properly. Make sure the CSS and the swf are in the same directory.

Create a CSS in Flash

Select the first frame of your Flash movie. The following code creates a text style for headline text and body text. Place the following code in the Actions panel:

```
var styles = new TextField.StyleSheet();
styles.setStyle("headline",
   {fontFamily: 'Arial,Helvetica,sans-serif',
    fontSize: '12px'}
);
styles.setStyle("bodyText",
   {fontFamily: 'Arial,Helvetica,sans-serif',
    fontSize: '10px'}
);
```

This CSS code can now be placed in the Actions panel in Flash. This example defines two styles, one for a sans-serif headline at 12 pixels, the other a sans-serif body text at 10 pixels.

Importing Graphics

Introduction

In addition to the vector drawing tools that allow you to create graphics and animation in Flash, you can also import artwork in other formats to use in your Flash movie. Flash has full native support for Adobe Photoshop, Adobe Illustrator, Adobe FXG, BMP, JPEG, GIF, and PNG files, the standard bitmapped graphics. However, you can also import EPS and PDF by using Adobe Illustrator. This allows you to import a variety of different graphic formats into your Flash production process.

Flash drawing tools create and edit vector objects, not pixels, so preparation is necessary for bitmapped graphics in a paint application outside of Flash, such as Adobe Photoshop. Fortunately, Flash allows you to convert a bitmapped graphic into a vector with the Trace Bitmap function. You can also use a bitmap as a fill for vector objects. An important thing to remember is that any bitmap used in your project can add considerable size to your Flash movie. Flash includes several procedures for optimizing these bitmaps on export, through compression settings applied globally, or specifically to each image.

What You'll Do

Understand Vector and Bitmap Graphics

Examine Import File Formats

Set Illustrator Import Preferences

Set Photoshop Import Preferences

Import Photoshop and Illustrator Files

Import Bitmaps

Import Fireworks PNG Files

Import Multiple Files

Copy Images from Other Programs

Edit Bitmaps in an Outside Editor

Set Bitmap Compression

Use Break Apart to Create Fill Patterns

Modify a Bitmap Fill

Edit a Bitmap with the Magic Wand

Use Trace Bitmap to Create Vector Shapes

Understanding Vector and Bitmap Graphics

Vector graphics are comprised of anchor points connected to each other by lines and curves, called vectors. These anchor points and vectors describe the contour and surface of the graphic with some included information about color, alpha, and line width. Because they are general descriptions of the coordinates of a shape, they are resolution-independent; that is they can be resized without any loss to the quality of the graphic. Resolution represents the amount of information contained within a linear inch represented by a grid.

Bitmapped graphics are made up of small, colored squares, called pixels that form a grid. Each pixel is given a specific color and a grid of these pixels forms a mosaic, which is your image. Because of this, bitmaps are dependent on resolution (the number of pixels in the grid). Resizing up or down forces pixels to be created or removed to accommodate the new grid size, which can result in a loss of image quality. In Flash, bitmaps look much better on the Stage when severely enlarged or reduced. The smoothing process makes the appearance of these bitmaps in the Flash authoring tool and in Flash Player now consistent.

Both vector and bitmap graphics have their strengths and weaknesses. Vector shapes are simple and graphic in nature. They are a good choice for creating high-contrast, geometric art or art with limited color shifts. If you need to implement artwork with a richer surface texture, color depth, and shading, like those qualities found in a photograph, a bitmap better suits this purpose. The strength of Flash as a content creator is that you can combine the strengths of both vector art and bitmapped art.

Bitmap Image

Vector Image

Examining Import File Formats

The following image files can be imported into Flash:

Image File Formats			
File Type	Extension	Windows	Macintosh
Adobe Illustrator	.ai	✓	✓
Adobe Photoshop	.psd	✓	✓
Adobe FXG (**New!**)	.fxg	✓	✓
AutoCAD DXF	.dxf	✓	✓
Bitmap	.bmp	✓	✓ (Using QuickTime)
Enhanced Windows Metafile	.emf	✓	
GIF and animated GIF	.gif	✓	✓
JPEG	.jpg	✓	✓
PNG	.png	✓	✓
Flash SWF Movie	.swf	✓	✓
Windows Metafile	.wmf	✓	✓
QuickTime Image	.qtif	✓	✓
TIFF	.tiff	✓	✓

Setting Illustrator Import Preferences

Flash allows you to set preferences to customize the way you import Adobe Illustrator (.ai) files. You can specify general options to specify whether to use the import dialog box, import objects outside the Illustrator artboard or import hidden layers. After you set the general options, you can set options for specific element types you want to import, such as text, paths, images, groups, and layers. The options you set are applied to all Illustrator files when you import them into Flash. However, you can change options in the Illustrator import dialog box.

Set Illustrator File Import Preferences

1. Click the **Flash** (Mac) or **Edit** (Win) menu, and then click **Preferences**.

2. Click the **AI File Importer** category.

3. Select from the following options:

    ◆ **General.**

        ◆ **Show Import Dialog Box.** Select to show AI File Importer dialog box.

        ◆ **Excludes Objects Outside Art Board.** Select to exclude object outside the artboard or crop area.

        ◆ **Import Hidden Layers.** Select to import hidden layers.

    ◆ **Import Text As.**

        ◆ **Editable Text.** Imports Illustrator text as editable text in Flash.

        ◆ **Vector Outlines.** Converts text to vector paths; use to preserve appearance.

        ◆ **Bitmaps.** Converts text into a bitmap; not editable.

        ◆ **Create Movie Clips.** Imports text into a movie clip; use to maintain blends, AI effects, and transparency.

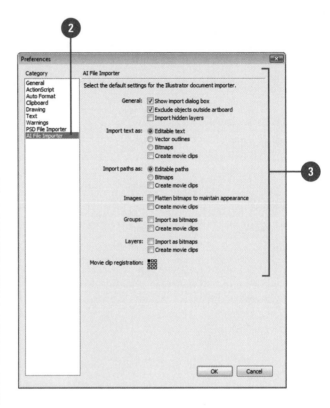

◆ **Import Paths As.**

    ◆ **Editable Paths.** Imports Illustrator path as editable in Flash.

    ◆ **Bitmaps.** Converts the path into a bitmap; use to preserve appearance of path; not editable.

    ◆ **Create Movie Clips.** Imports path into a movie clip symbol in Flash.

◆ **Images.**

    ◆ **Flatten Bitmaps To Maintain Appearance.** Converts an image into a bitmap; not editable.

    ◆ **Create Movie Clips.** Imports an image into a movie clip symbol in Flash.

◆ **Groups.**

    ◆ **Import As Bitmaps.** Converts all objects in the group into a bitmap; not editable.

    ◆ **Create Movie Clips.** Imports all objects into a movie clip symbol in Flash.

◆ **Layers.**

    ◆ **Import As Bitmaps.** Converts the layer into a bitmap; not editable.

    ◆ **Create Movie Clips.** Imports the layer into a movie clip symbol in Flash.

◆ **Movie Clip Registration.** Select the global registration point for movies and all other object types.

4 Click **OK**.

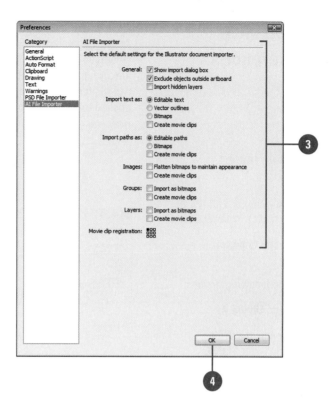

Setting Photoshop Import Preferences

Flash allows you to set preferences to customize the way you import Adobe Photoshop (.psd) files. You can set options for specific element layer types you want to import, such as images, text, paths, shapes, and groups. You can also set compression and quality publishing options for the imported Photoshop files. The options you set are applied to all Photoshop files when you import them into Flash. However, you can change options in the Photoshop import dialog box.

Set Photoshop File Import Preferences

1. Click the **Flash** (Mac) or **Edit** (Win) menu, and then click **Preferences**.

2. Click the **PSD File Importer** category.

3. Select from the following options:

   - **Import Image Layers As.**

     - **Bitmap Images With Editable Layer Styles.** Create a movie clip with a bitmap clipped inside.

     - **Flatten Bitmap Images.** Convert an image into a bitmap; not editable.

     - **Create Movie Clips.** Imports an image into a movie clip symbol in Flash.

   - **Import Text Layers As.**

     - **Editable Text.** Imports Photoshop text from the text layer as editable text in Flash.

     - **Vector Outlines.** Converts text to vector paths; the object is also converted to a movie clip.

     - **Flattened Bitmap Images.** Converts text into a bitmap; not editable.

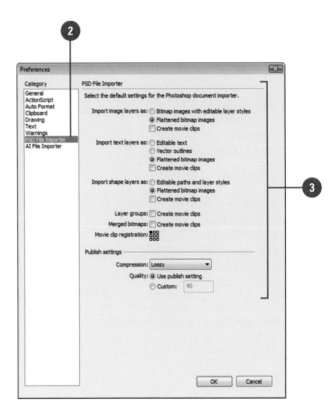

- **Create Movie Clips.** Imports the text layer into a movie clip symbol.

◆ **Import Shape Layers As.**

- **Editable Paths And Layer Styles.** Creates an editable vector shape with a bitmap clipped inside the vector shape.

- **Flatten Bitmap Images.** Converts an image into a bitmap; not editable.

- **Create Movie Clips.** Imports an image into a movie clip symbol in Flash.

◆ **Layer Groups.** Select the Create Move Clips check box to convert all groups into a movie clip in Flash.

◆ **Merged Bitmaps.** Select the Create Movie Clips check box to convert the shape layers into a movie clip in Flash.

◆ **Movie Clip Registration.** Select the global registration point for movies and all other object types.

◆ **Publish Settings.**

- **Compression.** Select the Lossy (JPEG) or Lossless (PNG/GIF) compression mode you want.

- **Quality.** For the Lossy compression, select the Use Publish Setting or Custom option; select the quality 1 to 100; the higher the setting, the greater quality, yet the larger the file size.

4 Click **OK**.

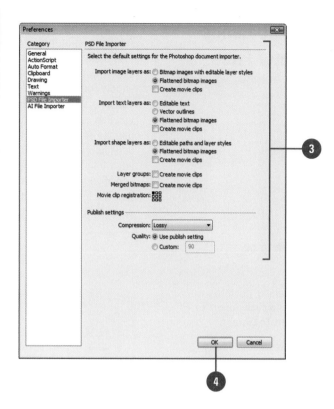

Importing Photoshop and Illustrator Files

Flash includes support for importing Adobe Photoshop (.psd) files and Adobe Illustrator files created in versions 6 through 10. When these files are imported, there are a number of options you can choose from. Before you import Photoshop and Illustrator files, you need to set import options in the Preferences dialog box. For Illustrator files, you can also specify whether you want to show an import dialog box where you can set import settings for specific parts of an Illustrator file. The options you set are applied to all Illustrator and Photoshop files when you import them into Flash. However, you can change options in the import dialog box. Some options in the Import dialog box are context-sensitive; that is, they only appear if they are relevant to the imported file. The import options are similar between Illustrator and Photoshop; when they differ, the options are noted.

Import a Photoshop or Illustrator File

1. Click the **File** menu, point to **Import**, and then click **Import To Stage** or **Import To Library**.

   ◆ Open and select the library where you want to import files.

2. Click the **Show** popup (Mac) or **Files Of Type** (Win), and then select **Photoshop**, **Adobe Illustrator** or **All Image Formats**.

3. Navigate to the drive or folder where the file is located.

4. Select the Photoshop or Illustrator file you want to import.

5. Click **Import** (Mac) or **Open** (Win).

   Flash inserts the image file or displays an import dialog box for files, where you can specify options for the specific files. If the Import dialog box opens, continue.

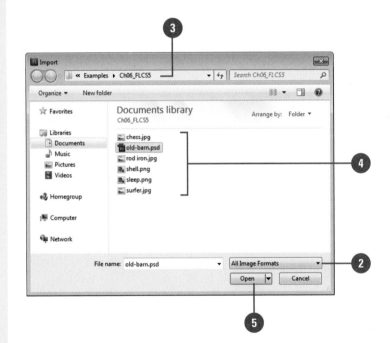

Did You Know?

You can import an Illustrator EPS or PDF using Illustrator CS4 or later. Open the file in Adobe Illustrator CS4 or later, save it as a CS4-compatible AI file, and then import into Flash as an AI file.

6 To generate a list of items from Illustrator now compatible with Flash, click **Incompatibility Report**.

7 Select the check boxes with the elements you want to import, select each element and set the related options you want; you may need to ungroup elements.

8 Click the **Convert Layers To** list arrow, and then click.

♦ **Flash Layers**. Click this option to convert the layers in the imported file into corresponding layers in the Flash Timeline.

♦ **Keyframes**. Click this option to convert the layers in the imported file into consecutive keyframes.

♦ **Single Flash Layer**. Click this option to flatten the layers in the imported file onto a single layer in Flash.

9 Select from the following options:

♦ **Place At Original Position**. Select to maintain the same positions from Illustrator or Photoshop to Flash.

♦ **Set Stage Size To Same Size As**. Select to set the Flash Stage to the same size as the Illustrator artboard or Photoshop canvas.

♦ **Import As Unused Symbols (AI)**. Select to import AI symbols not used as instances as unused symbols in Flash.

♦ **Import As A Single Bitmap Image (AI)**. Select to convert into a bitmap.

10 Specify the compression and quality settings you want (PSD).

11 Click **OK**.

Importing Bitmaps

You can import bitmaps of several file types directly into Flash to use in your Flash movie. It is important to remember that even though you can edit and resize bitmaps in Flash, the original bitmap will always be embedded in the exported Flash file. If file size is an issue, it is best to bring your bitmapped art in at the size you want to export it. For example, if your image is going to be 160 pixels by 160 pixels in the final movie, it is best to import it at this size and not resize it up or down in Flash. You will end up with higher-quality images and smaller files if you do this. You can import files using the Import To Stage or Import To Library methods. The Import To Stage method stores the bitmap in the Library and places a copy on the Stage, while the Import To Library method stores the bitmap in the Library and doesn't place a copy on the Stage.

Import a Bitmap to the Stage

1. Click the **File** menu, point to **Import**, and then click **Import To Stage**.

2. Click the **Show** popup (Mac) or **Files Of Types** list arrow (Win), and then select the format of the file you want to import.

3. Navigate to the drive or folder where the file is located.

4. Select the file you want to import.

5. Click **Import** (Mac) or **Open** (Win).

Did You Know?

You may not be able to see the images you've imported to the Stage at certain magnification levels. Flash aligns the top left-hand corner of the image at the 0,0 coordinate. If you are zoomed in, the image may have appeared outside the viewable area. Use the Hand tool to navigate around, zoom out, or press Shift+⌘+W (Mac) or Ctrl+Shift+W (Win) to toggle the Work Area off. This sets the zoom level to 100% and hides the Work Area.

For Your Information

Scaling Image Before Importing

Scaling bitmaps reduces the quality of the image, so it's best to import an image into Flash at the size you want it to be. If you need to scale an image in Flash, it's a good idea to import the image at a slightly larger size, so when you scale it down, loss of quality is minimized.

Import to the Library

1. Click the **File** menu, point to **Import**, and then click **Import To Library**.

2. Click the **Show** popup (Mac) or **Files Of Types** list arrow (Win), and then select the format of the file you want to import.

3. Navigate to the drive or folder where the file is located.

4. Select the file you want to import.

5. Click **Import To Library** (Mac) or **Open** (Win).

Did You Know?

You can quickly swap bitmaps. You can exchange an image on the Stage with another one from the Library. To swap one bitmap with another on the Stage, select the bitmap image on the Stage, open the Property Inspector, click Swap, select the image you want from the list of currently stored images in your document library, and then click OK.

Image is placed in the Library.

Importing Fireworks PNG Files

You can import Adobe Fireworks PNG files into Flash as editable objects or bitmap images. When you import a PNG file as a bitmap image, the file, including any vector data, is flattened, or rasterized, and converted to a bitmap. When you import a PNG file as an editable image, the file retains any vector data, bitmaps, text (with default anti-alias settings), filters (called effects in Fireworks) and guides. In Flash, you can retain Fireworks filters, blend modes, and text, and continue to modify them using Flash. When you import Fireworks files into Flash, PNG file graphic properties remain intact. You can also select multiple PNG files to import in a batch. When you batch PNG files, you select import settings one time. When you import a PNG as a flattened image, you can also edit the image in Fireworks directly from Flash. Flash updates the image with your changes from Fireworks creating easy round-trip edits.

Import and Edit Fireworks PNG Files

1. Click the **File** menu, point to **Import**, and then click **Import To Stage** or **Import To Library**.

2. Click the **Show** popup (Mac) or **Files Of Types** list arrow (Win), and then click **PNG File** or **All Formats**.

3. Navigate to the Fireworks PNG files you want to import, and then select one or more.

4. Click **Import** or **Import To Library** (Mac) or **Open** (Win).

5. To flatten the PNG file into a bitmap, select the **Import as a Single Flattened Bitmap** check box.

   IMPORTANT *To use round-trip editing, you need to flatten the PNG file into a bitmap. You cannot edit bitmaps from Fireworks PNG files imported as editable objects.*

6. Click the **Import** popup, and then click **Page** or other available options.

7. Click the **Into** popup, and then click **Current Frame As Movie Clip, New Layer** or other available options.

8 For objects and text, select one of the following:

◆ **Import As Bitmaps To Maintain Appearance**. Retains Fireworks fills, strokes, and effects in Flash.

◆ **Keep All Paths Editable**. Retains vector properties; however, some Fireworks fills, strokes, and effects are lost; places file and related files in a Fireworks Objects folder in the Library.

9 Click **OK**.

10 To edit a flattened PNG bitmap, right-click (Win) or control-click (Mac) the PNG/bitmap's icon in the Library, and then click **Edit with** and select an image editing program or click **Edit with Fireworks**.

◆ In the Edit Image dialog box, specify whether the PNG file or the bitmap file is to be opened.

◆ In Fireworks, edit the image, click **Done** or click the **File** menu, and then click **Update**.

Did You Know?

You can optimize PNG images in Fireworks for Flash. Images can increase the size of a movie so you want to optimize images to be as small as possible while still maintaining high quality. You can optimize bitmap and PNG images in Fireworks using round-trip editing from Flash. In Fireworks, specify options on the Optimize panel to optimize and compress images.

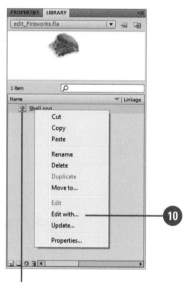

PNG file from Fireworks

Importing Multiple Files

Flash allows you to import multiple files simultaneously to save time. This is useful if you have many files to import. You can select multiple, non-sequential files in the Import dialog box. Choose to import to the Library or to the Stage directly. When you import to the Stage, the file is stored in the Library and a copy is placed on the Stage so you can begin editing it immediately. If you attempt to import a series of files that are numbered sequentially, Flash detects this and produces a dialog box to handle this. When sequential images are imported, they will appear in separate frames by order of the number in their file name. This is extremely useful for image sequences where a series of images forms an animation.

Import Multiple Files or a Sequence of Files

1 Click the **File** menu, point to **Import**, and then click **Import To Stage** or **Import To Library**.

2 Click the **Show** popup (Mac) or **Files Of Types** list arrow (Win), and then select the format of the file you want to import.

3 Navigate to the drive or folder where the file is located.

4 Select the first file you want to import.

5 To import multiple files, hold down the ⌘ (Mac) or Ctrl (Win) key and click additional files to select them.

6 Click **Import** (Mac) or **Open** (Win).

For a sequence of files, Flash detects that this image is part of a sequence and asks whether you want to import all of them at once.

7 Click **Yes**.

The numbered files are imported and placed on separate sequential keyframes on the selected layer in the Timeline.

Multiple files imported appear stacked on top of each other. Press down and drag with your mouse to reveal images underneath.

Each imported image appears on a separate frame sequentially.

Copying Images from Other Programs

You can paste a bitmap image from other image editing programs, such as Adobe Photoshop or Adobe Fireworks. Simply use the standard copying procedure in the program of your choice to place the bitmap into the clipboard, which is where the operating system dynamically stores information you copy, and then paste it into Flash directly on the Stage. Copying images from other programs works well for bitmaps. However, results are unpredictable when pasting vector graphics from other programs. Often they become corrupted when they are copied to the clipboard, depending upon the origin program or the operating system. It is best to use the Import command to import vector graphics into Flash.

Paste from the Clipboard

1. Copy the image to the clipboard in an image-editing program.

2. Launch or switch to Flash, and then open the Flash document in which you want to paste an image from the clipboard.

3. Select an unlocked layer or keyframe.

4. Click the **Edit** menu, and then click **Paste in Center** or **Paste in Place**.

   TIMESAVER *Press ⌘+V (Mac) or Ctrl+V (Win) to quickly paste in center from the clipboard; press ⌘+Shift+V (Mac) or Ctrl+Shift V (Win) to quickly paste in place from the clipboard.*

Image is pasted onto the Stage and placed in the Library.

Editing Bitmaps in an Outside Editor

You can edit a bitmap in its native program, such as Photoshop CS5 or Fireworks 3, or some other image editing tool. Once it is re-saved or updated to the hard drive, Flash automatically updates the bitmap back when you return to Flash (**New!**). If an image is moved to another location, you can manually update it. In addition, you can import another image to replace the bitmap in the Library. In either case, every copy of the bitmap used in the Flash movie (including bitmap fills) will update with these changes. This is a convenient way to make global changes to bitmap art included in your project.

Update an Image Edited Outside of Flash

1. Import a bitmap into Flash.

2. Open the **Library** panel.

3. Right-click (Win) or Control-click (Mac) the bitmap's icon, and then click **Edit with Photoshop CS5** or **Edit with Fireworks 3**.

   ◆ For other imaging programs, click **Edit With**, select an image-editing program, and then click **OK**.

4. In the image-editing program, modify the bitmap, click the **File** menu, and then click **Save** or **Update**, and then return to Flash.

   The bitmap is automatically updated in Flash.

5. To manually update an image or relink to a different location, right-click (Win) or Control-click the icon in the Library panel, click the **Properties**, click **Update**, and then click **OK**.

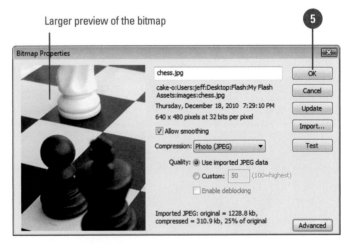

Larger preview of the bitmap

208 Chapter 6

Replace a Bitmap

① Open the **Library** panel, and then select the bitmap from the item list.

② Click the **Properties** icon in the bottom of the panel or double-click the bitmap file in the list.

③ Click **Import**.

④ Navigate to the replacement file on your hard drive.

⑤ Select the replacement file.

⑥ Click **Import** (Mac) or **Open** (Win).

⑦ Change the name and any other options you want.

⑧ Click **OK**.

Did You Know?

Flash preserves the path when you import a bitmap. When you import a bitmap into Flash, the path to that image is preserved in the Bitmap Properties. If you have moved the image to another directory on your hard drive and you want to update the file in the Library with the new changes, navigate to it by using the Import button in the Bitmap Properties window.

Image is replaced with new imported image. All copies used in the Flash movie update to this new image.

Setting Bitmap Compression

When you export a Flash movie, you can decide how much color information to include in each exported bitmap. This is called **compression**. The more compression you apply, the less color information is included and the lower the size and quality of the image. **Lossy** compression reduces the file size by removing color information, while **lossless** compression reduces the file size (not as much) without removing information. You can choose to set a global compression for all bitmap files used in a Flash movie or you can set a separate compression for each image. As with all image compression, file size needs to be weighed against image quality. It is always best to experiment until you get the results you want.

Set Compression for a Bitmap

1. Open the **Library** panel.

2. Select the bitmap from the Library item list in which you want to set compression.

3. Click the **Properties** icon in the bottom of the panel or double-click the bitmap file in the list.

4. Select the **Allow Smoothing** check box to anti-alias the edges of the image, making it appear smoother.

5. Click the **Compression** popup, and then select from the following options:

   ◆ **Lossless (PNG/GIF).** Compresses the image without losing any information; remains in its highest quality.

   ◆ **Photo (JPEG).** You can choose to use the compression information contained by selecting the **Use Document Default Quality** check box. By deselecting this feature you can set the level of JPEG compression applied to the bitmap. The values are 1-100. The higher the number, the less compression applied, producing a higher quality image.

6. Click **OK**.

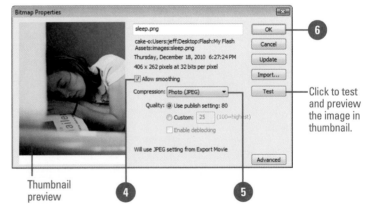

Click to test and preview the image in thumbnail.

Thumbnail preview

Using Break Apart to Create Fill Patterns

By default, when you import a bitmap into Flash and drag it to the Stage, you are limited in how you can edit it. Break Apart the image to remove the image from its bounding box and enable you to cut into the image, remove parts, select regions, and use it as a fill pattern. The bitmap is still linked to its parent in the Library. Any edit made to a bitmap only affects the copy on the Stage. For example, if you break an image and then edit it down to a tiny portion, in the exported movie the image appears exactly as you edited it. However, it will still have the same file size of the image you imported (less any compression you may have applied). It is always best to do your most severe editing in a bitmap or paint program outside of Flash.

Create a Bitmap Fill Pattern

1. Drag a copy of a bitmap to the Stage from the Library panel; make sure the bitmap is selected on the Stage.

2. Click the **Modify** menu, and then click **Break Apart**.

   TIMESAVER *Press ⌘+B (Mac) and Ctrl+B (Win) to quickly break apart a bitmap on the Stage.*

3. Click the **Eyedropper** tool on the Tools panel.

4. Position the eyedropper over the image, and then click to select it.

   The bitmap is a selected fill that you can use to fill vector shapes.

5. Click the **Rectangle** or **Oval** tool on the Tools panel.

6. Click and drag on the Stage to create a new shape with the bitmap fill.

Did You Know?

You can select the bitmap fill in the Color Mixer panel. In the panel, click Bitmap from the Fill Style popup, and then select a thumbnail fill (bitmaps from the Library appear).

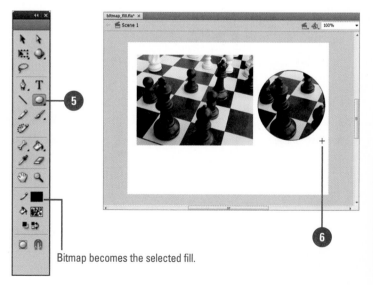

Bitmap becomes the selected fill.

Modifying a Bitmap Fill

Flash defaults to tiling a bitmap fill. Tiling is simply when an image is repeated in a grid until it fills the entire object. If you have applied a bitmap fill to a vector object, you can continue to edit its characteristics and placement. You can resize, skew, or rotate the fill or change its center point within the shape with the Gradient Transform tool. This tool allows you to dynamically make these changes when it is applied to any editable shape. As with most of the assets Flash stores in the Library, any change you make to the application of the fill does not affect the master object stored in the Library. In this way, bitmaps like video clips and sounds, behave similarly to symbols in that their master object is not affected. Although when you use a bitmap in your movie Flash refers to this as a copy, not an instance, because there are no built-in controls for bitmaps.

Change the Center Point

① Create a shape on the Stage with a bitmap fill.

② Click the **Gradient Transform** tool on the Tools panel.

The pointer changes to an arrow with a small gradient box in the right-hand corner.

TIMESAVER *Press F to quickly select the Gradient Transform tool.*

③ Click the shape to select it.

A bounding box appears on the tile.

④ Position the pointer over the white circle in the center of the bounding box.

The cursor becomes a Move icon.

⑤ Click and drag the center point to a new position.

The tile accommodates to the new position of the center point.

Bounding box

Bitmap fill in new location

Modify the Orientation and Size of a Bitmap Fill

① Create a shape on the Stage with a bitmap fill.

② Click the **Gradient Transform** tool on the Tools panel.

The pointer changes to an arrow with a small gradient box in the right-hand corner.

③ Position the pointer over the shape, and then select it.

A bounding box appears on the tile.

④ Do one of the following:

◆ **Bottom-left-corner square.** Drag this to resize the fill proportionally.

◆ **Left-center square.** Drag this to resize width of fill.

◆ **Bottom-center square.** Drag this to resize height of fill.

◆ **Top-right-corner circle.** Drag this to rotate fill.

◆ **Top-center circle.** Drag this to skew fill horizontally.

◆ **Right-center circle.** Drag this to skew fill vertically.

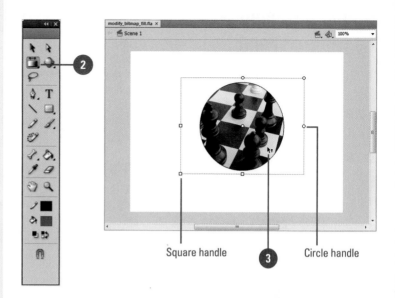

Square handle   ③   Circle handle

Resize proportionally   Resize width   Resize height

Rotate   Skew horizontally   Skew vertically

Samples of various fills

Editing a Bitmap with the Magic Wand

When you use Break Apart on a bitmap, the bitmap becomes a fill and its content is editable. You can select specific regions of it with any of Flash's selection tools and procedures. If you want to remove parts of the bitmap or replace them with different fills you can select those parts with the Magic Wand tool. The Magic Wand tool selects regions of similar colors. Clicking on other parts adds those parts to the selection. The color threshold (or sensitivity) for this tool can be set in the Magic Wand options popup menu.

Use the Magic Wand

1. Select a bitmap on the Stage.

2. Click the **Modify** menu, and then click **Break Apart**.

    TIMESAVER *Press ⌘+B (Mac) or Ctrl+B (Win) to quickly break apart a bitmap on the Stage.*

3. Click on the Stage to deselect the broken bitmap.

4. Click the **Lasso** tool on the Tools panel.

5. Click the **Magic Wand Mode** button in the Options section of the Tools panel.

    The pointer becomes a small magic wand.

6. Position the pointer over regions of the image you want to select.

    The color region you clicked on is selected. Subsequent clicks on other regions are added to the selection.

Color regions selected and deleted from bitmap fill.

Set the Magic Wand Options

1 Click the **Lasso** tool on the Tools panel.

2 Click the **Magic Wand Properties** button on the Tools panel.

3 Enter a color threshold between 0 and 200.

This number defines how close adjacent colors have to be to the selected color before they are added to the selection. A higher number selects a broader number of colors.

4 Click the **Smoothing** popup, and then select from the following options: **Pixels**, **Rough**, **Normal**, and **Smooth**.

This sets the smoothness of the edges of the selection.

5 Click **OK**.

Using Trace Bitmap to Create Vector Shapes

Flash provides a procedure to convert bitmaps into vector art. When Trace Bitmap is used, Flash interprets the pixel information in the bitmap and converts it into vector shapes. The results can be unpredictable in quality and have unwieldy file sizes if the bitmaps are very complex. However, there are several parameters in the Trace Bitmap dialog box that can be modified to strike a balance between file size and quality.

Trace a Bitmap

1 Drag a copy of a bitmap to the Stage from the Library panel; make sure the bitmap is selected on the Stage.

2 Click the **Modify** menu, point to **Bitmap**, and then click **Trace Bitmap**.

> **TROUBLE?** *The Trace Bitmap command is disabled if you select a broken bitmap (a bitmap fill).*

3 Specify values and options to determine how close the vector shape resembles the bitmap:

- **Color Threshold.** If the difference in the RGB color value for two pixels is less than the color threshold, the pixel colors are considered the same. Enter a value between 1 and 500. The higher the value, the lower the number of colors.

- **Minimum Area.** Determines how many neighboring pixels to include in the threshold calculation. Enter a pixel value between 1 and 1000.

- **Curve Fit.** Determines how smoothly Flash creates vector outlines.

- **Corner Threshold.** Controls whether to preserve sharp edges or create more smooth contours.

4 Click **OK**.

Vectorized bitmap

Creating Frame-by-Frame Animation

Introduction

Flash provides several methods for creating animation. In addition to shape and motion tweening, you can create frame-by-frame animations. The frame-by-frame method is derived from the traditional animation process whereby the content is redrawn on each frame with slight differences from the last frame. When these frames are played in sequence, there is an illusion of movement. In Flash, you utilize keyframes in the Timeline to accomplish this. A **keyframe** defines a change to the artwork placed on the Stage. There are a number of ways to create and edit keyframes, as they are editable objects. Keyframes can be moved, copied, and pasted to and from any Timeline in your Flash movie or between different Flash documents. Frame-by-frame animations can be previewed in the Flash development environment so you can quickly see the results and check your work as you animate. They can also be viewed in the Flash Player using the Test Movie options.

Additionally, there is an Onion Skin mode that allows you to see the active frame in context to the frames around it, making it easier to fine-tune keyframe changes. The versatility of the Timeline and the strength of the Flash Player allow you to implement animation in your movie and give it life.

What You'll Do

Understand Frame-by-Frame Animation

Create Keyframes

Convert Frames to Keyframes

Use Frame-Based Versus Span-Based Selection

Clear Keyframes Versus Removing Frames

Edit Keyframes

Create a Simple Frame-by-Frame Animation

Play an Animation

Use Onion Skinning

Modify Onion Skin Markers

Edit Multiple Frames

Understanding Frame-by-Frame Animation

Animation is the illusion of movement. It is comprised of a series of pictures, each slightly different from the last, that when played sequentially imply movement. Motion pictures work the same way. What you see when you view a film is a long strip of images played at specific intervals. In this way, the content in the pictures moves and seems to imitate real life.

Traditional cell animators draw a picture onto a frame of celluloid and then draw the same thing onto the next frame but with slight changes made to the drawing. Static parts of the scene (such as a background) are copied and only the objects that change are redrawn. In this way the process is more efficient.

The principles for animating in Flash have derived from this process. In Flash, you create frame-by-frame animations in the Timeline through the use of keyframes. Each keyframe defines a change on the Stage, and when played in succession, the content can seem to evolve, or move. When you export your movie, Flash will play these frames in succession at specific intervals depending on the frame rate you set. A good introduction to this concept, as well as the basics of animation, is the dissection a character walk cycle. When human beings walk, they are essentially repeating the same motion over and over again. In an animated walk cycle, the same thing occurs, though instead of drawing the cycle over and over again, the motion is spaced out so that the last frame (the last image drawn) meets up with the first frame. If this animation is looped, the character will seem to walk perpetually.

Keyframes define changes. Each frame displays a different part of the walk cycle.

Static elements such as the sidewalk span across multiple frames.

Frame-by-Frame Animation

Frame 1

Frame 2

Frame 3

Frame 4

Frame 5

Frame 6

Frame 7

Frame 8

Creating Keyframes

When art is placed on the Stage, it appears in a keyframe in the Timeline. A keyframe is represented as a black-bounded box with a small circle in it. By default, each layer in the Timeline has a keyframe on its first frame. An empty keyframe displays an empty or hollow circle, but when you place artwork or objects on the Stage, the bounding box becomes shaded and the small circle becomes a filled black dot. A keyframe can span multiple frames when there are no changes to the art. To make a change you create another keyframe. In this way, you can create animations or content that seems to move or change over time.

Create a Keyframe

1. Place art or an object on the Stage.

2. Click on a frame later in the Timeline.

3. Click the **Insert** menu, point to **Timeline**, and then click **Keyframe**.

   A new keyframe appears.

   TIMESAVER *Press F6 to add a keyframe or Control+click (Mac) or right-click (Win) the selected frame, and then click Add Keyframe.*

Did You Know?

You can remove content from a keyframe. Select a filled keyframe in the Timeline or the art on the Stage contained in that keyframe, and then press the Delete (Mac) or Backspace (Win) key.

Empty keyframe appears as a hollow circle.

When content is placed on the Stage, the hollow dot becomes a filled black dot.

New keyframe appears

Framespan

Create a Blank Keyframe

1. Click on a frame in the Timeline where you want to add a blank keyframe.

   IMPORTANT *You can only add a blank keyframe to a frame without an existing keyframe (sometimes called an inactive frame or keyspan).*

2. Click the **Insert** menu, point to **Timeline**, and then click **Blank Keyframe**.

   TIMESAVER *Press F7 to add a keyframe or Control+click (Mac) or right-click (Win) the selected frame, and then click Add Blank Keyframe.*

Blank keyframe appears

Increase the Keyframe Span

1. Click anywhere in a keyframe span.

   ◆ To insert multiple keyframes, select the number of frames you want.

2. Click the **Insert** menu, point to **Timeline**, and then click **Frame**.

   Repeat until you've increased the framespan to the length you need.

   TIMESAVER *Press F5 to add a frame or Control+click (Mac) or right-click (Win) the selected frame, and then click Insert Frame.*

Inserts one frame

A framespan increased by 10 frames

Did You Know?

You can decrease the keyframe span. Press Shift+F5 for each frame you want to remove.

Converting Frames to Keyframes

Any frame can be converted into a keyframe. As a time-saver, you can select a range of frames and convert them all into keyframes simultaneously. This is useful when you have many frames to convert. It is also a good technique for fine-tuning shape and motion tweens. After the tween has been applied, you can convert the frames in the tweened span into keyframes and edit them independently.

Convert Multiple Frames Into Keyframes

1. Click on a frame, and then drag to select a frame span.

2. Click the **Modify** menu, point to **Timeline**, and then click **Convert To Keyframes**.

   TIMESAVER *Press Ctrl+click (Mac) or right-click (Win) the selected frames, and then click Convert To Keyframes or Press F6 after selecting all of the frames you want to convert.*

Selected frames are converted into keyframes.

Did You Know?

You don't have to select a frame to add keyframes. If you place the playhead over a frame and add a keyframe or a blank keyframe, it appears without you having to select the actual frame. However, if you are working with multiple layers, Flash adds a keyframe to all layers at that frame if no frame is selected.

Using Frame-Based Versus Span-Based Selection

Depending upon how you like to work, you can choose between two selection modes in Flash. The default mode is frame-based selection. In this mode, frames are treated as individual elements. When span-based selection is chosen, Flash treats frames as part of a frame span, which means all of the frames adjacent to a keyframe are selected as a unit. You can accomplish the same tasks in either mode and you can switch between the two depending upon the task at hand.

Set the Frame Selection Style

1 Click the **Flash** (Mac) or **Edit** (Win) menu, and then click **Preferences**.

2 If necessary, click the **General** category.

3 Select the **Span Based Selection** check box to enable span-based selection or clear it to enable frame-based selection.

4 Click **OK**.

Did You Know?

You can select a single frame in span-based mode. Press ⌘+click (Mac) or Ctrl+click (Win) the frame. Likewise, to select a span of frames in frame-based mode, click the first or last frame in the span, and then drag until you've selected the entire span.

Frame-based selection:
Clicking once on a frame selects that frame

Span-based selection:
Clicking once on a frame selects the entire span

Clearing Keyframes Versus Removing Frames

Depending on what you are trying to accomplish, you can choose to remove a frame's status as a keyframe or remove the frame entirely. Clearing a keyframe preserves the length of the framespan and the overall duration of the animation on the layer. It simply turns the keyframe back into a regular frame and removes any changes the keyframe contained. Conversely, removing frames deletes the entire frame and shortens the framespan as well as the length of your animation in the Timeline.

Clear Keyframes

1. Click on the frame to select it or click and drag to select a range of frames.

2. Click the **Modify** menu, point to **Timeline**, and then click **Clear Keyframe**.

   Flash converts the keyframe back into a regular frame.

   TIMESAVER *Press Shift+F6 to clear keyframes.*

The keyframe is cleared

The duration is maintained

Remove Frames

1. Click on the frame to select it or click and drag to select a range of frames.

2. Click the **Edit** menu, point to **Timeline**, and then click **Remove Frames**.

   Flash removes the selected frame(s) and shortens the length of the animation.

   TIMESAVER *Press Shift+F5 to remove frames.*

The duration is shortened

Editing Keyframes

Keyframes are editable elements. You can add or remove content from a keyframe, move keyframes around by simply dragging, or copy and paste keyframes in the same Timeline, across scenes and even other Flash documents. Because keyframes are so versatile, you can continue to fine-tune your animations after they are created. When the playhead is placed on a frame, the content of that frame is displayed on your Stage. Selecting the keyframe in the Timeline selects all of the content on that keyframe on the Stage. Likewise, selecting any of your content on the Stage will select its corresponding keyframe. In this way, you can interactively edit the content in a keyframe or the keyframe's position in the Timeline and know what you are affecting.

Copy and Paste Keyframes

1 Click on the keyframe to select it or click and drag to select a keyframe and a range of frames.

2 Click the **Edit** menu, point to **Timeline**, and then click **Copy Frames**.

> **TIMESAVER** Press Option+⌥⌘+C (Mac) or Ctrl+Alt+C (Win) to copy frames.

3 Click on the frame where you want to paste the frames.

4 Click the **Edit** menu, point to **Timeline**, and then click **Paste Frames**.

> **TIMESAVER** Press Option+⌥⌘+V (Mac) or Ctrl+Alt+V (Win) to paste frames.

Frames are pasted starting on selected frame.

Drag and Drop Keyframes

1. Click on the keyframe to select it or click and drag to select a keyframe and a range of frames.

2. Click again on the selected frame(s), and then drag to a new area of the Timeline.

Did You Know?

It's important to understand the difference between the normal copy and Paste commands and the copy frames and Paste Frames commands. When you copy and paste frames you are copying the keyframes and in-between frames and the content contained in them. Pasting them preserves the structure and layout. If you select a keyframe and use the normal copy and paste commands ⌘+C and ⌘+V (Mac) or Ctrl+C and Ctrl+V (Win), you are only copying the content contained in that keyframe.

You can use drag and drop to copy frames. Press and hold down the Option (Mac) or Alt (Win) key as you drag frames, Flash copies them to a new location.

Move frames as you drag.

Frames are moved to the new location.

Press the Option key (Mac) or the Alt key (Win) to copy frames as you drag them.

The plus sign (+) modifier indicates a copy has been engaged.

Frames copied to the new location.

Creating a Simple Frame-by-Frame Animation

Flash incorporates the traditional animation technique with its use of keyframe-based animation. Artwork is placed in a keyframe in the Timeline and subsequent keyframes are created to record changes to the artwork. When played consecutively, these minute changes mimic movement as each keyframe describes an altered position or transform effect. Static art that does not change is stored on separate layers and can span the entire animation. In this way, you don't have to redraw the entire frame and you can quickly create complex animations.

Create a Frame-by-Frame Animation

1. Create a new Flash document or open an empty Timeline.

2. Click the first frame to select it.

3. Click the **Oval** tool on the Tools panel.

4. Click on the Stage, and then drag to draw a circle.

5. Click the second frame to select it.

6. Click the **Insert** menu, point to **Timeline**, and then click **Keyframe**.

   TIMESAVER *Press F6 to insert a keyframe.*

7. Select the second keyframe or double-click the circle on the Stage and drag it slightly to the right.

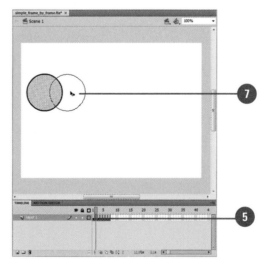

8 Click on the third frame to select it.

9 Repeat step 6.

10 Select the third keyframe or double-click the circle on the Stage and drag it slightly further to the right.

11 Continue to add keyframes and move the circle until it reaches the right edge of the Stage.

IMPORTANT *The more keyframes you add the smoother the animation is.*

12 Click the **Playhead** and move it across the frames to preview the movement of the circle.

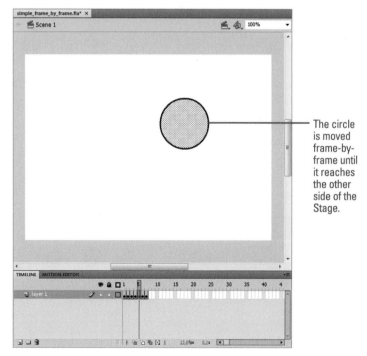

The circle is moved frame-by-frame until it reaches the other side of the Stage.

Playing an Animation

In addition to moving the playhead in the Timeline to view your animation, commonly called scrubbing, Flash provides a controller to navigate the Timeline. The Controller resembles the transport controls on a VCR and can be used in the same way. Additionally, you can export your Flash document into a Flash movie (a .swf file). You do this to see your Flash movie in its final state, as there are some elements that are not viewable in the Flash Development environment, such as animations contained in movie clip symbols and ActionScript functionality. To preview basic animations from their own Timeline, you can use the Controller to preview them.

Use the Controller to Play an Animation

1. Click the **Window** menu, point to **Toolbars**, and then click **Controller**.

2. To stop the animation, click **Stop**.

3. To rewind to the first frame of the animation, click **Rewind To Beginning**.

4. To step back one frame, click **Step Back**.

   TIMESAVER *Press the < key to step back a frame.*

5. To play or stop the animation, click **Play**.

   TIMESAVER *Press Return (Mac) or Enter (Win) to play if stopped or to stop if playing.*

6. To step forward one frame, click **Step Forward**.

   TIMESAVER *Press the > key to step forward a frame.*

7. To fast-forward to the end of the animation, click **Go To End**.

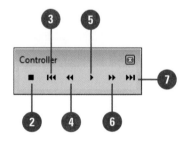

Test Animation in the Flash Player

1. Click the **Control** menu, point to **Test Movie**, and then click **Test**.

   The Test command tests the movie based on the current test option. Flash uses the document type the default until you change it.

   For the in Flash Professional test option, Flash exports the entire Timeline and any other scenes you've created into a SWF file that plays in the Flash Player.

   TIMESAVER Press ⌘+Return (Mac) or Ctrl+Enter (Win) to test a movie.

Current test option

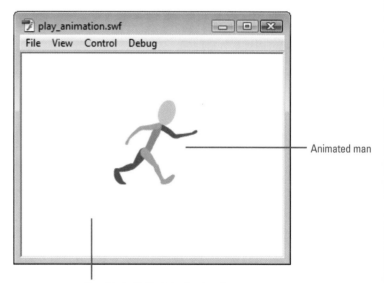

Animated man

Test Movie (in Flash Professional) exports the Flash movie with the SWF extension, which plays in the Flash Player.

Using Onion Skinning

Normally, the playhead shows one frame at a time—the frame it's placed on. As you play the Timeline, the Stage displays the content of one frame at a time, forming your animation. Onion Skinning mode allows you to view multiple frames simultaneously. This is useful for fine-tuning your animation, because you can see the content on the frames immediately preceding and following the active frame.

Activate Onion Skinning

1. Open a Timeline with a multiple frame animation.

2. Click the **Onion Skin Mode** button in the Status bar.

Onion skin markers appear in the area above the frame numbers and the area of the range of frames selected dims. The frames that precede the active frame and the frames that follow appear in varying degrees of shading on the Stage, becoming lighter the further they are from the active frame.

Onion Skinning allows you to see the content on all the frames.

Onion Skin Markers

Use Onion Skin Outlines

① Open a Timeline with a multiple frame animation.

② Click the **Onion Skin Outlines** button in the Status bar.

The frames that precede the active frame and the frames that follow appear as outlines on the Stage.

Did You Know?

You can only edit the active frame. This is the frame the playhead is on. The art that appears when Onion Skin (regular and outline) is enabled is for preview only.

Onion Skin Outlines mode

Modifying Onion Skin Markers

You can adjust the number of frames previewed in the onion skin by manually dragging the onion skin markers. These markers have draggable handles that set the beginning and end of the onion skin. The handles appear as brackets with small dots. Alternately, you can set the range of the markers from the Modify Onion Markers popup menu.

Set Onion Skin Markers Manually

1. Click the **Onion Skin Mode** button in the Status bar, if necessary

2. Click on the small dot on either end of the onion skin markers and then drag to include or exclude any consecutive frames in the onion skin.

Did You Know?

You can only edit the active frame in the onion skin. To edit other frames and maintain the selected frames, select Anchor Onion in the Modify Markers popup menu.

More frames are contained in the Onion Skin Markers, so more of the animation is seen simultaneously.

Set Onion Skin Markers in Modify Onion Markers Window

① Click the **Modify Onion Markers** button.

The Modify Onion Markers popup appears.

② Select from the following options:

◆ **Always Show Markers.** Keeps Onion Skin Markers visible in and out of Onion Skin mode.

◆ **Anchor Onion.** Maintains the selected frames even if you move the playhead.

◆ **Onion 2.** Shows two frames before and after the current frame.

◆ **Onion 5.** Shows five frames before and after the current frame.

◆ **Onion All.** Includes the entire duration of the Timeline in the markers.

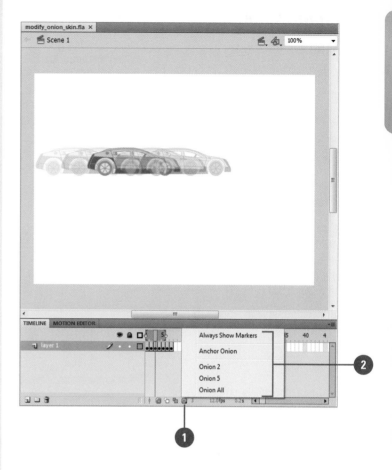

Onion Skin Markers

Command	Description
Always Show Markers	Keeps Onion Skin Markers visible in and out of Onion Skin mode.
Anchor Onion	Prevents the Markers from moving as you move your playhead.
Onion 2	Selects two frames before and after the active frame.
Onion 5	Selects five frames before and after the active frame.
Onion All	Selects all the frames in the Timeline.

Editing Multiple Frames

If you need to make changes to an entire animation or to a series of frames at once, you can select them in Edit Multiple Frames mode. When this feature is enabled, brackets appear similar to those in Onion Skinning mode. Drag them to select the range of frames you want to edit. This works well if you need to make global changes to your animation such as resizing it or changing its location. You can select an entire framespan or layer instead of moving or resizing the content on each individual frame separately.

Select Multiple Frames

① Open a Timeline with a multiple frame animation.

② Click the **Edit Multiple Frames** button in the Status bar.

③ Click and drag the markers until they include all the frames you want to select.

   All of the content in the selected frames appears on the Stage.

④ Click the **Selection** tool on the Tools panel.

   TIMESAVER *Press V to select the Selection tool.*

⑤ Drag a selection box around the content on the Stage.

   You can make changes to location, scale, effects, etc. All the selected frames will be affected.

   TIMESAVER *Press ⌘+A (Mac) or Ctrl+A (Win) to select all the content on all unlocked layers.*

Did You Know?

When Edit Multiple Frames is activated, it selects all of the frames on all layers contained in the markers. You must lock any layers you don't want included in the selection.

Animating with Motion Tweening

Introduction

In Flash, it's not necessary to draw every frame of an animation. You can set the position and attributes of your art in the beginning and ending frames, and Flash will create all of the frames in between. This is called **tweening**. A motion tween connects two keyframes, each with different effects or characteristics applied to them and then gradually "morphs" one into the other. Tweening allows you to quickly animate objects, apply fades, and gradually alter color, alpha, scale, and any other effect that can be applied to a symbol, group, or text object.

The span between the starting frame and ending frame of a motion tween is called the **tween span**. The tween span consists of a group of frames in a single layer with a blue background in the Timeline in which an object changes over time. Only one object, known as the **target object**, on the Stage can be animated in each tween span.

Once an animation is tweened, you can continue to edit it by adding or removing frames to make it move slower or faster, adjust effects, or control the inertia with ease-in and ease-out properties, adding further complexity. Motion tweening produces smaller files than frame-by-frame animation because Flash describes the motion mathematically, incrementally transforming the object in between the two keyframes.

Understanding Motion Tweening

Motion tweening allows you to apply smooth motion and transform effects, such as scale, position, rotation, and skew, to symbol instances (movie clip, graphic, and button) and text fields. Additionally, you can utilize Flash's advanced color effects to apply changes to color, alpha, and brightness.

Because these effects are applied to instances, they only affect the instance placed on the Stage. Its parent (original) symbol in the Library is not affected. Motion tweening produces the smallest file sizes of any of Flash's animation methods.

Flash use two different types of motion tweens: **classic tween** and **motion tween**. A classic tween uses several instances in keyframes of an object along with property keyframes to create a tween, while a motion tween uses one object instance over the entire span along with property keyframes to create a tween. A property keyframe is a frame within the motion tween where you define a value for a property. A motion tween is known as object based animation. Motion tweens are easy to create and provide precise control, while classic tweens are more complex to create and provide more advanced control. All motion tweens from Flash CS3 are classic tweens.

Tween Differences

There are several differences between classic and motion tweens.

Classic Tweens

- Use Keyframes and property keyframes to create tweens.
- Allow frame scripts.

- Allow only symbols (movie clip, graphic, and button) as a tweenable type. It converts all others (editable shapes, groups, and text objects) to a graphic symbol.
- Consist of groups of individually selectable frames in the Timeline.
- Apply eases to groups of frames between keyframes within the tween.
- Allow animation between two different color effects, such as tint and alpha transparency.
- Don't allow animation of 3D objects.
- Allow symbol swaps and setting the frame number of a graphic symbol to display in a property keyframe.

Motion Tweens

- Use one object instance and property keyframes instead of keyframes to create tweens.
- Don't allow frame scripts.
- Allow text as a tweenable type. It doesn't convert it to a symbol.
- Treat tween spans as a single object that you can stretch and resize in the Timeline.
- Apply eases across the entire length of a motion tween span.
- Apply only one color effect per tween.
- Allow animation of 3D objects.
- Don't allow symbol swaps and setting the frame number of a graphic symbol to display in a property keyframe.
- Convert all non-allowed object types (editable shapes and groups) to a movie clip symbol.

Motion Tweening of Scale and Alpha Changes

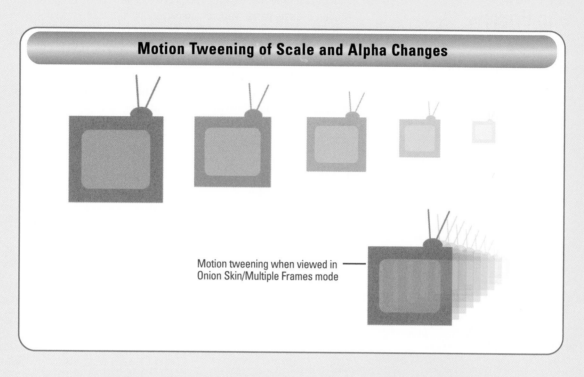

Motion tweening when viewed in
Onion Skin/Multiple Frames mode

Motion Tweening of Scale, Alpha, and Rotation Changes

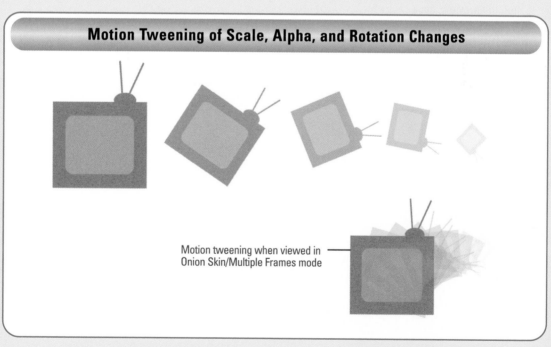

Motion tweening when viewed in
Onion Skin/Multiple Frames mode

Applying Motion Tween Presets

Motion Presets are ready-made motion tweens that you can apply to an object on the Stage. After you preview a motion tween in the Motion Presets panel, you can quickly apply it to a selected object. You can apply only one motion preset per object on the Stage. If you apply another preset to an object, it replaces the previous one. You can only apply a 3D motion preset to a movie clip instance, which is the only object type for 3D effects. Each motion preset contains a specific number of frames, which you can adjust later. In the Motion Presets panel, you can also create and save your own custom motion presets as well as import and export them (stored as XML files) to share with others.

Apply a Motion Tween Preset

1 Select a tweenable object (symbol instance or text field) on the Stage.

2 Click the **Window** menu, and then click **Motion Presets** to open the panel.

3 Select a preset in the Motion Presets panel.

A preview of the preset plays in the Preview pane at the top of the Motion Presets panel.

◆ To stop the preview, click outside the Motion Presets panel.

4 Click **Apply**.

◆ If you apply a motion tween to a non-tweenable object, a dialog box appears, asking you to convert it to a symbol.

The motion is set to start at the current position of the object on the Stage.

◆ To apply the preset so that the motion ends at the current position of the object on the Stage, hold down Shift, and then click **Apply**.

Preview pane

Save a Tween as a Custom Motion Preset

1. Select the tween span, object on the Stage, or the motion path on the Stage with the custom tween that you want to save as a preset.

2. Click the **Window** menu, and then click **Motion Presets** to open the panel.

3. Click the **Save Selection As Preset** button.

4. Type a name for the preset.

5. Click **OK**.

The new preset appears in the Motion Presets panel under Custom Presets. The preset is saved as an XML file in the Motion Presets folder, which you can locate by performing a search using Instant Search (Win) or Spotlight (Mac).

◆ To create a preview for the new preset, publish a SWF of the motion tween with the same name in the Motion Presets folder.

Did You Know?

You can import and export a motion preset. To import a motion preset, click the Options button on the Motion Presets panel, click Import, select the XML file, and then click Open. To export a motion preset, select the preset in the Motion Presets panel, click the Options button, click Export, specify a name and location, and then click Save.

You can delete a motion preset. Select the motion preset in the Motion Presets panel that you want to delete, and then click the Remove Item button.

Creating a Motion Tween

You can tween position, scale, rotation and other transform effects applied to symbols instances and text fields. A motion tween uses one instance over the entire span along with property keyframes, which you define with property values to modify the tween. You can change property keyframes on Stage, in the Property Inspector, or in the Motion Editor. You should have only one object when you apply the tween or the results will be unpredictable. Tweened frames must reside on the same layer in the Timeline. After you add a tween to a layer, Flash changes it to a tween layer, which you can no longer draw on. A tween layer can contain tween spans, static frames, and actions.

Create a Motion Tween

1. Select one or more objects to tween on the Stage.

   ◆ To create multiple tweens at once, place objects on multiple layers, and then select them all.

2. Click the **Insert** menu, and then click **Motion Tween**.

   ◆ If you apply a motion tween to a non-tweenable object, a dialog box appears, asking you to convert it to a symbol.

   Flash converts the layer containing the tweened object to a tween layer and creates a tween span in the layer.

3. To change the length of the tween span, drag either end of the tween span in the Timeline.

4. To add motion to the tween, click a frame within the tween span, and then drag the object on the Stage.

5. To tween 3D rotation or position, use the **3D Rotation** tool or **3D Translation** tool.

6. To remove a motion tween, select the tweened object, click the **Insert** menu, and then click **Remove Tween**.

7. To add another tween to an existing layer, drag a tween span from a different layer.

A black dot indicates a target object in the first frame.

Motion tween appears with a blue background.

Black diamonds indicate property keyframes and the last frame.

Adjusting Motion Tween Properties

Motion tweens can be fine-tuned in the Property Inspector or the Motion Editor. When a tweened object is selected, a number of options are enabled that you use to add complexity to your motion path. You can set motion tween properties to deal with position and size, set rotation direction and frequency, apply color and display blending effects, or control the easing in or out of the motion. The options you set in the Property Inspector are applied to the entire tween span.

Set Motion Tween Properties in the Property Inspector

1. Click the **Window** menu, and then click **Properties** to open the Property Inspector.

2. Select an object on the Stage with a tween applied.

3. Choose from the available settings; options vary depending on the selected tweened object:

   - **Ease.** Sets the motion speed in and out.

   - **Position and Size.** Sets the X and Y position, and the selection width and height.

   - **3D Position and View.** Sets the 3D X, Y, and Z position, 3D perspective selection width and height, perspective angle, and vanishing point.

   - **Rotation.** Sets the direction and frequency your object rotates. Select the **Orient To Path** check box to keep your object parallel to the guide relative to its center point.

   - **Path.** Sets the X and Y position, and the selection width and height.

   - **Color Effect.** Sets the color style effect: Brightness, Tint, Alpha, or Advanced.

   - **Display.** Sets the display blending effect, which includes Darken, Overlay, and Invert.

Editing Motion Tween Properties with the Motion Editor

The Motion Editor panel allows you to view and edit all tween properties and related keyframe properties. You can change the basic motion of the tween by changing the x-, y-, and z-axes, transform the skew and scale, apply color and filter effects, or add motion speed easing in or out. You can open the Motion Editor panel by using the Window menu. It appears next to the Timeline. When you select a tween space, a tweened object, or motion path, the Motion Editor panel displays tween property values in categories and a grid with a graph for each property.

Change the Motion Editor Display

1 Select an object on the Stage with a tween applied.

2 Click the **Window** menu, and then click **Motion Editor** to open the panel.

3 To change the display of the Motion Editor, do any of the following:

◆ **Display Properties.** Click the triangle next to a property category.

◆ **Expand/Collapse Property View.** Click the property name to toggle it.

◆ **Viewable Frames.** Sets the number of frame of a tween shown in the Motion Editor.

◆ **Graph Size.** Sets the size of the graph.

◆ **Expanded Graph Size.** Sets the expanded property view size of the graph.

◆ **Add Eases Options.** Adds an ease option to menus in the Motion Editor. Click the **Add** button on the Eases category, and then select an ease option.

Display properties

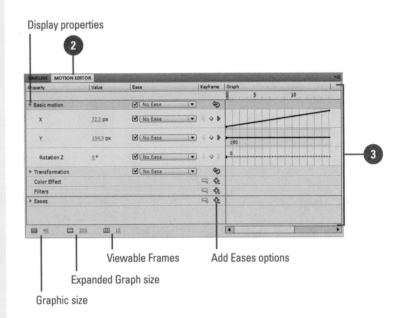

Graphic size

Expanded Graph size

Viewable Frames

Add Eases options

Set Motion Tween Properties in the Motion Editor

1. Select an object on the Stage with a tween applied.

2. Click the **Window** menu, and then click **Motion Editor** to open the panel.

3. Click the triangle to expand a category, and then specify any of the following:

   ◆ **Basic Motion.** Specify values for the x-, y-, and z-axes, and other related options.

   ◆ **Transformation.** Specify skew and scale values, and other related options.

   ◆ **Color Effect.** Click the **Add** or **Remove** button on the Color Effect category, and then select an option. Specify the color effect options you want.

   ◆ **Filters.** Click the **Add** or **Remove** button on the Filters category, and then select an option. Specify the filter options you want.

4. Select or clear the **Ease** check box to enable or disable it for a property or category, and then set an ease value. Positive values increase the ease at the end of the curve, while negative values increase the ease at the beginning of the curve.

5. To reset values for an option, click the **Reset Values** button.

Add and Remove buttons

Adding Color Effects and Filters

Wondering where Timeline Effects have gone in Flash. They are now a part of the Motion Editor. You can add many Timeline Effects by using filters in the Motion Editor. You can add filter effects, such as Drop Shadow, Blur, Glow, Bevel, Gradient Glow, Gradient Bevel, and Adjust Color, to a motion tween. You can also add color effects, such as Alpha, Brightness, Tint and Advanced Color, to a motion tween. You can apply more than one effect or filter to an object to create a different effect. If an applied color effect or filter doesn't work for you, you can remove it.

Add Color Effects and Filters to a Motion Tween

1. Select an object on the Stage with a tween applied.

2. Click the **Window** menu, and then click **Motion Editor** to open the panel.

3. Click the triangle to expand the Color Effect or Filters category.

4. Use any of the following:

   ◆ **Color Effect.** Click the **Add** button on the Color Effect category, and then select an option.

   The options include Alpha, Brightness, Tint, and Advanced Color.

   ◆ **Filters.** Click the **Add** button on the Filters category, and then select an option.

   The options include Drop Shadow, Blue, Glow, Bevel, Gradient Glow, Gradient Bevel, and Adjust Color.

5. Specify the options you want for the category; options vary depending on the color effect or filter that you choose.

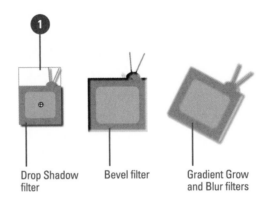

Drop Shadow filter   Bevel filter   Gradient Grow and Blur filters

Work with Color Effects and Filters

1. Select an object on the Stage with a tween applied.

2. Click the **Window** menu, and then click **Motion Editor** to open the panel.

3. Click the triangle to expand the Color Effect or Filters category.

4. Specify the options you want for the category; options vary depending on the color effect or filter that you choose.

5. To remove a color effect or filter, click the **Remove** button on the Color Effect or Filter category, and then select the effect or filter that you want to remove.

6. To reset values back to the default, click the **Reset Values** button for the effect or filter.

Working with Property Keyframes

When you select a tween space, a tweened object, or motion path, the Motion Editor panel displays tween property values in categories and a grid with a graph for each property. Each keyframe property for a specific property appears as a control point on the graph. You can add or remove a property keyframe at any time. Control points can be either smooth or corner points. When a point is smooth, Bezier handles appear, which you can adjust. Some properties in the Motion Editor are associated with each other, such as Scale X and Scale Y. You can use the Link icon to constrain values to match to each other.

Work with Property Keyframes

1. Select an object on the Stage with a tween applied.

2. Click the **Window** menu, and then click **Motion Editor** to open the panel.

3. Click the triangle to expand a category.

4. To work with property keyframes, do any of the following:

   ◆ View. Click the **Go To Previous Keyframe** or **Go To Next Keyframe** arrows.

   ◆ Add. Place the playhead where you want to property keyframe, and then click the **Add or Remove Keyframe** button.

   ◆ Remove. Right-click (Win) or Control-click (Mac) the control point in the graph, and then click the **Remove Keyframe**.

   ◆ Smooth or Corner. Alt-click (Win) or Command-click (Mac) the control point to toggle between smooth and corner.

   ◆ Link. Click the **Link** icon to constrain values to match for associated pairs. Click the icon again to unlink a pair.

Control points

Add or Remove keyframe

Go To Preview/next keyframe

Editing the Path of a Motion Tween

If you want to change the x-, y-, or z-axes, it's easier to make bigger adjustments in the motion path of a tween on the Stage and minor ones in the Motion Editor. You can move the entire motion path to another location on the Stage or edit individual points on the path. If segments within the path become to fast or slow, you can use the roving property for the x-, y-, and z- axes to make the speed consistent throughout the tween.

Edit the Path of a Motion Tween

1. Select an object on the Stage with a tween applied.

2. To make changes directly on the Stage, do any of the following:

   ◆ **Object Position.** Place the playhead in the frame you want to move, click the **Selection** tool, and then drag the target object to a new location.

   ◆ **Motion Path Position.** Click the **Selection** tool, click the motion path, and then drag the path.

   ◆ **Motion Path Size.** Click the **Free Transform** tool, click the motion path, and then drag a resize handle.

   ◆ **Motion Path Shape.** Click the **Selection** tool, click away from the motion path, and then drag any line segment on the path.

     Click the **Subselection** tool, click the path, and then drag a control point to move it, or click a control point, and then drag the Bezier handles of the control point to reshape it.

   ◆ **Delete Motion Path.** Click the **Selection** tool, double-click the motion path, and then press Delete.

   ◆ **Roving.** Right-click (Win) or Control-click (Mac) the tween span or an individual control point in a Motion Editor graph, and then click **Roving** to toggle on and off.

Path

Selection tool

Subselection tool

Free Transform tool

Copying Motion as ActionScript

If you have a complex animation in the timeline that you want to convert into ActionScript 3.0 code, you can use the Copy Motion as ActionScript 3.0 command to get the job done. When you use the command, Flash copies the properties that define the motion tween on the timeline and writes the ActionScript 3.0 code for you to apply to a symbol. You can apply the code as timeline code or in class files for the Flash document file.

Copy Motion as ActionScript 3.0

1. Create the animation using a symbol on the timeline in a layer that you want to copy as ActionScript 3.0 code.

2. Create a new layer.

3. Create a new symbol or drag another instance of your existing symbol on the Stage.

4. Select the entire animation that you want to copy on the animation layer of the timeline. Click the first frame, press Shift, and then click the last frame.

5. Right-click (Win) or Control-click (Mac) the animation, and then click **Copy Motion as ActionScript 3.0**.

6. Type an instance name to use in the ActionScript code. Enter the instance name of the instance that you want to apply the ActionScript code to.

7. Select your second instance that you added to layer 2 (from Step 2), and type the instance name you entered into the Properties panel.

8. Create a new layer (for the ActionScript), and select the first frame of that layer.

9. Open the Actions panel and paste the code into the Script pane.

   Before you test the animation, make sure layer 2 has the same number of frames as the animation layer.

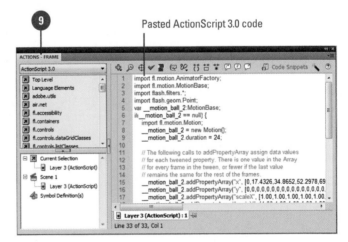

Pasted ActionScript 3.0 code

Animating with Classic Tweening

Introduction

In the previous Chapter you learned about motion tweening. In this Chapter, you'll learn about classic tweening. Tweening is an animation technique that creates the necessary in-between frames based on a starting and ending frame. A motion tween uses one object instance over the entire span along with property keyframes to create a tween, while a classic tween uses several instances in keyframes of an object along with property keyframes to create a tween. Classic tweens are more complex to create than motion tweens. However, if you're looking for a custom result, classic tweens provide more advanced control.

When you create an animation with classic tweening, there are some things you should know about. A classic tween:

◆ Uses Keyframes and property keyframes to create tweens.

◆ Allows frame scripts.

◆ Allows only symbols (movie clip, graphic, and button) as a tweenable type. It converts all others (editable shapes, groups, and text objects) to a graphic symbol.

◆ Consists of groups of individually selectable frames in the Timeline.

◆ Applies eases to groups of frames between keyframes within the tween.

◆ Allows animation between two different color effects, such as tint and alpha transparency.

◆ Doesn't allow animation of 3D objects.

◆ Allows symbol swaps and setting the frame number of a graphic symbol to display in a property keyframe.

What You'll Do

Work with Classic Tweening

Understand Frame and Instance Properties

Create a Classic Tween

Adjust Classic Tween Properties

Copy and Paste a Tween

Change the Length of a Tween

Change the Frame Rate

Reverse Frames

Add and Remove Keyframes from a Classic Tween

Scale and Rotation a Classic Tween

Add Color Effects to a Classic Tween

Create a Classic Motion Guide Layer

Animate Along a Classic Motion Guide

Orient Objects to a Classic Motion Path

Ease In and Out of a Classic Tween

Working with Classic Tweening

Classic tweening can only be applied to instances of symbols. When applying classic tweening to groups or text objects, Flash automatically converts them into symbols and stores them in the Library. When this happens, they appear in the Library named as Tween 1, Tween 2, etc. It is a good idea to convert them into symbols as the tweening is applied. When managing large projects with many assets it can become confusing to have assets named in this generic way. Of course you can always rename them by selecting the field in the Library and typing in a new name.

If your classic tweened animation doesn't behave as expected, there are a few things you can check. If the object disappears when you play the animation and only re-appears on the end keyframe, you may have more than one object on the keyframe. Make sure that only one object, or instance, is on each keyframe in the tweened span. Also, make sure that both instances are of the same object. Flash cannot motion tween two different objects. To "morph" different shapes into each other you must use shape tweening.

When classic tweening is applied to groups or text objects, Flash automatically converts them into symbols and names them incrementally in this generic fashion.

A dotted line in a tween span indicates that there is a problem with the tween. Makes sure there is only one instance (the same instance) on each keyframe.

Understanding Frame and Instance Properties

There is a difference between frame properties and instance properties. This is a source of initial confusion when dealing with animation tweens (both motion and shape). Because the Property Inspector is context-sensitive, it displays properties for many different objects in Flash, depending on which of these objects is selected.

Classic motion (and shape) tweens are applied to keyframes in the Timeline. Color and Transform effects are applied to instances on the Stage. To view the classic tween properties for a specific frame or keyframe, you must select that frame. It is here that you activate tweening and tell Flash what you are going to tween (such as scale or rotation). This needs to be differentiated from the effects you apply to the instances in the tweened keyframes. These are accessed in the Property Inspector and the Transform panel whenever any instance is selected on the Stage. For example, if you check scale as an option in the tween properties for a keyframe, a change in size only results if the size of one of the instances is changed. Conversely, if you want to tween a change in alpha, you can't do this by selecting either of the keyframes in a tween; you must select the instance on the Stage and apply the alpha change when the instance properties appear in the Property Inspector.

Frame Properties appear when a frame is selected in the Timeline.

Instance Properties appear when the instance is selected on the Stage.

Creating a Classic Tween

You can tween position, scale, rotation and other transform effects applied to symbols, groups, and text. Additionally, you can apply classic tweening to color and alpha changes. A classic tween connects two keyframes. You should have only one object in the keyframe when you apply the tween or the results will be unpredictable. Tweened frames must reside on the same layer in the Timeline.

Create a Simple Classic Tween

1. Create a new Flash document, and then click on the first frame of the Timeline.

2. Do one of the following:

   ◆ Draw a shape on the Stage with any of Flash's drawing tools and convert into a symbol.

   ◆ Drag an instance of a symbol from the Library.

3. Select the first frame.

4. Click the **Insert** menu, and then click **Classic Tween**.

5. Click frame 10 in the Timeline.

6. Click the **Insert** menu, point to **Timeline**, and then click **Frame**.

   Flash displays a dashed line in the framespan to indicate an incomplete or broken motion tween. It also tints the framespan a pale, bluish-purple to indicate that a motion tween has been applied.

   TIMESAVER *Press F5 to add frames, or right-click the frame, and then click Insert Frame.*

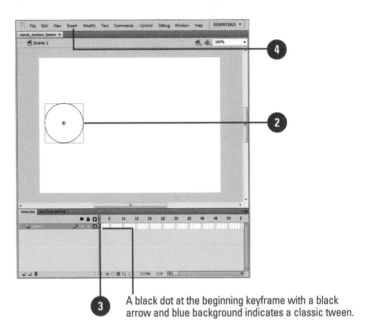

A black dot at the beginning keyframe with a black arrow and blue background indicates a classic tween.

Dotted line indicates a broken or incomplete tween.

7 Click and drag the object on the Stage at frame 10 to a new location.

Flash creates a second keyframe that is connected to the first with an arrow. This indicates the motion tween is complete.

8 Click the **Control** menu, point to **Test Movie**, and then click **Test**.

Flash gradually moves the object.

Did You Know?

You can add keyframes and then alter the position of the object on the Stage. Tweening can be applied to any two existing keyframes on the same layer. Select the first keyframe, click the Tweening list arrow in the Property Inspector, and then click Motion.

You can move keyframes around in the Timeline. Simply click to select it, and then click it again and drag it to a new location.

End keyframe is created when object is moved to a new position.

Motion tween viewed in Onion Skin mode.

Adjusting Classic Tween Properties

Classic tweens can be fine-tuned in the Property Inspector. When a tweened frame is selected, a number of options are enabled that you use to add complexity to your motion path. It is also where you remove an applied classic tween. Set the tween to deal with scale, set rotation direction and frequency, or apply inertia by easing in or out of the motion. Additionally, you can set orientation and snapping when using a motion guide. In Flash, you can customize easing in or out of a motion using the Edit button in the Property Inspector.

Set Classic Tween Properties

1. Click the **Window** menu, and then click **Properties** to open the Property Inspector.

2. Select a keyframe with motion tween applied.

3. Choose from the following settings:

   ◆ **Scale.** Check this when you are tweening scale changes.

   ◆ **Rotate.** Sets the direction and frequency your object rotates.

   ◆ **Orient To Path.** Use this when you have applied a motion guide layer. This keeps your object parallel to the guide relative to its center point.

   ◆ **Sync.** This synchronizes the animation contained in the symbol with the Timeline that contains it. Use this when your symbol's Timeline is not an even number of frames.

   ◆ **Snap.** Check to snap the object's registration point to a motion guide.

   ◆ **Edit.** This button allows you to create custom ease in and ease out transitions.

4. To remove a classic tween, click the **Insert** menu, and then click **Remove Tween**.

Edit

Rotate

Snap, Sync, Orient to path, and Scale

Set Ease Properties in a Classic Tween

1. Click the **Window** menu, and then click **Properties** to open the Property Inspector.

2. Select a keyframe with motion tween applied.

3. Click the **Ease** field, and then select the setting to set the speed at which your object eases in or out of its motion.

   A positive value eases in, a negative value eases out. A zero value evenly distributes motion across each frame.

No Easing

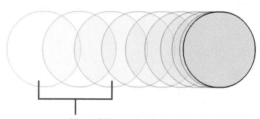

Motion is evenly distributed across frames.

Ease Out

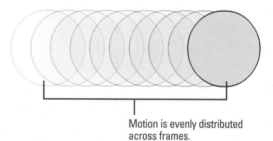

Most of the motion is applied to the beginning frames so the object appears to slow down as it stops.

Ease In

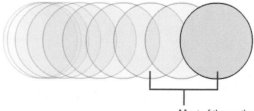

Most of the motion is applied to the end frames so the object appears to slowly accelerate.

Copying and Pasting a Tween

After you fine-tune a motion tween, you can copy and paste the frames, tween, and symbol information to another object. When you paste a motion tween, you can also specify the motion tween properties you want to apply, such as X and Y position, horizontal and vertical scale, color, filters, and blend. You can also override target scale, rotation, and skew properties. If you want to use a motion tween as ActionScript 3.0 in the Actions panel or other code-specific location, you can use the Copy As ActionScript command.

Copy and Paste a Motion Tween

1. Select the frames in the Timeline with the motion tween you want to copy. The frames you select need to be on the same layer. However, the selection can span a tween, empty frames, or two or more tweens.

2. Click the **Edit** menu, point to **Timeline**, and then click **Copy Motion**.

3. Select the symbol instance to receive the copied motion tween.

4. Click the **Edit** menu, point to **Timeline**, and then click **Paste Motion**.

   The frames, tween, and symbol information are inserted to match the original copied tween.

Motion pasted to instance

Paste Motion Tween Properties

1 Select the frames in the Timeline with the motion tween you want to copy.

2 Click the **Edit** menu, point to **Timeline**, and then click **Copy Motion**.

3 Select the symbol instance to receive the copied motion tween.

4 Click the **Edit** menu, point to **Timeline**, and then click **Paste Motion Special**.

5 Choose from the following settings:

◆ **X or Y Position.** Pastes how much to move in the X (horizontal) and Y (vertical) direction.

◆ **Horizontal or Vertical Scale.** Pastes the ratio between the current and the natural size in the horizontal (X) or vertical (Y) direction.

◆ **Rotation And Skew.** Pastes the rotation of the object.

◆ **Color.** Pastes the color values of the object.

◆ **Filters.** Pastes the filter properties of the object.

◆ **Blend Mode.** Pastes the blend properties of the object.

◆ **Override Target Scale or Rotation and Skew Properties.** Select to override the existing scale, or rotation and skew properties of the object. Clear to paste the properties relative to the target object.

6 Click **OK**.

For Your Information

Copying Motion As ActionScript 3.0

In addition to copying motion tweens in the Timeline, you can also copy motion tweens to the Actions panel or use them as ActionScripts. To accomplish this task, you use the Copy Motion As ActionScript command. This command copies the properties that define a motion tween in the Timeline as ActionScript 3.0. These properties include Position, Scale, Skew, Rotation, Transformation Point, Color, Blend Mode, Orientation To Path, Cache As Bitmap Setting, Frame Labels, Motion Guides, Custom Easing, and Filters. After you copy the properties, you can apply them to another symbol in the Actions panel or in the source files for the Flash document that uses ActionScript 3.0. To copy a motion tween as ActionScript 3.0, select the frames in the Timeline with the motion tween you want to copy, click the Edit menu, point to Timeline, click Copy Motion As ActionScript 3.0, type the name of the instance to attach the motion tween to, and then click OK. Flash generates ActionScript for the specific instance name. The code appears on the Clipboard for use in the Actions Panel or other place.

Changing the Length of a Tween

Tweens in Flash are editable after they have been created. You can continue to change their properties and position in the Timeline, and Flash redraws the tweened frames. To change the length of a motion or shape tween (that is, the time it takes to complete the tween), you can add or remove frames in the framespan. Essentially you are adjusting the amount of frames Flash uses in its calculation of the tween. Adding frames means it takes longer for the transformation to happen, while deleting frames shortens the time.

Add Frames to a Tween

① Click anywhere except the last keyframe on a motion or shape tweened framespan to place the playhead.

 ◆ To add multiple frames, select multiple frames in the Timeline.

② Click the **Insert** menu, point to **Timeline**, and then click **Frame**.

 TIMESAVER *Press F5 to add frames.*

Frame is added to tween span.

Duration of other tweens is maintained.

Remove Frames from a Tween

1. Click anywhere on a motion or shape tweened framespan to place the playhead.

   ◆ To remove multiple frames, select multiple frames in the Timeline.

2. Click the **Edit** menu, point to **Timeline**, and then click **Remove Frames**.

   TIMESAVER *Press Shift+F5 to subtract frames.*

Tween span is reduced by one frame.

Did You Know?

If no layer is selected, the entire Timeline increases or decreases when you add or remove frames. To constrain this action to one target layer, lock all other layers you don't want to affect, or simply select the frame in the tween you want to adjust.

Tweens with more frames will be smoother. The more frames you add to a tween, the smoother the animation plays, because Flash has more frames to split the motion between. However, if you add too many frames the animation may move so slowly that the illusion of movement could be hampered. It is best to experiment with the length of a motion or shape tween and the frame rate of your Flash movie until you get the results you are looking for.

Changing the Frame Rate

The frame rate describes the amount of frames the Flash Player will play each second. The higher you set the frame rate, the smoother your animations will play. Traditional animations play at a rate of 24 frames per second, the same rate at which film plays, while NTSC video plays at 29.97 frames per second. It is important to keep your audience in mind and what the destination of the Flash movie will be. For delivery via the Web, you should consider the processor speeds of the destination computers. If you set the frame rate too high, the computer may not be powerful enough to play all of the frames. When this happens, Flash will drop frames in order to stay in sync. Try to avoid this scenario because it can make your animations play choppily. Consider where your Flash movie is going to be played and choose accordingly. Avoid frame rates over 30 fps, and, for slower computers, you can go as low as 12 fps, which is the default frame rate in Flash.

Change Frame Rate

1 Click a blank area on the Stage.

2 Click in the **Frame Rate** field in the Property Inspector or at the bottom of the Timeline, and then type in a frame rate.

Did You Know?

You can also change the frame rate in the Document options window. Access this window by clicking the Document button in the Property Inspector or in the Modify menu.

The frame rate is ignored for FLV Flash video. You need to set its frame rate in the encoder or editing application.

Document settings appear in the Property Inspector when nothing is selected on the Stage or the Timeline.

The frame rate is also available to change at the bottom of the Timeline.

Reversing Frames

With a classic tween, use the Reverse Frames command to reverse the frames in the Timeline. You can access this action in the Modify menu and it will be applied to all selected frames. This works for animations created frame-by-frame or with motion or shape tweening applied. Flash changes the order of the frames so your animation plays backwards.

Reverse Frames

1 Click and drag on the range of the frame span or tween you want to reverse.

2 Click the **Modify** menu, point to **Timeline**, and then click **Reverse Frames**.

> **TROUBLE?** *If the tween is not preserved when you use the reverse frames command, you might not have applied motion or shape tweening to the end keyframe in the tween. Flash only requires you to apply tweening to the starting keyframe in a tween. It is implied that it tweens into the next (or end) keyframe. To fix this, do one of the following: (1) Before you reverse frames, select the end keyframe and apply Motion (for motion tweening) or Shape (for shape tweening) to it from the Property Inspector. (2) After you reverse frames, select the beginning keyframe (which use to be the end keyframe) and apply Motion (for motion tweening) or Shape (for shape tweening) to it from the Property Inspector.*

Frames before reversing

Click and drag to select a range of frames

Frames after reversing

Did You Know?

You can select an entire layer and reverse all the frames on that layer. To select an entire layer, click the layer name to select it, and then reverse frames.

Adding and Removing Keyframes from a Classic Tween

With a classic tween, you can add keyframes to a motion tween by simply dragging the object on the Stage on the frame on which you want the change (or keyframe) to be created or by using the Add Keyframe function in the Insert menu. For example, if you want the object to move to another coordinate before it reaches the end position, you can set another keyframe between them. In this way, you can animate shapes in several directions in the same motion tween. Alternately, you can clear a keyframe from the tween by selecting it and using the Clear Keyframe function in the Modify menu. In either case, the length of the tween is preserved; the frame's status as a keyframe is removed and Flash redraws the animation, connecting the keyframes located before and after.

Add a Keyframe to a Classic Tween

1. Click on a frame in a tweened framespan you want to add a keyframe to.

2. Click the **Insert** menu, point to **Timeline**, and then click **Keyframe**.

   TIMESAVER *Press F6 to insert a keyframe.*

> #### Did You Know?
>
> *You can click and drag the object on the Stage and move it to another coordinate.* Flash automatically creates a keyframe on the active frame if the playhead is in a motion tweened framespan.

Keyframe is added

Remove a Keyframe from a Classic Tween

1. Click on the keyframe you want to remove in the motion tween.

2. Click the **Modify** menu, point to **Timeline**, and then click **Clear Keyframe**.

   The keyframe is cleared but the duration of the tween is preserved. The first and last keyframe are automatically reconnected and Flash redraws the tween.

   TIMESAVER *Press Shift+F6 to remove the keyframe.*

Keyframe is removed

Duration is maintained

Scaling and Rotating a Classic Tween

With a classic tween, any change made to an object on either keyframe can be tweened. Included are any changes made to the scale or rotation of objects on either keyframes in a tweened span. Simply alter the size or rotation of the instance on either frame, and Flash gradually tweens these properties. To change scale, you must select the scale option in the Property Inspector, while rotation has several options to choose from, including clockwise and counter-clockwise rotation, and frequency of rotation.

Change Scale During a Classic Tween

1. Open a document with a tweened animation or create a new one.

2. Select the first keyframe in the tween to open the Motion settings in the Property Inspector.

3. Select the **Scale** check box in the Property Inspector.

4. Change the size of the object on either keyframe with any of Flash's transform methods including the Free Transform tool, the Transform panel or the transform options in the Modify menu.

5. To preview the animation, drag the playhead in the Timeline, or click the **Control** menu, point to **Test Movie**, and then click **Test**.

   Flash gradually increases or decreases the size of the object.

   TIMESAVER *Press* ⌘+Return *(Mac) or Ctrl+Enter (Win) to test it.*

First keyframe   Last keyframe

Scale and position changes tweened

Change Rotation During Classic Tween

1 Open a document with a tweened animation or create a new one.

2 Change the rotation of the object on either keyframe with any of Flash's transform methods including the Free Transform tool, the Transform panel or the transform options in the Modify menu.

3 In the Property Inspector, click the **Rotation Options** list arrow, and then select a rotation property:

- ◆ **None.** This is the default setting. No rotation is applied.

- ◆ **Auto.** Rotates the object in the direction requiring the least motion.

- ◆ **CW.** Rotates the object clockwise. Enter the number of times you want the object to rotate.

- ◆ **CCW.** Rotates the object counter-clockwise. Enter the number of times you want the object to rotate.

4 To preview the animation, drag the playhead in the Timeline, or click the **Control** menu, point to **Test Movie**, and then click **Test**.

Flash gradually rotates the object in the direction indicated.

First keyframe

Last keyframe

Rotation and position changes tweened

Adding Color Effects to a Classic Tween

With a classic tween, any color effect that can be applied to an instance can be transformed in a motion tween. You can tween any color properties applied to either the starting or ending keyframe. For example, if the starting keyframe in a motion tween is tinted red and the ending keyframe is tinted yellow, Flash will gradually change the tint of the object from red, through shades of orange to the final tint of yellow. Use these properties to create any number of color effects in your animations. Additionally, you can tween the alpha of an object to make it appear to fade on and off the Stage.

Add Color Effects to a Classic Tween

1. Open a Timeline with a tweened animation or create a new one.

2. Select the object on the Stage on either keyframe in the tween.

3. Click the **Color Styles** list arrow in the Property Inspector, and then select an effect: **Brightness**, **Tint**, **Alpha**, or **Advanced**.

4. Drag the slider to set the percentage of the Color Styles applied or enter a value in the entry field.

   TROUBLE? *If the Color styles don't appear in the Property Inspector, you may have selected the keyframe in the Timeline and not the object on the Stage.*

5. To preview the animation, drag the playhead in the Timeline, or click the **Control** menu, point to **Test Movie**, and then click **Test**.

   Flash applies the tint gradually between the two keyframes.

See Also

See "Creating a Motion Tween" on page 242 for information on creating a motion tween.

First keyframe
Alpha of 100%

Last keyframe
Alpha of 0%

Alpha and position tweened

Creating a Classic Motion Guide Layer

If you want to implement motion that is smoother, or that follows a curve or some specific path, you can create a motion guide. A motion guide has its own layer just above the layer containing the object. Flash allows you to draw a line that you want your object to follow with any of the built-in drawing tools. Because this layer is a guide, it will be invisible in the exported Flash movie.

Create a Classic Motion Guide

① Select the layer containing the classic motion tween.

② Right-click (Win) or Control-click the layer containing the classic tween, and then click **Add Classic Motion Guide**.

Flash creates a new layer above the selected layer and indents the affected layer.

TIMESAVER *Press Control+click (Mac) or right-click (Win) the layer you want to add a motion guide to, and then click Add Motion Guide.*

③ Click on the motion guide layer to select it.

④ Draw a line on the Stage with any of Flash's drawing tools to define the path your object will follow.

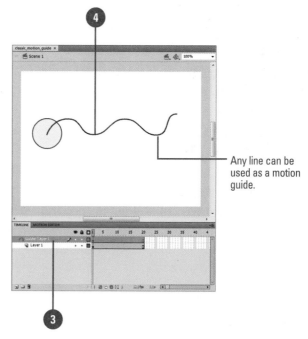

Any line can be used as a motion guide.

Animating Along a Classic Motion Guide

Turn snapping on to easily animate along a classic motion guide. The center point of the object must be on the classic motion guide path for it to work, and snapping ensures that this happens. Once the classic motion guide is created, all you have to do is drag the object in the first and last frames of the tween to the classic motion path you drew and Flash will draw the in-between frames along this path.

Animate Along a Classic Motion Path

1 Create a classic motion guide.

2 Click on the first keyframe of the motion tween, and then click and drag the object on the Stage onto the start of the motion path.

The object snaps to the motion path.

TROUBLE? *If the object doesn't snap to the motion path, verify that the Snap setting is turned on in the Property Inspector for this frame. The objects on both the beginning and ending keyframe must be snapped to the motion guide line for the motion to follow the guide line.*

3 Click on the last keyframe of the motion tween, and then click and drag the object on the Stage onto the end of the motion path.

The object follows the line you drew located in the motion guide layer.

See Also

See "Creating a Classic Motion Guide Layer" on page 269 for information on creating a motion guide.

Orienting Objects to a Classic Motion Path

When objects are tweened along a classic motion path, they remain in their native orientation regardless of the path. For certain objects, such as a circle, this is ok. For more complex objects, you must rotate the object so that it follows the path in a more naturalistic way. A good example of this sort of orientation in motion is in the path a car takes while driving down a road-the car must rotate gradually as the road curves to remain parallel with the road, and so, avoid disaster. Flash can do this work for you when you set the Orient To Path option in the motion tween settings.

Animate Along a Classic Motion Path

1. Animate an object along a classic motion guide.

2. Click on the first keyframe of the motion tween to select it.

3. Select the **Orient To Path** check box in the Property Inspector.

   The object will automatically rotate to remain parallel with the motion guide.

See Also

See "Animating Along a Classic Motion Guide" on page 270 for information on creating animation using a motion guide.

Tweening along a motion guide without orientation can seem unnatural.

Orient to Path makes sure the baseline is always parallel.

Easing In and Out of a Classic Tween

With a classic tween, you can customize easing in or out of a motion tween using the Edit button in the Property Inspector. The ease in and out of a motion tween is the rate at which the change of location is applied to an object. You can make an object move back and forth on the Stage within a single tween or create more complex tweens. Flash displays a graph representing the degree of motion in frames over time. The percentage of change is the vertical axis and the number of frames is the horizontal axis. The rate of change of the object is indicated by the slope of the graph's curve.

Set Ease In and Out Motion Tween Properties

1 Click the **Window** menu, and then click **Properties** to open the Property Inspector.

2 Select a keyframe with motion tween applied.

3 Click the **Edit** button in the Property Inspector.

4 Select or clear the **Use One Setting For All Properties** check box. Select it (default) to customize one curve, clear it to customize a curve for each curve property (Position, Rotation, Scale, Color, and Filters).

If cleared, use the Property list arrow to select a curve.

5 Click a point on the ease line to add a control point, and then drag the control point to change ease in and out. You can add and change multiple points.

6 Drag a tangent point (hollow circles on the sides of a control point) to further change ease in and out.

7 Click the **Play** or **Stop** buttons to try the customized ease settings.

8 To reset setting to the default, click **Reset**.

9 Click **OK**.

Last keyframe at 100%

First keyframe at 0%; square handles (control points) represent frame indicators.

Click a control point (square handle) to display its keyframe and % of change.

Animating with Shape Tweening

Introduction

Shape tweening works similarly to motion tweening. It follows the same structure of keyframing in the Timeline. You can animate many of the same changes such as alpha, color, scale, and position, though its main purpose is to transform the shape of an object into another shape. Whereas motion tweening is applied to groups and symbols, shape tweening must be applied to an editable shape. You can determine whether an object is editable by selecting it with the Selection tool—if it doesn't have a bounding box when selected, shape tweening can be applied. The reason for this is that when you convert a shape into a symbol, you are essentially protecting it from editing by storing it in its own Timeline. To apply shape tweening to a symbol, you must enter symbol editing mode and apply it to the shape contained inside the symbol. Shapes are created with any of Flash's drawing tools, such as the Oval or Rectangle tools. By making changes to the shape with any of Flash's editing tools, you can change the contours of the shape (for example, turn a circle into a square) and then use shape tweening to make this change happen gradually over time. Because the results of a shape tween can be unpredictable, you can set shape hints to let Flash know how to proceed with the tween. This is useful when you are working with complex shapes such as letterforms. In all cases you should only tween one shape at a time in a tweened span for best results.

In addition to shape tweening, you can also animate shapes using Inverse Kinematics (IK), which allows you to stretch and bend shape objects and link groups of symbol instances to make them move together in naturalistic ways using an internal structure of bones to create character animation.

What You'll Do

Use Shape Tweening

Create a Shape Tween

Add and Remove Keyframes from a Shape Tween

Change Shape Positions with Shape Tweening

Change Shape Position and Form Simultaneously

Adjust Shape Tween Properties

Change Shape Tweening Color and Alpha Options

Use Shape Hints

Create Animation Using ActionScript

Use Inverse Kinematics

Add Bones to an Armature

Edit Armatures and Bones

Bind Bones

Using Shape Tweening

You can use shape tweening when you need to alter the form of any editable shape gradually. Place artwork in a keyframe and then use any of Flash's drawing and editing tools to adjust the contours of a shape on another keyframe. When you apply shape tweening, Flash draws the frames in-between the two keyframes so that the object appears to "morph" between the two states. To provide even more control, you can use shape hints.

Using the Polystar Tool

Shapes created with
the Polystar tool

Using Shape Hints

Break apart letterforms
for shape tweening

Creating Complex Animations

For best results, tween shapes separately on different layers.

Creating a Shape Tween

In most cases, you can easily shape tween any two simple shapes. Geometric forms such as lines, rectangles and circles yield the best results. Because Flash draws the tweened frames mathematically, the simpler the shape, the more likely it will tween without any problems or without having to apply corrections such as shape hints. Experimentation is the key. As long as both keyframes contain an editable shape, Flash will attempt to morph one object into another. Use any of Flash's drawing tools or import a vector shape from another vector drawing program. If you want to apply a shape tween to grouped artwork or a symbol, you can break apart the group or enter symbol editing mode and apply the shape tween to any editable shape in the symbol's Timeline. You can quickly view your animation by exporting it with the Test command (in Flash Professional). By default, Flash loops animations in the Flash Player.

Create a Shape Tween

1 Create a new Flash document.

2 With any of Flash's drawing tools, draw a shape on the Stage at frame 1.

3 Select the first frame.

4 Click the **Insert** menu, and then click **Shape Tween**.

Square drawn on Frame 1

5 Select frame 10.

6 Click the **Insert** menu, point to **Timeline**, and then click **Blank Keyframe**.

Flash tints a shape-tweened span a pale green.

TIMESAVER *Press F7 to add a blank keyframe.*

7 With any of Flash's drawing tools, draw a different shape on the Stage at frame 10.

8 Click the **Control** menu, point to **Test Movie**, and then click **Test**.

The shape on frame 1 slowly transforms into the shape on frame 10.

TIMESAVER *Press ⌘+Return (Mac) or Ctrl+Enter (Win) to test it.*

5

Circle drawn on Frame 10

Shape tween span is tinted a pale green

Beginning Shape on Frame 1

Tweened frames

Ending Shape on Frame 10

Tweened frames

Adding and Removing Keyframes from a Shape Tween

The procedure for adding or removing keyframes in a shape tween is similar to that of motion tweens except for one crucial difference. In a motion-tweened framespan you can drag the object on the Stage and a new keyframe is automatically created. In shape-tweened spans, the object is only selectable on a keyframe. To add additional locations or shape changes along a shape-tweened span, you must add the keyframe first and then edit the shape. You can do this by using the Add Keyframe function in the Insert menu. Once the keyframe is added, the shape at that point in the framespan becomes editable.

Add a Keyframe to a Shape Tween

1 Place the playhead between any two shape tweened keyframes.

2 Click the **Insert** menu, point to **Timeline**, and then click **Keyframe**.

   TIMESAVER Press F6 to insert a keyframe.

Keyframe is added

Remove a Keyframe from a Shape Tween

1. Click on the keyframe you want to remove in the shape tween.

2. Click the **Modify** menu, point to **Timeline**, and then click **Clear Keyframe**.

   The keyframe is cleared but the duration of the tween is preserved. The first and last keyframes are automatically reconnected, and Flash redraws the tween.

   TIMESAVER *Press Shift+F6 to remove the keyframe.*

Keyframe is removed

Duration is maintained

Changing Shape Positions with Shape Tweening

To create a shape tween you need to draw or place an editable shape in a keyframe. Use any of Flash's drawing tools or import a vector shape from another vector drawing program. If you want to apply a shape tween to grouped artwork or a symbol, you can break apart the group or enter symbol editing mode and apply the shape tween to any editable shape in the symbol's Timeline. You can quickly view your animation by exporting it with the Test command (in Flash Professional). By default, Flash loops animations in the Flash Player.

Animate a Ball with Shape Tweening

1. Create a new Flash document.

2. Select the **Oval** tool on the Tools panel.

3. Set the **Stroke Color** to None.

4. On the first frame, draw a circle on the left side of the Stage.

5. Select the first frame.

6. Click the **Insert** menu, and then click **Shape Tween**.

7. Click frame 20 in the Timeline.

8. Click the **Insert** menu, point to **Timeline**, and then click **Keyframe**.

   Flash tints a shape-tweened span a pale green.

   TIMESAVER *Press F6 to add a keyframe.*

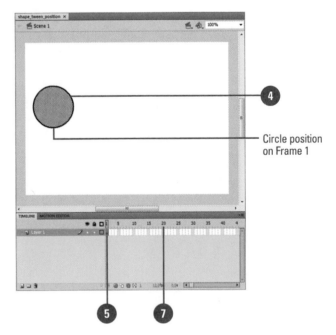

Circle position on Frame 1

9. Select the **Selection** tool on the Tools panel.

10. Select the circle on frame 20 and drag it to the right side of the Stage.

11. Click frame 40 in the Timeline, and then add another keyframe.

12. Select the circle shape on frame 40 and drag it back to the left side of the Stage.

13. Click the **Control** menu, point to **Test Movie**, and then click **Test**.

The ball animates back and forth across the screen.

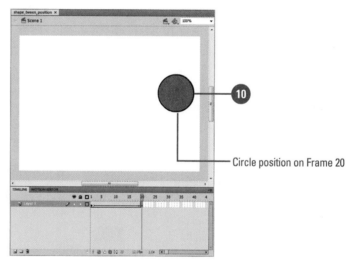

Circle position on Frame 20

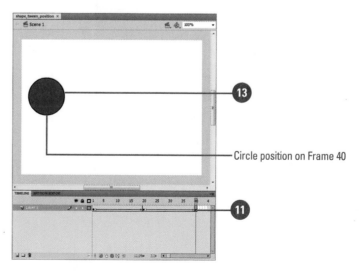

Circle position on Frame 40

Changing Shape Position and Form Simultaneously

Many of the same motion effects can be applied using either motion or shape tweening. What differentiates shape tweening from motion tweening is that shape tweening is applied to editable shapes. You can change the form of the shape on either keyframe and these changes will be applied gradually by Flash across the tween, slowly morphing one into the other. Additionally, you can combine movement with this tweening process, so your shape can change its shape as it changes its location.

Combine Shape Tweening and Movement in a Ball Animation

1. Create a shape tween of a moving ball that begins on the left side of the Stage, hits the right side of the Stage, and then returns to the left.

2. Click to place the playhead between the first and second keyframes in the shape tween.

3. Click the **Insert** menu, point to **Timeline**, and then click **Keyframe**.

4. Select the **Selection** tool on the Tools panel.

5. Place the pointer on the left edge of the shape and pull it to create a tail off the circle.

   The shape must be deselected on the Stage to pull the edges of the shape.

Shapes must be deselected to pull the edges.

Small curve icon indicates editable curve.

New keyframe placed at Frame 10.

6 Click to place the playhead between the second and third keyframes in the shape tween.

7 Click the **Insert** menu, point to **Timeline**, and then click **Keyframe**.

8 With the **Selection** tool still selected, place the pointer on the right edge of the shape and pull it to create a tail off the circle.

9 Click the **Control** menu, point to **Test Movie**, and then click **Test**.

The ball stretches as it animates back and forth across the screen.

See Also

See "Changing Shape Positions with Shape Tweening" on page 280 for information on animating a moving ball.

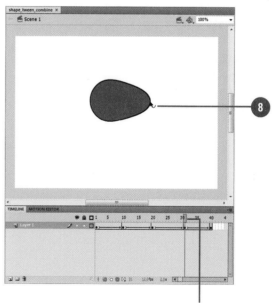

New keyframe placed at Frame 30.

Adjusting Shape Tween Properties

When shape tweens are applied to keyframes, the Property Inspector enables several options for controlling how Flash draws the tweened frames. Settings such as easing in and easing out enable you to control how the shape changes are distributed across the frames in the tween. Frame Blending allows you to set preferences to let Flash know which qualities to maintain during the tween.

Set Shape-Tween Properties

1. Click the **Window** menu, and then click **Properties** to open the Property Inspector.

2. Select a keyframe with shape tween applied.

3. Choose from the following settings:

   ◆ **Ease**. This sets the speed at which your object eases in or out of its motion. A positive value eases in, a negative value eases out.

   ◆ **Blend**. The Distributive option smoothes out the tweened shapes, while the Angular option preserves corners and straight lines in the shape tweens.

Changing Shape Tweening Color and Alpha Options

Because shape tweening can only be applied to editable shapes, you can't use the same color style effects that are available to instances. Instead, you must make these changes directly to the shape using the color palettes, the Color panel, or the Swatches panel. When shape tweening is applied, differences in color and alpha are tweened along with any shape changes. This applies to strokes as well as fills.

Change Shape-Tween Color

1 Select the beginning or ending keyframe in a shape tween or select the shape on the Stage.

2 Click the **Window** menu, and then click **Color**, if necessary.

   TIMESAVER *Press Shift+F9 to open the Color panel.*

3 Make changes to the shape's stroke and fill colors by entering values in the RGB, HSB, and Alpha fields, or by using the list arrows to the right of these fields.

4 Click the **Control** menu, point to **Test Movie**, and then click **Test**.

   The shape color changes as the shape tweens.

Color Picker
Fill Color
Stroke Color

Did You Know?

You can use any palette available to change the color of a shape in a tween. In addition to the Color Mixer, there are palettes located on the Tools panel, Property Inspector, and Swatches panel.

See Also

See "Modifying Instance Color Styles and Blends" on page 158-159 for more information on working with color and alpha options.

Using Shape Hints

Sometimes it isn't possible to predict how some, more complicated, shapes will tween. To exercise greater control over the tweening process, you can set shape hints to guide how Flash draws the in-between frames. You simply specify a beginning shape hint and then a corresponding end shape hint. In this way, Flash will know which parts of the shape in the first keyframe will transform into which parts in the end keyframe. Even with shape hints enabled, the results can be unpredictable, but you will have a greater control over the process.

Set Shape Hints

1. Create a shape tween of a simple shape into a complex shape.

2. Click to place the playhead on the first frame of the shape tween.

3. Click the **Modify** menu, point to **Shape**, and then click **Add Shape Hint**.

   A small red, circle with a small letter on it appears in the center of the shape. The first letter is "a". Shape hints appear in alphabetical order "a, b, c...". You can use up to 26 hints in one tween.

   TIMESAVER *Press Shift+⌥⌘+H (Mac) or Ctrl+Shift+H (Win) to insert a shape hint.*

4. Drag the shape hint to an area of the shape you want to control.

5. Click to place the playhead on the last frame of the shape tween.

   The corresponding shape hint appears as a small green circle with a corresponding letter that matches the beginning hint.

Beginning shape hint "a"

Place start shape hints on problem areas.

End shape hint "a"

Place end shape hints on corresponding areas.

Animation without Shape Hints

Animation with Shape Hints

6 Drag the corresponding end shape hints to the part of the shape that corresponds to the placement of the beginning shape hint.

"a" should correspond with "a", "b" should correspond with "b", etc.

7 Move the playhead back to the first frame.

8 Repeat steps 3, 4, 5, 6, and 7 until you have set and placed shape hints on all areas of the shape you want to control.

9 Click the **Control** menu, point to **Test Movie**, and then click **Test**.

The shape hints help make complex shape tweens more predictable.

Did You Know?

You can remove shape hints. Drag shape hints off the Stage or click the Modify menu, point to Shape, and then click Remove All Hints.

You should place your shape hints consecutively in a clockwise or counter-clockwise direction. Placing shape hints out of order can confuse Flash and often produces unwanted results.

Creating Animation Using ActionScript

In addition to creating animation using the Timeline and Property Inspector, you can also use ActionScript to animate movie clips, buttons, text, and components. You can animate any instance name with ActionScript. For an ActionScript 3.0 example, see Project 4, "Modifying an Object with ActionScript in the Workshops, available at *www.perspection.com*. For ActionScript 2.0, you can animate an object over time and change any ActionScript property, such as scale, rotation, color, and transparency. ActionScript provides two events that work well for animation: onEnterFrame and setInterval. The onEnterFrame event is a continuously executing event based on the frame rate of your movie until you stop (delete) it. The setInterval event is a continuously executing event for only a certain period of time. The one disadvantage of these actions is the large use of memory and CPU, so you need to clear it.

◆ **onEnterFrame event.** The following example is a frame script that animates a movie clip to the right until it reaches the position it should be in:

```
myMovieClip.onEnterFrame=function()
{
        if(this._x<300)
          {
                this._x+=10;
          }
        else
          {
delete this. onEnterFrame;
```

◆ **setInterval event.** This event requires two parameters: funtionName and an interval (amount of time in milliseconds between executions). If your interval is smaller than your frame rate, the screen cannot refresh. If your interval is greater than your frame rate, it executes as close as possible. The following example moves a TextArea component to the right every 10 milliseconds until it has reached its final location:

```
myInternval=setInterval(textAreaMove, 10);
function textAreamove()  {
        if (textAreaInstance._x<300)  {
                textAreaInstance._x += 10;
        } else
        clearInterval(myInterval);
        }
}
```

Using Inverse Kinematics

Inverse Kinematic (IK) allows you to stretch and bend shape objects and link groups of symbol instances to make them move together in naturalistic ways using an internal structure of bones to create character animation.

You can add bones to the interior of a shape or to separate symbol instances. When you move one bone, the other connected bones move in relation to the one that initially moved. A chain of bones is called an **armature**, which is either linear or branched in structure.

There are two types of Inverse Kinematic animation: those with symbols and those with shapes. For the symbol type, you link them together as a chain. For the shape type, you add bones inside the shape.

When you add bones to a shape or symbol instance, Flash creates a new layer called a **pose layer**. For a shape, Flash also converts the selected shapes and bones into an IK shape object. Each pose layer can contain only one armature. The first bone in an armature is the root bone. It appears with a circle around the head of the bone. Each bone has a head, the round end, and a tail, known as the pointed end.

After you add bones to an armature, you can change the position and length of a bone, delete bones, and edit objects containing bones.

When you're ready to animate an armature, all you need to do is add frames to the pose layer and reposition the armature on the Stage to create a keyframe. Keyframes in pose layers are called **poses**. To insert a frame in a pose layer, right-click (Win) or Option-click (Mac) a frame in a pose layer to the right

of any existing frames, and then click Insert Frame. To add a pose to a frame, right-click (Win) or Option-click (Mac) the frame in the pose layer, and then click Insert Pose. After you insert a pose, you can use the Selection tool to change the configuration of the armature. If you want to change the length of the animation, drag the last frame of the pose layer to the right or left in the Timeline to add or remove frames.

You can adjust the speed of an armature animation in frame around each pose by applying an easing motion. To add easing to frames in a pose layer, click a frame in a pose layer, open the Property Inspector, click the Ease popup, select an ease option, and then enter an ease strength value (0-100, where 0 is no easing and 100 is the most easing).

Inverse Kinematics

Adding Bones to an Armature

With Inverse Kinematic (IK), you can use bones to create two types of IK animations: those with symbols and those with shapes. For the symbol type, you link them together as a chain. For the shape type, you add bones inside the shape. When you add bones to a shape or symbol instance, Flash creates a new pose layer. For a shape, Flash also converts the selected shapes and bones into an IK shape object. The first bone in an armature is the root bone. It appears with a circle around the head of the bone. Each bone has a head, the round end, and a tail, known as the pointed end.

Add Bones to a Shape

1 Create one or more filled shapes and arrange them the configuration you want.

2 Select the entire shape on the Stage.

3 Click the **Bone** tool on the Tools panel.

4 Click inside the shape, and then drag to another location within the shape.

While you drag, a bone appears. When you connect the points, a solid bone appears between them. Flash converts the selected shape into an IK shape object and moves it to a new pose layer in the Timeline.

5 To add another bone, drag from the tail of the first bone to another location in the shape.

As you add bone instances, Flash moves each one to a new pose layer in the Timeline.

6 To create a branched armature, click the head of an existing bone, and then drag to create a new branch of the first bone.

Armature layer

Add Bones to a Symbol

1 Arrange the instances in the configuration you want.

2 Click the **Bone** tool on the Tools panel.

3 Click the symbol instance that you want as the root or head of the armature.

4 Drag the symbol instance to another symbol instance to connect it.

While you drag, a bone appears. When you connect the symbols, a solid bone appears between the symbols. As you add bone instances, Flash moves each instance to a new pose layer in the Timeline.

5 To add another bone, drag from the tail of the first bone to the next symbol instance you want to add to the armature.

6 To create a branched armature, click the head of an existing bone, and then drag to create a new branch of the first bone.

You can add as many branches as you want.

Did You Know?

You can move an armature. Select the IK shape object with the Selection tool, and then drag any of the bones to move it.

Symbols

Editing Armatures and Bones

After you add bones to an armature, you can change the position and length of a bone, delete bones, and edit objects containing bones. An armature can only be edited in pose layers that contain an initial pose in the first frame in which the armature appears in the Timeline. To edit the armature, you need to delete any additional poses after the first frame of the armature. You can bone properties, such as motion speed, joint rotation and motion, and springiness (life-like movement) (**New!**), in the Property Inspector.

Edit Armatures, Bones, and Related Objects

1. Select the bones and associated objects you want:

   ◆ **Bone.** Click the **Selection** tool, and then click a bone. You can Shift-click to select multiple bones.

   ◆ **Armature.** Double-click a bone.

   ◆ **IK Shape.** Click the shape.

   ◆ **Symbol Instance.** Click the instance.

2. To move bones, do any of the following:

   ◆ **Bone.** Drag a bone.

   ◆ **IK Shape.** Select the shape, and then change its X and Y position in the Property Inspector.

   ◆ **Bone End in IK Shape.** Click the **Subselection** tool, and then drag the end of the bone.

   ◆ **Bone Joint, Head, or Tail.** Use the Transform panel to move the transformation point of the symbol instance.

   ◆ **Rotate a Bone.** Shift-drag a bone to rotate it with its child bones without moving the parent bone.

3. To delete bones, do either of the following:

   ◆ **Bone.** Select the bones you want to delete, and then press Delete.

Selection tool

Symbols

Armature layer

Transform panel

- ◆ **IK Shape or Symbol Instance.** Select the shape or symbol, click the **Modify** menu, and then click **Break Apart**.

4 To edit an IK shape, do any of the following:

- ◆ **Move the Position of a Bone.** Drag a bone endpoint to move the position of a bone without changing the IK shape.

- ◆ **Display Control Points of the Boundary.** Click the stroke of the IK shape.

- ◆ **Move Control Point.** Drag the control point.

- ◆ **Add Control Point.** Click a part of the stroke without any control points. You can also use the Add Anchor Point tool on the Tools panel.

- ◆ **Delete Control Points.** Click a control point to select it, and then press Delete. You can also use the Delete Anchor Point tool on the Tools panel.

5 To set motion constraints, open the Property Inspector, and then specify the options you want (see table for details) to move or constrain joints, disable bone rotation around joints, constrain the rotation of a bone, make a bone stationary, limit the motion speed of a bone, or adjust the springiness (**New!**) to bones.

- ◆ **Enable or Disable Spring Options.** Select the pose layer in the Timeline, and then select or deselect the **Enable** check box in the Spring section of the Property Inspector.

4 IK shape

Bone Properties

Properties	Options
Location	Displays the X and Y position, length, and angle. Specify a speed percentage.
Joint: Rotation	Select the Enable check box to allow joint rotation. Select the Constrain check box to constrain the Min and Max angles of rotation.
Joint: X or Y Translation	Select the Enable check box to allow the bone to move along the X or Y axis. A two-headed arrow appears to indicate that X or Y axis motion is enabled. Select the Constrain check box to limit the amount of motion along the X or Y axis.
Spring	Specify the Strength (stiffness) (**New!**) of the bone spring. The higher the Strength, the stiffer the spring. Specify the Damping (rate of decay) (**New!**) of the spring effect. The higher the Damping, the faster the spring diminishes and the animation ends. A 0 value equals full strength.

Binding Bones

When the stroke of an IK shape doesn't distort in the way you want, you can use the Bind tool to edit the connections between individual bones and shape control points to create the appearance you desire. By default, the control points of an IK shape are connected to the bone that is nearest them. The Bind tool allows you to change it. You can bind multiple control points to a bone and multiple bones to a control point.

Bind Bones to Shape Points

◆ **Highlight Control Points Connected to a Bone.** Click the **Bind** tool, and then click a bone.

   The connected points are highlighted in yellow while the selected bone is highlighted in red.

◆ **Add Control Points.** Select a bone, and then Shift-click an unhighlighted control point.

◆ **Remove Control Points.** Ctrl-click (Win) or Option-click (Mac) a control point that is highlighted in yellow.

◆ **Highlight Bones Connected to a Control Point.** Click the **Bind** tool, and then click the control point.

   The connected bones are highlighted in yellow while the selected control point is highlighted in red.

◆ **Add Other Bones to a Control Point.** Select a control point, and then Shift-click a bone.

◆ **Remove a Bone from a Control Point.** Select a control point, and then Ctrl-click (Win) or Option-click (Mac) a bone that is highlighted in yellow.

Binded bones to shape points

Control points

Bind tool

Creating Masks

Introduction

You can create mask layers to show and hide parts of your artwork on the Stage. A mask works like a window blocking out everything but a certain area that you define. Any shape, symbol or text object can be used as a mask. The shape you place in a mask layer defines the area that will be visible in the linked layers below it. You can animate a mask to reveal the content on a layer in stages or animate the art in the layer beneath the mask. It is useful for spotlighting and controlling the shape of the viewable area. Masks are great tools for keeping the boundaries of the art on your Stage neat and controlled. They are also useful for cropping and experimenting with different borders and layouts, because you don't have to edit your art, you simply edit the mask. When creating a mask layer, it is important not to mix elements. For example, don't use an editable shape and a group on the same mask layer group everything together or break the groups into editable shapes. For the most consistent results, use ungrouped, editable shapes in the mask layer.

Understanding Masks

You use a mask in Flash to control what is viewable on a layer. Whatever you paint or draw onto a mask layer defines the viewable area on any layer it is linked to. Essentially, the shape you place on the mask layer acts like a window to the layers linked beneath it.

To link a layer, you simply drag it into the linked set. When a layer is linked to a mask it displays a tinted icon and is indented underneath the mask layer. Masks are useful for cropping artwork on the Stage, and animated masks can create interesting visual effects.

Draw any shape or shapes on a mask layer to limit the visible area of any layer linked to it.

Mask layer   Linked layer

The mask layer and all linked layers must be locked to activate the mask.

understand_masks* ×

Scene 1   100%

Shapes drawn on the mask layer define the visible area.

understand_masks* ×

Scene 1   100%

understand_masks* ×

Scene 1   100%

understand_masks* ×

Scene 1   100%

Creating a Mask Layer

Any layer can be converted into a mask layer. A **mask layer** only affects the linked layers beneath it, and there is no limit to the number of layers that can be included. Once a mask layer is created, you can drag other layers beneath it to link them. It is important to keep in mind that too much masking can affect performance in the Flash Player, especially when objects in the masked layers or the mask itself are animated.

Create a Mask Layer

1. Create a new Layer in the Timeline or select an existing one.

   The layer you select will be the one converted into a mask. If you want to mask the selected layer, create a new layer above this layer and select it.

2. Click the **Modify** menu, point to **Timeline**, and then click **Layer Properties**.

3. Click the **Mask** option from the Layer Type list.

4. Click **OK**.

   A blue masking icon appears on the layer.

Layer 2 becomes a mask layer indicated by masking icon.

5 Click the layer name of the layer directly beneath the mask layer, and then drag the layer slightly up to link it to the mask.

TIMESAVER *Press Control+click (Mac) or right-click (Win) the Layer Name area of the layer you want to convert into a mask, and then click Mask. When you use this method, Flash converts the layer into a mask and then automatically links it to the layer directly beneath it.*

Drag layer 1 slightly up until the gray bar appears. This links it to the mask layer.

Mask layer

Layer is linked to the mask layer. It appears in the Timeline indented under the mask layer with a tinted icon.

Drawing a Mask

You can use any filled shape as a mask. Flash ignores gradients, lines, and the content in bitmaps—in all cases it just deals with the whole shape. Use any of Flash's drawing tools to create a shape that will define the viewable area of the linked layers below. Keep in mind that mixing elements at different levels (editable shapes and symbols, for example) can produce unexpected results. Try to use only one type of element in any one mask: editable shapes, symbols, or groups.

Create a Mask Layer

① Click to select the mask layer.

② If the mask layer is locked, click on the **lock** icon in the Lock Layer column to unlock it.

③ Draw a shape with any of Flash's drawing tools or drag a symbol from the Library.

The area of the shape drawn, or symbol used, is the area that will be the visible area of the linked layer(s) beneath the layer mask.

Circle shape

Any shape or shapes drawn on the mask layer defines what is visible in the linked layers beneath.

Activating a Mask

To activate a mask, you simply lock it and any of the linked layers beneath it. Linked layers are indented in the Layer Name region and have tinted blue icons. You can lock and unlock a mask and its layers to edit them and see the effects of the mask in the Flash development environment. You can also use the Test command (in Flash Professional) to view the masking effects in the Flash Player.

Activate a Mask

1. Open a document with a masked layer.

2. Click the **black dot** in the lock column of the mask layer to lock it.

   The dot changes to a lock icon.

3. Click this dot on each linked layer to lock all of them and see the masking effect.

   TIMESAVER *You can click the Lock icon at the top of the lock layers column to lock all the layers in your Timeline simultaneously.*

Shapes drawn on the mask layer define the visible area.

Editing a Mask

Masks are editable. Which type of element you are using in the mask layer defines the procedure for editing: editable shapes can be modified with Flash's drawing tools, while groups and symbols must be edited in their own editing modes. Regardless, Flash only concerns itself with the fill area. Changes to color, alpha, and other such attributes are ignored. To edit a mask, you must first unlock it. To view your changes, simply re-lock the mask layer and all of its linked layers.

Edit a Mask

1 If the mask layer is locked, click on the **lock** icon in the Lock Layer column to unlock the layer and enable it for editing.

2 Edit the shape of the mask or, if using a group or symbol, enter the group or symbol's editing mode.

3 Re-lock the mask layer and any linked layers to view changes.

Add or delete shapes, or draw new ones with any of Flash's drawing tools.

Removing a Mask

To remove a mask layer entirely, select it and then click the Delete Layer icon. You can also convert a mask layer back to a normal layer in the Layer Properties dialog box. Additionally, you can remove linked layers from a mask layer set by dragging them out of the indented set.

Remove a Mask

1. Click on the mask layer to select it.

2. Click the **Modify** menu, point to **Timeline**, and then click **Layer Properties**.

3. Click the **Normal** option from the Layer Type list.

4. Click **OK**.

   The mask layer is converted into a normal layer.

   TIMESAVER *Press Control+click (Mac) or right-click (Win) the Layer Name area of the mask layer you want to convert back into a normal layer, and then click Mask to deselect it.*

Mask layer becomes a Normal layer.

Adding Layers to a Mask

Add layers to an existing mask by dragging them to any region within the masked layer hierarchy. Simply drag it between layers already linked, drag it under the mask layer, or drag it slightly up toward the bottom of a masked layer set. There is no limit to the number of layers that can be contained in a mask. Additionally, you can remove linked layers by dragging them out and above the mask layer set.

Link Additional Layers to a Mask

1. To add additional layers to a mask, do one of the following:

   ◆ Click and drag the layer below the mask.

   ◆ Click and drag the layer until it touches the bottom of a layer already linked to the mask.

Any layer can be added to an existing mask layer set.

Did You Know?

You can change the order of the linked layers. Masked layers behave the same as other layers. Click and drag the layers to reorder them in the indented set.

To add a layer to the bottom of the mask set, click and drag slightly below the set to link it.

To add a layer to the top of or between the linked layers of the mask set, click and drag the layer into the indented set.

Layers linked to the mask.

Remove a Linked Layer from a Mask

1. Click on the linked layer, and then drag it above the masked layer.

   The layer will no longer be linked to the mask and the indentation disappears.

Select the layer you want to remove.

Select the layer you want to remove. Drag it above the mask layer until a gray bar appears.

Layer is no longer linked to the mask.

Animating a Mask Layer

To create special effects such as a spotlighting effect or a gradual reveal of artwork on the Stage, you can animate a mask. Use any form of animation such as frame-by-frame animation or a shape or motion tween. The path of the shape or object on the mask layer will reveal the art below as it passes over it. Transforms to scale and position work well as well as shape tweens to editable objects. Other effects such as color and alpha will be ignored.

Animate a Mask

1. Place artwork in a linked layer.

2. Click on the first frame of the layer's mask layer in the Timeline.

3. Do one of the following:

   ◆ Draw a shape on the Stage with any of Flash's drawing tools.

   ◆ Drag an instance of a symbol from the Library.

4. Select the first frame with the shape or symbol.

5. Click the Insert menu, and then click **Classic Tween** (when using symbols) or **Shape Tween** (when using editable shapes).

6. Click frame 12 in the Timeline.

7. Click the **Insert** menu, point to **Timeline**, and then click **Keyframe**.

   TIMESAVER *Press F6 to add a keyframe.*

8. Transform the object with any of Flash's editing procedures: scale, skew, position, or in the case of shape tweening, edit the shape of the object.

9. Lock the mask layer and linked layer to see the effect.

Frame   1   3   5   7   9   10

Tweened scale changes on the mask layer reveal the photograph located on the linked layer beneath the mask in stages.

Working with Sounds

Introduction

Incorporating audio can really bring life to a Flash movie; however, the effect is very subtle. For example, most people would not be able to tell you the background music playing behind their favorite movie, but try leaving the sound out and they'll immediately notice. This makes audio a powerful influence on the viewers of your Flash movies. Adobe understands the power of audio and gives you the ability to import audio in a variety of formats, including ASND, MP3, WAV, AIF, and AU. If you want more control over your audio, you can edit sounds in Adobe Soundbooth directly from Flash. You can use on-clip controls to make fast edits and intuitive, task-based tools to clean up recordings, polish voice-overs, customize music, modify sound effects, apply high-quality filters, and much more.

There are two types of sounds: **event** sounds and **stream** sounds. An event sound needs to download completely before it starts to play, while a stream sound starts to play as soon as enough data downloads for the first few frames. Event sounds continue to play until they are done or you explicitly stop them. Steam sounds are synchronized to the Timeline for playing on a Web site.

Flash audio can be controlled using Flash's version of JavaScript, called ActionScript, and it even gives you the ability to load streaming MP3 files. Add to that the ability to choose between mono and stereo, and you can further reduce the size of your audio files (mono audio files are half the size of stereo). The one drawback to using audio is that it produces a much larger file (even compressed audio files are relatively large), but even this can be reduced to a minimum by using shared audio libraries. Since audio files create large Flash movies, use sounds when they are necessary to the design of the Flash movie, and remember that sometimes silence is golden.

What You'll Do

Import Audio

Use Audio on the Timeline

Load a Sound from a Shared Library

Use Audio with ActionScript

Load a Streaming MP3 File

Sync Sounds to the Timeline

Add Effects and Looping Sounds

Publish Documents Containing Audio

Edit Sounds

Edit Sounds Using Soundbooth

Importing Audio

When working with Flash, understand that Flash will let you import audio in a variety of formats. However, Flash has no way to record or create sounds; you can do it with Adobe Soundbooth. Therefore, audio must come from external sources. You can use the sample Sounds library that comes with Flash or conduct audio searches on the Internet using your favorite search engine to find a lot of audio files. One other consideration is creating your own audio, using your computer, an attached microphone, and a bit of imagination. Flash supports the following sound formats: ASND (from Adobe Soundbooth), WAV, AIFF, MP3, Sound Designer II (Mac), Sound Only QuickTime Movies, AU, and System 7 Sounds (Mac). When you import an audio file to Flash's Stage, you will first need to have a specific layer and keyframe selected. When you work on a Flash project, it might be beneficial to bring audio files directly into Flash's Library. That way you have easy access to them when needed. Any unused audio files are purged when you publish the Flash movie.

Import Audio Files to the Stage

1. Select a keyframe in the Timeline in which you want the audio file placed.

   IMPORTANT *You should always place audio files in a separate layer. This gives you easy access and control over the audio file once it's been placed on the Stage.*

2. Click the **File** menu, point to **Import**, and then click **Import To Stage**.

3. Navigate to the drive or folder location with the files you want.

4. Select one or more audio files to import.

   To select more than one file, click an audio file, then hold down the Shift key and click another file to select contiguous audio files, or hold down the ⌘ (Mac) or the Ctrl key (Win), and then click to select non-contiguous audio files.

5. Click **Import** (Mac) or **Open** (Win).

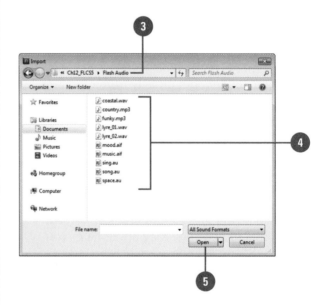

For Your Information

Using QuickTime for Sound

In addition, many formats that are not easy to import can be converted using the QuickTime plug-in. Point your browser to *www.quicktime.com* and download this free plug-in. You can also purchase QuickTime Pro to perform a wider range of conversions. In addition, you can perform limited conversions for free at *www.itunes.com*.

Import Audio Files to the Library

1. Open and select the library where you want to import your audio files.

2. Click the **File** menu, point to **Import**, and then click **Import To Library**.

3. Navigate to the drive or folder location with the files you want.

4. Select the audio file or files you want moved into the Library.

5. Click **Import To Library** (Mac) or **Open** (Win).

Did You Know?

You can sync sound to a Timeline animation. Select the sound on the Stage, and then change the Sync option on the Properties panel to Stream. Flash will force the animation to sync to the timing of the audio file even if it has to drop video frames to keep up.

See Also

See "Using Audio on the Timeline" on page 310-312 for information on importing audio using an external library.

Sound wave

Current audio in library

Sample Sounds library

For Your Information

Audio files

Audio files are embedded directly into the Flash movie. When you publish the Flash movie, by default, all audio files are embedded with the movie. Therefore, the Flash SWF file becomes a self-contained movie file without the need to access the original audio files.

Using Audio on the Timeline

Once you've imported audio files into the active document's Library, it's a simple matter to transfer the file to the Timeline. Flash's Timeline is actually a frame-by-frame representation of the Stage. For example, if you select frame 23 on the Timeline, the Stage displays the contents of the 23rd frame on the Stage. Audio, however, does not have a visible Stage object, so when you add an audio file to the Timeline, the effects are only apparent on the Timeline, not the Stage. Flash's Library holds all of the audio files that you've imported into the active Flash document. No matter how many times you use that audio file in the source document, Flash only needs to save it one time in the published Flash movie. In addition to the main Library, you can also use audio from the Sounds library that comes built-in to Flash. One of Flash's powerful features is the ability to use audio files from other Flash libraries. External Flash libraries are simply Flash source documents, which have an active Library. This gives you the ability to create libraries of audio files and use them over and over again.

Add Audio Using the Library or Sound Library

1. Open the library that you want to use:

    ◆ **Library.** Click the **Window** menu, and then click **Library**.

    TIMESAVER *Press* ⌘+L (Mac) or Ctrl+L (Win) to open the Library panel.

    ◆ **Sound Library.** Click the **Window** menu, point to **Common Libraries**, and then click **Sounds**.

2. Select a layer and keyframe in the Timeline in which you want the audio file placed.

3. Drag the audio file from the Library directly onto the Stage.

    Flash places the audio file in the selected keyframe.

Library

Sound library

Audio file placed on the keyframe.

Add Audio Using an External Library

1. Click the **File** menu, point to **Import**, and then click **Open External Library**.

2. Navigate to the drive or folder location with the files you want.

3. Select a Flash document that contains an active Library.

4. Click **Open**.

5. Drag items from the external Library directly to the Stage.

6. Drag items from the external Library to the active document's Library.

   IMPORTANT *When you drag an object from an external Library onto the Stage of the active Flash document, it is automatically added to the active document's Library.*

Did You Know?

You can use a single Library panel for all open documents. When you open multiple documents, Flash now consolidates all the libraries into a single Library panel. Click the list arrow button (located at the top of the Library panel) to select from any available library.

See Also

See "Working with the Library Panel" on page 136 for information on using the single library panel and other options.

Loading a Sound from a Shared Library

By default, Flash embeds audio files directly into the published (.swf) file. You have the option of loading audio files from a common Library. This gives you the advantage of using the same sounds in several Flash movies at the same time. For example, you create a Web site using fifteen separate Flash movie files, and each one uses the same background music. Rather than embed the same sound fifteen times, you can simply load the sound, when needed, from a common Library. Shared libraries are simple Flash documents that are set up to share their files between several Flash movies. The process is easy, and the rewards are great, and you don't increase the file size of Flash movies using shared Library elements. Once you've created and defined a Flash document as a shared Library, you can use the items in other Flash movies without increasing the size of the Flash published .swf file.

Create a Shared Audio Library

1. Create a new Flash document.

2. Add the audio files to the document's Library. They do not have to be placed on the Stage.

3. Click the **File** menu, and then click **Save**. Use a distinctive name for the source document.

4. Select an audio file in the Library.

5. Click the **Library Options** button, and then click **Properties**.

6. Select the **Export For Runtime Sharing** check box.

   ◆ If the check box is not available, clear the **Import for runtime sharing** check box.

7. Enter a distinctive name for the Identifier field or use the default.

8. Enter the name of the published document into the URL field.

9. Click **OK**.

   Repeat steps 4 through 9 until all the audio files are correctly linked.

10. Click the **File** menu, and then click **Publish** to create the Flash .swf file.

11. Close the original source file.

Work with Shared Audio Libraries

1. Click the **File** menu, point to **Import**, and then click **Open External Library**.

2. Select the shared Library, and then click **Open**.

   The items in the external Library will be grayed out, indicated they are sharable items.

3. Drag the audio files from the external Library to the Library of the active document.

4. To display or change link properties for an audio, double-click the audio icon in the Library, click **Advanced** (if necessary), view or change link options, and then click **OK**.

   When you publish the Flash .swf file, the audio files will be drawn from the common Library, without increasing the size of the Flash movie.

Did You Know?

A Flash Library can be shared with other designers. Since a Library is simply a Flash movie with Library elements, you can create common libraries of often-used elements, and then give them to other designers. When you're working with two or more designers, this is a great way to maintain consistency on a complex project.

External Library (Shared)

Active Library

Linkage settings for audio

Using Audio with ActionScript

Sound is a great motivator. For example, a particular piece of music can make you happy, or it can make you sad. In addition, sounds can pull out childhood memories and stir emotions. Sound is a powerful tool, however, different people react differently to sounds, therefore it's important that you think carefully about the sounds you add to your movies. It's equally important to understand how you can control your movies using using ActionScript 3.0 code or ActionScript Behaviors in ActionScript 2.0.

Load a Sound from the Library with ActionScript 3.0

1. Create or open a Flash document (ActionScript 3.0).

2. Click the **Window** menu, click **Library** to open the Library panel, and then select an audio file from the available Library items.

3. Right-click (Win) or Command-click (Mac) the audio sound, and then click **Properties**. Click **Advanced**, if necessary.

4. Enter a distinctive name for the Identifier field or use the default.

5. Select the **Export For ActionScript** check box.

6. Leave the other fields at their default values, and then click **OK**.

7. Click Frame 1 in a layer.

8. Click the **Window** menu, and then click **Actions**.

9. Type the ActionScript code shown in the illustration:

10. Click the **Control** menu, point to **Test Movie**, and then click **Test**.

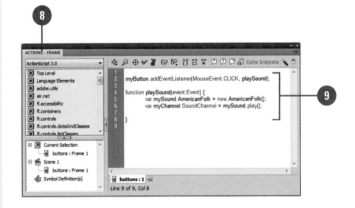

Load a Sound from the Library with an ActionScript Behavior

① Create or open a Flash document (ActionScript 2.0).

② Click the **Window** menu, click **Library** to open the Library panel, and then select an audio file from the available Library items.

③ Click the **Library Options** button, and then click **Properties**. Click **Advanced**, if necessary.

④ Select the **Export For ActionScript** check box.

⑤ Enter a distinctive name for the Identifier field or use the default.

⑥ Leave the other fields at their default values, and then click **OK**.

⑦ Click the **Window** menu, and then click **Behaviors** to open the Behaviors panel.

⑧ Select a button object on the Stage or Timeline keyframe.

⑨ Click the plus (+) sign, located in the upper-left portion of the Behaviors panel, point to **Sound**, and then click **Load Sound From Library**.

⑩ Enter the name of the audio file in the Linkage ID field.

⑪ Enter a unique name in the instance field.

⑫ Select the **Play This Sound When Loaded** check box.

⑬ Click **OK**.

⑭ Select an Event to trigger the sound. If the audio file was added to a Timeline frame, the event field will be disabled.

⑮ Click the **Control** menu, point to **Test Movie**, and then click **Test**.

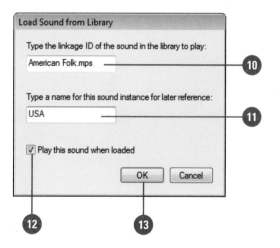

Loading a Streaming MP3 File

You can load an MP3 music audio file using a built-in Flash behavior. The advantage to this process is that the file is loaded when needed, and it never increases the size of the original Flash movie. Flash performs a calculation on audio files as they are loading. When it has enough of an audio file, it begins playing, while it continues to download the remaining information in the background. For large audio files, this cuts down on long wait times and keeps the visitor from becoming bored. Streaming MP3 files are not part of a pre-existing Flash movie, they're just available from a common location.

Load a Streaming MP3 File with ActionScript 3.0

① Create or open a Flash document (ActionScript 3.0), and then select a button object on the Stage.

② Open the **Properties** panel.

③ Enter a distinctive name for the object in the Instance field, such as *myButton*.

④ Click Frame 1 in the actions layer.

⑤ Click the **Window** menu, and then click **Actions**.

⑥ Enter the script as shown in the illustration:

⑦ Click the **Control** menu, point to **Test Movie**, and then click **Test**.

See Also

See Project 2, "Loading and Formatting Text" in the Workshops, available at www.perspection.com, for Action-Script 3.0 code to load external text.

Load a Streaming MP3 File with an ActionScript Behavior

① Create or open a Flash document (ActionScript 2.0), and then select a button object on the Stage or Timeline keyframe.

② Click the plus (**+**) sign, located in the upper-left portion of the Behaviors panel, point to **Sound**, and then click **Load Streaming MP3 File**.

③ Enter the URL to the source MP3 file.

④ Enter a unique name in the identifier field.

⑤ Click **OK**.

⑥ If you selected a button object, select an Event to trigger the sound.

⑦ Click the **Control** menu, point to **Test Movie**, and then click **Test**.

Did You Know?

You can stop all sounds using an ActionScript Behavior. Create or open a Flash document (ActionScript 2.0) that contains playing audio files, place a button object on the Stage, and then select it. Click the plus (+) sign in the Behaviors panel, point to Sound, and then click Stop All Sounds. Click OK. Select an Event to stop the sound.

Syncing Sounds to the Timeline

When you sync a sound to the Timeline, you're essentially instructing Flash how to play the sound. Syncing sounds is a fundamental operation because choosing the wrong sync operation can drastically change how the sound plays out during the execution of the Flash movie. Flash gives you the ability to choose a separate sync operation for each individual sound file. When you place the sound on the Timeline, the Properties panel displays the audio properties for the selected sound and lets you define individual properties for every sound in your Flash document. For example, you have a background music sound that's located in several scenes, and you want to make sure it doesn't play on top of itself (Sync: Stop). Or, you have a narration that you want perfectly synced to an animation on the Timeline (Sync: Stream).

Sync Sounds to the Timeline

1. Select the keyframe on the Timeline containing the sound you want to sync.

2. Click the **Window** menu, and then click **Properties** to open the Property Inspector.

3. Click the **Sync** list arrow, and then select from the following options:

   ◆ **Event.** When you select Event (default) the sound plays when the record head reaches the keyframe containing the sound, and continues to play until the end of the sound. If the record head reaches another keyframe that contains the same sound, it will begin playing on top of the original sound.

   ◆ **Start.** Doesn't allow the sound to play on top of itself.

   ◆ **Stop.** Stops a sound if it is already playing, without affecting any other sounds.

   ◆ **Stream.** The Stream Sync creates sounds synchronized to the Timeline. This is useful for matching sounds to a particular visual event in the movie. If the video can not keep up with the audio, Flash will automatically drop video frames to keep the audio synchronized.

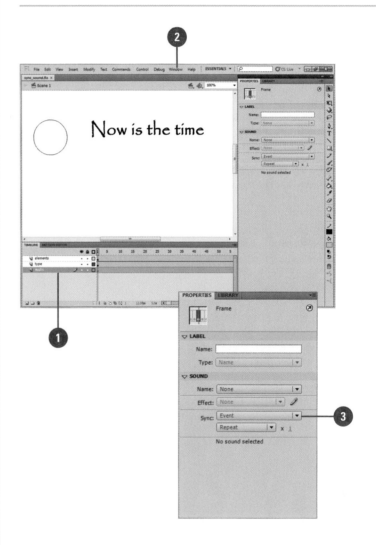

Adding Effects and Looping Sounds

Once a sound is imported into Flash and placed on the Timeline, you can add sound effects and determine the number of loops. When you loop a sound, you're instructing the Flash movie to repeat the sound a given number or times, or to loop the sound forever. Some sounds loop better than others. For example, you create some background music, and you want it to continue to play for as long as the visitor is on that particular page, but you don't want the sound to have a definable beginning or end. In addition to loops, you can also add effects to a sound, including fades in and out, and fade to the left or right channel. The effects applied will only modify the selected audio file. Each copy of an audio file dragged into a Flash movie is controlled independently.

Add Effects and Loop Sounds

1. Select the keyframe on the Timeline containing the sound you want to change.

2. Click the **Window** menu, and then click **Properties** to open the Property Inspector.

3. To add effects to the sound, click the **Effect** list arrow, and then select an option:

   - **Left Channel/Right Channel.** Plays sound in the left or right channel.

   - **Fade Left To Right/Fade Right To Left.** Changes sounds from one channel to the other.

   - **Fade In.** Increases volume.

   - **Fade Out.** Decreases volume.

   - **Custom.** Creates custom in and out sound points using the Edit Envelope.

4. To loop a sound, click the list arrow, and then select an option:

   - **Loop.** Click **Loop** to force the sound into an infinite loop.

   - **Repeat.** Click **Repeat**, and then enter the number of times you want the sound to loop (up to 65,535).

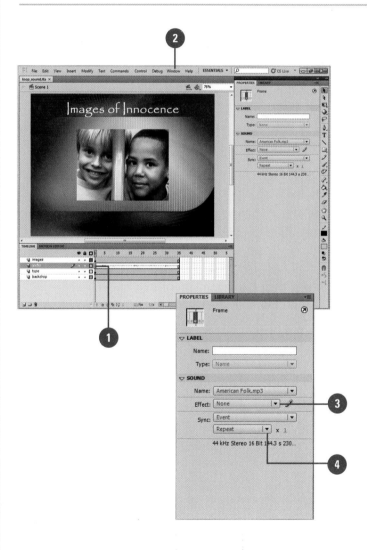

Publishing Documents Containing Audio

Sooner or later, you're going to want to export your Flash movie that contains audio as an SWF file. The process of publishing is relatively painless; however, there are a few considerations as to the compression of the files, which will be important to the size and playability of the Flash movie. Publishing requires knowledge of where the document will be used. For example, if the document is to be streamed over the Internet, and your visitors have relatively low bandwidth, you would want to choose compression settings that would significantly reduce the size of the audio files. It's possible that the Flash document is intended for playing off a CD/DVD; in that case, you could increase the compression settings. When you're designing a Flash document, it's imperative that you understand the end game and design the document toward that goal. Always remember that you can design a Flash document, but it's your visitors that ultimately will see, and use it.

Publish Sound Documents

1. Click the **File** menu, and then click **Publish Settings**.

2. Click the **Formats** tab, and then select the **Flash (.swf)** check box.

3. Click the **Flash** tab.

4. Click the **Set** buttons for Audio Stream or Audio Event.

5. Select other sound options as desired:

   ◆ Select the **Override Sound Settings** check box to override any sound settings applied to the individual sound files within the active Flash document.

   ◆ Select the **Export Device Sounds** check box to export sounds suitable for devices, such as mobile devices, instead of the library sound.

6. Click the **Compression** list arrow, and then select from the following options:

   ◆ **Disable.** Turns off all sound compression options and instructs Flash not to export sounds.

   ◆ **ADPCM.** Performs minor compression to the audio files.

- **MP3.** Creates audio files, especially music files, with excellent quality in a small file size.

- **Raw.** Leaves the sounds intact without any compression schemes applied.

- **Speech.** Creates optimized files for the human voice.

7. Select the **Convert Stereo To Mono** check box for the ADPCM and RAW compression formats.

8. Based on your Compression selections from step 5, select the following options:

- **Sample Rate.** Available for ADPCM, Raw, and Speech compression. The higher the sample rate the better the quality, but the bigger the file.

- **ADPCM bits.** Higher bit values translate into better quality audio, but larger file sizes.

- **Quality.** Available for MP3 compression. The Best option gives the finest quality, but produces a larger file.

- **Bit Rate.** Available for MP3 compression. The higher the value, the better the quality and the bigger the file.

9. Click **OK**.

10. Select the **Override Sound Settings** check box to take priority over the individual settings applied to the audio files.

11. Select the **Export Device Sounds** check box to export device sounds with the published Flash movie.

12. Click **OK**.

Editing Sounds

Flash is not a major sound editing application. For example, you can't trim or cut audio files, nor can you enhance audio or reduce hum and background noises. Flash expects all that to be done before you import the file. However, you do have some control over when the sound begins and ends (time in, and time out), and you do have control over the volume (fade in and fade out). Making sure that your audio file is clean and smooth flowing will help with the quality of your audio file.

Work with Edit Envelope

1. Select a keyframe on the Timeline that contains an audio file.

2. Click the **Window** menu, and then click **Properties** to open the Property Inspector.

3. Click the **Edit** button.

4. Click the **Effect** list arrow, and then select a channel, fade, or custom effect.

5. Drag the **Time In** marker to the right to change where the audio file begins.

6. Drag the **Time Out** marker to the left to change where the audio file ends (the Time Out marker appears at the end of the audio file).

7. Click the **Envelope** lines to adjust the volume on the right or left channels.

8. Use the **Zoom** buttons to increase or decrease the size of the audio file in the edit window.

9. Click the **Play** or **Stop** buttons to test the changes to the audio file.

10. Click the **Time Marker** buttons to change the marker code from frames to seconds.

11. Click **OK** to save your changes.

IMPORTANT *Adjusting an audio file using Edit Envelope only impacts the select instance of the audio file. The original audio file (in the Library) is unaffected by these changes.*

Editing Sounds Using Soundbooth

Adobe Soundbooth is a program that allows you to record and modify sound files. If you have Soundbooth installed on your computer, you can edit imported sounds in Soundbooth directly from within Flash. When you're done editing the sound file in Soundbooth, you can save the file and your changes automatically appear in Flash. If you change the name or format of a sound after editing it, you'll need to re-import the modified file back into Flash. You can edit all different sound file formats in Soundbooth. If you want to non-destructively edit sounds, then use the default sound file format (ASND) in Soundbooth for the best results.

Edit a Sound Using Adobe Soundbooth

1. Click the **Window** menu, and then click **Library** to open the Library panel.

2. Right-click (Win) or Control-click (Mac) the sound file you want to edit, and then click **Edit with Soundbooth**.

   The sound file opens in Adobe Soundbooth.

3. Edit the sound file using Soundbooth tools and commands.

   ◆ Use Help in Soundbooth to edit the sound file the way you want.

4. When you're done, save the sound file in Soundbooth. Click the **File** menu, and then click **Save**.

   ◆ To save the changes in a non-destructive format, save the file using the ASND file format, the default in Soundbooth.

   ◆ If you change the name or format of a sound after editing it, you'll need to re-import the modified file back into Flash.

5. Quit (Mac) or exit (Win) Soundbooth to return to Flash and view the edited version of the sound file in the Library panel.

Working with Video

Introduction

The Flash Video Import Wizard lets you import a video clip as a file that is streamed from a Flash server, progressively downloaded from a Web server, embedded (stored in movie) or linked (stored out of movie). It guides you through the steps for the specific deployment method. During the import process, you have the ability to compress the video using user-defined profiles, or preset values, set cue points, and trim excess video. It's important to understand that although Flash can import a video file, it can't make the quality of the video any better than the original. If you receive your video from outside sources, there is little you can do; however, if you're the one shooting the footage, pay close attention to lighting, camera angles, and distractions within the video. The more time and attention you spend taking the video, the better the video will be when imported into Flash. If you do need to tweak a video file, video-editing applications such as Adobe's Premiere (Mac/Win), and Apple's Final Cut Pro (Mac) are excellent choice for the budding movie director.

If you have a video-editing application and Flash, you can create a movie against a blue screen and then mask the area out using alpha channel masks. They do this in the movies all the time. The process involves opening the image within a video-editing application, and creating the transparency using a specific color (referred to as blue or green screening), using luminosity levels, or actually creating a mask in an image-editing application such as, Adobe Photoshop, and then importing the mask. When you open the movie in Flash, any other background you place behind the movie will replace the original green screen.

What You'll Do

Use the Video Import Wizard

Work with Video on the Stage

Work with Video on the Timeline

Use Movie Clips with Video Files

Add Cue Points to a Video

Use Video with ActionScript

Control Video Through Movie Clips

Use the FLV Playback Component

Work with the Video Encoder

Work with Alpha Channel Masks

Export as a QuickTime Video

Export as a FLV File

Using the Video Import Wizard

Importing video into Flash is not much more difficult than importing a graphic or audio file. The Video Import Wizard is Flash's way of helping you through the process of importing video files into Flash. When you import video, the Wizard lets you import a video clip as a file that is streamed from a Flash server, progressively downloaded from a Web server, embedded (stored in movie) or linked (stored out of the movie). It guides you through the steps for the specific deployment method. During the import process for some methods, you have the ability to compress the video using user-defined encoding profiles, set cue points, and trim excess video. You can choose to accept the Wizard's recommendations or make changes. You can also attach movie playback controls with different looks, known as **skins (New!)**. The Wizard seamlessly uses the Skinning component to attach movie controls.

Use the Video Import Wizard

1 Click the **File** menu, point to **Import**, and then click **Import Video**.

◆ For the FLV format, use **Import To Library** since the file is native to Flash and doesn't need to be encoded.

Flash saves the video in the active document's Library.

2 Select a video file location option:

◆ Click the **On Your Computer** option, click **Browse** to manually locate the video file.

Choose a video method from the following options:

◆ Load external video with playback component.

◆ Embed FLV in SWF and play in timeline.

◆ Import as mobile device video bundled in SWF.

◆ Click the **Already deployed to a web server, Flash Video Steaming Service, or Flash Media Server** option, and then enter in the file's URL.

3 Click **Next**.

Skinning options

4 Options vary depending on the deployment method; select the ones you want.

◆ **Skinning.** Specify the appearance and position of the play controls (**New!**); additional skins added.

◆ **Embedding.** Specify a symbol type, and other embedding options.

5 Click **Next**.

6 Click **Finish**.

Flash will automatically create an FLV component, and drop it into the active layer on the Timeline. Flash places the external video on the Stage with the first frame of the video (**New!**) and playback controls at the bottom.

7 Click the **Control** menu, point to **Test Movie**, and then click **Test**.

See Also

See "Working with the Video Encoder" on page 340 for information on Flash video encoding settings.

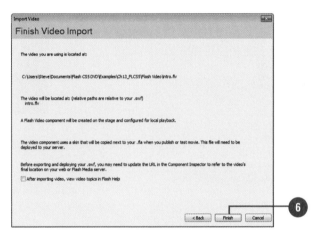

Supported Import Video Formats

Extension	Description
.flv, f4v	Adobe Flash Video
.mp4, .m4v, .avc	Moving Picture Experts Group
.mov, .qt	QuickTime
.3gp, .3gpp, .3gp2, .3gpp2, .3g2	3GPP/3GPP2 for Mobile Devices

Working with Video on the Stage

When you import video into a source document, Flash places the external video on the Stage with the first frame of the video (**New!**) and playback controls at the bottom. You can use the playback controls on the Stage to play and work with the video (**New!**). In addition, you can make changes to video settings in the Properties panel as you work with the video on the Stage. In the Properties panel, you can change the position and size, alignment, skin, volume, autoplay, and cuepoints. You can no longer change video properties in the Component Inspector panel on the Parameters tab (**New!**).

Move a Video File Directly to the Stage

1. Open a Flash document (.fla) that contains one or more video files.

2. Select the video.

3. Use the playback controls to work with the video.

4. Click the **Window** menu, and then click **Properties** to open the Properties panel.

5. Use the Properties panel to change the options you want.

   - **align.** Specify FLV file alignment in the player.

   - **autoPlay.** Select or deselect to automatically play the FLV file.

   - **cuePoints.** Specify a string with the cue points for the video.

   - **isLive.** Select or deselect whether the FLV is streaming live.

   - **preview.** Creates a preview for authoring purposes.

- **scaleMode.** Select an option to maintainAspectRatio, noScale, or exactFit.

- **skin.** Select a skin for the FLV video player.

- **skinAutoHide.** Select or deselect to automatically hide or show the skin.

- **skinBackgroundAlpha.** Specify a background alpha channel for the skin.

- **skinBackgroundColor.** Specify a background color for the skin.

- **source.** Specify the path to the video source file.

- **volume.** Specify a volume setting for the video.

6 Click the **Control** menu, point to **Test Movie**, and then click **Test**.

Skin for the FLV player

Working with Video on the Timeline

When you import video into a source document, Flash stores a copy of the video in the active document's Library. Even if you import the video directly to the Stage, Flash will still place a copy in the Library. It's always best to import video files first into the Library; that way you have control of the video and how it's brought onto the Stage. Moving a video file directly to the Stage is the easiest way to incorporate video into a Flash movie. In fact, once the video file has been imported into Flash, it's a simple drag and drop operation. However, video files should always be held within a separate layer. That gives you control over the display of the video and lets you place other Flash elements in other layers.

Move a Video File to the Stage from the Timeline

1. Open a Flash FLA document that contains one or more video files in the Library or use the Video Import Wizard.

   IMPORTANT *To work directly with video files on the Timeline, you will have to Import them using the Embed video in SWF and play in Timeline (see Using the Video Import Wizard).*

2. Click the **Window** menu, and then click **Library** to open the Library panel.

3. Click the **Insert Layer** button, name the new layer video_1, and then select the new layer.

4. Drag the video file from the Library onto the Stage.

5. Click **Yes**, if prompted to a dialog box indicating how many frames the video file will occupy on the Stage.

6. Click the **Control** menu, point to **Test Movie**, and then click **Test**.

Video file in the Library

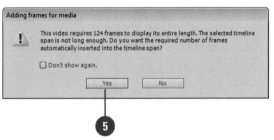

Using Movie Clips with Video Files

While placing a video file directly onto the Stage may be an easy way to bring a video file into a Flash movie, the best way to control video is to first place it into a movie clip, and then drag the movie clip onto the Stage. That gives you control of the clip with two Timelines: the Timeline on the Stage, and the Timeline of the movie clip.

Use Movie Clips with Video Files

1. Click the **Window** menu, and then click **Library** to open the Library panel.

2. Click the **Insert** menu, and then click **New Symbol**.

3. Name the new symbol.

4. Click **Type** list arrow, and then click **Movie Clip**.

5. Click **OK**.

6. Drag a video file from the Library into the movie clip Library.

7. Click **Yes** when Flash instructs you as to how many frames the video file will occupy in the movie clip.

8. Return to the current scene by clicking the **Scene** button, located in the upper-left corner of the Flash window.

9. Click the **Insert Layer** button, and name the new layer video_1.

10. Select the new layer.

11. Drag the movie clip from the Library onto the Stage.

    The movie clip occupies a single frame.

12. Click the **Control** menu, point to **Test Movie**, and then click **Test**.

Adding Cue Points to a Video

A cue point is a marked moment in time within a video clip. Cue points enable you to access different segments of a video clip. With Flash video, you can create and manage ActionScript cue points in the Properties panel (**New!**). You can add or delete a cue point, rename a cue point, adjust the time, and add or delete ActionScript parameters. If you want to reuse existing ActionScript cue points, you can also import and export them in the XML file format using the Import ActionScript Cue Point or Export ActionScript Cue Point buttons.

Work with Cue Points in a Video

1 Open a Flash FLA document that contains one or more video files in the Library or use the Video Import Wizard.

2 Select the video.

3 Click the **Window** menu, and then click **Properties** to open the Properties panel.

4 Click the **Cue Points** arrow to expand the panel.

5 To work with ActionScript cue points, do any of the following:

   ◆ **Find a Cue Point.** Enter a keyword in the Search box, and then press Enter (Win) or Return (Mac).

      ◆ To clear the search, click the **Close** button in the Search box.

   ◆ **Add a Cue Point.** Use the playback controls to position the video where you want to create a cue point, and then click the **Add ActionScript Cue Point** button.

   ◆ **Delete a Cue Point.** Select the cue point, and then click the **Delete ActionScript Cue Point** button.

   ◆ **Rename a Cue Point.** Click the cue point name to select it, rename it, and then press Enter (Win) or Return (Mac).

Playback controls

6 To add or delete ActionScript parameters, do any of the following:

- ◆ **Add Parameter.** Click the **Add Cue Point Parameter** button. Click the parameter name or value to change them.

- ◆ **Delete parameter.** Select the the parameter, and then click the **Delete Cue Point Parameter** button.

7 To export or import ActionScript cue points, do any of the following:

- ◆ **Export Cue Points.** Click the **Export Cue Points** button, specify a filename and location, and then click **Save**.

  The exported file also includes any navigation and event cue points which are embedded in the video

- ◆ **Import Cue Points.** Click the **Import Cue Points** button, select the cue points XML file, and then click **Open**.

Cue point controls

Import

Did You Know?

ActionScript cue points are different than encoded cue points. Encoded cue points are ones you add when encoding video with Adobe Media Encoder.

See Also

See "Working with the Video Encoder" on page 340 for more information on working with encoded cue points.

Using Video with ActionScript

Playing a video file inside a Flash movie is one thing, controlling the movie, or better yet, letting your visitors control the movie is something quite different. Control of a movie requires knowledge of Flash's ActionScript language. ActionScript is a control language that instructs Flash what to do, and when to do it. For example, you could create an ActionScript that instructs Flash to play or stop a movie, or you could add buttons to move the video backward or forward, one frame at a time. One way to display video in a Flash Movie is to drag it directly from the Library to the Timeline. Once the video is on the Timeline, ActionScripts can be created to start and stop the video. Since you're using the active document's Timeline to control the video, any other layers containing animation sequences on the Timeline will stop and start along with the video.

Control Video from the Timeline

1 Create or open a Flash document, create a new layer to hold the video file, and then select the layer.

2 Drag the video file from the Library to the Stage.

3 Create a new layer to hold the navigation buttons, and then select the layer.

4 Drag the Play, Stop, and Rewind buttons into the Navigation layer from the Library, and then place them underneath the video.

5 Click the **Window** menu, and then click **Actions** to open the Actions panel.

6 To display scripting language commands for the scripting language you want to use, click the **Language** button, and then select the language you want.

Did You Know?

You can check the syntax of any script with the click of a button. Click the Check Syntax button, located at the top of the Actions panel, and Flash will check the syntax of the script.

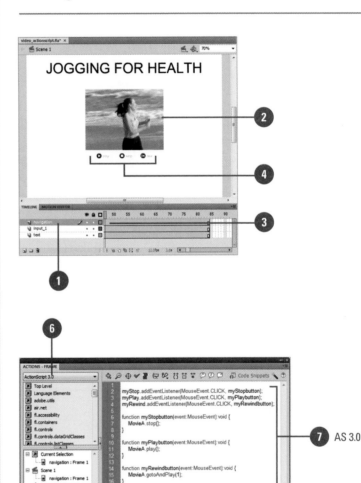

7 Do either of the following depending on the ActionScript version:

- ◆ **ActionScript 2.0.** Select the Play, Stop, and Rewind buttons individually, and then enter the ActionScript 2.0 script as shown in the illustration.

- ◆ **ActionScript 3.0.** Click Frame 1 in a layer, and then enter the ActionScript 3.0 script as shown in the illustration.

IMPORTANT *ActionScript is a relatively easy language to learn, but it is also a very unforgiving language. For example, the gotoAndStop script must be written exactly as shown, including the capital "A" and "S". While ActionScripting, remember to keep an eye on syntax.*

8 Click the **Control** menu, point to **Test Movie**, and then click **Test**.

IMPORTANT *Although working with embedded video is a common practice, large video files can cause audio sync problems when the file is published and played. It's always wise to thoroughly test your published documents.*

7 AS 2.0

AS 2.0 - Stop

AS 2.0 - Rewind

Did You Know?

Flash contains several sets of pre-designed buttons. Click the Window menu, point to Common Libraries, and then click Buttons. Flash's button Library contains folders with dozens of buttons, including arcade buttons and buttons for controlling a Flash movie.

Controlling Video Through Movie Clips

While it's an easy matter to drag a video file onto the Stage and then use start and stop ActionScripts to control the playing of the video, it's better to create a movie clip, and then load the video file into the clip. It's a bit more work, but the additional rewards are great. For example, you can instruct a movie clip to stop playing without affecting anything else on the Stage. As a matter of fact, you can have as many movie clips on the Stage as you want, and each one can be controlled individually. It's exactly that kind of control that leads to awesome Flash movies. To control a video using a movie clip you will need to have a flash document that contains one or more video files, in the Library.

Control Video Through Movie Clips

1 Create or open a Flash document, click the **Insert** button, and then click **New Symbol**.

2 Name the symbol, and then click the **Movie Clip** option.

3 Click **OK**.

4 Drag a video file from your Library into the movie clip symbol.

5 Click the **Scene** button to return to the Stage of the active scene.

6 Create a new layer to hold the video, and then select the layer.

7 Drag the movie clip to the Stage, and then select the clip.

8 Enter a unique Instance name in the Property Inspector.

IMPORTANT *The Instance name you enter will be used in the ActionScript to identify the movie clip to the button object "with (instance name)".*

9 Create a new layer to hold the navigation buttons, and then select the layer.

10 Drag Play, Stop, and Rewind buttons into the Navigation layer from the library, and then place them underneath the video.

11 Click the **Window** menu, and then click **Actions**.

12 To display scripting language commands for the scripting language you want to use, click the **Language** button, and then select the language you want.

13 Do either of the following depending on the ActionScript version:

♦ **ActionScript 2.0.** Select the Play, Stop, and Rewind buttons individually, and then enter the ActionScript 2.0 script as shown in the illustration.

♦ **ActionScript 3.0.** Click Frame 1 in a layer, and then enter the ActionScript 3.0 script as shown in the illustration.

IMPORTANT *ActionScript is a relatively easy language to learn, but it is also a very unforgiving language. For example, the gotoAndStop script must be written exactly as shown, including the capital "A" and "S". While ActionScripting, remember to keep an eye on syntax.*

14 Click the **Control** menu, point to **Test Movie**, and then click **Test**.

13 AS 3.0

13 AS 2.0

AS 2.0 - Stop

AS 2.0 - Rewind

Using the FLV Playback Component

Instead of importing video into Flash, you can also use the FLVPlayback components to dynamically play external FLV files in Flash Player. The FLVPlayback component is the display area (made up of a customizable skin with playback controls) in which you view video. Simply export your movie as an FLV file from Flash or a video editing programs using the FLV Export plug-in, and then use the FLVPlayback component in Flash to play it back. If you want to include closed captioning (W3C standard XML format Timed Text), you can use the FLVPlayback Captioning component

Work with the FLV Playback Component

1. Create or open a Flash document.

2. Click the **Window** menu, and then click **Components** to open the Components panel.

3. Click the **Video** arrow to expand the list.

4. Drag the **FLVPlayback** component onto the Stage, and then select the component.

5. Click the **Window** menu, and then click **Properties** to open the Properties panel.

6. Click the **Edit Source** button.

7. Click the **Browse folder** icon, navigate to and select the FLV video file that you want to use, and then click **Open**.

8. Select the **Match source dimensions** check box to use the same video size as the file.

9. Click **OK**.

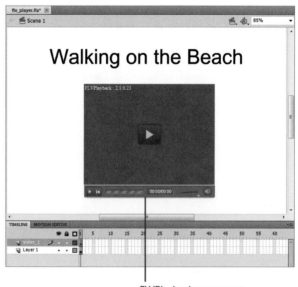

FLVPlayback component

10 Use the Properties panel to change the options you want.

◆ **align.** Specify FLV file alignment in the player.

◆ **autoPlay.** Select or deselect to automatically play the FLV file.

◆ **cuePoints.** Specify a string with the cue points for the video.

◆ **isLive.** Select or deselect whether the FLV is streaming live.

◆ **preview.** Creates a preview for authoring purposes.

◆ **scaleMode.** Select an option to maintainAspectRatio, noScale, or exactFit.

◆ **skin.** Select a skin for the FLV video player.

◆ **skinAutoHide.** Select or deselect to automatically hide or show the skin.

◆ **skinBackgroundAlpha.** Specify a background alpha channel for the skin.

◆ **skinBackgroundColor.** Specify a background color for the skin.

◆ **volume.** Specify a volume setting for the video.

11 Click the **Control** menu, point to **Test Movie**, and then click **Test**.

Working with the Video Encoder

To improve workflow for those of us who love to work with video, Adobe Media Encoder includes a stand-alone video encoder that you can install on a computer dedicated to video encoding. The Adobe Media Encoder lets you batch process video encoding, allowing you to encode several video clips, using different codecs at the same time. The Adobe Media Encoder also lets you edit video clips, add cue points (to trigger other actions), and crop (change viewable area of video) and trim (edit beginning and end points) the video.

Work with the Video Encoder

1. Open the Adobe Media Encoder CS5.

   ◆ Use the Start menu (Win) or Applications folder (Mac).

   ◆ If you're importing a video, click **File**, point to **Import**, click **Import Video**, and then click **Launch Adobe Media Encoder**.

2. Click **Add** to add video files to the batch list.

   ◆ Click the **File** menu, and then click **Add Adobe Premiere Pro Sequence** or **Add Adobe After Effects Composition** to add these file types.

3. Select the video that you want to change settings.

4. Click **Duplicate** to make a copy of the selected video file, which saves the same video file using different compression settings.

5. Click **Remove** to remove the selected video file from the batch list.

6. Click the **Format** menu, and then select a format with which to encode the video or audio clip.

   The selected format displays a list of available presets designed for the delivery format.

7. Click the **Preset** menu, and then select an encoding preset for your intended application.

8 Click the **Output** filename, specify a location and file name for the encoded file or use the default filename from the source clip.

9 Click **Settings**.

The Export Settings dialog box appears, displaying tabs for Source and Output.

10 Click the **Source** tab.

11 Select the **Export Video** check box, click the **Video** tab, and then specify a frame rate, and other video options.

12 Select the **Export Audio** check box, click the **Audio** tab, and then select a kbps data rate, quality setting, and other options.

13 Click the **Crop** button, enter edge values to crop the video, and then drag the in and out point markers below the scrubber bar to set the video trim points.

Click the **Output** tab to preview the cropped image. Use the **Crop Setting** list arrow to select an option.

14 Use the cursor to move the playback head to the frame location you want to embed, click **Add Cue Point**, and then specify the type of cue point you want.

15 Click **OK**.

16 Click **Start Queue** to begin batch processing all the files in the batch list. Click **Stop Queue** to halt the process.

The status column provides information for each video during the encoding process.

Audio tab

Video tab

Working with Alpha Channel Masks

One of the cool features in Flash is its ability to work alpha channel masks. Alpha masks are typically created within video-editing applications, such as Apple's Final Cut Pro or Adobe's Premiere. The process involves opening the image within the video-editing application and creating the transparency using a specific color (referred to as blue or green screening), using luminosity levels, or actually creating a mask in an image-editing application such as Adobe Photoshop, and then importing the mask. For example, you could film yourself against a green screen, and then mask those areas out. When you open the movie in Flash, any other background you place behind the movie will replace the original green screen. They do this in the movies all the time.

Work with Alpha Channel Masks

1. Open your video-editing application, and create a specific alpha channel mask.

   The mask represents the areas of the movie for which you want to maintain transparency.

2. Use your video-editing Export command and then select the Flash FLV format.

3. Click **Options** or select options for exporting a Flash FLV file.

   ◆ If Options is not available, open the Adobe Media Encoder (from the desktop), add the FLV file to the queue select a FLV preset format, and then open the Export Settings dialog box. Click the **Edit** menu, and then click **Export Settings**.

   The Export Settings dialog box appears, displaying tabs for Source and Output.

4 Click the **Source** tab.

5 Select the **Export Video** check box.

6 Click the **Video** tab.

7 Select the **Encode Alpha Channel** check box.

8 Click **OK**.

9 Click **Save** to save the file.

10 Open Flash Professional.

11 Click the **File** menu, point to **Import**, and then click **Import Video**.

12 Use the steps outlined in "Using the Video Import Wizard" on page 326.

13 Move to the Timeline and create a new layer directly underneath the video layer, and name it backdrop.

14 Place an image in the backdrop layer.

15 Click the **Control** menu, point to **Test Movie**, and then click **Test**.

When you view the movie, the areas designated as transparent by the alpha channel mask will display the contents of the backdrop layer, directly through the running video.

See Also

See "Using the Video Import Wizard" on page 326 for more information on using the Video wizard.

See "Working with the Video Encoder" on page 340 for information on Flash video encoding settings.

FLV masked movie   Backdrop image

Exporting as a QuickTime Video

Flash makes it easy to export a Flash document to a QuickTime video using the QuickTime Export Settings dialog box. By default, Flash creates a QuickTime video of the complete source document with the same dimensions. However, you can change the export options. In the QuickTime Export Settings dialog box, you can set movie dimensions, ignore stage color, specify when to stop exporting and where to store temporary data, and set advanced QuickTime settings. The advanced QuickTime settings are set for optimal playback. If you have experience using QuickTime, you can set the advanced settings to customize the results you want.

Export Flash as a QuickTime Video

1. Click the **File** menu, point to **Export**, and then click **Export Movie**.

2. Click the **Format** popup (Mac) or **Save As Type** list arrow (Win), and then click **QuickTime (*.mov)**.

3. Type the new file name.

4. Navigate to the drive or folder location where you want to save the document.

5. Click **Save**.

   The QuickTime Export Settings dialog box opens.

6. If available, specify the width and height in pixels you want for the QuickTime video.

   ◆ To maintain the same ratio of width and height, select the **Maintain Aspect Ratio** check box.

7. To create an alpha channel using the Stage color, select the **Ignore Stage Color (Generate Alpha Channel)** check box.

   The alpha channel is encoded as a transparent track, letting you overlay the exported QuickTime movie on top of other content to alter the background color or scene.

Supported Export Video Formats

Extension	Description
.swf	Shockwave movie
.avi	Audio Video Interleaved
.mov	QuickTime
.gif	Animated GIF
.wav	Audio WAV
.jpg, .jpeg, .gif, .png	Sequence of images for JPEG, GIF, or PNG

8 Click the **When Last Frame Is Reached** or **After Time Elapsed** option and then specify the time you want in the format (hh:mm:ss.msec), where hh is hours, mm is minutes, ss is seconds, and msec is milliseconds.

9 Click the **In Memory** or **On Disk** option to specify where you want to store temporary data.

10 Click **QuickTime Settings**.

11 Select the **Video** check box, and then click the buttons where you want to make video option changes.

◆ **Settings.** Select video compression type, quality, frame rate, and data rate.

◆ **Filter.** Select a video filter, such as blur, emboss, sharpen, and special effects.

◆ **Size.** Select a standardized size, such as NTSC, PAL, etc.

12 Select the **Sound** check box, and then click the buttons where you want to make audio option changes.

◆ **Settings.** Select sound compression, sample rate, sample bit size, and usage (mono or stereo).

13 To optimize for Internet streaming, select the **Prepare For Internet Streaming** check box, and then select the option you want.

14 Click **OK**.

15 Click **Export**.

16 Upon completion, click **OK**.

Exporting as a FLV File

The FLV (Flash Video) file format allows you to import or export a static video stream including encoded audio. For example, you could use the FLV format to save video for use with communications applications, such as video conferencing. When an FLV clip is exported with streaming audio, the audio is compressed using the Streaming Audio settings in the Publish Settings dialog box, and the file is compressed. FLV files can be used with Flash's new media components to create streaming video files directly in a Flash movie. In order to use the FLV format, you must first set up the video files for exporting. Any Flash document that contains video clips will work. When FLV video files are played back, they're handled as a progressive download—Progressive downloads begin playing as soon as a certain percent of the complete file has been transferred. The playback is not as quick as that provided by streaming video, but it's not as slow as complete file download formats such as the MPEG video.

Export Video Clips into the FLV File Format

1. Select a video clip in the Library panel.
2. Click the **Libraries Options** button, and then click **Properties**.
3. Click **Export**.
4. Enter a name for the exported file.
5. Select a location where it will be saved.
6. Click **Save**.
7. Click **OK**.

Did You Know?

You can use the Property Inspector to modify a Flash FLV video clip. Drag the FLV video file onto the Stage, select the video clip, and then open the Property Inspector. The Property Inspector lets you give the clip an instance name; change the width, height, and registration point of the clip; and even swap a video clip with another video clip.

Using Basic ActionScripts

Introduction

Flash's programming language is called ActionScript. **ActionScript** lets you create detailed instructions on how the Flash movie will perform. Flash CS5 allows you to build applications using two different versions of ActionScript, either ActionScript 1.0 & 2.0 or ActionScript 3.0.

In this chapter, you'll learn the basics of ActionScript along with scripting as it relates to ActionScript 2.0. In the next chapter, you'll learn about scripting as it relates to ActionScript 3.0. ActionScripts can use an event to trigger the specific action. Say you create a button, and you want the ActionScript to trigger an instruction that will stop the movie, but only when the user clicks the button object. The defined event is the user clicking his mouse, and the action would be to stop playing the movie. ActionScript is a relatively easy language to learn, but a very precise language to code, so pay close attention to the syntax.

The good news is that once you master the language and the syntax, the full power of Flash is available to you. You can create ActionScripts that are triggered (the event) by specific data, or information typed in by a visitor. You can even create ActionScripts that are sensitive to variables such as date and time. Flash helps you by giving you functions (English-like script) and as your ActionScript skills grow, you can even create and call your own functions. Each new version of Flash moves the ActionScripting language closer and closer to JavaScript. The power of Flash is fully realized when you write ActionScripts and incorporate them in your Flash documents.

What You'll Do

View the Actions Panel

Set ActionScript Preferences

Understand Properties and Methods

Apply Properties and Methods to an Object

Use Dot Syntax

Understand Data Types

Use Functions

Use Conditional Statements

Attach a Mouse Event to a Button

Work with Frame Events

Work with Clip Events

Attach a Clip Event to a Movie Clip

Work with Loops

Use For Loops

Work with ActionScript Behaviors

Viewing the Actions Panel

The Actions panel is gives the Flash designer control of a Flash document by allowing him/her to create and edit actions for an object or frame. To use the Actions panel, select an object on the stage, or select a frame on the Timeline, click the Window menu, and then click Actions. Scripts can be typed directly into the Actions panel using the Script pane, or augmented by using a list of installed Actions in the Toolbox.

- **Toolbox.** Supplies a list of all installed actions, either ActionScript 1.0 & 2.0 or ActionScript 3.0

- **Script pane.** Enter the Actions into the Script pane.

- **Script Navigator pane.** Gives reference to all the Scripts in the active movie.

- **Current Script tag.** Indicates which script is being edited.

- **Pin Script.** Adds a tab for a selected script.

- **Options menu.** Contains options that control and format the Actions panel.

- **Add Statement.** Lets you add script elements to the current action.

- **Find, and Find and Replace.** Searches the active script.

- **Insert Target Path.** Inserts a specific target clip into the action.

- **Check Syntax.** Checks the current action for syntax errors.

- **Auto Format.** Cleans up the script by auto indenting.

- **Auto Close Bracket.** When you type an open bracket {, Flash automatically adds the corresponding close bracket }. (**New!**)

- **Show Code Hint.** Gives you hints to the syntax of the action as you type.

- **Debug Options.** Add or remove breakpoints into the action to pause on the specified line of code.

- **Collapse and Expand.** Collapse between braces, collapse selection, or expand all.

- **Comments.** Apply a block or line comment.

- **Code Snippet.** Code Snippets provides ActionScript 3.0 code segments to use in scripts. (**New!**)

- **Script Assist for 3.0.** Script assist provides a visual interface for editing scripts (syntax completion and parameter descriptions).

- **Help.** Provides online help.

Setting ActionScript Preferences

Since ActionScripting is so important, Flash gives you the ability to control the Actions panel through preferences. ActionScript preferences give you the ability to control the font and size of the text typed into the Actions panel, as well as using syntax coloring to help you visualize the code. You can also set AutoFormat preferences to specify the automatic formatting you want for your ActionScript code.

Set ActionScript Preferences

1. Click the **Flash** (Mac) or **Edit** (Win) menu, and then click **Preferences**.

2. Click the **ActionScript** category.

3. Select from the following options:

   ◆ **Automatic Close Brace.** Select to automatically insert a close bracket. (**New!**)

   ◆ **Automatic Indentation.** Instructs Flash to perform syntax indentation.

   ◆ **Tab Size.** Enter a value for the number of spaces used.

   ◆ **Code Hints.** Gives you on-screen hints as you type.

   ◆ **Delay.** Delay before showing a code hint. (0 to 4 seconds)

   ◆ **Font.** Select a font and size for the ActionScript text.

   ◆ **Open/Import and Save/Export.** Select UTF-8 or Default encoding for open and import operations (UTF-8 is best).

   ◆ **Reload Modified Files.** Click to be prompted when Flash needs to reload a modified file.

   ◆ **Class Editor.** Select an editor or Ask to be prompted. (**New!**)

   ◆ **Syntax Coloring.** Choose the syntax-coloring scheme.

   ◆ **Language.** Click ActionScript 2.0 or ActionScript 3.0 to modify the ActionScript sub-settings.

4. Click the **Auto Format** category.

5. Select format check boxes and view the effect in preview.

6. Click **OK**.

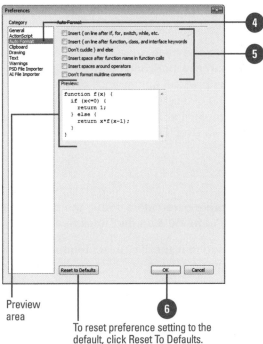

Preview area

To reset preference setting to the default, click Reset To Defaults.

Understanding Properties and Methods

Objects in Flash are defined using two primary identifiers: properties and methods. The **properties** of an object define its characteristics. In the real world, a house would be an object, and its properties would be things like its color, style, and number of windows and doors. In Flash, it would be written something like this:

```
house.color = "green";
house.style = "ranch";
house.windows = "12";
house.doors = "2";
```

In this example, the word *house* is a unique instance name for the house object, and the words *color*, *style*, *windows*, and *doors* represent the properties assigned to this instance. Think of an instance as a copy of a Library item. When you create a movie clip, the object is created in Flash's Library. When you return to the Stage, you can then drag the movie clip from the Library to the Stage (technically, you're moving a Library symbol, created using the movie clip behavior). Once the movie clip is moved to the Stage, it is defined as an instance of the original Library item. When you select an instance on the Stage, Flash's Properties panel lets you give it a unique name. In the previous example, "house" is the unique name.

Giving a Library symbol a unique name gives you a lot of control. For example, you could move two instances of the same movie clip onto the Stage, give each of them its own unique name (house1, house2) in the Properties panel, and then define different properties for each one. Something like this:

```
house1.color = "green";      house2.color = "blue";
house1.style = "ranch";      house2.style = "tudor";
house1.windows = "12";       house2.windows = "8";
house1.doors = "2";          house2.doors = "4";
```

In Flash, most objects have properties. For example, the MovieClip object has property values such as transparency, horizontal and vertical position, and visibility. You might define properties loosely as the physical appearance of a movie clip, as it appears on the Flash Stage. A **method** instructs the object to perform some task. A method is a function that is part of a class definition. For example, if a DVD player is an object, then the methods would be something like: play, record, and stop. Flash methods are written like this:

```
play();
record();
stop();
```

Some methods require parameters within the parenthesis. The following method instructs the play head to move to frame 6 on the Timeline and stop: gotoAndStop(6);

Attaching the method to a specific object requires identifying the object in the ActionScript code: myDVD.gotoAndStop(6);

ActionScript is a language, and just like learning any foreign language, all the words and syntax might seem strange at first; however, the longer you work with the language, the simpler it becomes.

Applying Properties and Methods to an Object

Once you've gotten the hang of writing ActionScripts, the next step is to apply properties and methods to objects in a Flash document. You can have an object and let your visitor control its color. Changing the color is an example of changing an object's properties. To make an object change color, you will need a Flash document that contains a MovieClip and button symbols. An easy script translation would be: Flash, when my visitor clicks (release) on the button, I want you to assign a new color to an object that I gave a unique instance name (change it), and I'm defining that property as objectColor, and change the color (setRGB) to red (0x990000). When you attach ActionScripts to buttons, you're not limited to just a single use. For example, you could drag three instances of the same button symbol on the Stage and repeat the previous code with one exception: change the SetRGB value of one to (0x990000) for red, another to (0x009900) for green, and the third one to (0x000099) for blue.

Apply Properties and Methods

1. Drag the movie clip onto the Stage.

2. Enter a unique instance name in the Properties panel.

3. Drag the button symbol onto the Stage, and then select the symbol.

4. Click the **Window** menu, and then click **Actions** to open the Actions panel.

5. Enter the script (ActionScript 2.0) as shown in the illustration.

   ◆ ActionScript 3.0 example files are available on the Web at *www.perspection.com*.

6. Click the **Control** menu, point to **Test Movie**, and then click **Test**.

7. Click the button to change the color of the object to red.

See Also

See "Creating Invisible Buttons" on page 153 for information on creating invisible buttons.

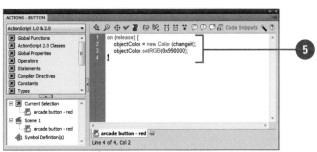

Using Dot Syntax

ActionScript, just like any human language, has rules you should follow. However, in ActionScripts, you have to follow the rules or it won't work. One of the more important rules to follow is the use of dot syntax. The use of dots (.) in a script serves several purposes. First, is to specify the target path to a particular Timeline. For example, **_root.america.kansas.wichita** defines a movie clip on the main (_root) Timeline with the name america, containing a movie clip named kansas, which in turn contains a movie clip named wichita. Dot syntax is used to create a road map for Flash to follow. Dot syntax is a separator between two or more parts of a Flash script.

Another use of dot syntax is to change the properties and methods for a specific object. Since ActionScript, by definition is an object-oriented language, Flash performs its responsibilities by instructing an object to do something (method), or by changing a property. For example, **star._rotation = 90;** instructs Flash to rotate the MovieClip instance named *star*, 90 degrees (property). To instruct the star MovieClip instance to play (method), you would enter the following code: **star.play();**

Movie Clip with Instance Name: *MovieA*

ActionScript 2.0

Understanding Data Types

When you use ActionScripts, you have the ability to work with data. Data can be information entered in by a visitor in an input data field, or it can be computer information such as the current position of the mouse, or the date and time. When you work with data, you have 4 possible data types:

- **String.** Allows for the entering of text values.

- **Number.** Allows for the entering of numeric values.

- **Boolean.** A Boolean state has two values; typically true or false.

- **Object.** Serves as a storage device for any data type, including other objects.

Use Data Types to Control Information

Since data types control the type of information that can be entered into a data field, you can use them to validate the data someone is entering. For example, you want to create a calculator to convert between degrees Fahrenheit and Celsius. To do this, you will need an input field for someone to enter the current temperature in Fahrenheit, a button that would perform the calculation, and then a dynamic text field for the result, and one for an error message.

1. Select the Input Field, and then give it a unique variable name in the Properties panel.

2. Select the Error Dynamic Text Field and give it a unique variable name in the Properties panel.

3. Select the Results Dynamic Text Field, and give it a unique variable name in the Properties panel.

4. Select the button instance, and then enter a script into the Actions panel (see the example file for script details).

When the movie is played, the visitor will enter a value into the data field, and it will be evaluated as to whether it's purely numeric. If it isn't, an error message will display in the dynamic error field. If the field contains numbers, then the calculation will perform the conversion and display the results displayed in the output field.

Error Message using text

Error Message using a blank field

Correct data...no error message

Using Functions

A **function** is a block of ActionScript code that can be reused anywhere in a SWF file. If you pass values as parameters to a function, the function will operate on those values. A function can also return values. Flash contains built-in functions that let you access certain information and perform certain tasks, such as getting the version number of Flash Player hosting the SWF file (getVersion()). Functions that belong to an object are called methods. Functions that don't belong to an object are called top-level functions and are found in the Functions category of the Actions panel.

Each function has its own characteristics, and some functions require you to pass certain values. If you pass more parameters than the function requires, the extra values are ignored. If you don't pass a required parameter, the empty parameters are assigned the undefined data type, which can cause errors when you export a script. To call a function, it must be in a frame that the playhead has reached.

To call a function, simply use the function name and pass any required parameters. The following code describes a common syntax for creating functions:

```
function firstFunction (x, y, z) {

    // place all actions here;

}
```

Calling a Function

Functions begin with the word function, followed by the name of the function (user-defined). The area enclosed by parenthesis is used for passing parameters to the function actions. If the parameters are left blank, you're essentially creating a generic function that will function the same way every time it's called. If the function contains parameters, it will perform in a unique way each time it's called. When you call a function, you're instructing Flash to execute all of the actions within that function. Therefore, if firstFunction contained 20 actions, all of them would be executed by using a single line of script. To call a function, simply add this line to the action:

```
myFunction ();
```

Passing Parameters to a Function

If the function has been defined to accept parameter information, you can use the following line of script:

```
myFunction (parameter 1, parameter2);
```

Once a Function is defined, it can be called anytime it's needed. Therefore, it's a good practice to define all of your functions in frame 1 of the active Flash document. That way they can be called anytime after that.

Using Conditional Statements

Conditional statements in ActionScript are a critical part of interactivity. They let you program a script based on any number of conditions. For example, in the morning, you say good day, or good morning to someone you meet. In doing so, you made a conditional choice.

ActionScript does the same thing. You can create an ActionScript that checks the time of day. If it's before noon, Flash responds with a Good Morning message. If it's from noon to 5, Flash says Good Afternoon, or from 5 till midnight, Flash says Good Evening. This type of condition is known as an if/else condition. If this happens, do this... else do that. Since a variable can be almost anything you can measure on a computer, and a conditional statement is made up of two or more variables, ActionScript can be taken to a point where it almost thinks for itself. The previous example could be expressed in flow charting the following way:

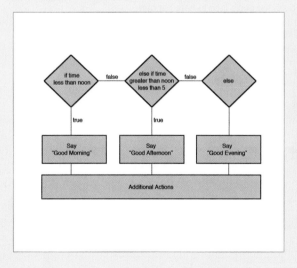

Typically, when you're creating a conditional statement, you're comparing one element against another using operators. The following operators are available to create conditional statements:

- ◆ == Checks for equality between two values (is time of day equal to 5).

- ◆ != Checks for inequality between two values.

- ◆ < Checks for less than (is value A less than value B).

- ◆ > Checks for greater than (is value A greater than value B).

- ◆ <= Checks for less than or equal to between two values.

- ◆ >= Checks for greater than or equal to between two values.

- ◆ && Checks for a logical AND (if day == "Friday" && time > 5).

- ◆ || Checks for a logical OR (if day == "Saturday" || day == "Sunday").

Using these operators to check between two or more values, you can create complex ActionScripts that react differently based on the available data. To create a dynamic field that checks the time, and responds with the appropriate answer, you would enter the following code:

```
if (time > "0000 &&  time < 1200) {
    response = "Good Morning";
} else if (time >1200 && time < 1700) {
    response = "Good Afternoon";
}else if (time > 1700 && time < 2400);
    response = "Good Evening"
}
```

Attaching a Mouse Event to a Button

Attaching a mouse event to a button is probably the easiest of all the event handlers. For example, you have a movie clip of a dog that contains a barking audio file. When the movie clip plays, the dog barks. The trick is to have the dog bark when the visitor rolls their mouse over the dog's face. To do this, you will need to create an invisible button and then attach the mouse event to the invisible button.

Attach an Event to a Button

1. Click the **Insert** menu, and then click **New Symbol**.

2. Select the **Button** type, and then name the symbol.

3. Click **OK**.

4. Create a blank keyframe in the Hit state of the button, and then create a shape.

   Leave the Up, Over, and Down states blank.

5. Exit the Symbol editing mode, and then return to the Stage.

6. Drag a movie clip onto the Stage.

7. Create a new layer, and then name the layer.

8. Drag the invisible button onto the Stage, and then place it over the area of the image you want to use as a button.

9. Enter the script (ActionScript 2.0) as shown in the illustration.

   ◆ ActionScript 3.0 example files are available on the Web at *www.perspection.com*.

   When the visitor rolls into or out of the invisible button, the rollOver or rollOut event handlers will trigger the playing or stopping of the dog movie clip.

10. Click the **Control** menu, point to **Test Movie**, and then click **Test**.

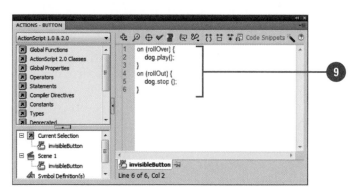

Working with Frame Events

Frame event handlers are easy to understand. When an action is attached to a frame, the action is triggered when the play head hits the frame. For example, you want to create a frame event that swaps images on the Stage, and you want the images to swap every 40 frames. You can attach an ActionScript that swaps the image, and place the action every 40 frames. When the play head hits the frame, the action executes. When you attach an ActionScript to a frame, you'll need a blank keyframe on the Timeline, and it is strongly recommended that you always place ActionScripts in a separate layer from access and control. In addition, if you're planning to swap images in a Flash movie, it's always best to use a blank movie clip (called a placeholder) to hold the images.

Attach an ActionScript to a Frame

1. Drag a blank movie clip onto the Stage, and then select the clip.

2. Give the movie clip a unique instance name in the Properties panel.

3. Create a new layer, and then name the layer.

4. Create blank keyframes at frame numbers 1, 21, 41, and 61.

5. Select a frame, click the **Insert** menu, point to **Timeline**, and then click **Blank Keyframe**.

6. Select frame 1, and then enter the script (ActionScript 2.0) as shown in the illustration.

    ◆ ActionScript 3.0 example files are available on the Web at *www.perspection.com*.

7. Select frames 21, 41, and 61, and then repeat the script, except change the name of the image you want to load (image_b.jpg, image_c.jpg, image_d.jpg).

8. Click the **Control** menu, point to **Test Movie**, and then click **Test**.

Working with Clip Events

If you're working with ActionScript 2.0 (not supported in ActionScript 3.0), you can attach clip events to movie clips, which triggers an action specified in the onClipEvent handler. Event handlers, also known as event listeners, control when events in Flash occur. When you create a script, some event will be invoked to trigger that particular action. You might want a specific movie clip to stop playing when another movie clip loads on the Stage, or when the user clicks or moves their mouse.

The Clip Event is one of a series of event handlers that Flash uses to create actions within a Flash movie. You can attach event handlers directly to a button or movie clip instance by using the onClipEvent() or the on() handlers. The onClipEvent() handles movie clip events, and on() handles button events. To use an on() or onClipEvent() handler, attach it directly to an instance of a button or movie clip on the Stage, and then specify the event you want to handle for that instance. For example, the following on() event handler executes whenever the user clicks the button the handler is attached to.

```
on(press) {
    trace("The button has been pressed.");
}
```

You can specify two or more events for each on() handler, separated by commas. The ActionScript in a handler executes when one of the events specified by the handler occurs. For example, the following on() handler attached to a button will execute whenever the mouse rolls over or out of the button.

```
on(rollOver, rollOut) {
    trace("mouse rolled in or out");
}
```

If you want different scripts to run when different events occur, you have the option to attach more than one handler to an object. You can attach onClipEvent() handlers to the same movie clip instance. The first would execute when the movie clip first loads (or appears on the Stage); the second executes when the movie clip is unloaded from the Stage.

```
onClipEvent(load) {
    trace("loaded");
}
onClipEvent (unload) {
    trace("unloaded");
```

Assigning a Clip Event using the Behaviors panel.

Assigning a Clip Event directly in the Actions panel.

Attaching a Clip Event to a Movie Clip

For ActionScript 2.0, you can only attach an onClipEvent() to a movie clip instance that has been placed on the Stage. You can't attach an onClipEvent() to a movie clip instance that is created at runtime; for example, using the attachMovie() method. However, you can still attach multiple event handlers. Using different event handlers within the same Flash document do not conflict with each other. You could have a button with an on(press) handler that tells the SWF file to play, and the same button can have an onPress method, for which you define a function that tells an object on the Stage to rotate. When the button is clicked, the SWF file plays, and the object will rotate. Being able to consolidate different event handlers with a single instance gives you greater control, as well as less Stage clutter.

Attach an onClipEvent to a Movie Clip

1. Create or open a Flash document (ActionScript 2.0), place a movie clip on the Stage, and then select the movie clip.

2. Give the movie clip a unique instance name in the Properties panel.

3. Move down the Timeline and add a keyframe at frame 80.

4. Click the **Insert** menu, point to **Timeline**, and then click **Keyframe**.

5. Add a second movie clip to the Stage, and then select the second movie clip.

6. Enter the script as shown in the illustration.

7. Click the **Control** menu, point to **Test Movie**, and then click **Test**.

   When the playhead hits frame 80 it loads the second movie clip. The loading of the movie will trigger the onClipEvent handler, and stop the playing of the movie clip with the unique instance name of movie2.

Working with Loops

Loops allow Flash to perform an action repeatedly. You can use a loop to create a dynamic drop-down menu, validate data, search for text, duplicate movie clips, and even detect collisions in games that have projectiles and objects. **Conditional statements** let you execute an action based on a specific condition. You can have a specific action continue to loop until a certain condition is met. For example, continue to search for a specific text string until it is found or the end of the text document is reached. Loops come in two forms—While loops and For loops. While loops wait for a specific condition to start or stop the loop. That may sound similar to the For loop, with one exception: The For loop is self-contained, and the While loop works with an external condition, or one outside the scope of the loop.

◆ **While Loops.** While loops continue to execute while a certain condition exists (keep looping or searching) until a specific value is reached.

```
i = 4;
while (var i > 0) {
    my_mc.duplicateMovieClip("newMC" + i, i );
    i--;
}
```

◆ **For Loops.** For loops are self-contained counters. For example, loop (repeat the action)   ten times and then stop.

```
x = x;
for (x=0; x<=10, ++x) {
    myClip.duplicateMovieClip ("myClip" + x, x);
    myClip._rotation =45 + x * 10;
}
```

When you create a Looping action, you can further control the loop by using the following loop exceptions:

◆ **Continue.** The continue exception lets you stop the current loop from performing its actions and jump directly to the next cycle of the loop.

◆ **Break.** The break exception is used to exit a loop, even if the original condition that is driving the loop is still true.

For example, if you create a While loop using the following script:

```
total = 0;
i = 0:
while (++i <=20) {
    if (i == 10) {
        continue;
    }
    total +=i;
}
```

The results would be a script that executes and adds 1 to total; unless the value of i equaled 10. This would create a sequence of numbers 1 2 3 4 5 6 7 8 9 11 12 13 14 15 16 17 18 19 20. If you had used the break exception in place of continue, the values would read: 1 2 3 4 5 6 7 8 9. Therefore, it loops whether For or While are controlled by internal or external conditions, and using a break or continue exception gives you further control over the loop.

Using For Loops

The For loop works with an increasing or decreasing numeric value. For example, you could use a For loop to create several copies of a movie clip on the Stage. Letting the For loop control movie clips to the Stage is far more efficient than having to move them one at a time. In addition, the visitor can control when the items appear on the Stage using a button.

Use For Loops

1. Drag a movie clip from the Library to the Stage, and then select the movie clip.

2. Enter a unique instance name for the movie clip in the Properties panel.

3. Place a button on the Stage, and then select the button.

4. Enter the script (ActionScript 2.0) as shown in the illustration.

   ◆ ActionScript 3.0 example files are available on the Web at *www.perspection.com*.

When you play the movie, clicking on the button causes the action to loop 10 times. Each time it loops, it duplicates the original movie clip and rotate it by 45 degrees plus the current value of x times 10.

Did You Know?

You can use a For Loop to pause a Flash movie. Select a value, instruct the loop to increment by 1, and then loop until the value is reached. Use a loop timer for such items as a Flash slide show, where you want the slides to display on the stage for a given number of seconds before moving to the next slide.

Working with ActionScript Behaviors

Behaviors are time-savers because they give you sections of ActionScript 2.0 code (not supported in ActionScript 3.0; see Code Snippets in the next Chapter) for common Flash tasks. Behaviors are a great way to introduce yourself to the wonderful world of ActionScripting without having to write all the code. For example, if you want to add a Play ActionScript to a button, you can do it using the Add button in the Behaviors panel, or you can write out the code on your own; see the example code below. Using Behaviors, as opposed to writing the code by hand, is not better, it's simply faster. The more time you save doing common Action-Scripting tasks using Behaviors, the more time you will have for the creative process.

Using the Behaviors Panel

You use the Behaviors panel to apply the behavior to a triggering object, such as a button. You specify the event that triggers the behavior, such as releasing the mouse. Next select a target object, such as the movie clip instance, and then select settings for behavior parameters, such as a frame number or label, or a relative or absolute path. Flash comes with built-in behaviors, such as Load Graphic, Duplicate Movieclip, and GotoAndPlay At Frame Or Label. To add and configure a

behavior, select a trigger object, and then step through the following general instructions (steps may vary depending on the behavior):

1 Click the **Window** menu, and then click **Behaviors**.

2 Click the **Add (+)** button, and then select a behavior from the menu.

3 If necessary, select settings for the behavior parameters, and then click **OK**.

4 Under Event, click **On Release** (the default event), and then select a mouse event from the menu.

Add button   Click to select a mouse event.

Behavior parameters

Example Play ActionScript 2.0 code

```
on (release) {
    if(this.video_1._parent._currentframe == this.video_1.parent._totalframes){
        this.video_1parent.gotoAndPlay(1);
    } else {
        this.video_1._parent.play();
    }
}
```

Working with ActionScript 3.0

Introduction

Do you like Flash games and cool features on YouTube, like jumping from standard view to HD? There are two faces to Flash: the one you see and then the complex scripting engine, called ActionScript, you don't. Without ActionScript Flash would not be interactive. ActionScript is the scripting language built within Flash that allows you to build interactive solutions. Any Flash movie where you need to click, drag or pause requires the use of ActionScript to instruct Flash what to do. ActionScript is the core to all interactivity and logic built into Flash.

The release of Flash CS3 introduced ActionScript 3.0, a significant overhaul of the scripting language. Older versions of ActionScript ran slowly with large and complex scripts. ActionScript 3.0 changed this. ActionScript 3.0 is up to 10x faster than ActionScript 2.0 and brings a whole lot more functionality to the party. ActionScript 3.0 adopted a true object-oriented approach to development, a technique that allows Flash applications to compete with solutions developed with Microsoft's .NET or Oracle's Java. ActionScript 3.0 dramatically extends what can be accomplished by increasing the speed of Flash through the Flash Player 9 and 10. With ActionScript 3.0 and Flash Player 10.1, you can deliver Flash solutions to more desktops, devices and systems than ever before. ActionScript 3.0 is now the default scripting language in Flash CS5.

In this chapter, you'll learn why ActionScript 3.0 is a programming language you will want to start using, what has changed from earlier versions of ActionScript, what is the same and how you can make your applications rock by using ActionScript 3.0. The only challenge you have is to decide what to develop first.

What You'll Do

Use Object-Oriented Programming

Enable Flash to Execute Solutions Faster with AVM 2.0

Use ActionScript 3.0

Change ActionScript 3.0 Settings

Insert Code with Code Hints

Insert and Create Code Snippets

Develop Solutions Built with the DOM3 Model

Work with Classes

Work with Objects and Classes

Use NameSpaces in your Projects

Control Data

Manipulate XML with E4X

Use Regular Expressions

Control Text

Draw with the Shape Class

Extend Flash with Open Source Libraries

Using Object-Oriented Programming

Objects are the key to understanding object-oriented programming. In object-oriented programming (OOP), an object is just as real as an object in this world. For example, your dog, or even your computer are objects that exist in the real world. Real-world objects share two characteristics with objects in the computer world: They have a specific state and behavior. For example, dogs have a state such as their name, color, breed, and if they're hungry. Dog behaviors would be: barking, fetching, and wagging their tails. All objects in the real and computer worlds have a behavior and a state.

Computer objects are modeled after real-world objects in that they also have a specific state and behavior. A **class** is a representation of an object that stores information about its data type, state, and behaviors. A class can include three types of characteristics: properties, methods, and events. A **property** represents different data associated with an object. A **method** is an action that can be performed by an object. An **event** is a system, application, or user action, such as a mouse click, that triggers an action related to an object.

After you create a class, you can also create new classes based on the existing one, known as **subclassing** or extending a class. The subclass inherits all the properties and methods of the parent class, known as the **superclass**. For example, you could create a superclass called Parents, and a subclass called Children. Inheritance allows one class definition (subclass) to include all the functionality of a different class definition (superclass). You can also additional methods and properties to the subclass as well as override methods inherited from a superclass, which is

called **polymorphism**. Inheritance and subclassing are very useful for large projects where you can share similar functionality and reduce the amount of code.

An object maintains its state using one or more variables. A **variable** is an item of data named by an identifier, and an object performs its behavior with methods. Everything an object understands (its state) and what it can do (its behavior) is expressed by the variables and the methods within that object.

An object that represents a speeding car would have variables that instruct the object as to speed, direction, and color. These variables are known as instance variables because they contain the state for a particular object, and in object-oriented terminology, a particular object is called an **instance**. In addition to its variables, the car would have methods assigned to change speed and turn on the lights. These methods are formally known as instance methods because they inspect or change the state of a particular instance.

• Speed = "fast"
• Direction = "north"
• Color = "yellow"

• Change Speed (faster or slower)
• Lights (on or off)

Variables   Methods

Enabling Flash to Execute Solutions Faster with AVM 2.0

Flash Player, the plug-in you install in your Web browser to play back Flash SWF files, is the key to success in building fast applications. To compile and then run any ActionScript in your Flash movies the Flash Player uses a tool called the ActionScript Virtual Machine, or AVM. For ActionScript 1.0 and 2.0, the Flash Player uses AVM 1.0. Flash Player 9 introduced a new AVM, called AVM 2.0, that is dedicated to running just ActionScript 3.0 SWF files. To put it simply: AVM 2.0 rocks. It makes your code zip along.

AVM 2.0 is critical to Adobe's future success with Flash. With AVM 2.0, you can build applications that have the speed and complexity of traditional desktop applications. Examples of this include Adobe's WorkFlow Lab, a tool that allows you to develop complex Workflow solutions and competes directly with Microsoft's desktop tool Visio; Adobe Story, a tool that allows you to script rich media and video productions; and Kuler, a sophisticated color management tool. Using these tools has the same feel and responsiveness as traditional desk top application. But they are not. They are all running in Flash.

Developing ActionScript 3.0 solutions that are targeted at the AVM 2.0 rendering engine ensures you'll have highly optimized Flash solutions. While ActionScript 3.0 is not required for content that runs in Adobe Flash Player 9 or later, it allows performance improvements that are available only with the AVM 2.0. ActionScript 3.0 code can execute up to ten times faster than legacy ActionScript code.

Flash Player 9 supports AVM 1.0 for backward compatibility with existing and legacy content. Flash Player 7 and 8 only support AVM 1.0 and not AVM 2.0. However, there are a few things you need to know about compatibility. A SWF file cannot combine ActionScript 1.0 or 2.0 with ActionScript 3.0 code, and ActionScript code can load an SWF file with ActionScript 1.0 or 2.0, but it cannot access the file's variables and functions (except you can use the loadMovieNum() command and pass a level parameter). If you have ActionScript 1.0 or 2.0 code and want to use version 3.0 code, you need to migrate all the old code to version 3.0. If you want to use behaviors, you need to use ActionScript 2.0; behaviors are not available for ActionScript 3.0.

Virtual Machines and JavaScript

Web Browsers use virtual machines to run JavaScript. JavaScript is a kissing cousin to ActionScript. Both technologies are structured on the international ECMA-262 scripting format, or ECMAScript as it is often referred too. Web browsers such as Google's Chrome, Apple's Safari, Mozilla's Firefox and Microsoft's Internet Explorer all use Scripting JVM's (JavaScript Virtual Machines) to render content. Many of these companies have even given their JVM engine's cool code names, such as V8 for Chrome, SquirrelFish for Safari and TraceMonkey for FireFox. Unfortunately, Microsoft win's the prize for least inspired name by calling their JVM just JS, for JavaScript. Of course, Adobe's AVM 2.0 is a close second. Any chance of getting a cool code name for AVM 3.0, Adobe?

Using ActionScript 3.0

ActionScript 3.0 has undergone significant changes. This does not mean that if you have worked with Flash ActionScript 1.0 or 2.0 that you will be completely lost, but it will require that you learn new ways to use your code.

Understanding ActionScript 3.0

ActionScript 3.0 is a robust programming model (completely up-to-date with the latest release of the ECMAScript standard) familiar to developers with a basic knowledge of object-oriented programming. If you have developed for other programming languages, such as Java, C++ or C#, then you have heard of this term. Object-oriented programming allows you break your code into objects that can be easily re-used. With object-oriented programming, it's easier to manage an application that has a collection of smaller files than one large file.

There are number of changes that will take a while to get used. The main changes are:

- ActionScript is located in Class files or in the Timeline.
- Code design is truly object oriented.
- You cannot add ActionScript directly to movie clips or buttons instances.
- Triggering events has changed.
- Loading data has changed.
- XML is managed differently.

Some other enhancements include more run-time exceptions for common error conditions, added use of run-time type information, improved use of properties and classes with sealed classes, added use of method closures for event handling, added use of industry standard ECMAScript for XML, more support for regular expressions, and added primitive types (int and uint).

There are a score of smaller changes. As you dive directly into ActionScript 3.0 you will find a learning curve as you move from ActionScript 2.0. Is it all worthwhile to go through the pain? Absolutely. ActionScript 3.0 is simply so much faster and more powerful that it is worth the undertaking.

Working with ActionScript 3.0

There are two ways in which you can work with ActionScript. The first method is to add ActionScript to the Timeline. This will be familiar to earlier Flash developers. A good practice to get into is to have a layer in that Timeline that is dedicated to just working with ActionScript. Adobe recommends that you label the ActionScript label "Actions." Locking the "Actions" layer will prevent you from accidentally adding movie clips into it.

The second method is to insert ActionScript into Flash files with a Class file. Class files have a long history in the development world. With a Class file you can now specify both Public and Private Classes. Using the Private keyword restricts the use of the attribute defined in just that class and not shared with other classes. This is useful as you develop instruction that needs to be executed privately in a closed environment.

Other major changes include:

- Developing Solutions Built with the DOM3 event model.
- Using Namespaces in your projects.
- Controlling Data.
- Controlling Text.
- Drawing with the Shape Class.
- Ability to easily work with external ActionScript Libraries.

ActionScript 2.0 and 3.0 Similarities

With all of the changes between ActionScript 3.0 and 2.0 it's important to remember that there is a lot of functionality that is the same between them. For instance you still use the following in the same way:

- Variables
- Math object
- If/Else Statements
- Switch Statements
- String
- Date to control the use of date and time
- Array to build a structured collection of data
- Boolean to specify a true or false

The following works in ActionScript 2.0 and ActionScript 3.0:

```
var str:String = new String("Hello, ");

var str2:String = new String("World");

trace (str + str2);
```

You can see that the overall syntax structure is the same between both versions of ActionScript. You still end your code with curly brackets, your variable names are still case sensitive, your variable names cannot start with a number and you still use number class objects the same way.

For specific details about using an ActionScript language, click the Help menu, click Flash Help, and then look in the *Programming ActionScript 2.0 or 3.0* or the *ActionScript 2.0 or 3.0 Language and Components Reference* online chapter.

Extending ActionScript with Open Source Libraries

The core to ActionScript 3.0 is that it can be easily extended. To this end, you can use dozens of great Open Source Libraries that can be used to extend the functionality of Flash. Great examples are:

- **Box2D Physics Engine** (*http://box2dflash.sourceforge.net/*).

- **CoreLib** (*http://code.google.com/p/as3corelib/*) a collection of basic utilities such as MD5 hashing, JSON serialization and advanced data parsing.

- **Syndication Library** (*http://code.google.com/p/as3syndication lib/*) a library that allows you to parse all ATOM and RSS feeds easily.

- **AlivePDF** (*http://www.fpdf.org/*) a library that allows you to convert your Flash screen content to PDF.

These are some of the best Libraries you can use. Each comes with its own level of documentation.

Extending ActionScript with C/C++

ActionScript can be extended using C/C++. The Open Source project Brajeshwar.com (http://brajeshwar.com/2008/cc-to-action-script-compiler/) is a project that allows you to take C++ programs and compile them to run in Flash. As an Example, they were able to take the C++ version of Quake, convert it and run it in Flash. That is darn impressive and could not be done with ActionScript 2.0.

Changing ActionScript 3.0 Settings

To take advantage of the new powerful AVM 2.0 and ActionScript 3.0 you must be publishing your Flash movies to target Flash Player 9 or later. Adobe has done a great job of ensuring that the latest release of the Flash Player is installed on your computer. For instance, with the release of Flash Player 9, Adobe installed a feature that automatically updates your Player on your PC, Mac users receive updates through the Mac OS update tool and—as part of Flash Player 10.1—will now receive automatic updates as soon as new releases are available. Flash Player 10.1 will help your Flash movies to play back more efficiently on Mac based computers, especially for mobile devices, such as an Android, Palm Pre or BlackBerry phones. Flash Player 10.1 dramatically optimized code for the Cocoa Framework, it uses Apple's Core Animation to render animation). Mobile users simply have not been able to view Flash. Now they can. To change which Flash Player you are targeting you need to open the Publish Settings and modify the Flash Player settings.

Change Publishing Setting for ActionScript 3.0

1. Click **File**, and then click **Publish Settings**.

   The default settings on the Formats tab include Flash and HTML.

2. Click the **Flash** tab.

3. Click the **Player** list arrow, and then click **Flash Player 9** or **Flash Player 10**.

4. Click the **Script** list arrow, and then click **ActionScript 3.0**.

5. Click the **HTML** tab.

6. To publish settings for a specific subversion (an update to a main release) of the selected Flash Player, select the **Detect Flash Version** check box, and then enter the Flash Player subversion you want. For example, 10.1.52. This uses SWObject2 for version detection and embedding SWF into Web pages. (**New!**)

7. Click **OK**.

   You are ready to start developing a ActionScript 3.0 Flash movie that uses AVM 2.0.

Change ActionScript 3.0 Settings

1. Click **File**, and then click **ActionScript Settings**.

2. To create a document class, enter the filename of the ActionScript file without the .as extension.

3. Specify the frame where the class definition resides.

4. Specify any of the following options:

   - **Strict Mode.** Select to to report compiler warnings as errors.

   - **Warnings Mode.** Select to report warnings for issues when updating ActionScript 2.0 to ActionScript 3.0.

   - **Automatically declare state instances.** Select to automatically declare instances on the Stage.

   - **Dialect.** Select ECMAScript or ActionScript 3.0 (Recommended).

5. Click any of the following tabs:

   - **Source path.** Specify the location of the external ActionScript files that contain the class definition.

   - **Library path.** Specify the location of pre-compiled ActionScript code, which resides in the SWC files.

   - **Config constants.** Specify any configuration constants for use with conditional compilation.

6. Click **OK**.

See Also

See "Creating a New Document" on page 12 for more information on creating an ActionScript 3.0 FLA document.

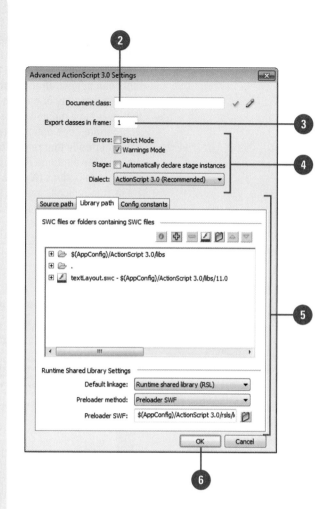

Inserting Code with Code Hints

Code hints makes it easy to insert and edit code accurately. With Code hints, you don't have to remember all of the objects, methods, and properties used in ActionScript. As you enter to type code, you can display the Code Hints popup menu to help you enter it correctly (**New!**). Code hints can appear after the dot (.) following a statement or command, where a property or method needs to appear next, or between parentheses [()] in a method name. The Code Hints popup menu displays appropriate code options based on the currently entered code. When you enter code that refers to a custom ActionScript 3.0 class, you can also display the Code Hints popup menu to help you access the appropriate code options (**New!**). When you use a custom class in a script, Flash automatically imports the related code for its use. Code hinting also works for nested class references, and all classes included in a SWC file.

Use Code Hints

1. Create or open a Flash document.

2. Open the **Actions** panel or Script window.

3. Place the insertion point where you want to add code.

4. Start to type the code you want, and then press Control+Spacebar (Win) or ⌘+Spacebar (Mac) or click the **Show Code Hint** button on the toolbar to manually display the code hints popup menu.

5. Scroll through the list by using the scroll bar or pressing the Up Arrow and Down Arrow keys.

6. To insert a code hint, double-click an item, or select it and then press Enter (Win) or Return (Mac).

   ◆ Press Esc to dismiss the list of code hints.

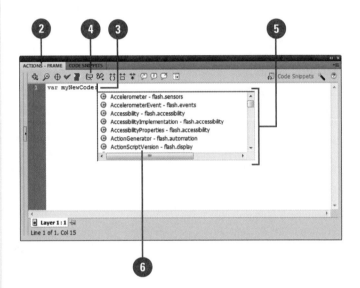

See Also

See "Setting ActionScript Preferences" on page 349 for information on enabling code hinting.

Use Code Hints for Custom Classes

1. Create or open a Flash or class document (ActionScript 3.0).

   ◆ Store the custom classes in the same folder as the document.

2. Open the **Actions** panel or Script window.

3. Place the insertion point where you want to add code.

4. Start to type the code you want, and then press Control+Spacebar (Win) or ⌘+Spacebar (Mac) or click the **Show Code Hint** button on the toolbar to manually display the code hints popup menu.

5. Scroll through the list by using the scroll bar or pressing the Up Arrow and Down Arrow keys.

6. To insert a code hint, double-click an item, or select it and then press Enter (Win) or Return (Mac).

   ◆ Press Esc to dismiss the list of code hints.

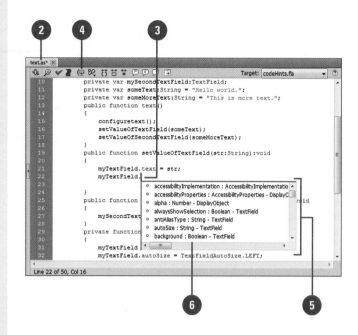

Did You Know?

You can reload code hints without restarting Flash. Open the Actions panel, click the Options menu, and then click Reload Code Hints.

You can save time with Auto close-bracket insertion. When you type an open bracket { in the Actions panel or Script window, Flash automatically adds the corresponding close bracket }. (**New!**)

Code Hinting for Custom Classes

Properties	Options
Type *this*	Code hints for that same class
Type *new+<space>*	Displays a list of available classes and packages
Type *import+<space>*	Displays a list of all the built-in packages and custom packages

Inserting and Creating Code Snippets

As you build Flash documents for ActionScript 3.0, it's almost a certainty that you will use elements over and over again. Flash created a solution that makes it easier to reuse elements called Code Snippets (**New!**). Snippets offer a simple and convenient method of creating reusable code, which especially helpful for those transitioning from ActionScript 2.0 to ActionScript 3.0. They are composed of bits of code and/or content along with comments for usage that you can save, edit, use, and reuse as often as you want. You can use a pre-defined code snippet supplied by Flash or create your own in the Code Snippets panel (**New!**).

Insert a Code Snippet

1. Select the object or Timeline frame in the Flash document where you want to insert/apply the code snippet.

2. Open the **Code Snippets** panel.

3. Click the **arrow** icon next to the folder (Actions, Timeline Navigation, Animation, Load and Unload, Audio and Video and Event Handlers) to display the snippet you want to insert.

4. Select the snippet you want to insert.

5. Click the **Add to current frame** button in the Code Snippets panel.

   TIMESAVER *You can also drag a snippet from the Code Snippets panel directly onto an element, or double-click the code snippet in the Code Snippets panel. In the Actions panel, you can click the Code Snippets button.*

6. Click **Yes** to convert your selection to a movie clip, if necessary.

   A new ActionScript is added to a new layer, labeled Actions, in the Timeline.

New layer with ActionScript

Click to Play/Stop Sound snippet code

Create a Code Snippet

1. Open the **Code Snippets** panel.

2. Click the **Options** button in the Code Snippets panel, and then click **Create New Code Snippet**.

3. Type a title and tooltip.

4. Type the code you want to use in the Code box or click **Auto-fill** to insert the code selected in the Actions panel.

5. Select or clear the **Automatically replace instance_name_here when applying code snippet** check box.

6. Click **OK**.

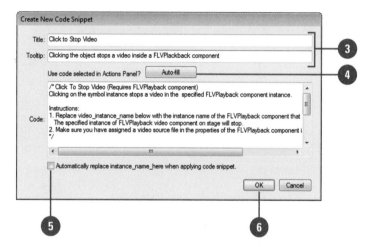

Did You Know?

You can edit an existing code snippet. In the Code Snippets panel, select the snippet you want to edit, click the Options button, click Edit Code Snippets XML, make the changes you want, click the File menu, click Save, and then click the Close button in the Code Snippets tab.

You can copy a code snippet to the clipboard. In the Code Snippets panel, select the snippet you want to copy, click the Copy to Clipboard button, and then click OK, if necessary. Now, you can paste it into the Actions panel or ActionScript file.

For Your Information

Importing and Exporting Code Snippets

If you want to share code snippets with others, you can import or export one or more from the Code Snippets panel. To import a code snippet, click the Options button in the Code Snippets panel, click Import Code Snippets XML, select the XML file, and then click Open. To export a code snippet, select the snippet you want to export in the Code Snippets panel, click the Options button, click Export Code Snippets XML, type a name, specify a location, and then click Save.

Developing Solutions Built with the DOM3 Event Model

ActionScript 3.0 now supports the ECMAScript, DOM3, event model syntax. In laymen's terms, this means that you now use the Listener object to detect when you interact with your Flash movie using either a keyboard, mouse, or the new gesture interfaces used in touching the screen directly.

This is a big move from ActionScript 2.0. As an example, the following script is ActionScript 2.0 that instructs a Movie Clip to jump to frame 25 of a movie:

ActionScript 3.0 uses Listeners to trigger when an event occurs. Listeners are more complex to work with, but, give you more flexibility. There are essentially two parts to a Listener. The first is a function that describes what is going to happen when you trigger an event. The second is the Listener that waits for a specified event to happen, such as mouse clicking on a button.

The following steps adds an ActionScript 3.0 event that mimics the same event as the ActionScript 2.0 example above.

Use ActionScript 3.0

1. Click the **File** menu, click **New**, click **ActionScript 3.0**, and then click **OK**.

2. Create a new Movie clip on the Stage with the name *myMovie*.

3. Create a new layer in the Timeline with the name *Actions*, and then select the layer.

4. Open the **Actions** panel, create the function, and then add the listener that triggers the function.

The function is called *gotoFunction* and the parenthesis dictates that it is looking for a mouse driven event. There is only one instruction in the function, the *gotoAndStop* function that moves the Timeline to frame 25.

The first part of the Listener, *myMovie*, instructs ActionScript to target the movie clip object on the Stage. The second part of the Listener, *addEventListener*, instructs Flash that you are using the Listener object. The parenthesis has two parts that explain that the event is a mouse event and to use the function gotoFunction.

The ActionScript 3.0 event model gives you flexibility to write more complex scripts and to extend the functionality of the event model beyond traditional mouse and keyboard interfaces. To do this you use the core object class controlling events on the screen called the EventsDispatcher class. Through this you can not only leverage standard events such as mouse clicks and the keyboard, but you can extend the class with your event types.

Working with Classes

A common design pattern in Object Oriented programs separates design, programming and data elements. Flash CS5 adds this functionality with the inclusion of Classes. A Class is a packaged document that you can use to explain how UI components, business logic and data elements are to interact.

A Class is a separate ActionScript file that is associated with the main Flash file and movie clips. You can use Flash CS5 as the Class file editor or your favorite text editor such as Eclipse, Notepad or Textedit. A Class file is only a text file. It is very easy to create entire Flash movies using just Class files and not even add any content into a traditional timeline.

Create a Simple Class File

1. Click the **File** menu, click **New**, click **ActionScript 3.0**, and then click **OK**.

2. Click the **File** menu, and then click **Save** to save the file with the name *helloWorld.fla*.

3. Open the **Properties** panel.

4. Click the **Edit Class Definition** button (pencil icon) in the Property inspector, enter a new class with the name *helloClass*, and then click **OK**.

   A new ActionScript file named *helloClass.as* opens with the following ActionScript 3.0 script.

4. Remove the line that says //constructor code and replace it with:

   trace ("Hello, World");

5. Click the **File** menu, and then click **Save** to save the Class file.

6. In the Flash document, click the **Control** menu, point to **Test Movie**, and then click **Test** to view the results.

   The words "Hello, World" posted to the Output panel.

Classes provide you a way in which you can create public and private class elements. The difference between the two is related to how you use the data. For instance, a public property can be shared throughout your whole Flash movie. A private property can only be used within the class it is defined in.

Add Classes to Movie Clips

You can also add separate class references directly to Movie Clips in your Library.

1. Open the **Library** panel.

2. Right-click (Win) or Control-click (Mac) a Movie Clip, and then click **Properties**.

3. In the Properties dialog box, click **Advanced** if necessary, and then select the **Export For ActionScript** check box.

4. Click **OK**.

A class is automatically created for the symbol using the name of the Movie Clip. You can now modify the Class file for the Movie Clip in your favorite text editor.

Working with Objects and Classes

With ActionScript 3.0, you specify a class definition, either document or object level, to work with objects using ActionScript code. To create your own class, you need to follow a certain syntax. First, you enter a package statement to indicate where your class will be found. Then, you enter a class statement to define the name of the class. At this point, you define each property in the class by using variables, and each method by using functions. When you define a class element, such as a property or method, you can also specify an attribute. A private attribute can be called only by code within the class, while a public attribute can be called by any code in the program. After you define a class, you can define a subclass that inherits all the properties and methods of the parent class, or superclass. In the subclass, you can add methods and properties and override others from the superclass, known as polymorphism. If you want to trigger actions based on events, you can use the EventDispatcher class to keep track of event listeners and notify them of events.

Work with Objects and Classes in ActionScript

1. Create or open a Flash document (ActionScript 3.0).

2. Open the **Properties** panel.

3. Click the Stage.

4. In the Class field, type the name of the ActionScript file to create a document class definition.

    IMPORTANT *Be sure not to include the .as extension.*

5. Open the **Library** panel.

6. Right-click (Win) or ⌃⌘-click (Mac) the object you want to control in ActionScript, and then click **Properties**.

7. Click **Advanced**, if available. (Button name changes to Basic.)

8. Enter a name for the object.

9. Select the **Export for ActionScript** check box.

    The Class appears with the same name as the object, and the Base class appears with object type.

Class definitions

10 Click **OK**.

11 If prompted, click **OK** to define the new class.

12 Click the **File** menu, and then click **Save**.

13 Click the **File** menu, and then click **New**.

14 Click **ActionScript File**.

15 Click **OK**.

16 Click the **File** menu, and then click **Save As**.

17 Navigate to the folder with the Flash document, and then name the file (same as the one in Step 4).

18 Click **Save**.

19 In the Actions panel, enter the script as shown in the illustration.

IMPORTANT *ActionScript 3.0 is case-sensitive, so upper- and lower-case make a difference.*

20 Click the **File** menu, click **Save**, and then close the ActionScript file.

21 Click the **Control** menu, point to Test Movie, and then click **Test**.

Did You Know?

You can define accessor methods. For advanced ActionScripting, you can also define accessors methods, which are a cross between a method and property (defined like a method, yet creates an instance like a property).

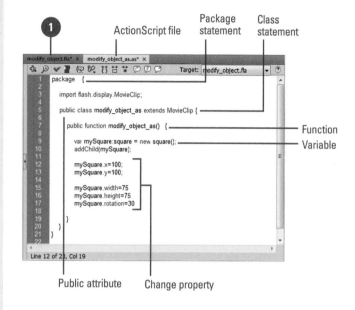

ActionScript file — Package statement — Class statement — Function — Variable — Public attribute — Change property

---

Common Syntax in ActionScript 3.0

Command	Description
Dot syntax	Access the properties and methods of an object. myDotEx.method ();
Slash syntax	Not supported in ActionScript 3.0.
Literals	A value that appears directly in your code. "text", true, false, 10
Semicolon (;)	Terminates (ends) a statement. var a:int = 2;
Parentheses	Indicates order of operation, evaluates a series of expressions, or pass parameters.
Comments	Documents code. Single-line comments begin with //, while multi-line comment begin with /* and ends with */.
Keywords	Reserved words you cannot use as identifiers. as, class, const, if, var, true, in
Constants	A fixed value. const MINIMUM:int = 0; ActionScript defines constants with all CAPS with words separated by an underscore. const MOUSE_DOWN:String = "mouseDown";

Using Namespaces in your Projects

Namespaces are ways in which you can define the visibility of properties you are creating. This is commonly used in XML when you are importing documents using a URI indicator.

You can also use the NameSpace as a way to overload your objects. The principle in overloading is to create several methods that have the same name but differ in the types of input and output they generate.

The following example is built using a Class called NamespaceExample. The role of this class is to pull in an XML document and step through the formatting of the code. Using Namespaces you can instruct Flash where to find a definition of the document type you are using, in this case an RSS formatted document type.

① Click the **File** menu, click **New**, click **ActionScript 3.0**, and then click **OK**.

② Open the **Properties** panel.

③ Click the **Edit Class Definition** button (small pencil icon) in the Properties inspector, enter a new class with the name *NamespacesExample*, and then click **OK**.

A new ActionScript file named *NamespacesExample.as* opens.

④ Create a simple RSS formatted XML document. You can use the following formatted RSS document:

```
<rdf:RDF
xmlns:rdf="http://www.w3.org/1999/02/22-rdf-syntax-ns#"
xmlns="http://purl.org/rss/1.0/"

xmlns:dc="http://purl.org/dc/elements/1.1/"
>
```

```
<channelrdf:about="http://www.xml.com/cs/xml/query/q/19">
<title>This is an RSS feed</title>
<link>http://www.bbc.co.uk/</link>
<description>This is a test RSS document.</description>
<language>en-us</language>
<items>
<rdf:Seq>
<rdf:li
rdf:resource="http://www.bbc.co.uk/"/>
 </rdf:Seq>
</items>
</channel>
<item rdf:about="http://news.bbc.co.uk/">
  <title>BBC News Center</title>
  <link>http://news.bbc.co.uk</link>
  <description>Welcome to the BBC News Center</description>
  <dc:creator>BBC</dc:creator>
  <dc:date>2010-02-12</dc:date>
</item>
<item
rdf:about="http://www.bbc.co.uk/radio">
  <title>BBC Radio Center</title>
  <link>http://www.bbc.co.uk/radio</link>
  <description>Welcome to the BBC Radio Center</description>
  <dc:creator>BBC</dc:creator>
  <dc:date>2010-02-12</dc:date>
</item> </rdf:RDF>
```

5 Open the NamespacesExample Class, and then define the package with a public class named *NamespacesExample* that will extend the functionality of the Sprite object.

```
package
{
    import flash.display.Sprite;

    public class NamespaceExample extends
Sprite
```

6 Insert the Namespace reference that describes how to use RSS XML.

```
{
    private var rss:Namespace = new
Namespace("http://purl.org/rss/1.0/");

    private var rdf:Namespace = new
Namespace("http://www.w3.org/1999/02/22-
rdf-syntax-ns#");

    private var dc:Namespace = new
Namespace("http://purl.org/dc/elements/1.1/
");

    public function NamespaceExample()
```

7 RSS has several standard XML types. You are going to extract the following: title, creator, date, link and description. Each of these items will be formatted in accordance to the namespace called RSS. You will see in the third line of the ActionScript that you reference the RSS namespace.

```
private function parseRSS(rssXML:XML):Array
    {
    default xml namespace = rss;

    var items:XMLList = rssXML.item;

    var arr:Array = new Array();

    var len:uint = items.length();
```

```
    for (var i:uint; i < len; i++)
    {
arr.push({title:items[i].title,
creator:items[i].dc::creator,
date:items[i].dc::date, link:items[i].link,
description:items[i].description});

        }
    return arr;

    }
```

8 Add a Public function that will use the RSS namespace and send the content to the Output panel:

```
public function NamespaceExample()
    {
        var myXML:XML = getRSS();

        var rssItems:Array =
parseRSS(myXML);

        var len:uint = rssItems.length;

        for (var i:uint; i < len; i++)
        {
        trace(rssItems[i].title);
trace(rssItems[i].creator);

        trace(rssItems[i].date);

        trace(rssItems[i].link);

trace(rssItems[i].description);

        }

    }
```

9 Click the **Control** menu, point to **Test Movie**, and then click **Test** to see the RSS feed results sent to your Output panel.

Namespaces are an effective way to manage your control over XML data. As with all core classes in Flash, you can extend the Namespace to use it in conjunction with other objects and data types.

Controlling Data

There are several key ways to control data in ActionScript 3.0. They include Arrays, Shared Objects and XML. An Array is the first method you are likely to use in your ActionScript code. The role of an Array is to create a list of data types in your code. For example, you may want to list the colors red, green, blue and orange. To do this you need to define a new variable with the data type of Array:

```
var colorArray:Array = new Array("red", "green", "blue", "orange");
```

You can see in this script that a set of four items have been inserted into the Array. You can access the data in the Array with the following trace statement:

```
trace (colorArray);
```

The "push" property will allow you to add a new item into your array:

```
colorArray.push("purple");
```

To remove the last item of an Array you can use the Pop property.

```
colorArray.pop();
```

What you will find is that Arrays are great for manage simple lists. Additional properties allow you to remove specific values, to count the number of values you have and to sort your lists. For more complex data you will want to leverage the Local Data Storage or XML.

When you are counting the number of values in an Array you have to remember that Arrays always start with 0. For instance, if you have five items in an array and tell the array to pull item 1, it will pull the second item. This is because the first item has the registered value of 0.

If you are developing an AIR solution you can take advantage of the SQL database built right into AIR. The SQL database comes with support for the creation of tables, stored procedures and SQL statements.

Using Flash Cookies

The Flash Player can also store data locally in very much the same way that a cookie can be stored in a Web browser. Flash does not call this cookies but Shared Objects. An example of Share Object ActionScript 3.0 is:

```
var mySO:SharedObject = SharedObject.getLocal("myFlashCookie");
```

```
mySO.data.now = new Date().time;
```

```
trace(mySO.data.now);
```

The Share Object is declared and given a name where it will be stored on the local computer. You can now effectively target data to this space that can be accessed if this computer comes back to this page at a later date.

Manipulating XML with E4X

Flash has supported XML in one fashion or another since Flash 5. Have you worked with XML in ActionScript 2.0? It's not pretty. To our relief, ActionScript 3.0 now supports the ECMA XML standard called E4X. You can now more easily step through your XML documents. You can also change the value of items into an XML document. What this means is that you can load an XML document and then modify the content. For instance, you can change Yellow to Blue.

Import an XML Document as a Data Type

1. Before you can import an XML document, you need to create one. You can use the following code and save it as an XML document with the name *colors.xml*.

```
<?xml version="1.0"  encoding="UTF-8"?>
<pallette>
<color>Orange</color>
<color>Red</color>
<color>Yellow</color>
</pallette>
```

2. Click the **File** menu, click **New**, click **ActionScript 3.0**, and then click **OK**.

3. Click the **File** menu, and then click **Save** to save the FLA file to the same folder as the XML document.

4. The first step is to create a new object to manage the XML:

```
var myXml:XML;
```

5. The next step is to create a new URLLoader file that will load the XML file:

```
var xmlLoader = new URLLoader();
```

```
xmlLoader.addEventListener
  (Event.COMPLETE,onXMLLoaded);
```

```
xmlLoader.load
  (new  URLRequest("colors.xml"));
```

6. At this point you have loaded the XML successfully into Flash. You can test this by adding the following function to trace the contents of the XML document into your OutPut window.

```
function onXMLLoaded(e:Event):void{
    myXml = new XML(e.target.data);
    trace(myXml);
}
```

7. You can now easily pull out a specific value. For instance, add the following to the onXMLLoaded function to extract the third value in the XML file:

```
trace(myXml..color[2]);
```

The double dots after the variable myXML allows you to step to the second value of your XML document. All of this is so much easier to accomplish with E4X than with ActionScript 2.0.

Using Regular Expressions

Patterns are everywhere as you develop your code. This is clearly seen with the use of Regular Expressions, a method for describing the pattern of data you are looking to use. Using Regular Expressions you can now easily format form fields to correctly capture date, ZIP or Credit Card numbers.

To validate data meets a simple pattern you need to create a string variable:

```
var myColor = "Orange";
```

Now create a new regular expression that is looking for a simple pattern. In this instance, the pattern is that the myColor string value must start with an "O":

```
var colorRegExp:RegExp = /O/;
```

You can write a trace script to test your movie:

```
trace( colorRegExp.test( myColor ) );
```

The value in the Output panel is True.

Let's extend what you can do with Regular Expressions by adding a pattern that looks for an email address. Start by adding a new email string with a valid email address:

```
var email:String = "mdavid@matthewdavid.ws";
```

Next, create a new Regular Expression that is looking for a pattern structure in your email:

```
var emailRegExp:RegExp = /^([a-zA-Z0-9_-]+)@([a-zA-Z0-9.-]+)\.([a-zA-Z]{2,4})$/i;
```

The pattern is looking for a combination of alpha-numerical-special character formats separated by an "@" sign and suffix "." Add the following trace statement to see whether or not the pattern works:

```
trace( "Is this email valid? " + emailRegExp.test( email ) )
```

Test the movie to view the following response in the Output panel:

Is this email valid? True

Change the email address to just "Matthew David" a pattern that does not match the Regular Expression. When you test the movie you will see that the Regular Expression returns a false response.

You can also get great information on how to structure regular expressions at: *http://www.regular-expressions.info*.

Controlling Text

In many ways you do not need to work on the Stage at all when using ActionScript 3.0. All visual objects can be programmatically created. The easiest way to see this is in using the Text object to create dynamic text fields on the Stage.

Create a Dynamic Text Field

1 Click the **File** menu, click **New**, click **ActionScript 3.0**, and then click **OK**.

2 Open the **Properties** panel.

3 Click the **Edit Class Definition** button (small pencil icon) in the Properties inspector, enter a new class with the name *text*, and then click **OK**.

A new ActionScript file named *text.as* opens.

4 Add the libraries to be imported into your file:

import flash.display.Sprite;

import flash.text.TextField;

import flash.text.TextFieldAutoSize;

import flash.text.TextFormat;

5 Insert a private variable that will be used to define the dynamic text:

private var myTextField:TextField;

6 The following creates a basic string you can insert into your texftfield:

private var someText:String = "Hello world.";

A private function is used to define the physical position of the textfield on the screen.

7 Declare the text field as a new object, and then use the X and Y properties to place the text on the screen:

private function configuretext():void

```
{
        myTextField = new TextField();
        myTextField.y = 200;
        myTextField.x = 100;
```

8 A textFormat object is used to format the visual properties of the text. For instance, the following textFormat object sets the font to "_sans", the color black and font size 15:

var format:TextFormat = new TextFormat();

format.font = "_sans";

format.color = 0x000000;

format.size = 15;

myTextField.defaultTextFormat = format;

addChild(myTextField);

9 The final two public functions tie the text string to the new formatted text field:

public function text()

```
{
        configuretext();
        setValueOfTextField(someText);
}
```
public function setValueOfTextField
(str:String):void

```
{
        myTextField.text = str;
}
```

10 Click the **Control** menu, point to **Test Movie**, and then click **Test** to display a text string added to your screen.

Creating a dynamic text field on the Stage with ActionScript allows you more control over the text on the Stage than using traditional methods.

Drawing with the Shape Class

As with the text object, you can create images dynamically in ActionScript 3.0. There are several different types of image you can create that include traditional Movie Clips and Graphics. You can now also create a new type of image called a Sprite. Essentially, a Sprite is the same as a Movie Clip with the exception that it does not contain timeline functionality. Sprite's can be created by invoking the new Sprite Object Class and then adding properties to the object.

```
shapeExample.as
                                    Target: shape.fla
1   package {
2       import flash.display.DisplayObject;
3       import flash.display.Graphics;
4       import flash.display.JointStyle;
5       import flash.display.LineScaleMode;
6       import flash.display.Shape;
7       import flash.display.Sprite;
8       public class ShapeExample extends Sprite {
9           private var size:uint          = 80;
10          private var bgColor:uint        = 0xFFCC00;
11          private var borderColor:uint    = 0x666666;
12          private var borderSize:uint     = 0;
13          private var cornerRadius:uint   = 9;
14          private var gutter:uint         = 5;
15          public function ShapeExample() {
16              doDrawCircle();
17              doDrawRoundRect();
18              doDrawRect();
19              refreshLayout();
20          }
21          private function refreshLayout():void {
22              var ln:uint = numChildren;
23              var child:DisplayObject;
24              var lastChild:DisplayObject = getChildAt(0);
25              lastChild.x = gutter;
26              lastChild.y = gutter;
27              for (var i:uint = 1; i < ln; i++) {
Line 1 of 60, Col 1
```

Add a Square Shaped Sprite to the Stage

1 Add the following ActionScript to create a new Sprite with the name *myFirstSprite*.

var myFirstSprite:Sprite = new Sprite();

addChild(myFirstSprite);

2 The following ActionScript formats the size, fill/outline color, and position of the Sprite:

myFirstSprite.graphics.lineStyle(3,0xFF6600);

myFirstSprite.graphics.beginFill(0xFF0000);

myFirstSprite.graphics.drawRect(0,0,100,100);

myFirstSprite.graphics.endFill();

3 Click the **Control** menu, point to **Test Movie**, and then click **Test** to view the rectangle on the screen.

4 The following ActionScript applies a fade in transition effect to your new Sprite.

myFirstSprite.addEventListener
    (Event.ENTER_FRAME, fadeInSprite);

myFirstSprite.alpha = 0;

function fadeInSprite(event:Event)

{

    myFirstSprite.alpha += 0.01;

    if(myFirstSprite.alpha >= 1)

    {

    myFirstSprite.removeEventListener
    (Event.ENTER_FRAME, fadeInSprite);

    }

}

You can do a lot with ActionScript constructed images. Working with the all the different objects available to you in ActionScript 3.0 you have almost no limits to what you can create using Flash.

Developing iPhone Apps

Introduction

Apple has this device called an iPhone. Have your heard of it? Of course you have. There is even a good chance you have an iPhone. While the iPhone itself is an amazing piece of technology, it is the software that makes the iPhone really great.

The challenge in developing applications for the iPhone is that you need to know how to develop using Apple's Cocoa Touch framework and the programming language Objective C. One of the most interesting and talked about features in Flash CS5 is Adobe's inclusion of a tool that converts your Flash movies to files that will run on any iPhone OS device without needing to know Objective C. You just need to apply the Flash and ActionScript knowledge you already have. A new tool in Flash CS5, called the iPhone Packager, converts files into valid iPhone applications.

Before you can create an iPhone App there are several activities you need to complete so you can develop in Flash CS5. They are (1) Become a Certified Apple Developer, (2) Create a Development and Developer P12 certificate, and (3) Register your development iPhone with Apple.

In this chapter, you'll get an overview for how to start developing for the iPhone using Flash CS5 including deploying an App to the iTunes App Store.

What You'll Do

Become an Apple Certified Developer

Register an iPhone and other Apple Testing Devices

Create App's ID

Create a Developer's Provisioning Profiles

Create and Publish an iPhone App

Control the Accelerometer

Save Images to the Camera Roll

Understand the Limitations of Flash

Identify Devices to Deploy an Ad Hoc App

Create an Ad Hoc Distribution Profile

Package an Ad Hoc App

Use iTunes Connect to Publish an App

Use Screen Orientation in an App

Use Geolocation in an App

Use Multitouch in an App

Becoming an Apple Certified Developer

The iPhone OS has rapidly become the mobile operating systems against which all other mobile systems, such as Android, Windows Mobile 7, BlackBerry, WebOS and Symbian, are all compared to. There is a very good reason for this: the iPhone OS is rock solid. Each App you develop for the iPhone OS will run on an ever increasing number of products shipping from Apple. They include the iPhone 3G and 3GS, iPod Touch and the iPad. All of your Flash CS5 applications (**New!**) will run on these devices. To be able to develop applications for the iPhone you do need to become a registered Apple developer. The cost is only $99 a year and this gives you the ability to load applications up to the iTunes App Store. Yes, you heard me right; it only costs $99 a year to load as many apps as you can develop into the iTunes App Store. This is an amazing deal. Similar programs run by Nintendo to develop apps for their Wii Wares store start in the low thousands of dollars.

Become an Apple Certified Developer

① Open your Web browser on the Mac, and then go to the iPhone Dev Center site:

◆ *http://developer.apple.com /iphone*

IMPORTANT *Use a Mac for these steps. later work can be done on a Windows computer.*

② Click the **Register** link on the Web page.

③ Follow the registration process; either use an existing iTunes Account or create a new account to register with the site.

◆ Upon completion, you'll receive an email confirmation.

④ Go to *http://developer.apple.com /iphone/manage/certificates* to download and install your Apple iPhone Development Certificate.

⑤ Open the Keychain to view your Apple iPhone Development Certificates: a Developer and a Distribution Certificate.

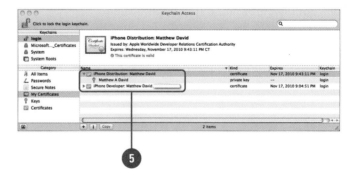

6 Control-click on the Developer Certificate, and then click **Export Certificate**.

7 Navigate to the location where you want to save the certificate.

8 Click the **File Format** list arrow, and then click **Personal Information Exchange (.p12)**.

9 Click **Save**.

10 Enter a strong password for your App, and then remember it as you'll need it later.

11 Repeat Steps 6-10 to export the Distribution Certificate in the Personal Information Exchange (.p12) format.

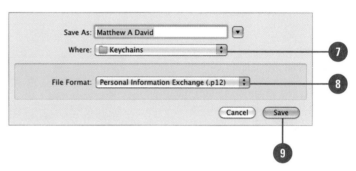

Did You Know?

You can use the P12 Certificates on Windows. You can copy the P12 Developer and Distribution Certificates to a disc and use them on a Windows computer. Creating the P12 Personal Information Exchange Certificates can be done on a Windows computer, but it requires the use of third party software such as OpenSLL. It is not easy. You are much better off starting with a Mac (find a friend, if you need to) and then moving to a Windows computer for your future Flash CS5 iPhone development needs.

For Your Information

Developing Apps on Macs and Windows

Amazingly, Adobe is the only company that allows you to develop iPhone Apps on Windows. All you need to accomplish this is to use a P12 Developer and Publishing certificate. The easiest way to get a P12 certificate is from a Mac computer. Just ask a friend if you can create an account on their Mac and then register yourself with Apple's Development program and create your own P12. After that you can copy the P12 certificate onto your Windows machine and develop the iPhone Apps.

Registering an iPhone and Other Apple Testing Devices

The hardest part of developing apps for the iPhone is not the code you develop, but ensuring you have all of your i's and t's dotted and crossed per Apple's rigorous registration process. One small step in the wrong direction and your App will not compile or install correctly. It is worth taking your time to go through the setup process (**New!**). After you have your P12 Certificates you will need to register your test iPhone with Apple. You can register up to 100 devices per year. The developer account ID, registered device and P12 certificates are needed for all apps your want to sell in the iTunes App Store. You can register iPhone's, iPod Touches and iPads.

Find your iPhone's Unique Identifier

1. Connect your test iPhone/iPod Touch to your computer.

2. Open iTunes, and then select your device from the list to view the Summary tab information.

3. Click the Serial Number next to your device.

   The number changes to an Identifier (UDID) number, which is. about 40 alpha-numeric characters long.

4. Copy the UDID number.

5. Open your Web browser, and then go to the Devices page on the iPhone Developer site:

   ◆ http://developer.apple.com /iphone/manage/devices /index.action

6. Click the **Add Devices** button.

7. Paste in the UDID number and then enter a name for your device.

   ◆ Suggestion: you may want to choose something like "iPhone Development" or "iPod Touch Gen 3 Development."

Creating App ID's

The App ID is a unique identifier Apple uses to identify your App from the tens of thousands of Apps in the iTunes App Store. There are ten's of thousands of applications in the iTunes App Store with more in constant development. Part of your registration process is to assign your App an ID, called the App ID. The App ID (**New!**) will be connected to your certificate and to the development and publication profiles you generate. You control the name of the App, but behind the scenes, Apple associates it an unique ID, called a Bundle Seed ID. Apple will know what your App is when it comes time for you to submit your App to iTunes.

Create an App ID

1. Open your Web browser, and then go to the App ID page on the iPhone Developer site:

   ◆ *http://developer.apple.com /iphone/manage/bundles /index.action*

2. Click the **New App ID** button.

3. Enter a new App name you can find easily, such as *WorldlyWordSearch*; the name has to be all one word.

4. Enter a Bundle Seed ID.

   ◆ The convention is to reverse your Web site address and add your Apps name at the end. For example, *com.pearson. worldlywordsearch*; the name has to be all one word.

5. Click **OK**.

Creating a Developers Provisioning Profiles

A provision profile is a document which is associated with your App and developer certificate for either development or iTunes App distribution. There are three types of Provisioning Profiles (**New!**) you can use: Developer, Distribution to Ad Hoc and Distribution to iTunes App Store. You will cover how to use the Distribution Profiles later in the chapter. For now, let's focus on creating Developer Profiles.

Create a Developer Profile

1. Open your Web browser, and then go to the Provisioning Profiles page on the iPhone Developer site:

   ◆ http://developer.apple.com /iphone/manage/provisioningpr ofiles/index.action

2. Click the **Development** tab.

3. Click the **New Profile** button.

4. Enter a meaningful Profile name.

   A convention that is gaining popularity is to use the prefix "Dev" followed by the App ID, such as *DevWorldlyWordSearch*.

5. Select the check box with your name in the Certificates list.

6. Click the **App ID** list arrow, and then select your App ID.

7. Select your test device from the devices listed.

8. Click the **Submit** button.

   Your developer profile takes about 30 seconds to generate.

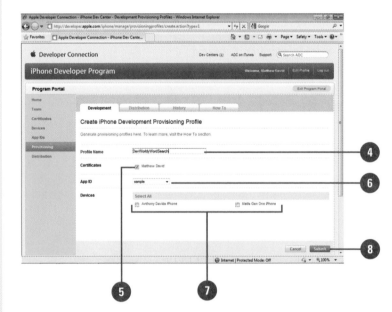

9 Click **Download** (Mac) or **Save** (Win), and then save the Developer profile to your desktop.

The file will have the extension "mobileprovision"

10 Connect your test iPhone to iTunes.

11 Drag the downloaded Developer Profile onto iTunes, and then sync your iPhone.

This adds the Developer Profile to your testing device.

For Your Information

Developing Icons for your iPhone Apps

In preparation for your iPhone App there are four PNG images you need:

       29.png – a file that is 29x29 pixels

       57.png – a file that is 57x57 pixels

       512.png – a file that is 512x512 pixels

       Default.png – this place holder file that is used while your App is loading. It is important the file starts with a capital "D".

You can create all of these files using Adobe Fireworks.

Creating and Publishing an iPhone App

With all of these tasks completed you are now ready to complete your first iPhone App. Sometimes it seems like a world full of red tape where you need to dot your i's and cross your t's, but you do get to the point where you can develop applications for your iPhone using Flash CS5 (**New!**). You need to go through the steps of creating a Developer Certificate, registering your test iPhone, creating an App ID, and downloading a developers profile in order to develop for any iPhone development tool; this is not just a unique Flash CS5 feature. Flash CS5, however, does allow you to very easily create the final iPhone App.

Create and Publish an iPhone App

1 In Flash, click the **File** menu, click **New**, click **iPhone OS**, and then click **OK**.

A new movie opens with the size 320x480 pixels.

2 Create an iPhone App using Flash tools.

3 Open the **Properties** panel.

4 Click the iPhone Settings **Edit** button.

The iPhone Settings dialog box opens, displaying three tabs: General, Deployment and Icons.

5 Click the **General** Tab.

6 Enter an Output file name, such as *wordsearch.ipa*.

7 Enter the App Name that you want to appear on the iPhone, such as *Word Search*. You are limited to 11 characters.

8 Enter an version number for the App, such as *1.0*.

9 Click the **Aspect Ratio** list arrow, and then select a display option: Portrait or Landscape view.

10 Select or deselect any of the following options:

♦ **Full Screen**. Select to force your App to take up all of the screen space on your phone;

deselect to show information at the top of your iPhone, including carrier signal, WiFi connection, time and battery life, will be visible in your App.

◆ **Auto Orientation.** Select to change the orientation of your App as the iPhone is rotated.

11 Click the **Rendering** list arrow, and then click an acceleration option, **Auto**, **CPU**, or **GPU**.

12 Click the **Add** button (+) in Included Files, and then select the Default.png file. The Default.png file displays when your App starts to run and disappears when your App has loaded.

13 Click the **Deployment** tab.

14 Click **Browse**, and then select your Developer P12 certificate file, and then enter your password.

15 Click **Browse**, and then select the developer Provisioning Profile you downloaded.

16 Enter the full name of the App ID you created in the iPhone Developer Center.

17 Select the **Quick Publishing For Device Testing** option.

18 Click the **Icons** tab.

19 Locate and add the 29.png, 57.png and 512.png file.

20 Click **Publish**.

Flash launches the iPhone Packager tool and generates (6-10 minutes) an IPA iPhone App file in the same folder as your Flash files.

21 Locate the IPA file, and then drag the file onto iTunes and sync your device. When the sync completes you will be able to launch your App from your iPhone.

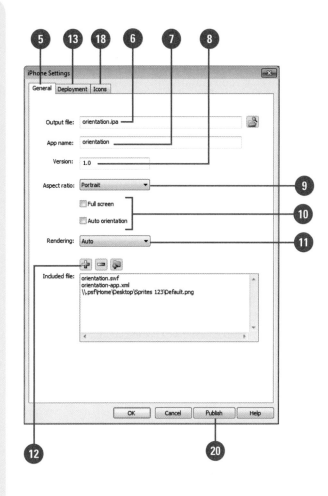

For Your Information

Playing Back Video

You can play back video in the iPhone, but there is a caveat. The only types of video that you can add to your iPhone Apps are Sorenson and ON2 VP6 video formats. If you want to use H.264 then you need to essentially post the video to a URL string so it pops up in Mobile Safari.

Controlling the Accelerometer

With the release of the Flash Player 10.1 and Adobe Integrated Runtime, AIR 2.0, the Flash team added several new core API features (New!). Access to a devices Accelerometer is one of those. The role of the Accelerometer is to detect when you move your phone. The Accelerometer is a listener that is triggered when it is used. The following example adds an Accelerometer listener to your iPhone App.

Add an Accelerometer Listener

1. Create a new iPhone App and add the necessary development properties in the iPhone settings.

2. Add a dynamic text field to the Stage with the name *myTextField* in the Properties panel.

3. Create a new layer on the Timeline with the named *Actions*, and then select the Actions layer.

4. Open the **Actions** panel.

5. Add code to import the libraries for the Accelerometer to work correctly:

   ```
   import flash.events.AccelerometerEvent

   import flash.sensors.Accelerometer;
   ```

6. Add code to create a new Accelerometer object:

   ```
   var acc1:Accelerometer = new Accelerometer()
   ```

7. Add a boolean object to test if the Accelerometer works or not:

   ```
   var isSupported:Boolean =
       Accelerometer.isSupported;

       checksupport();
   ```

8. Add a function that contains the event listener, which waits for the Accelerometer to be triggered:

   ```
   function checksupport():void {

    if (isSupported) {

     myTextField.text = "Accelerometer feature
       supported";

   acc1.addEventListener
   (AccelerometerEvent.UPDATE, updateHandler);

   } else {

     myTextField.text = "howdy ";    }

   }
   ```

9. Add a function that posts a message to the text field to tell what direction the device has moved to:

   ```
   function
   updateHandler(evt:AccelerometerEvent):void {

   myTextField.text = String("at: " + evt.timestamp
     + "\n" + "acceleration X: " + evt.accelerationX
     + "\n" + "acceleration Y: " + evt.accelerationY
     + "\n" + "acceleration Z: " +
   evt.accelerationZ);
   ```

10. Publish and package your file into an iPhone App and test it on your iPhone.

The Accelerometer gives you new ways for your customers to interface with your applications beyond touchscreen controls. The Accelerometer works great on the iPhone but the same code can be used for Adobe AIR apps running on Google's Android OS, Palm's WebOS and RIM's BlackBerry phones. Yes, that's right. Develop one App and have it deployed to multiple mobile devices.

Saving Images to the Camera Roll

Adobe does give you access to some core iPhone specific tools. One of those is the ability to add a function that will save an image of the screen to the Camera Roll (**New!**). The following example saves a screen image to the Camera Roll in an iPhone App.

Save a Screen Image to Camera Roll

① Click the **File** menu, click **New**, click **iPhone OS**, and then click **OK**.

② Create a new Movie Clip on the Stage with the name *snapShot*.

③ Add the following event Listener to:

snapShot.addEventListener(MouseEvent.CLICK, myScreenShot);

④ Add the following function that takes a screen shot of your iPhone:

function myScreenShot
(event:MouseEvent):void

{

if (CameraRoll.supportsAddBitmapData)

{

var cameraRoll:CameraRoll = new CameraRoll();
cameraRoll.addEventListener(ErrorEvent.ERROR, onCrError);

cameraRoll.addEventListener(Event.COMPLETE, onCrComplete);

var bitmapData:BitmapData = new BitmapData(stage.stageWidth,stage.stageHeight);

bitmapData.draw(stage);

cameraRoll.addBitmapData(bitmapData);

}

else

{

trace("not supported.");

}

}

⑤ Publish and package your file into an iPhone App and test it on your iPhone.

Understanding the Limits of Flash

There are some limitations to using the iPhone Packager for Flash CS5 (New!). The first is that you cannot load external SWF movies. You can, however, load external JPG and PNG files and sound files such as MP3.

There are also performance problems between different versions of the iPhone. For instance, the iPhone 3GS is literally twice as fast as the iPhone 3G and original iPhone. There some simple tricks you can do to speed up things. The following code will prevent event Bubbles starting:

```
override public function
    dispatchEvent(evt:Event):Boolean {

if (hasEventListener(evt.type) || evt.bubbles) {

return super.dispatchEvent(evt);

}

return true;

}
```

A second optimization trick you can do is to restrict your use of vector based images inside of Flash. Use PNG formatted images where possible. The good news is that that the iPhone has great support for PNG files.

If you do need to use vector images you can fool the iPhone into thinking it's a bitmap image by using the cahceAsBitmapMatrix.

1 Create a new image. Add code import the Flash Geom Matrix:

```
import flash.geom.Matrix;
```

2 Create a new shape:

```
var my_shape :MyShape = new MyShape();
addChild(my_shape);
```

3 Add the cachasBitmap property to ensure that all objects that create are cached:

```
my_shape.cacheAsBitmap = true;

my_shape.cacheAsBitmapMatrix = new
Matrix();
```

4 Create images on the screen that the iPhone thinks are bitmaps.

A final significant limitation is the use of audio files. Audio files can have a short delay between an event happening and the sound playing. This is because the audio file is not in the iPhone's cache for playback. You can avoid this by exporting your audio file to be triggered in the first frame of your movie.

What Flash Does Not Allow You To Do

Adobe has gone to great lengths to allow you to build applications for the iPhone using traditional Flash tools. BUT (and it is a big BUT) there are some things that Flash does not allow you to do using the iPhone Packager.

The biggest challenge you will have is the inability to use ActionScript 1.0 and 2.0. All of your apps must be developed using ActionScript 3.0. There are tens of thousands of great ActionScript 1.0 and 2.0 apps that can not be published to the iPhone due to the ActionScript 3.0 limitation.

You also have to be careful using video. Only Flash Video will work. You can use a URL link to load a MPEG4 video, but this is really a cheat as you are running the video through the iPhone's Mobile Safari Web browser.

If you are familiar developing iPhone Apps using the iPhone SDK then you may expect core iPhone Cocoa Touch kits available to you in Flash. This includes the StoreKit (for "in App purchase"), GameKit, MapKit and other rich media tools. These useful kits are simply not available to the Flash developer.

The good news is that Adobe is well aware that the Flash CS5 iPhone Packager is not complete. Expect releases for the iPhone Packager to keep coming during the lifecycle of Flash CS5.

Identifying Devices to Deploy an Ad Hoc App

Ad Hoc is a method for deploying your App to up to 100 iPhone, iPod Touch and iPad devices. The Ad Hoc method (**New!**) is a solution that allows you to deploy your apps to a small group of friends and co-workers without the App appearing in the iTunes App Store. The method for creating the application is very similar to deploying an App for deployment to the iTunes App store. There are three steps you need to be able to successfully deploy an App using Ad Hoc: Identify each device you will be deploying your Ad Hoc App too; creating an Ad Hoc provisioning license; and packaging your Ad Hoc App.

Collect and Add Deployment Device IDs

① Contact each person you will be deploying your App to and ask them to connect their iPhone, iPod Touch or iPad to their Mac or Windows computer.

② Ask them to open iTunes, select their device, and then view the Summary tab information.

③ Ask them to click the Serial Number next to their device.

The number changes to an Identifier (UDID) number.

④ Ask them to copy the UDID number, and then send it to you.

⑤ Open your Web browser, and then go to the Devices page on the iPhone Developer site:

◆ http://developer.apple.com /iphone/manage/devices /index.action

⑥ For each trusted device, click the **Add Devices** button on the Web page, paste in the UDID number and then enter a device name.

IMPORTANT *You can only have 100 identified devices per year. You cannot add and remove devices to keep your list at 100. When you have added the 100th device you have to wait a year before you can remove a device and add a new one.*

Added trusted devices

Creating an Ad Hoc Distribution Profile

The first step is to identify the devices you will be deploying your Ad Hoc App to. The next step is to create the profile you will need to use when you are building your Application for Ad Hoc deployment. The Ad Hoc Distribution method (**New!**) removes the hassle of having to wait for your App to be approved by Apple (which can take days to weeks to complete). To be able to take advantage of the Ad Hoc deployment process you need to first create an Ad Hoc Distribution Profile. Creating the Ad Hoc Profile is very similar to the profile you will create when you submit your App to the iTunes Store. The one big difference is you need to have a list of all the unique iPhone's and iPod Touch devices you will be sending your final App too.

Create an Ad Hoc Distribution Profile

1. Open your Web browser, and then go to the Provisioning Profiles page on the iPhone Developer site:

   ◆ *http://developer.apple.com /iphone/manage/provisioningpr ofiles/index.action*

2. Click the **Distribution** tab.

3. Click the **New Profile** button.

4. Click the **Ad Hoc** option.

5. Enter a profile name for your App.

6. Click the **App ID** list arrow, and then select the App ID that matches the App you want to deploy using Ad Hoc.

7. Select the devices (from the list of ones you entered) you want to deploy using Ad Hoc.

8. Click the **Submit** button.

   Your Ad Hoc profile takes about 30 seconds to generate.

9. Click **Download** (Mac) or **Save** (Win), and then save the Ad Hoc profile to your desktop.

   At this point, you're ready to create your Ad Hoc iPhone App.

Packaging an Ad Hoc App

The final step you need to take is to package your Flash movie into an iPhone App using the Ad Hoc profile (**New!**). The final step in creating your Ad Hoc App is to package your Flash App for distribution. The Ad Hoc distribution process is very similar to the final App Store Packaging publication process. There are some differences. The main change is that you must use the Ad Hoc Profile you created in the previous section. Without the Ad Hoc Profile your Ad Hoc deployment method will not work correctly.

Publish and Package an Ad Hoc App

1. In Flash, open the iPhone App you want to publish and package as an Ad Hoc App.

2. Open the **Properties** panel.

3. Click the iPhone Settings **Edit** button.

    The iPhone Settings dialog box opens, displaying three tabs: General, Deployment and Icons.

4. Click the **Deployment** tab.

5. Click **Browse**, and then select your Published P12 certificate file, and then enter your password.

6. Click **Browse**, and then select the Ad Hoc Distribution Profile you downloaded.

7. Click the **Deployment – Ad Hoc** option.

8. Click **Publish**.

    Flash launches the iPhone Packager tool and generates (6-10 minutes) an IPA iPhone App file in the same folder as your Flash files.

10. Locate the IPA file and send it to anyone in the Ad Hoc Provisioning Profile list. Ask them to drag the file onto iTunes and sync their device. When the sync completes you will be able to launch your App from your iPhone.

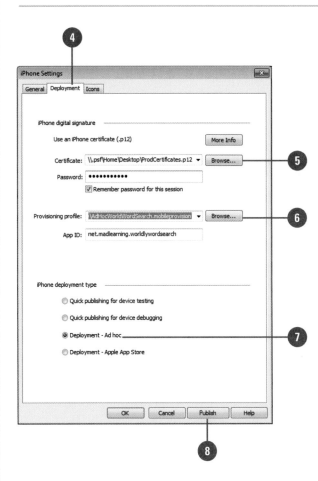

Packaging an App for the iTunes App Store

Apple's iTunes Store is an amazing success story. 133,000 Apps and 3 Billion downloads in 20 months is nothing to sneeze at. There are many stories of companies making millions from Apple. But, before you can get any money, you need to have your App ready for deployment. The method for packaging your Flash file into an iPhone App for distributing to the iTunes store is very similar to the Ad Hoc process with the exception that you only need to create a distributing profile and create your iPhone IPA file from Flash CS5 (**New!**).

Publish and Package an iPhone App

1. Open your Web browser, and then go to the Provisioning Profiles page on the iPhone Developer site:
   - http://developer.apple.com /iphone/manage/provisioningpr ofiles/index.action

2. Click the **Distribution** tab.

3. Click the **New Profile** button.

4. Click the **App Store** option.

5. Enter a profile name for your App.

6. Click the **App ID** list arrow, and then select the App ID that matches the App you want to deploy.

7. Click the **Submit** button.

   Your profile takes about 30 seconds to generate.

8. Click **Download** (Mac) or **Save** (Win), and then save the App Store profile to your desktop.

9. In Flash, open the iPhone App you want to publish and package as an App Store App.

10. Open the **Properties** Panel.

11. Click the iPhone Settings **Edit** button.

    The iPhone Settings dialog box opens, displaying three tabs: General, Deployment and Icons.

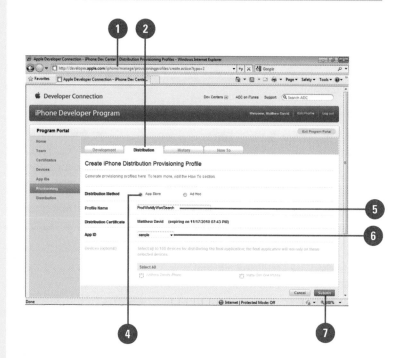

12 Select the **Deployment** tab.

13 Click **Browse**, and then select your Published P12 certificate file, and then enter your password.

14 Click **Browse**, and then select the App Store Distribution Profile you downloaded.

15 Click the **Deployment – Apple App Store** option.

16 Click **Publish**.

Flash launches the iPhone Packager tool and generates (6-10 minutes) an IPA iPhone App file in the same folder as your Flash files.

17 Locate the IPA file and then change the extension of the file from IPA to ZIP.

Both file formats are container formats. That is, they contain all of the files needed for the App to run; iTunes Connect only accepts files in the ZIP format.

At this point, your App is ready for deployment to the iTunes App Store.

Did You Know?

Ad Hoc is a great way to easily deploy apps to a small group of users. It is not a good solution for deploying apps to a large number of users. If you want to deploy your App to a large number of users then you will need to take advantage of Apple's powerful iTunes App Store.

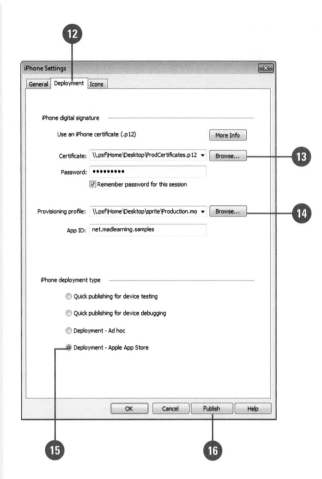

Using iTunes Connect to Publish an App

You are now very close to having an App available on the iTunes store. Can't you feel the rush! You could be selling thousands of apps in a matter of a few days. The gap between you and riches is Apple's iTunes Connect publishing tool. You are very close now. You will be using a new Web site to upload your final iPhone Apps. The site is called iTunes Connect (*https://itunesconnect.apple.com/*). In every sense, iTunes Connect is your business relationship with Apple. The site allows you to set up your contracts, tax records, banking information, review sales trends, download financial report and manage your In App Purchases. You will need to complete these sections in order to sell your App in iTunes. This section is going to focus on the important part of iTunes Connect: Managing your Applications (**New!**).

Use iTunes Connect to Publish your App

1 In Flash, create your iPhone App, publish and package it, and then change the extension from IPA to ZIP.

2 Convert the 512x512 PNG pixel image into a JPG image. Label the new file 512.jpg.

3 Take a screen shot of your App as it appears in your iPhone. When your App is playing on your iPhone, press the Home and Sleep buttons at the same time (screen flashes) to take a screen shot of your App.

The image is stored to your Camera Roll and is exactly the same size Apple needs.

Did You Know?

You can download Apple's Developer Guide. Open your Web browser, go to the Manage Your Application page on iTunes Connect, and then click the download link to save the PDF file.

4 Open your Web browser, and then go to the iTunes Connect page, and then use your Apple Developer ID and Password to log into the site:

◆ *https://itunesconnect. apple.com*

5 Click **Manage Your App** from iTunes Connect.

6 Add anew application or edit an existing one.

◆ Add New App. Click the **Add New Application** button to start the process of creating a new iTunes App.

◆ Edit Existing App. Double-click the application icon.

When you're done editing your App settings, click **Save Changes**.

There are several screens you need to complete to upload your App to iTunes.

7 If prompted, click the **Yes** or **No** option to specify whether your App contains encrypted data.

◆ For a first App, click **No** to keep the process simple. In the future, you can experiment with different settings.

8 Click the **Continue** button when you have completed the page.

The next page allows you to add product overview information about your App. For the most part, the content you enter on this screen can be edited after your App has been submitted.

Continue Next Page

Link to download the Developer Guide

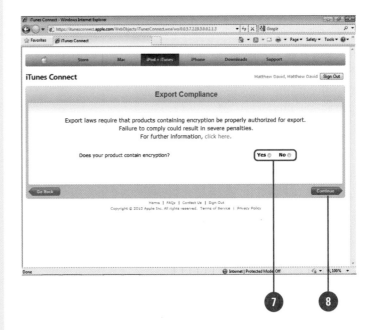

9 Enter or change information about your App. The information includes the following:

  ◆ Name and description.

  ◆ Product primary and secondary categories.

  ◆ Copyright, version number, and SKU number.

  ◆ Keywords. Use for search engines (up to 100 characters).

  ◆ URLs. Application/support URL and support email.

10 Click the **Continue** button when you have completed the page.

The next page allows you to add a rating for your App.

11 Click options to answer the 10 questions to determine a rating.

12 Click the **Continue** button when you have completed the page.

The next page allows you to upload all of your App files.

13 Click the **Choose File** button to upload your App files:

  ◆ Upload the ZIP'd IPA file for the Application.

  ◆ Upload the 512.jpg for the Large 512x512 Icon.

  ◆ Upload a 480x320 jpg image for the Primary Screenshot.

  ◆ Add 1-4 480x320 jpg images for the Additional Screenshots.

The upload will take about 20 minutes. The upload is checking for some basic settings such as including the correct profile.

A green check mark appears for each successfully loaded image. A red cross appears when something is wrong.

14 Click the **Continue** button when you have completed the page.

The next page allows you to specify availability and pricing for your App.

15 Specify an Availability Date and Price Tier.

◆ **Availability Date.** Specifies when your App goes on sale.

◆ **Price Tier.** Select a price tier level; you do not get to select a specific price for your App.

This removes the pain of selling with different currencies. A Tier 2 App will be $0.99 in the US, 59 pence in England and AU$1.29 in Australia. There are over 70 different currencies that Apple manages for you.

16 Click the **Continue** button when you have completed the page.

The next page allows you to specify localization for your App.

17 Specify the localization settings you want for your App.

18 Click the **Continue** button when you have completed the page.

19 At this point, review all of your content, and then click the **Submit** button.

◆ When you're done editing your App settings, click **Save Changes**.

Did You Know?

Faster iTunes App Submission. Apple has done a lot to improve the review process for new apps. Today it only takes 5-7 days for an App to be approved and appear in iTunes.

Using Screen Orientation in an App

The iPhone has one characteristic that you will not see on a desktop or laptop computer: it can be easily rotated. Determining orientation can allow you to add interesting effects to your iPhone Apps (**New!**). For instance, the default Stocks tool on your iPhone will show you the numbers of a particular stock when you hold your phone in portrait; switch the phone to landscape and the content changes to a line chart illustrating how the stock is performing. This trick is accomplished through the iPhone being able to detect the orientation of the device. The iPhone can detect Orientation in four distinct directions:

- Default – Portrait
- Rotation Left – Landscape
- Rotation Right – Landscape
- Upside Down – Portrait, upside down

ActionScript contains a special class called the Orientation Class, which allows you to control content on the screen depending on the orientation of the device.

Use the Screen Orientation Class

① Create a new iPhone App, apply the appropriate provisioning profiles, and then save the file with the name *iPhoneOrientation.fla*.

② Add a dynamic text box to the Stage with the name *myTxt*, and then apply the _Sans font.

③ Open the **Actions** Panel.

④ Add a listener and function that changes the content of the text box based on the orientation of the device (see illustration).

⑤ Publish and package your file into an iPhone App and test it on your iPhone. Rotate your iPhone to see the text change on your iPhone.

```
stage.addEventListener(StageOrientationEvent.ORIENTATION_CHANGE,onChangeOrientation);

function onChangeOrientation(event:StageOrientationEvent):void
{
    switch (event.afterOrientation)
    {
        case StageOrientation.DEFAULT :
            myTxt.text = "Portrait";

            break;
        case StageOrientation.ROTATED_RIGHT :
            myTxt.text = "Rotated Right";

            break;
        case StageOrientation.ROTATED_LEFT :
            myTxt.text = "Rotated Left";

            break;
        case StageOrientation.UPSIDE_DOWN :
            myTxt.text = "Upside Down";

            break;
    }
}
```

In addition to using ActionScript to control the orientation of your phone, you can also have the whole movie auto-orientate as a default setting in your iPhone Settings screen. On the whole, however, you have much tighter control over your content is you use ActionScript to control the orientation of specific movies, sprites and objects over the auto-orientation Boolean setting.

For Your Information

Loading Files Into the iPhone

The Loader Class allows you to load external content into your Flash Player. For the most part, this still works when you package your Flash movie for the iPhone. For instance, you can still load MP3, Sorenson Flash video and PNG files. There is, however, one exception: you cannot load SWF files that contain ActionScript into your movies. This is a pain as a lot of Flash designers like to break up their movies into smaller, individual SWF files and then you use a shell SWF to package it all together. Hopefully that will change in future releases.

Using Geolocation in an App

Mobile devices are meant to move. With GeoLocation services, you can figure out your current location. So, when someone asks you "Where are you?" you can tell them.

The following example shows how to add Adobe AIR 2.0 GeoLocation Class (**New!**) to your iPhone App. This sample is stripped down to a simple Class file, which can give you an idea of how you can use this in other Apps.

Add GeoLocation Services

① Create a new iPhone App, apply the appropriate certificates and profiles, and then save your file with the name *iPhoneGeolocation.fla*.

② Add a dynamic Classic Text box to the Stage with the name *myTxt*, and then apply the _Sans font.

③ Create a new Class for the App with the name *iPhoneGeolocation*.

④ Save the ActionScript file with the name *iPhoneGeolocation.as*.

⑤ Add code to import the class files that allow you to use the Geolocation objects:

import flash.events.GeolocationEvent;

import flash.sensors.Geolocation

⑥ Create a new geolocation variable that you can use:

private var myGeo:Geolocation;

⑦ Create a simple If/Else statement that detects whether or not the geolocation services can be used.

The iPhone always gives the user of the iPhone a choice to whether or not you can use the Geolocation services. If you do not allow geolocation to be used a message will be posted to the text field informing the user that a location could not be detected. If you do, however, allow the user to use geolocation then a new listener event will be triggered and then re-run 10x/second.

⑧ Add a function triggered by the geolocation listener:

⑨ Publish and package your file into an iPhone App and test it on your iPhone.

How Does the iPhone Know Your Location?

There are three ways to detect your location. The most accurate method uses the Global Position Satellites (GPS) built into the iPhone 3G and 3GS. The second method uses Cell Tower Triangulation where the location of the device is determined by using 3 or more Cell Tower's. This method can be used by all iPhones and 3G enabled iPad's. The third method uses a WiFi hotspot, which is similar to the Cell Tower Triangulation but is only accurate to within a few hundred feet. All iPhone OS devices (iPhone, iPod Touch and iPad) support WiFi hotspot geolocation services.

Using Multitouch in an App

By default, Flash assumes that you are using a mouse to touch the screen. This actually works OK for many iPhone Apps and allows you to take the same code you have developed for other Flash movies and move it into your iPhone projects. That's OK, but what about those cool iPhone gestures (**New!**) you see people using to swipe content? Flash can do that, too.

For the iPhone, Flash supports the following Multitouch gestures:

◆ TransformGestureEvent.GESTURE_PAN

◆ TransformGestureEvent.GESTURE_ROTATE

◆ TransformGestureEvent.GESTURE_SWIPE

◆ TransformGestureEvent.GESTURE_ZOOM

Each gesture is used as an interactive event in a Listener. This means that you can take your knowledge of Listeners and quickly apply it to iPhone Apps. The following example shows you how to add a swipe gesture that will trigger a movie clip to fade onto the screen.

Use the Multitouch Class

① Create a new iPhone App, apply the appropriate development profiles and certificates, and then save the file with the name *iPhoneMultitouch.fla*.

② Draw a rectangle on the Stage, and then convert the rectangle into a Movie Clip with the name *myMovie*.

③ Open the **Actions** panel.

④ Add code to import the class libraries:

import flash.ui.Multitouch;

import flash.ui.MultitouchInputMode;

⑤ Set the default Alpha value for the Movie Clip to 0:

myMovie.alpha = 0;

⑥ Add a listener and function that enable the Movie Clip to fade onto the screen (see illustration).

⑦ Publish and package your file into an iPhone App and test it on your iPhone.

```
ACTIONS - FRAME

                                                      Code Snippets

1   import flash.ui.Multitouch;
2   import flash.ui.MultitouchInputMode;
3   myMovie.alpha = 0;
4
5   function fadeIn(event:Event)
6   {
7       myMovie.alpha += 0.01;
8       if (myMovie.alpha >= 1)
9       {
10          myMovie.removeEventListener(TransformGestureEvent.GESTURE_SWIPE, fadeIn);
11      }
12  }
13  myMovie.addEventListener(TransformGestureEvent.GESTURE_SWIPE, fadeIn);

Layer 1 : 1
Line 13 of 13, Col 71
```

Debugging a Movie

Introduction

Flash provides several enhancements that make it easier for you to debug scripts using the ActionScript language. The features include new language elements, improved editing and debugging tools, and the introduction of a more object-oriented programming language; however, not all debugging problems reside in an ActionScript. Debugging a Flash movie is similar to a mechanic attempting to fix the engine on a car. He can hear a knocking or pinging sound, but he's not sure what's causing it, so he brings out his debugging tools to help locate the problem.

A Flash movie is not a car, however, there are similarities. If the movie is not doing what you want: Maybe it's running too slow, or your movie crashes after playing a specific scene; you can bring out Flash's debugging tools to help locate (and fix) the problem. When you design a Flash movie, the fonts, colors, video and audio (if any), along with the overall construction of the movie are very right-brain techniques (your creative side at work). When you debug a Flash movie, you're using a very logical approach to the problem. Like the car mechanic, you're listening for that annoying pinging sound. Flash will not only help you locate the problem, its array of debugging tools will help you fix it and get you back speeding down the electronic highway.

Flash's debugging tools include the Debug workspace (ActionScript 3.0) or Actions panel (ActionScript 2.0) and the Movie Explorer, where you can set breakpoints, view variables, and see how they react during the play of the movie. Flash uses a different debugger for ActionScript 3.0 files than it does for ActionScript 2.0 files. The debugger functionality is similar, but the look and feel is different. The debugger for ActionScript 3.0 uses the Debug workspace while ActionScript 2.0 uses the traditional Actions panel.

What You'll Do

Debug Concepts

Debug with the ActionScript Editor

Use the Movie Explorer

Debug for ActionScript 3.0

Resolve Compiler Errors

Debug for ActionScript 2.0

View Variables

Add Variables to the Watch List

View Properties

Set Breakpoints

Step Through Code

Debug Manually

Debugging Concepts

When you debug a movie, you're not just looking for the obvious problems; you're attempting to see if you can find anything that might happen. Depending on the complexity of the movie, hidden problems can be difficult to find. For example, if you're calling video files into a Flash movie, are all your paths to the files correct? It may function fine when you're testing on your computer, but will it still work when you move it to a CD or Web server? Test it and find out. Here are a few things to consider when going into the debug phase of a Flash Movie:

◆ **Paths to file.** If you're importing external SWF files, image files, video, or audio files into a Flash movie, the best approach is to create a folder to hold the entire Flash project, and then create sub-folders within that folder to hold the movie assets. When you move the Flash project, move the entire folder. That way, all the path names stay correct, and you always know where everything is, at all times.

◆ **Short, descriptive file names.** Computers allow for file names of unlimited length; however, that does not mean that you need to use large file names. Large file names are harder for you to type in, and there is a greater chance for errors. Use short, descriptive names.

◆ **Use smart naming conventions.** Since file names display alphabetically, it's not a bad idea to come up with similar names for similar file types. For example, car_1.jpg, car_2.jpg, car_3.jpg. The name and extension describe (in general terms) the content of the file and file type and will display one after the other. Smart naming conventions won't make your Flash project any better, but they will help to organize some of the confusion that comes with a complicated Flash project.

Project folder

◆ **Test and debug often.** Debugging does not start at the end of a project, it begins as soon as you click the File menu, and then click New. Flash lets you test a movie whenever you choose. Just click the Control menu, point to Test Movie, and then click Test (to test the entire Flash movie), or click Test Scene (to test just the active scene). When you test a scene or movie, Flash creates a temporary SWF file and then runs the movie in a version of the Flash plug-in. Flash publishes the test movie using the settings in the Publishing dialog box. If there is a problem, you can use the Debugger to diagnose the problem, so you can fix it. Just click the Debug menu, point to Debug Movie, and then click Debug.

◆ **Bandwidth.** If a project is going out to the Internet, make sure that the size of the finished movie isn't so large that your

visitors have to wait a long time for it to download. It's possible you might want to include a pre-loader to entertain the audience while they're waiting.

◆ **Planning is the key.** If you want your Flash movie to look good, work without error, and be completed in the least amount of time, then plan, plan, and then plan some more. Use the carpenter's adage: Measure Twice... Cut Once. University studies show that planning a project, before you start, cuts the project completion time by 20 percent. Planning involves thinking about what you want to accomplish (what's the message), research and gather all the files and things you'll need to complete the project, and think about where the project will be used (Internet, CD). In addition, a well-planned project will cut down your debugging time by over half.

Smart file naming conventions

Debugging with the ActionScript Editor

The ActionScript editor allows you to edit and debug scripts. When you're debugging a Flash movie, the traditional wisdom is to try to push it until it breaks, and then figure out why it broke. However, once you find out what's broken, it's very possible that you're going to have to work on the ActionScript's that drive the movie. That's where the Actions panel comes into play. The designers of Flash included editing and debugging features to make debugging easier. You can quickly set and remove breakpoints using the Debug Options button to check different parts of your code to determine if it's working correctly. You can also work in the Actions panel in Script Assist mode—supported by ActionScript 2.0 and ActionScript 3.0 (attached to a frame)—in which you filled in options and parameters to create code or access the Code Snippets panel (**New!**) to insert ActionScript 3.0 code. It is a great way for novice ActionScript coders to learn programming. To make working with code easier, you can use collapse and expand buttons to show and hide sections of code. In addition, you can use buttons to quickly add comments to a line or a block of code to document your work.

Use the ActionScript Editor

1. Click the **Window** menu, and then click **Actions** to open the ActionScript Editor.

2. **Script Assist**. Click the Script Assist button to view, write, and edit scripts using a visual interface that includes syntax completion and parameter descriptions.

   ◆ To insert ActionScript 3.0 code, click **Code Snippets** to access the panel (**New!**).

3. **Word wrapping**. Click Word Wrap on the Options menu in the Actions panel to enable or disable word wrapping.

4. **Viewing context-sensitive Help**. When your pointer is positioned over an ActionScript element in the Actions toolbox or in the Script pane, you can click the Reference button in the context menu to display an element help page.

5. **Importing scripts**. Click Import Script on the Options menu in the Actions panel, the imported script is copied into the script at the insertion point.

Breakpoints

6 **Single-click breakpoints**. To add a debugging breakpoint before a line of code in the Debugger panel or the Script pane of the Actions panel, click in the left margin.

7 **Pinning multiple scripts**. You can pin multiple scripts within a FLA file along the bottom of the Script pane in the Actions panel.

8 **Script navigator.** The Script navigator is a visual structure of your Flash FLA file; you can navigate through the file to locate the ActionScript code.

9 **Integrated Script window for editing external files**. You can use the ActionScript editor in a Script window (separate from the Actions panel) to write and edit external script files.

10 **Syntax coloring**. Syntax coloring utilizes a user-defined set of colors to display the code entered into the Script pane. Click the Flash (Mac) or Edit (Win), and then click Preferences. Click the ActionScript category to modify the syntax coloring.

11 **Instant Syntax Checking**. Click the Check Syntax button to get an instant evaluation of the current script.

12 **Code Hint**. Click the Show Code Hint button to have Flash help you enter code.

13 **Debug Options**. Click the Debug Options button to set and remove breakpoints.

14 **Collapse and Expand**. Click the Collapse Between Braces, Collapse Selection, or Expand All buttons.

15 **Comments**. Click the Apply Block Comment, Apply Line Comment, and Remove Comment buttons.

Selected code

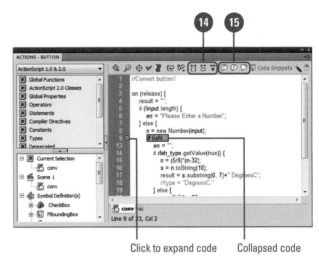

Click to expand code   Collapsed code

Using the Movie Explorer

Flash's Movie Explorer gives you an easy way to view and organize the contents of an .fla document, and even select elements for modification. It contains a display list of currently used elements, arranged in a tree hierarchical structure. The Movie Explorer gives you the ability to filter which categories of items in the document are displayed: text, graphics, buttons, movie clips, actions, and imported files. You can even display selected categories as individual scenes, concise symbol definitions, or both. When you select an item in the Movie Explorer panel, the item will be selected in the Flash document. If you double-click on an ActionScript, Flash opens the script in the Actions panel. If you double-click on a Library item, Flash opens the item in the Library.

Use the Movie Explorer

1. Click the **Window** menu, and then click **Movie Explorer** to open the panel.

2. Click the Movie Explorer **Options** menu, and then select from the following options:

   ◆ **Go To Location.** Takes you to the selected layer, scene, or frame in the active document.

   ◆ **Go To Symbol Definition.** Takes you to the symbol definition for a symbol that is selected in the Elements area.

   ◆ **Select Symbol Instances.** Takes you to the scene containing instances of a symbol that is selected in the Definitions area.

   ◆ **Find In Library.** Select to highlight the selected symbol in the document's Library.

   ◆ **Rename.** Select to enter a new name for a selected element.

   ◆ **Edit In Place.** Select to edit a selected symbol on the Stage.

   ◆ **Edit In New Window.** Select to edit a selected symbol in a new window.

   ◆ **Show Movie Elements.** Displays document elements organized into scenes.

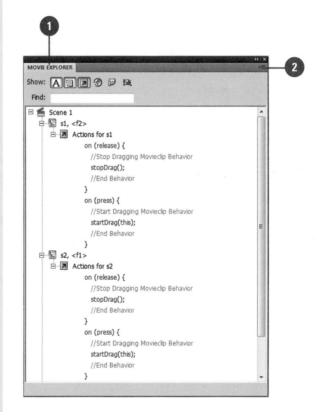

◆ **Show Symbol Definitions.** Select to display all the elements associated with a symbol.

◆ **Copy All Text To Clipboard.** Select to copy selected text to the Clipboard.

◆ **Cut, Copy, Paste, And Clear.** Select to perform these functions on a selected element.

◆ **Expand Branch.** Select to expand the navigation tree at the selected element.

◆ **Collapse Branch.** Select to collapse the navigation tree at the selected element.

◆ **Collapse Others.** Select to collapse the branches in the navigation tree not containing the selected element.

◆ **Print.** Select to print the hierarchical display list currently displayed in the Movie Explorer.

③ The Show buttons give you the option to show or hide different elements of the movie. These options will only impact the Movie Explorer, not the Flash Stage.

◆ **Show Text**

◆ **Show Buttons, Movie Clips, and Graphics**

◆ **Show ActionScripts**

◆ **Show Video, Sounds, and Bitmaps**

◆ **Show Frames and Layers**

④ Click the **Customize Which Items To Show** button to customize what items display in the Movie Explorer window.

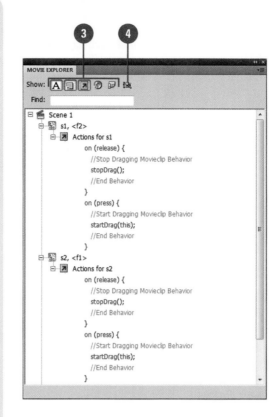

Debugging for ActionScript 3.0

The designers of Flash included editing and debugging features to make debugging easier. You can quickly set and remove breakpoints to check different parts of your code to determine if it's working correctly. Flash uses a different debugger for ActionScript 3.0 files (FLA or AS) than it does for ActionScript 2.0 files. The functionality is similar, but the look and feel is different. The debugger for ActionScript 3.0 uses the Debug workspace that displays the Debug Console, Variables, and Output panels along with the Actions panel or Script window. The Debug Console displays the call stack, scripts containing the functions in the call stack, and contains buttons to step through the code. The call stack shows the current list of nested function calls ready for execution. The Variables panel displays variables and their current values. When a problem is encountered, Flash displays the line of code in the Compiler Errors panel. Double-click the error to view it in the code.

Use the Debugger for ActionScript 3.0

1 Create or open a Flash document (ActionScript 3.0).

◆ To debug an ActionScript 3.0 file (AS), open the file in the Script window, select the associated Flash file from the Target menu.

2 Click the **Debug** menu, point to **Debug Movie**, and then click **Debug**.

◆ You can access debugging commands on the Debug menu.

3 Add or remove breakpoints to interrupt the execution of the scripting code.

◆ **Add.** Click in the left margin next to the line of code.

◆ **Remove.** Click the breakpoint in the left margin.

4 To step through the code line by line or step in and out of functions, use any of the following:

◆ **Step into code line by line.** Click the **Step In** button in the Debug Console panel.

◆ **Step over a function call.** Click the **Step Over** button in the Debug Console panel.

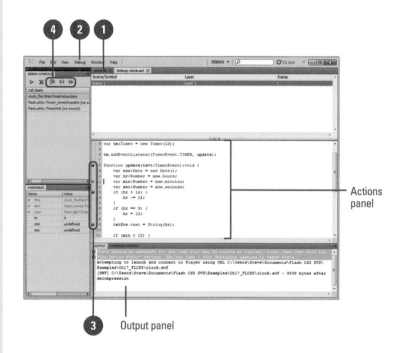

Actions panel

Output panel

- ◆ **Step out of a function call.** Click the **Step Out** button in the Debug Console panel.

- ◆ **Resume normal code execution.** Click the **Continue** button in the Debug Console panel.

5 To view the individual scripts that contain each function, double-click the script name in the call stack in the Debug Console panel.

6 To view variable values, click the **Options** button on the Variables panel, and then click one of the following:

- ◆ **Show Constants.** Displays the values constants.

- ◆ **Show Statics.** Displays variables for the class instead of instances of the class.

- ◆ **Show Inaccessible Member Variables.** Displays variables that are inaccessible to other classes or namespaces.

- ◆ **Show Additional Hexadecimal Display.** Displays hexadecimal values instead of decimal values.

- ◆ **Show Qualified Names.** Displays variable types with both the package name and the class name.

7 To edit the values of variables in the Variables panel, double-click the value, enter a new value, and then press Enter (Win) or Return (Mac).

8 If an error occurs, double-click it in the Compiler Errors panel.

9 To exit debugging mode, click the **End Debug Session** button in the Debug Console panel. To change workspaces, click the Workspace menu, and then select one.

Continue

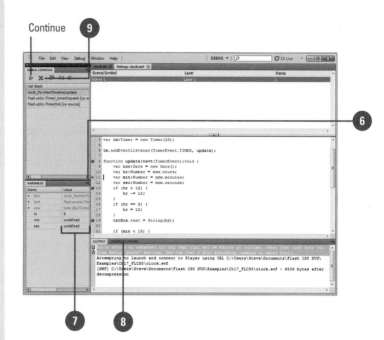

Resolving Compiler Errors

When a problem is encountered, Flash displays the location and description of the warnings and errors in the Compiler Errors panel. In the Compiler Errors panel, you can show or hide warnings or errors (**New!**), scroll through each one (**New!**), and display/highlight them in the code (**New!**). You can also manage the types of compiler warning that appear in the Compiler Errors panel by setting options in the Publish Settings dialog box. Two options are available: Strict Mode and Warnings Mode. Strict Mode reports warnings as errors, while Warnings Mode reports extra warnings for discovering incompatibilities when updating ActionScript 2.0 code to ActionScript 3.0.

Resolve Compiler Errors

1. Create or open a Flash document (ActionScript 3.0).

2. Click the **Control** menu, point to **Test Movie**, and then click **Test**.

   If an error occurs, the Compiler Errors panel opens displaying the errors found during the execution.

3. Open the **Compiler Errors** panel.

4. In the Compiler Errors panel, use the following options to resolve compiler errors:

   ◆ **View Warnings or Errors in the Code.** Select the warning or error, and then click the **Go To Source** button, or double-click the warning or error to display it in the Actions panel.

   ◆ **Display Warnings or Errors.** Click the **Go To Previous** or **Go To Next** button. The code line with the error highlights in the Actions panel.

   ◆ **Clear Warnings and Errors.** Click the **Clear** button.

   ◆ **Show or Hide Warnings or Errors.** Click the **Warning(s)** or **Error(s)** button at the bottom of the Compiler Errors panel.

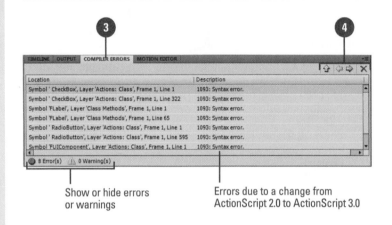

Show or hide errors or warnings

Errors due to a change from ActionScript 2.0 to ActionScript 3.0

Source of error from the Compiler Errors panel

Control Compiler Warnings

1 Create or open a Flash document (ActionScript 3.0).

2 Click the **File** menu, and then click **Publish Settings**.

3 Click the **Flash** tab.

4 Click the **Settings** button for ActionScript 3.0

5 Select the **Strict Mode** check box to report warnings as errors.

6 Select the **Warnings Mode** check box to report extra warnings for discovering incompatibilities when updating ActionScript 2.0 code to ActionScript 3.0 code.

7 Click **OK**.

8 Click **OK**.

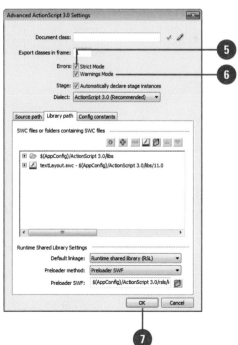

Debugging for ActionScript 2.0

Flash provides several tools for testing Flash files (ActionScript 2.0). The Debugger panel lets you find and locate errors hidden in an .swf file, while it's running in the Flash Player. You must view your SWF file in a special version of Flash Player called the Flash Debug Player (installed automatically when you install the Flash application). The Debugger panel shows a hierarchical display list of movie clips currently loaded in the Flash Player. You can then use the Debugger to display and modify variables and property values as the .swf file plays. You can insert breakpoints to stop the .swf file and step through the ActionScript code line-by-line. You can even use the Debugger panel to test files on a Web server in a remote location. The Debugger lets you set breakpoints in your ActionScript that stop the Flash Player, and then lets you step through the code as it runs. You can then go back to your scripts and edit them so that they produce the correct results. The Debugger will show you where the problems are, but it doesn't fix them.

Use the Debugger for ActionScript 2.0

1. Create or open a Flash document (ActionScript 2.0).

2. Click the **Debug** menu, point to **Debug Movie**, and then click **Debug**.

3. The Code View panel displays a message indicating the movie is paused.

4. Click the **Continue** button to start the movie.

5. Click the **Stop Debugging** button to turn off the Debugger panel.

6. Click inside the code, and then click the **Toggle Breakpoint** button to add or remove a breakpoint at the insertion point of the cursor.

   Breakpoints stop the movie from playing and allow you to step through the code line-by-line.

7. Click the **Remove All Breakpoints** button to remove all the breakpoints from the code.

8. Click the **Step Over**, **Step In**, and **Step Out** buttons to step through each line of an ActionScript.

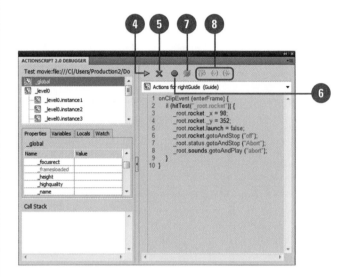

For Your Information

Testing Your Movie

When you use the Test command to test movies that implement keyboard shortcuts, click the Control menu, and then click Disable Keyboard Shortcuts. This prevents Flash from interpreting keystrokes, and lets them pass through to the player. For example, you can have a Flash document that uses Ctrl+U to display a file or video. However, Flash uses Ctrl+U to display the Preferences panel. If you don't Disable Keyboard Shortcuts, pressing Ctrl+U in the Flash player will actually open Flash Preferences.

Viewing Variables

When you work in the debugger, you have the option of viewing any variables used in the Flash movie. The Variables tab (ActionScript 2.0) or Variables panel (ActionScript 3.0) displays the names and values of any global and variables in the .swf file. If you change the value of a variable, you can see the change reflected in the .swf file while it runs. This gives you the ability to test new data variables and their impact on the Flash player document.

View Variables

1. Click the **Debug** menu, point to **Debug Movie**, and then click **Debug**.

2. Select the movie clip containing the variable from the display list.

3. Select an item in the display frame to view the variables' names and values.

4. Click the **Continue** button to observe the variables as the Flash movie runs.

5. Click the **Variables** tab (ActionScript 2.0) or open the Variables panel (ActionScript 3.0).

    IMPORTANT *The display list updates automatically as the .swf file plays. When a movie clip is removed from the .swf file at a specific frame, the movie clip, variable and variable name are removed from the display list in the Debugger panel. This lets you focus on the current variables. When you're viewing a complex Flash movie that contains a lot of variables, only having to view the current variables cuts down on the visual clutter and helps you to focus on the immediate problem.*

Variables panel (ActionScript 3.0)

Adding Variables to the Watch List

In any complex Flash movie, there will probably be a set of critical variables that you want to keep an eye on. You can monitor critical variables in a controllable way by marking them to appear in the Debugger panel Watch list (ActionScript 2.0). The Watch list displays the absolute path to the variable and its current value, and just like the Variables tab, you can enter a new variable value at any time during the debugging process. If you add a local variable to the Watch list, its value appears only when Flash Player is stopped at a line of ActionScript where that variable is in scope. All other variables appear while the .swf file is playing. If the Debugger can't find the value of the variable, it will list the value as undefined.

Add Variables

1. In a Flash document (ActionScript 2.0), click the **Debug** menu, point to **Debug Movie**, and then click **Debug**.

2. Click the **Variables** or **Locals** tab, and then select a variable.

3. Click the **Debugger Options** button, and then click **Watch**.

4. Click the **Watch** tab.

5. Click the **Debugger Options** button, and then click **Add Watch**.

6. Enter the target path to the variable name and the value in the fields.

   IMPORTANT *To remove variables from the Watch list, select a variable on the Watch tab, click the Debugger Options button, and then click Remove Watch.*

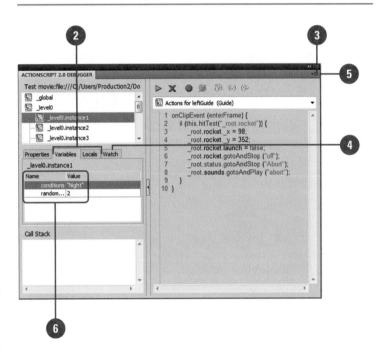

Viewing Properties

The Properties tab in the Debugger panel displays all property values of any movie clip on the Stage. Properties are modifiable script elements such as _alpha (controls transparency) or _rotation (controls the rotation of an object). The Properties tab lists all the properties including their current values. You can then view and adjust the values as the Flash movie is running to judge their impact. This gives you a tremendous amount of control over the debugging process.

View Properties

1. In a Flash document (ActionScript 2.0), click the **Debug** menu, point to **Debug Movie**, and then click **Debug**.

2. Select an available movie clip from the Display list.

3. Click the **Properties** tab to view all the properties, and their associated values.

4. Double-click on a value, and then enter a new value in any available property.

5. Click the **Continue** button to view how the Properties change as the Flash movie executes.

> **IMPORTANT** *The Property value is picky about what you enter. For example, you can enter a value of 100 or text within quotes such as: "newvalue", but you cannot enter expressions such as: y + 12, or an array of values such as: 1, 2, 3.*

Setting Breakpoints

Breakpoints are instructions to the Debugger to halt the running of a Flash movie. For example, you're watching how the .swf file plays using the debugger, however, it's moving so fast it's difficult to watch everything. By inserting a breakpoint, you instruct the Debugger to halt the movie, and any variables and properties will display the values associated with that point in time. You can then change the values, and instruct the Debugger to continue playing the movie, using the modified values.

Set Breakpoints

1. Click the **Debug** menu, point to **Debug Movie**, and then click **Debug**.

2. Click in the left margin next to the line of code where you want the breakpoint (red dot) to appear.

   ◆ You can also click the **Toggle Breakpoint** button (ActionScript 2.0) to add/remove a breakpoint.

3. To remove a breakpoint, click the existing breakpoint (red dot) in the left margin.

4. Click the **Continue** button to begin playing the Flash .swf file.

   The Debugger will stop the movie at each breakpoint.

Did You Know?

You can set or remove breakpoints in the Actions panel. In the Actions panel (ActionScript 2.0), click in the line you want, click the Debug Option button, and then select a command to set or remove breakpoints.

You cannot set a breakpoint on a comment line. If you set a breakpoint in a comment (or empty line) in the Actions panel, the breakpoint will be ignored by the Debugger.

Toggle Breakpoint

Breakpoint

ActionScript 3.0

Breakpoints

Stepping Through Code

When you open the Debugger, the Flash Player is automatically paused. This gives you the opportunity to set breakpoints in the script (see previous lesson: Setting Breakpoints). Once the breakpoints are set, you can click the Continue or Play button, and the Debugger will play the .swf file until it encounters a breakpoint. When a breakpoint is reached, the Debugger again pauses the movie. You now have the option to step in, out, or through the breakpoint script.

Step Through Code

1 Click the **Debug** menu, point to **Debug Movie**, and then click **Debug**.

2 Add breakpoints by clicking in the left margin next to the line of code where you want the breakpoint. To remove a breakpoint, click it.

3 Click the **Continue** button.

Flash will stop at the first breakpoint.

4 Select from the step options:

◆ **Continue**. Click to leave the line at which the player is stopped and continue playing.

◆ **Stop Debugging**. Click to deactivate the Debugger, but continue to play the SWF file.

◆ **Step In**. Click to step into and execute a function (works only for user-defined functions).

◆ **Step Out**. Click to move out of a function (works only if you are currently stopped in a user-defined function).

◆ **Step Over**. Click to skip over a line of code.

IMPORTANT *If you want to know where the Debugger stopped, keep an eye on the yellow arrow. A yellow arrow along the left side of the Debugger's code view indicates the line at which the Debugger stopped.*

Current breakpoints

Continue   Stop Debugging

The Yellow Arrow indicates where the Debugger stopped.

Debugging Manually

Debugging a Flash movie manually means exactly what it implies. You can open the movie and take it for a test drive. Debugging a movie manually gives you a chance to be the visitor, and experience your movie exactly as they would. When you manually test a Flash movie, you want to experience the wait time for downloading, you want to forget that you created this masterpiece, and you want to come at it just as if you were a first-time viewer. A Flash movie is composed of text, video, audio, images, animation, and ActionScript. Your visitors will never see the ActionScript code, and most do not care how it was written; but they will care if it doesn't work properly. For example, your visitor clicks a button to load a video file, and the video never loads, or it takes so long to load that they get bored and leave. Problems like these are what manual debugging can solve.

Debug Manually

① Click the **Control** menu, point to **Test Movie**, and then click **Test** to test the entire Flash movie, or click **Test Scene** to test the active scene.

> **IMPORTANT** *Flash uses the settings described in the Publish Settings dialog box to test the movie. Use different settings such as Flash plug-in, to test the movie against earlier versions of the Flash plug-in.*

② Test the movie for any structural failures. Click all the buttons, and then do all the things you think a visitor would do.

③ Note any problems on paper (remember this is manual) in a list, called a debug, or edit list. The list can then be used to edit the document, using Flash's standard editing tools.

Click and test all the buttons and input fields.

See Also

See Chapter 20, "Publishing a Movie" on page 477 for information on modifying publishing settings.

For Your Information

Debugging Flash Player

When Adobe Flash is installed, the debug version of the Adobe Flash Player is installed for the application as well as any browser specified. While this debug version of the player can be very useful when authoring, there may be situations where the standard player is desired. If you would like to uninstall the debug player, point your browser to: *http://www.adobe.com/support/flash/ts/documents /remove_player.htm*, and then follow the on-screen instructions. You can then point your browser to: *http://www.adobe.com/shockwave /download/download.cgi?P1_Prod_Version=ShockwaveFlash*, and download the current version of the player.

Adding and Modifying Components

Introduction

Components are building blocks that you can use to create interactive, dynamic Flash documents. Think of a component as a movie clip with modifiable parameters, which are set during the design of a Flash document, and ActionScript APIs (APIs allow you to customize the component at runtime). Since components are reusable, they give developers the ability to share code between projects. You can use components created by Adobe, download components created by other developers or, with a bit of practice create your own components. Since components are rooted in ActionScript code, Flash comes with a set of components for ActionScript 2.0 and another one for ActionScript 3.0, and you cannot mix components in the same Flash document.

Suppose you want to create a list of options from which a visitor would be able to click and choose. You can open the Actions panel, and then create the list by typing in about forty or more lines of script, or you can use Flash's built-in component to create the list. The difference is not in the quality of the list, but the amount of time it took to create it. Spending less time on creating dynamic, interactive Flash elements gives you more time to concentrate on design features. To a Flash visitor, it's not about the code or how long it took you to create it, it's about the design, and it will always be about the design.

What You'll Do

Understand Basic Components

Add a Text Input

Add a Combo Text Box

Add a Check Box

Add a Radio Button

Add a Text Area

Add a Button

Add a List

Add a Label

Add a Data Grid

Use a Local Data Provider

Add a Loader

Add a Numeric Stepper

Add a Progress Bar

Add a Scroll Pane

Create and Modify Bindings

Modify Schema

Modify Component Attributes

Use Components to Build a Form

Understanding Basic Components

Components are composed of two elements: a movie clip and parameters, allowing you to modify the components' appearance and behavior. Components run the gamut from a radio button to a scroll pane. Components equalize the designer's playing field, enabling anyone to build complex applications, even if they do not have a complete understanding of the ActionScript language. As easy as it is to simply drag the component you need from the Components panel onto the Stage, it is just as easy to customize the look and feel of components to suit your design needs.

Components let you easily and quickly build strong applications with a consistent appearance and behavior. Each component comes with predefined parameters, located in the Property Inspector (**New!**), which let you

control how the object looks and operates. Each component also includes a set of API (application programming interface) methods and properties that allows you to set parameters and additional options at runtime. This is typically accomplished by adding the scripts to Frame 1 in the Flash Timeline. It is said that Flash components finally allow for the separation of coding and design.

Using the Components Panel

Components are added to the Stage using the Components panel. To add a component to the Stage, you open the Components panel, expand the Components list, and then drag a component icon onto the Stage. Since components are based on ActionScript code, Flash comes with a set of components for

Components panel

Flash Components

Loader component in the Property Inspector

Available Settings

ActionScript 2.0 and another one for ActionScript 3.0, and you cannot mix components in a Flash document. You specify the components type by selecting an ActionScript version in the Publishing Settings dialog box.

There are three categories of components for ActionScript 2.0—user interface, media, and video—and three categories of components for ActionScript 3.0—Flex, user interface and video. ActionScript 3.0 provides similar components as ActionScript 2.0. However, the parameters associated with a component may vary. User interface components allow you to interact with an application (RadioButton, Checkbox, and TextInput). Video components allow you to add video playback controls, such as FLVPlayback, FLVPlayback with captioning, Back, Forward, Mute, Pause, Play, Play/Pause, Seek Bar, Stop, and Volume Bar. Media components (ActionScript 2.0) allow you to play back and control streaming media (MediaController, MediaPlayback, and MediaDisplay).

After you add an instance of a component to a Flash document (drag a component to the Stage), you can give the component a unique instance name using the Property Inspector and then use the Component Inspector panel to set and view information for the instance.

Using the Component Inspector

Once the component is on the Stage, it is controlled through the Component Inspector panel. The Component Inspector panel has three tabs: Parameters, Bindings, and Schema. Each tab gives you modifiable elements to help control the look and functionality of the component. The Parameters tab (now moved to the Property Inspector (**New!**)) lists the most commonly used properties; others parameters can be added using the ActionScript panel. The Bindings tab gives you

a way to bind, or link two or more components together. For example, you can bind an external database to a display component for on-screen viewing of the data. The Schema tab contains a list of a component's bindable properties, data types, internal structure, and other special attributes.

Using the Accessibility Panel

When you work with Flash components, you can create Flash content that is accessible to users with disabilities using Flash accessibly features. As you design accessible Flash applications, consider how your users will interact with the content. Visually impaired users might rely on additional technology, such as screen readers, while hearing-impaired users might read text and captions in the document. To make a Flash Component accessible, click the Window menu, point to Other Panels, and then click Accessibility to open the Accessibility panel. For more information on creating accessible compliant documents, open your browser and visit *www.w3.org/WAI/*, or for information on Flash, open your browser and visit *www.adobe.com/*, go to the Flash Exchange, and then type the word "accessibility" in the keyword field.

Accessibility panel

Working with the Component Inspector

The power of a component is its ability to change. Components can be modified directly in the Component Inspector panel, or they can be modified dynamically, as the Flash movie runs. The Component Inspector panel has three areas to modify a component— Parameters, Bindings, and Schema. These three tabs allow you to attach components to data files, change or modify the text on a button, or create drop-down menus and lists.

Setting Parameters Options

After adding an instance of a component to a Flash document, you can name the instance at the top of the Property Inspector, and then specify the parameters for the instance using the options and fields under Component Parameters in the Property Inspector (New!).

Each component has parameters that you can set to change the instance's appearance and behavior. A parameter is a property or method that appears in the Property Inspector. The most commonly used properties and methods appear as authoring parameters; others can be set using ActionScript. Authoring parameters represent common things such as the label attached to a Button component, or items displayed when using the List component. If you set a parameter using ActionScript, it will override any value set while authoring.

Understand that each component will have its own unique parameters, and changing parameters in the Property Inspector only changes the selected instance. Parameters include the ability to change an instance's

Component Parameters in the Property Inspector

Bindings tab

font, color, and size. You can add additional parameters by selecting the instance on the Stage and typing the script into the Actions panel. If you add the script to Frame 1 in the Timeline, you can create global changes to instance parameters.

Setting Binding Options

Data Binding is a concept where the property of one component can be bound to the property of another component: if the property of the one component changes, so will the property of the other component or components. The Bindings tab defines a link between two endpoints, a source (external data file, movie clip, graphic) and a destination component (DataGrid, Loader, Label). It listens for changes to the source endpoint and copies the changed data to the destination endpoint each time the source changes.

Setting Schema Options

Schemas are important because they help create a communication link between other components, using the Bindings tab. A component's schema simply represents the properties and fields that are available for data binding. Each property or field contains settings that control validation, formatting, type conversion, and other features that affect how data binding and the data management components handle the data of a field.

The Schema tab lets you view the schema for the selected component. Schema is basically a list of the component's binding properties, their data types, their internal structure, and other special attributes, depending on the selected component. This is the information

that the Bindings tab needs in order to handle your data correctly. For example, you can click the Schema tab, define the binding component (DataGrid), and then use the Bindings tab to link the DataGrid component to the external XML file.

The top portion of the Schema tab displays bindable properties associated with the selected component, while the bottom portion of the Schema tab displays detailed information about the selected schema item (selected from the top portion of the Schema tab), and gives you the ability to view or edit them.

Schema tab

Adding a Text Input

The TextInput component works with the ActionScript TextField object. Once a TextInput component is added to the Stage, you can use styles to customize the font, size, and color. A TextInput component can be formatted using HTML, or even as a password field that disguises the text. When a TextInput field has focus, visitors can use the arrow keys to move through information in the field, and they can use the tab key to move the focus to the next object, or Shift+Tab to move to the previous object. TextInput fields can be used to hold information. For example, you could use a group of TextInput components as the basis for creating an interactive form for fields such as: name, address, city, state, and zip code.

Add a TextInput Component

1. Open the **Components** panel.

2. Click the **User Interface** arrow to expand the list.

3. Drag the **TextInput** component onto the Stage, and then select the component.

4. Open the **Properties** panel, and then click the **Component Parameters** arrow to expand it.

5. Select from the following Text Input parameters:

   ◆ **editable.** When you select the check box, the field can be edited. If you select false, the field can be selected but not edited.

   ◆ **password (2.0)** or **display AsPassword (3.0).** When you select the check box, text entered into the field appears as dots. If you select false, text typed into the field appears as typed.

   ◆ **text.** Click the Value field, and then enter the text that will appear in the field when the Flash document opens.

- **maxChars.** Click the Value field, and then enter a numerical value indicating the max characters allowed in the TextInput field.

- **restrict.** Click the Value field, and then enter any characters that cannot be entered into the TextInput field.

- **enabled.** When you select the check box, the field can be edited. If you select false, the field appears grayed out and is not selectable or editable.

- **visible.** When you select the check box, the field can be viewed. If you select false, the field is invisible.

- **minHeight (2.0).** Click the Value field, and then enter a minimum height for the TextInput box.

- **minWidth (2.0).** Click the Value field, and then enter a minimum width for the TextInput box.

6 Click the **Control** menu, point to **Test Movie,** and then click **Test**.

IMPORTANT *Although you can change the size of any component using the Free Transform tool, since the TextInput component is a single-line component, changing its height does not impact how many lines of text you can type.*

TextInput
component

Adding a Combo Text Box

The ComboBox component creates a drop-down list of selectable options. They can be either static or editable. The static ComboBox component allows a user to make a single selection from a drop-down list. An editable ComboBox component lets users enter text into a text field located at the top of the list, as well as selecting an item from a drop-down list. A ComboBox component is composed of three subcomponents: Button, TextInput, and List components. When a visitor selects an item, the label of the selection is automatically copied to the text field at the top of the combo box. The ComboBox component is an excellent way to offer several choices to a user, without the necessity of them having to type in a response. For example, a ComboBox could be used to list all of the states in the union in a drop-down box, giving the user the chance to select his home state. When the ComboBox displays in a Flash document, it appears as a single line; clicking the triangle to the right of the line expands the box and displays all the available options.

Add a ComboBox Component

1. Open the **Components** panel.

2. Click the **User Interface** arrow to expand the list.

3. Drag the **ComboBox** component onto the Stage, and then select the component.

4. Open the **Properties** panel, and then click the **Component Parameters** arrow to expand it.

5. Select from the following ComboBox parameters:

   ◆ **data (2.0)** or **dataProvider (3.0)**. Click the Edit button, and then enter an array in the Values dialog box. Click the plus (+) sign to add values and the minus sign (-) to remove a value. Data values are used to populate the drop-down list.

   ◆ **editable**. When you select the check box, the field can be edited. If you select false, the field can be selected but not edited.

ComboBox component

◆ **labels (2.0).** Click the Edit button, and then enter an array in the Values dialog box. Click the plus (+) sign to add values, and the minus sign (-) to remove a value. Data values are used as the selectable items in the list.

◆ **rowCount.** Click the Value field, and then enter a number to determine the maximum height of the drop-down list.

◆ **enabled.** When you select the check box, the items in the list can be selected. If you select false, the field appears grayed out and is not selectable.

◆ **prompt (3.0).** Click the Value field, and then enter a prompt message text.

◆ **visible.** When you select the check box, the field can be viewed. If you select false, the field is invisible.

◆ **minHeight (2.0).** Click the Value field, and then enter a minimum height for the ComboBox box.

◆ **minWidth (2.0).** Click the Value field, and then enter a minimum width for the ComboBox box.

IMPORTANT *If there is not enough room for the ComboBox to open without hitting the bottom of the document, it will open up instead of down.*

6 Click the **Control** menu, point to **Test Movie,** and then click **Test.**

When you click the Select Your Country list arrow, the list will open, and a selection can be made by clicking on one of the available options.

Click to add values

Use to add, remove and order values

Enter values

Adding a Check Box

A check box is simply a square box that the user can select or deselect. When it is selected, a check mark appears in the box. When a selected check box is clicked, the check mark is removed. The state of a CheckBox component does not change until the mouse is released over the component.

Add a CheckBox Component

1. Open the **Components** panel.

2. Click the **User Interface** arrow to expand the list.

3. Drag the **CheckBox** component onto the Stage, and then select the component.

Did You Know?

You can control the state of a CheckBox component without the mouse. If the CheckBox component has focus (selected), pressing the Spacebar selects or deselects the check mark.

CheckBox component

4 Open the **Properties** panel, and then click the **Component Parameters** arrow to expand it.

5 Select from the following CheckBox parameters:

- **enabled (3.0).** When you select the check box, the items in the list can be selected. If you select false, the field appears grayed out and is not selectable.

- **label.** Click the Value field, and then enter a label for the check box.

- **labelPlacement.** Click the Value field, and then select between right, left, top, or bottom for the placement of the label text.

- **selected.** When you select the check box, the field appears with a checkmark, or deselect the check box, the field appears without a check mark.

- **visible (3.0).** When you select the check box, the field can be viewed. If you select false, the field is invisible.

6 To change the width and height of the check box component, select the component, and then drag a resize handle to change the width and height.

7 Click the **Control** menu, point to **Test Movie,** and then click **Test**.

Click in the CheckBox component to add a check mark, and then click a second time to remove the check mark.

Adding a Radio Button

The RadioButton component lets you do something that the CheckBox component cannot do: force a user to make a single choice within a set of choices. The RadioButton component must be used in a group of at least two RadioButton instances, and only one member of the group can be selected at any given time. Selecting one radio button in a group will deselect the currently selected radio button in the group. For example, a radio button options for Gender can be Male, Female. There can be only one answer to that question, so you would group the two items using RadioButton components.

Add a RadioButton Component

1. Open the **Components** panel.

2. Click the **User Interface** arrow to expand the list.

3. Drag one or more **RadioButton** components onto the Stage, and then select one at time.

4. Open the **Properties** panel, and then click the **Component Parameters** arrow to expand it.

Did You Know?

A visitor can control a radio button selection with the keyboard. Click the Tab key until one of the buttons within the group receives focus (is selected), and then use the left and right arrow keys to change the selection within the group. Having the ability to use the keyboard makes Flash components compliant with the current rules on accessibility as set by the U.S. Congress.

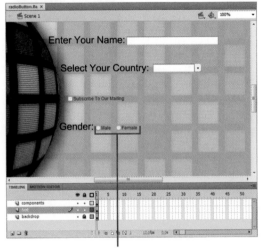

RadioButton component

5 Select from the following RadioButton parameters:

- ◆ **data (2.0)** or **value (3.0)**. Click the Value field, and then enter a value that will be used to populate the RadioButton.

- ◆ **groupName.** Click the Value field, and then enter a group name for the button. When you associate a group name to several RadioButton components, the visitor will only be able to select one button in the group.

- ◆ **label.** Click the Value field, and then enter a label for the RadioButton.

- ◆ **labelPlacement.** Click the Value field, and then select between right, left, top, or bottom for the placement of the label text.

- ◆ **selected.** When you select the check box, the field appears selected. If you deselect the check box, the field appears unselected.

- ◆ **enabled (3.0).** When you select the check box, the items in the list can be selected. If you deselect the check box, the field appears grayed out and is not selectable.

- ◆ **visible (3.0).** When you select the check box, the field can be viewed. If you deselect the check box, the field is invisible.

6 Click the **Control** menu, point to **Test Movie**, and then click **Test**.

Since the RadioButton components both use the same Group name, you can only select one button.

Adding a Text Area

The TextArea component works with the ActionScript TextField object. Once a TextArea component is added to the Stage, you can use styles to customize font, size, and color. In addition, a TextArea component can be formatted using HTML. If this sounds similar to the TextInput component, you're right. In fact, the major difference between a TextInput and a TextArea field is the ability of the TextArea field to generate multiple lines. TextArea fields can be used to hold information. For example, you can use a TextArea component to create a comment or a suggestion field on an interactive form.

Add a TextArea Component

1. Open the **Components** panel.

2. Click the **User Interface** arrow to expand the list.

3. Drag the **TextArea** component onto the Stage, and then select the component.

4. Open the **Properties** panel, and then click the **Component Parameters** arrow to expand it.

5. Select from the following TextArea parameters:

   ◆ **condenseWhite (3.0).** When you select the check box, it removes extra white space (spaces, line breaks) in a text field. If you deselect the check box, the white space remains.

   ◆ **editable.** When you select the check box, the field can be edited. If you deselect the check box, the field can be selected but not edited.

   ◆ **html (2.0).** When you select the check box, it allows HTML to control the formatting of the data. If you deselect the check box, the field cannot be modified using HTML.

   ◆ **text.** Click the Value field, and then enter the initial text that will appear in the TextArea component.

TextArea component

- **wordWrap.** When you select the check box, the text typed by the visitor wraps in the TextArea box. If you deselect the check box, the text will not wrap.

- **maxChars.** Click the Value field, and then enter the maximum number of characters that can be typed into the TextArea component.

- **restrict.** Click the Value field, and then enter any characters that cannot be entered into the TextArea field.

- **enabled.** When you select the check box, the field can be edited. If you deselect the check box, the field appears grayed out and is not selectable, or editable.

- **visible.** When you select the check box, the field can be viewed. If you deselect the check box, the field is invisible.

- **minHeight (2.0).** Click the Value field, and then enter a minimum height for the TextArea.

- **minWidth (2.0).** Click the Value field, and then enter a minimum width for the TextArea.

- **horizontal** or **vertical ScrollPolicy (3.0).** Click the Value field, and then select auto, on, or off to show or hide scroll bars.

6 Click the **Control** menu, point to **Test Movie**, and then click **Test**.

In the example, visitors can type as much information as needed, and when the box fills up, scroll bars appear to the right of the box; allowing them to maneuver up and down through the document.

Adding a Button

The Button component is a clickable rectangular button, which can be resized. If you desire, you can add a custom icon to the Button component. In addition, you can change the behavior of a Button component from push to **toggle**. A toggle button stays pressed when clicked and returns to its up state when clicked again. All of these options are accomplished through the Component Inspector panel.

Add a Button Component

1. Open the **Components** panel.

2. Click the **User Interface** arrow to expand the list.

3. Drag the **Button** component onto the Stage, and then select the component.

4. Open the **Properties** panel, and then click the **Component Parameters** arrow to expand it.

5. Select from the following Button parameters:

   ◆ **icon (2.0).** Click the Value field, and then enter the full path name to an icon file.

   ◆ **emphasized (3.0).** When you select the check box, it adds a border around the button. If you deselect the check box, the button is normal.

   ◆ **label.** Click the Value field, and then enter a label for the Button component.

   ◆ **labelPlacement.** Click the Value field, and then select between right, left, top, or bottom for the placement of the Button component text.

   ◆ **selected.** When you select the check box, the button appears selected. If you deselect the check box, the button is normal or deselected.

Button component

- **toggle.** When you select the check box, the button, when selected, returns a true value. If you deselect the check box, the button returns false when selected.

- **enabled.** When you select the check box, the button can be clicked. If you deselect the check box, the button is grayed out and cannot be clicked.

- **visible.** When you select the check box, the Button can be viewed. If you deselect the check box, the Button is invisible.

- **minHeight (2.0).** Click the Value field, and then enter a minimum height for the Button.

- **minWidth (2.0).** Click the Value field, and then enter a minimum width for the Button.

6 Click the **Control** menu, point to **Test Movie**, and then click **Test**.

In the example, when you click the button, it changes color, just like a typical rollover button. You could now attach an ActionScript to the button to load another scene or movie.

Adding a List

The List component is a scrollable box that lets users select one or more items in the list. Lists are similar to the ComboBox component, except List components can be formatted to display all of the available items at once, where as the ComboBox component uses a drop-down (or up) feature to display the items only when requested (clicking the triangle button to the right of the list).

Add a List Component

1. Open the **Components** panel.

2. Click the **User Interface** arrow to expand the list.

3. Drag the **List** component onto the Stage, and then select the component.

4. Open the **Properties** panel, and then click the **Component Parameters** arrow to expand it.

   IMPORTANT *The List component reduces the clutter of a typical data screen by allowing you to control the height of a data box. For example, if you wanted a visitor to select their home State from a list, you wouldn't want all 50 States permanently displayed on the screen. You would create a more manageable box size, and make the visitor scroll up or down to select the correct State.*

5. Select from the following List parameters:

   ◆ **data (2.0)** or **dataProvider (3.0).** Click the Edit button, and then enter an array in the Values dialog box. Click the plus (+) sign to add a value, and the minus sign (-) to remove a value. Data values are used to populate the list labels.

   ◆ **enabled (3.0).** When you select the check box, the field can be clicked. If you deselect the check box, the field is grayed out and cannot be clicked.

List component

◆ **labels (2.0).** Click the Edit button, and then enter an array in the Values dialog box. Click the plus (+) sign to add a value, and the minus sign (-) to remove a value. Data values are used as the selectable items in the list.

◆ **multipleSelection (2.0)** or **allowMultipleSelection (3.0).** When you select the check box, the visitor can select more than one item in the list. If you deselect the check box, the visitor can only select a single item.

◆ **rowHeight (2.0).** Click the Value field, and then enter a number to determine the spacing between items in the list. The higher the value, the more space between items.

◆ **horizontal or vertical ScrollPolicy (3.0).** Click the Value field, and then select auto, on, or off to show or hide scroll bars.

◆ **horizontal or vertical Line or Page ScrollSize (3.0).** Click the Value field, and then enter a number for the scroll size.

◆ **visible (3.0).** When you click the Value field, and select true, the list can be viewed. If you select false the list is invisible.

6 Click the **Control** menu, point to **Test Movie**, and then click **Test**.

In the example, click on a Chapter, and then select that chapter. You can now attach an ActionScript to the list to load the correct chapter.

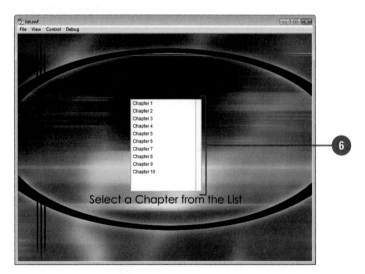

Adding a Label

A Label component consists of a single line of text. You can specify that a label be formatted with HTML. You can also control alignment and sizing of a label. Label components do not have borders, nor do they contain input that can be changed by the user. They are simply text information. Labels can be used to identify data input fields, or they can contain visitor information important to the understanding of a form. Labels can change what they display, as the Flash movie plays.

Add a Label Component

1. Open the **Components** panel.

2. Click the **User Interface** arrow to expand the list.

3. Drag one or more **Label** components onto the Stage, and then select the component, one at a time.

4. Open the **Properties** panel, and then click the **Component Parameters** arrow to expand it.

5. Select from the following Label parameters:

   ◆ **autoSize.** Click the Value field, and then select between left, center, right, or none. The autoSize parameter uses this information when automatically resizing the text.

   ◆ **condenseWhite (3.0).** When you select the check box, it removes extra white space (spaces, line breaks) in a text field. If you deselect the check box, the white space remains.

   ◆ **enabled (3.0).** When you select the check box, the field can be edited. If you deselect the check box, the field appears grayed out and is not selectable, or editable.

Label component

◆ **html (2.0).** When you select the check box, it allows HTML to control the formatting of the text. If you deselect the check box, the field cannot be modified using HTML.

◆ **text.** Click the Value field, and then enter the text that will appear in the field when the Flash document opens.

◆ **selectable (3.0).** When you select the check box, the field text is selectable. If you deselect the check box, the field text is not selectable.

◆ **visible.** When you select the check box, the field can be viewed. If you deselect the check box, the field is invisible.

◆ **minHeight (2.0).** Click the Value field, and then enter a minimum height for the Label.

◆ **minWidth (2.0).** Click the Value field, and then enter a minimum width for the Label.

◆ **wordWrap (3.0).** When you select the check box, the text typed by the visitor wraps in the TextArea box. If you deselect the check box, the text will not wrap

6 Click the **Control** menu, point to **Test Movie**, and then click **Test**.

In the example, the Label components represent visitor information in which the labeling fields require visitor input.

Adding a Data Grid

The DataGrid component allows you to create strong data-enabled displays and applications. You can use the DataGrid component to create a recordset (retrieved from a database query in ColdFusion, Java, or .Net) using Adobe Flash Remoting and display it in columns. You can also use data from a data set or from an array to fill a DataGrid component. The DataGrid component includes horizontal scrolling, event support (including event support for editable cells), sorting capabilities, and performance optimizations. The data for a grid can come from a recordset that is fed from a database query in Adobe ColdFusion, Java, or .Net using Flash Remoting, a data set or an array. To pull the information into a DataGrid, you set the DataGrid.dataProvider property to the recordset, data set, or array.

Add a DataGrid Component

① Open the **Components** panel.

② Click the **User Interface** arrow to expand the list.

③ Drag the **DataGrid** component onto the Stage, and then select the component.

④ Enter a unique instance name for the DataGrid component in the Property Inspector.

⑤ Select Frame 1 in the actions layer in the Timeline.

⑥ Open the **Actions** panel, and then enter the script as shown in the illustration.

The Flash Remoting recordset recordSetInstance is assigned to the dataProvider property of myDataGrid.

DataGrid component

Did You Know?

You can resize or copy the DataGrid. Select the Transform tool from the toolbox, and then use the resize nodes to change the width and height. To copy the DataGrid, select the Selection tool, hold down the Alt key (Win), Option key (Mac), and then drag the component.

Modify DataGrid Options

1. Select the DataGrid component.

2. Open the **Properties** panel, and then click the **Component Parameters** arrow to expand it.

3. Select from the following DataGrid parameters:

   - **editable.** When you select the check box, the field can be edited. If you deselect the check box, the field can be selected but not edited.

   - **mutipleSelection (2.0) or allowMultipleSelection (3.0).** When you select the check box, the visitor can select more than one item. If you deselect the check box, the visitor can only select a single item.

   - **headerHeight (3.0).** Click the Value field, and then enter a header height.

   - **rowHeight.** Click the Value field, and then enter a number to determine the spacing between items in the list. The higher the value, the more space between items.

   - **horizontal or vertical ScrollPolicy (3.0).** Click the Value field, and then select auto, on, or off to show or hide scroll bars.

   - **horizontal or vertical Line or Page ScrollSize (3.0).** Click the Value field, and then enter a number for the scroll size.

   - **resizableColumns (3.0).** When you select the check box, columns are resizeable.

   - **showHeaders (3.0).** When you select the check box, headers are displayed.

   - **sortableColumns (3.0).** When you select the check box, columns are sortable.

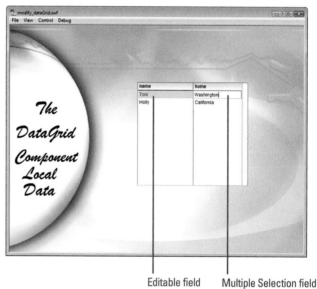

Editable field   Multiple Selection field

Using a Local Data Provider

The DataGrid component lets you provide data using a local (embedded in the document) data provider. The data is read into the grid from a pre-written ActionScript, and since Flash components are on the Stage, the ActionScript would typically be entered into the first frame of the Flash Timeline. It's smart programming to create a separate layer to hold the ActionScript for the DataGrid. That way you have much easier access to the script.

Use a Local Data Provider

1. Open the **Components** panel.

2. Click the **User Interface** arrow to expand the list.

3. Drag the **DataGrid** component onto the Stage, and then select the component.

4. Enter a unique instance name for the DataGrid component in the Property Inspector.

5. Select Frame 1 in the actions layer in the Timeline.

6. Open the **Actions** panel, and then enter the script as shown in the illustration.

7. Click the **Control** menu, point to **Test Movie**, and then click **Test**.

The name and home fields are the column headings for the DataGrid component, and the values fill the cells in each row.

DataGrid component

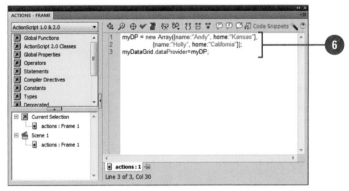

Did You Know?

You can use a Data Provider. Data Provider, such as adding data within an ActionScript, makes the Flash document display the same data every time the Flash document is displayed. You can always modify the data as the movie plays, by adding additional ActionScript instructions on the Timeline, and therefore, create a more dynamic Data Provider.

Adding a Loader

The Loader component is a container that can display a .swf or a .jpg. You use the Loader component when you want to pull in external content into a Flash movie. For example, you can bring in a product introduction (.swf) or a company logo (.jpg) at the beginning of a movie. In addition, you can scale the contents of the loader, or resize the loader itself, to accommodate the size of the contents. By default, the contents are scaled to fit.

Add a Loader Component

1. Open the **Components** panel.

2. Click the **User Interface** arrow to expand the list.

3. Drag the **Loader** (2.0) or **UILoader** (3.0) component onto the Stage, and then select the component.

4. Select the **Free Transform** tool to size the Loader to the dimensions of the image file.

5. Open the **Properties** panel, and then click the **Component Parameters** arrow to expand it.

6. Enter the path to the JPG or SWF file in the contentPath value (2.0) or source (3.0) field.

7. Click the **Control** menu, point to **Test Movie**, and then click **Test**.

   Flash displays the selected image in the Loader component.

Loader component

Adding a Numeric Stepper

The NumericStepper component allows a user to step through an ordered set of numbers. The component consists of a number displayed beside small up and down arrow buttons. You can decide the maximum and minimum values along with the step value. When the visitor clicks the up or down buttons, the value changes until the maximum or minimums are reached. As its name implies, the numeric stepper component only handles numbers, text or special characters are not allowed. The NumericStepper component has many uses; for example, a site that books rooms for a major hotel chain would use a stepper for letting the visitor indicate how many people are staying, or an airline for how many people are flying.

Add a NumericStepper Component

1. Open the **Components** panel.

2. Click the **User Interface** arrow to expand the list.

3. Drag the **NumericStepper** component onto the Stage, and then select the component.

4. Open the **Properties** panel, and then click the **Component Parameters** arrow to expand it.

    IMPORTANT *The NumericStepper component can be used to change the properties of items on the stage. You could link a NumericStepper instance to the property value of a dynamic text box, and then use the stepper to change the size of the text. This can be useful for people who require larger, readable text.*

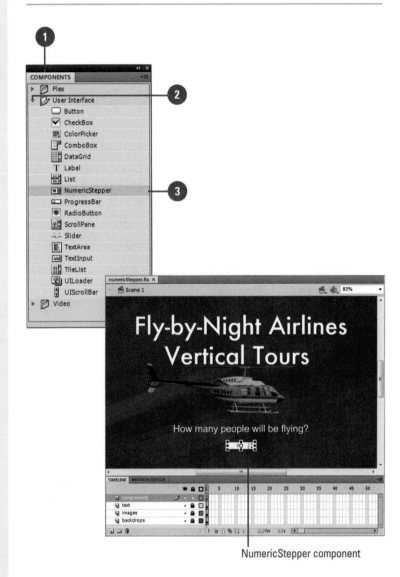

NumericStepper component

5 Select from the following NumericStepper parameters:

◆ **maximum.** Click the Value field, and then enter the maximum value associated with the NumericStepper.

◆ **minimum.** Click the Value field, and then enter the minimum value associated with the NumericStepper.

◆ **stepSize.** Click the Value field, and then enter a numerical value for stepping between numbers. For example, a stepSize value of 2, would cause the values to step by 2 (2, 4, 6, 8).

◆ **value.** Click the Value field, and then enter the first number value that appears in the NumericStepper.

◆ **enabled.** When you select the check box, the field can be selected. If you deselect the check box, the field appears grayed out and is not selectable.

◆ **visible.** When you select the check box, the field can be viewed. If you deselect the check box, the field is invisible.

◆ **minHeight (2.0).** Click the Value field, and then enter a minimum height for the NumericStepper.

◆ **minWidth (2.0).** Click the Value field, and then enter a minimum width for the NumericStepper.

6 Click the **Control** menu, point to **Test Movie**, and then click **Test**.

Adding a Progress Bar

The ProgressBar component is a necessity for Flash documents that require a long time to download, because they display the loading progress while a user waits. Web designers live under what is called the "ten-second rule." What that implies is that visitors to your Web site have very little patience, and they want to see things happening. When you add a ProgressBar component, the visitor sees a moving representation (a bar), letting them know the information is being downloaded.

Add a ProgressBar Component

1 Open the **Components** panel.

2 Click the **User Interface** arrow to expand the list.

3 Drag the **ProgressBar** component onto the Stage, and then select the bar.

4 Give the ProgressBar component a unique instance name in the Property Inspector.

5 Open the **Properties** panel, and then click the **Component Parameters** arrow to expand it.

6 Click the **Mode** list arrow, and then click **Event**.

Did You Know?

The ProgressBar component doesn't make a good preloader. A preloader is a custom progress bar that shows the loading status of an entire movie, and is usually smaller in file size than the ProgressBar component.

The loading process can be determinate or indeterminate. A determinate progress bar is linear, tracking progress over time. Use this when the amount of content is known. Indeterminate progress bar is used when the amount of content is unknown.

ProgressBar component

7 Drag a Loader component from the Components panel onto the Stage.

8 Give the Loader component a unique instance name in the Property Inspector.

9 Select the ProgressBar component.

10 Open the **Properties** panel, and then click the **Component Parameters** arrow to expand it, and then enter the instance name of the Loader into the Source value field.

11 Select Frame 1 in the actions layer in the Timeline.

12 Open the **Actions** panel, and then enter the script as shown in the illustration that will load a .jpg, or .swf file into the Loader component.

When executed, the ProgressBar component will display a horizontal bar, and the percentage of the file that's loaded.

13 Click the **Control** menu, point to **Test Movie**, and then click **Test**.

When executed, the ProgressBar component will display a moving horizontal bar, and a percentage which displays how much of the file has loaded.

IMPORTANT *Notice that you're not adding scripts to the components on the Stage. The key is that these components are activated by scripts in Frame 1 on the Timeline, and are identified by using unique instance names for each component.*

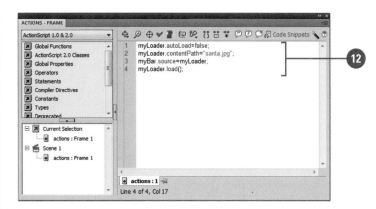

Adding a Scroll Pane

The ScrollPane component can be used for displaying large movie clips, .jpg files, and .swf files that need a scrollable area to display, or that you want to confine to a specific area on the Flash Stage. You have the ability to display images in a limited area, using scroll bars, and the content loaded into the ScrollPane can be from a local location, or over the Internet.

Add a ScrollPane Component

1. Open the **Components** panel.

2. Click the **User Interface** arrow to expand the list.

3. Drag the **ScrollPane** component onto the Stage, and then select the pane.

4. Open the **Properties** panel, and then click the **Component Parameters** arrow to expand it.

5. Select from the following ScrollPane parameters:

   ◆ **contentPath (2.0)** or **source (3.0)**. Click the Value field, and then enter the full path name to the movie clip, .jpg, or .swf file.

   ◆ **hLineScrollSize (2.0)** or **horizontalLineScrollSize (3.0)**. Click the Value field, and then enter the number of pixels to move the content when the left or right arrow in the horizontal scroll bar is pressed.

   ◆ **hPageScrollSize (2.0)** or **horizontalPageScrollSize (3.0)**. Click the Value field, and then enter the number of pixels to move the content when the track in the horizontal scroll bar is pressed.

   ◆ **hScrollPolicy (2.0)** or **horizontalScrollPolicy (3.0)**. Click the Value field, and then select whether the horizontal scroll bar is always present (on), never present (off), or appears automatically according to the image size (auto).

ScrollPane component

- **scrollDrag.** Click the Value field, and then select whether there is scrolling when a user presses and drags within the ScrollPane (true), or no scrolling (false).

- **vLineScrollSize (2.0)** or **verticalLineScrollSize (3.0).** Click the Value field, and then enter the number of pixels to move the content when the up or down arrow in the vertical scroll bar is pressed.

- **vPageScrollSize** or **verticalPageScrollSize (3.0).** Click the Value field, and then enter the number of pixels to move the content when the track in the vertical scroll bar is pressed.

- **vScrollPolicy (2.0)** or **verticalScrollPolicy (3.0).** Click the Value field, and then select whether the vertical scroll bar is always present (on), never present (off), or appears automatically according to the size of the image (auto).

- **enabled.** When you select the check box, the field can be selected. If you deselect the check box, the field appears grayed out and is not selectable.

- **visible.** When you select the the check box, the field can be viewed. If you deselect the check box, the field is invisible.

- **minHeight (2.0).** Click the Value field, and then enter a minimum height for the ScrollPane.

- **minWidth (2.0).** Click the Value field, and then enter a minimum width for the ScrollPane.

6 Click the **Control** menu, point to **Test Movie**, and then click **Test**.

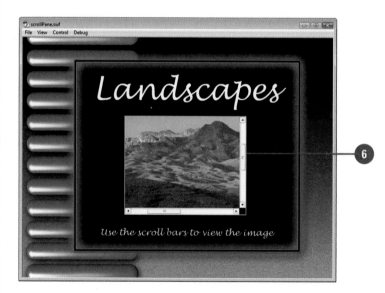

Creating Bindings

Data binding is a simple way of connecting Flash components to each other. Components can be viewed as containers that transfer information (images, text, numbers, video, graphics) from one to the other. In the Component Inspector panel, the Bindings tab controls the two containers, so that when property X of component A changes, it will copy the new value to property Y of component B. You can do data binding within the Component Inspector panel using the Bindings tab. The Bindings tab lets you add, view, and remove bindings for the selected component. Although data binding works with any component, its main purpose is to connect Component panel UI components to external data sources. These external data sources are available as components with properties, which you can bind to other component properties. The Component Inspector panel is the main tool that is used within Flash for data binding. It contains a Schema tab for defining the schema for a component and a Bindings tab for creating bindings between component properties. The following example demonstrates how to create basic data binding by connecting one UI component to another.

Create Bindings

1. Open the **Components** panel.

2. Click the **User Interface** arrow to expand the list.

3. Drag the **NumericStepper** component onto the Stage, and then select the component.

4. Give the NumericStepper a unique instance name in the Property Inspector.

5. Drag a second NumericStepper onto the Stage, and then give it a unique instance name.

6. Select the first NumericStepper component.

7 Open the **Component Inspector** panel, and then click the **Bindings** tab.

8 Click the **Add Binding (+)** button to add a binding.

9 In the Add Binding dialog box, select **Value**.

10 Click **OK**.

11 Move to the Name/Value section, located at the bottom of the Bindings tab.

12 Click the **Bound To** item under Name, and then click the **Magnifying Glass** icon.

13 In the Bound To dialog box, select the **NumbericStepper** component B.

14 Click **OK**.

15 Click the **Control** menu, point to **Test Movie**, and then click **Test**.

When you click the up and down buttons on the first NumericStepper, the value changes automatically in the second NumericStepper.

IMPORTANT *You can use the Bindings tab to link two or more components together. If you want to add another component, just click the Add Binding (+) button to bind a second, or third component. There is no limit to the number of components that can be bound together.*

Modifying Bindings

Once you create a binding between two components or between a component, such as a DataGrid, and an external file, you can control the binding through the binding options. For example, you may not want the exchange of data either way, or you may wish to control what type of data is entered or received. The Binding options, located on the Bindings tab, give you several author-controllable options.

Modify Bindings

1. Open the **Components** panel.

2. Click the **User Interface** arrow to expand the list.

3. Drag the **NumericStepper** component onto the Stage, and then select the component.

4. Give the NumericStepper a unique instance name in the Property Inspector.

5. Drag a **TextInput** component onto the Stage, and then give it a unique instance name.

6. Select the NumericStepper component.

7. Open the **Component Inspector** panel, and then click the **Bindings** tab.

8. Click the **Add Binding (+)** button to add a binding.

9. In the Add Binding dialog box, select **Value**.

10. Click **OK**.

11 Move to the Name/Value section, located at the bottom of the Bindings tab.

12 Click the **Bound To** item under Name, and then click the **Magnifying Glass** icon.

13 In the Bound To dialog box, select the **TextInput** component.

14 Click **OK**.

15 Click the **Control** menu, point to **Test Movie**, and then click **Test**.

If you click the up and down arrows on the NumericStepper, the value in the TextInput field changes. If you enter a value into the TextInput field and press Return or Tab, the value in the NumericStepper changes.

16 Close the Flash movie, and then select the NumericStepper.

17 Select **Value** at the top of the Component Inspector panel, click the **Directions** option, and then change the value from in/out to out.

18 Click the **Control** menu, point to **Test Movie**, and then click **Test**.

If you click the up and down arrows on the NumericStepper, the value in the TextInput field changes. If you enter a value into the TextInput field and press Return or Tab, the value in the NumericStepper no longer changes.

IMPORTANT *Data binding is supported only between components that exist in Frame 1 of the main Timeline, Frame 1 of a movie clip, or Frame 1 of a screen.*

Modifying Schema

To modify the schema of a component, you must first select an instance of the component. For example, if you want to modify the schema of a DataGrid component panel, you first select the component, open the Component Inspector panel, click the Schema tab, and then make the changes. Each component has its own unique schema, and changing parameters in the Component Inspector panel only changes the selected instance.

Modify Schema

① Select a unique instance of a component on the Stage.

② Open the **Component Inspector** panel.

③ Click the **Schema** tab.

④ Click the **Add A Component Property (+)** button to add additional fields to the schema list.

⑤ Click the **Add A Field Under The Selected Field (+)** button to add an additional field that's nested within the selected field.

⑥ Click the **Delete The Selected Field Or Property (-)** button to remove the selected field or property from the schema.

⑦ Select an item in the upper portion of the Schema tab, and then modify its options in the lower portion of the Schema tab.

Did You Know?

The Schema tab displays data based on the selected component. Although all components have properties, by default, the Schema tab only displays properties that contain dynamic data. Dynamic data properties are called bindable properties. Flash lets you bind to any property by adding it to the schema panel yourself (using the Add Field (+) button), or using ActionScript code.

Modifying Component Attributes

You can write ActionScript code to change the properties for any Flash component instance. For example, you can change the color of text of a label instance named myLabel using the following code:

myLabel.setStyle("color", "0x990000")

The preceding code would instruct Flash to change the color of the text used in the Label component instance named *myLabel* to red. Changes to the properties of a component can be attached to the instance on the Stage (influences only the one instance), or they can be used to globally change all instances, by placing the script in Frame 1 on the Timeline.

Modify Component Attributes

1. Open the **Actions** panel.

2. Select an instance or Frame 1 on the Timeline.

3. Enter the script as shown in the illustration.

4. Click the **Control** menu, point to **Test Movie**, and then click **Test**.

   The following table is a list of the available ActionScript options for changing the attributes of a component instance.

Did You Know?

You can customize a component. Some of the components, such as Scroll bars, include a skin, or look and feel, which you can customize to suit your own artistic nature. See Project 1, "Creating and Customizing Scrollable Text," in the Workshops (available on the Web at *www.perspection.com*) for a step by step example.

Available Flash Attributes

backgroundColor	marginLeft
borderColor	marginRight
borderStyle	scrollTrackColor
buttonColor	shadowColor
color	symbolBackgroundColor
disabledColor	symbolBackgroundDisabledColor
fontFamily	symbolBackgroundPressedColor
fontSize	symbolColor
fontStyle	symbolDisabledColor
fontWeight	textDecoration
highlightColor	textIndent

Using Components to Build a Form

When you create a form, you're incorporating all the various Flash components onto the Stage. Flash components make creating a form easy; however, there are still design considerations to be made. For example, what information do you need to extract from your visitors, and how will you receive it? Does your audience primarily speak and read English, or do you need to make the form multi-lingual (that's possible by creating label components that display text in a language selected by the visitor). And what about handicap and accessibility standards, how do you handle them? Yes, Flash does make the creation of a form easy, but you are still responsible for the overall design, and that includes images, backgrounds, colors, fonts and sizes, readability, and accessibility. The following Flash document is an example of incorporating multiple components to create an interactive form.

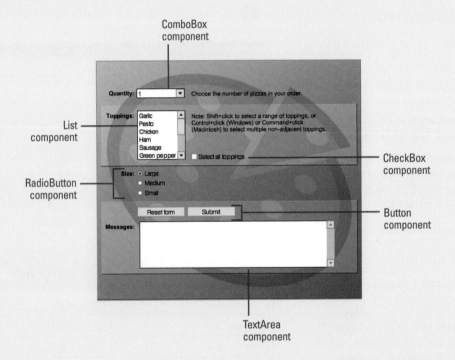

When you create a form, it is a good programming practice to isolate components onto separate layers. That way, they're easier to locate and edit, and you can always lock the component's layer to prevent accidental tampering.

Automating Your Work

Introduction

The History panel helps you work more efficiently in Flash. As you work, the History panel tracks all the steps you take in Flash. With the History panel, you can undo or redo steps to correct mistakes, replay selected steps for new tasks to streamline repetitive work, and record steps for replay from the Commands menu to automate your work. In addition, Flash allows you to use Object-level undo modes. Which means you can undo steps to a specific object without having to undo the changes made to other main objects on the Stage.

You can open the History panel from the Other Panels submenu on the Window menu. Each step you take in the active document during a work session appears on a separate line in the History panel. You can undo or redo a single step or series of steps quickly with the Undo/Redo slider, which you can drag up to undo a series of steps or drag down to redo a series of steps. You can also select a series of steps in the History panel and replay them to the same object or to a different object in the document.

Do you often repeat the same series of steps? Rather than repeat the same actions, you can work faster by saving the entire series of steps as a command on the Commands menu, which you can reuse again and again. Flash stores the commands you save for future use. After you save steps as a command, you can select the command name on the Commands menu to run it, or use the Manage Saved Command dialog box to rename or delete commands.

Due to the complex nature of some steps, such as adding a gradient to a shape or modifying document size, Flash cannot replay or save (as a command) all steps in the History panel. For these steps, a red X appears in the icon for a step in the History panel. Even though Flash cannot replay or save all steps, it can undo and redo all steps.

What You'll Do

Examine the History Panel

Use the History Panel

Work with Object-Level Undo Mode

Undo and Redo Steps

Replay Steps

Save Steps and Use Commands

Copy Steps Between Documents

Examining the History Panel

The History panel helps you automate and streamline the way you work in Flash. As you work in Flash, the History panel is tracking all your steps for the entire document or only on individual or all objects behind the scenes. With the History panel, you can do any of the following:

◆ Undo or redo steps to correct mistakes.

◆ Replay selected steps for new tasks to streamline repetitive work.

◆ Record steps for replay from the Commands menu to automate your work.

The History panel doesn't replace the Undo, Redo, and Repeat commands on the Edit menu, it simply tracks every step you perform in Flash. When you undo or redo one or more commands, the History panel displays the results; the Undo/Redo slider moves

according to the commands you select.

You can open the History panel using the Window menu like any of the other panels in Flash. Each step you take in the active document during a work session (since you created or opened the document) appears on a separate line in the History panel. The first step you perform in a work session appears at the top of the list and the last step appears at the bottom. If a red X appears in the icon for a step, it indicates Flash cannot save or replay the step. Unlike other panels in Flash, the History panel includes a slider on the left side that you can use to undo/redo steps; the Undo/Redo slider initially points to the last step you performed. The bottom of the History panel includes buttons to replay selected steps, copy selected steps to the Clipboard, and create a command from selected steps. The Options menu displays commands, such as Clear History, specific to the History panel.

Options menu

Undo/Redo slider

Replay selected steps

Copy selected steps to Clipboard

Create command from selected steps

Completed steps

Completed steps in document

Using the History Panel

You can use the Window menu to open the History panel like any of the other panels in Flash; the History panel appears on the Other Panels submenu. Each step you take in the active document during a work session appears on a separate line in the History panel. Steps you take in other Flash documents don't appear in other History panel lists. If you no longer need the steps in the History panel, you can erase the entire list. When you close a document, Flash clears the History panel.

Open and Close the History Panel

◆ To open the History panel, click the **Window** menu, point to **Other Panels**, and then click **History**.

TIMESAVER *Press ⌘+F10 (Mac) or Ctrl+F10 (Win) to open the History panel.*

◆ To close the panel, click the **Close** button, or click the **Options** menu, and then click **Close Panel**.

Close button

Clear the History Panel

① Open or expand the **History** panel.

② Click the **Options** menu, and then click **Clear History**.

③ Click **Yes** to confirm the operation.

④ When you're done, click the **Close** button on the History panel.

Options menu

Working with Object-Level Undo Mode

The History panel allows you to keep track of the changes made in Flash on a per-object basis. When this mode is activated in the General Preferences dialog box, each object on the Stage and even objects in the Library panel have their own undo list. Think about just what this means. You can now undo the changes you make to an object without having to undo changes to any other object.

Set Object-Level Undo

1 Click the **Flash** (Mac) or **Edit** (Win) menu, and then click **Preferences**.

2 Click the **General** category.

3 Click the **Undo** list arrow, and then click **Object-Level Undo**.

4 Click **OK** to confirm changing from Document to Object level undo will delete your current undo history.

5 Click **OK** to set object level undo or click **Cancel** to keep document level undo.

As you work, Flash keeps a per-object record of the history of each main Flash object.

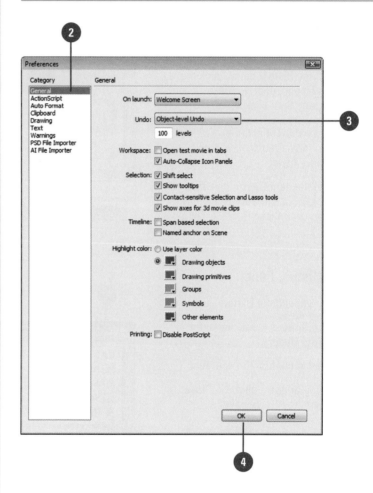

Work with Object Level Undo

1. Set object level undo in General preferences, and then open a new or existing Flash document.

2. Begin working with an object.

    As you work, Flash keeps a per-object record of the history of each main Flash object.

3. Open the **History** panel.

4. Use the Undo, Redo, or Repeat commands on the Edit menu.

    TROUBLE? *You cannot undo some object-level actions, such as working in a library or a scene. Check Flash Help for specifics.*

Undoing and Redoing Steps

You can undo or redo a single step or a series of steps quickly with the History panel. The History panel contains the Undo/Redo slider which you can drag up to undo (restore previous steps) a series of steps, or drag down to redo (restore steps you've undone) a series of steps. You can also undo and redo previous steps one at a time using the Undo and Redo commands on the Edit menu. When you use these commands, the steps in the History panel change based on the command results. The History panel and the Undo command can undo steps up to a maximum number (from 2 to 9999) set in the General tab of the Preferences dialog box.

Undo Steps with the History Panel

1. Open or expand the **History** panel.

2. Drag the **Undo/Redo** slider up until the slider points to the last step you want to keep.

   TIMESAVER *Position the pointer in the gray area to the left of a step, and then click the gray area to make the slider point to the step.*

   Flash undoes and grays out each selected step, starting from the bottom.

3. When you're done, click the **Close** button on the History panel.

Did You Know?

You can undo steps using the Undo command. Click the Edit menu, and then click Undo, or press ⌘+Z (Mac) or Ctrl+Z (Win).

See Also

See "Examining the History Panel" on page 466 for information on different elements in the History panel.

Drawn polygon shape removed with undo.

Redo Steps with the History Panel

1. Open or expand the **History** panel.

2. Drag the **Undo/Redo** slider down until the slider points to the last step you want to redo.

    Flash redoes and removes the gray highlighting for each selected step.

3. When you're done, click the **Close** button on the History panel.

Did You Know?

You can redo steps using the Redo command. Click the Edit menu, and then click Redo, or press ⌘+Y (Mac) or Ctrl+Y (Win).

You can change the number of undo levels for the Undo command. Click the Flash (Mac) or Edit (Win) menu, click Preferences, click the General tab, enter a number (from 2 to 9999) in the Undo Level box, and then click OK.

For Your Information

Saving Documents After Using Undo

When you delete an object in a document, the file size of the document doesn't change. The document still includes the size of the object you just deleted to preserve the possibility you might want to undo the step and restore the deleted item. If you know that you don't want the steps in the History panel, you can use the Save And Compact command on the File menu to clear the History panel, reduce the file size, and save the document. If you want to save the document and keep the steps in the History panel for the current session, use the Save command on the File menu.

Replaying Steps

You can replay steps from the History panel to the same object or to a different object in the document. You can replay steps only in the order in which you performed them; you can't rearrange the order of the steps in the History panel. If a red X appears in the icon for a step, it indicates Flash cannot save or replay the step. The Repeat command on the Edit menu allows you to apply your previous step to another object. For example, if you fill a shape with a color or pattern, you can fill another shape with the same color or pattern by selecting the other shape and using the Repeat command.

Replay Steps to the Same Object or Another Object

1. Open or expand the **History** panel.

2. Select the steps you want:

   ◆ **One step.** Click a step.

   ◆ **Adjacent steps.** Drag from one step to another or click the first step, hold down the Shift key, and then click the last step.

   ◆ **Nonadjacent steps.** Hold down the ⌘ (Mac) or Ctrl (Win) key, and then click steps.

3. Select the same object used in the History steps or another object.

4. Click **Replay** in the History panel.

   The steps are replayed in order, and a new step called Replay Steps appears in the History panel.

5. When you're done, click the **Close** button on the History panel.

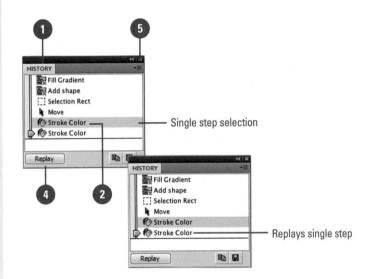

Single step selection

Replays single step

Multiple step selection

Replay multiple steps

> ### See Also
>
> *See "Copying Steps Between Documents" on page 476 for information on replaying steps in a different document.*

Repeat the Previous Step on Another Object

① Select an object, and then perform a command.

② Select another object to which you want to perform the same previous command.

③ Click the **Edit** menu, and then click **Repeat**.

The command is performed on the selected object.

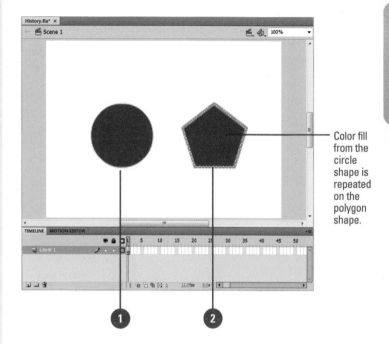

Color fill from the circle shape is repeated on the polygon shape.

For Your Information

Changing the View in the History Panel

The Options menu in the History panel allows you to change the way you view steps. You can view steps in the History panel with scripting arguments or JavaScript commands. Even if you are not a programmer, you can get a better idea about the functionality of each step by looking at the scripting argument or JavaScript commands. If you want to view scripting arguments or JavaScript commands in the History panel as you need it without having to change the view each time, you can view the information as a tooltip. To change the view, click the Options menu in the History panel, point to View, and then click a view option: Default (steps only), Arguments In Panel, JavaScript In Panel, Arguments In Tooltip, or JavaScript In Tooltip.

Saving Steps and Using Commands

The History panel records the steps you take in the order in which you performed them in Flash. If you perform the same set of steps several times while you work on a document, you can save the steps in the History panel as a command on the Commands menu, which you can reuse again and again. Flash stores the commands you save for future use (even if you close the document). Some steps, including selecting a frame or modifying a document size, can't be saved as commands, but they can be undone and redone. If a red X appears in the icon for a step, it indicates Flash cannot save or replay the step. After you save steps as a command, you can run, rename, or delete commands.

Save Steps as a Command

1 Open or expand the **History** panel.

2 Select the steps you want to save.

3 Click the **Save As Command** button in the History panel.

4 Enter a name for the command.

5 Click **OK**.

The command is available on the Commands menu and saved as a JavaScript file with the extension JSFL in the Commands folder, which is located in Adobe\Flash CS5\First Run\.

6 When you're done, click the **Close** button on the History panel.

Did You Know?

You can delete a name from the Command menu. Click the Commands menu, click Manage Saved Commands, select the command you want to remove, click Delete, click Yes, and then click OK.

Run a Command

1️⃣ Click the **Commands** menu.

2️⃣ Click a command name from the list.

Did You Know?

You can run JavaScript or Flash JavaScript commands. Click the Commands menu, click Run Command, navigate to the script file, and then click Open.

Edit the Names of Commands

1️⃣ Click the **Commands** menu, and then click **Manage Saved Commands**.

2️⃣ Select a command to rename.

3️⃣ Click **Rename**.

4️⃣ Enter a new name for the command.

5️⃣ Click **OK**.

6️⃣ Click **OK**.

Did You Know?

You can download commands from the Web. The Flash Exchange Web site contains commands developed by other users you can download (some for a fee) and use in your documents. Click the Commands menu, and then click Get More Commands to quickly access the Adobe Web site.

Copying Steps Between Documents

Each document only tracks its own set of steps in the History panel. When you close a document, Flash clears the History panel. If you want to use a set of steps in another document, you need to copy them from one History panel and paste them to another document. You can use the Copy Steps button on the History panel or the same command on the Options menu to complete the task. When you paste steps into another document, Flash replays the steps and the History panel shows the steps as only one step called Paste Steps (Mac) or Paste (Win).

Copy Steps Between Documents

1. Open a document containing the steps you want to copy.

2. Open or expand the **History** panel.

3. Select the steps in the History panel you want to copy.

4. Click the **Copy Steps** button in the History panel.

5. Open the document into which you want to paste the steps.

6. Select the objects to which you want to apply the steps.

7. Click the **Edit** menu, and then click **Paste In Center**.

   The steps play in the document as Flash pastes the steps into the History panel of the document. The steps appear in the History panel as a single step called Paste Steps (Mac) or Paste (Win).

8. When you're done, click the **Close** button on the History panel.

Steps pasted into the History panel of another document.

Publishing a Movie

Introduction

When you design a Flash movie, you're actually working with two documents: a source document FLA, and a publish document SWF. The source document is the working document that the Flash application uses to edit the movie data. The published document is the compressed player document that, once created, can be inserted into an HTML document, burned onto a CD, DVD, or DVS, or played directly from your hard drive, external drive, or network drive.

You can publish a Flash document in one step, by clicking the File menu, and then clicking Publish. However, before publishing, it's a good idea to first check the publish settings by clicking the File menu, and then clicking Publish Settings. Using the Publish Settings dialog box, you can easily change the way your file is published. For example, the default settings for publishing a Flash document are to publish using the latest Flash plug-in, and to create an HTML container document to hold and play the published movie. Additional options include the ability to generate a JPEG, GIF, or PNG image of a selected frame in the Flash source document. You can even create a self-running player document for Macintosh or Windows. Publishing is not only necessary to create a Flash movie; it can be used to test the movie using different settings.

Once the correct publish settings are found, you can export the settings into a separate file, and then use them on new Flash documents. This not only makes the publishing process fast, it gives you consistency between documents.

What You'll Do

Publish Considerations

Modify Publish Settings

Specify Flash Options

Specify Adobe AIR Options

Insert File Information

Specify HTML Options

Specify GIF Options

Specify PNG Options

Specify JPEG Options

Create a Projector

Create a Publishing Profile

Edit Profile Properties

Export and Import a Profile

Duplicate a Profile

Preview or Test a Movie

Use the Bandwidth Profiler

Export a Movie to Different Formats

Print from the Flash Player

Publishing Considerations

Publishing a Flash movie is the last step in a long journey from inception to the final product. Along the publishing road, you'll encounter detours, and stoplights and even get lost once in awhile. However, if you've had the foresight to plan your project, then the journey becomes one more of pleasure than pain.

Planning a project requires knowledge of where the final published document is headed. You might be designing a Flash movie, where the intended audience is the Web, or it could be a project where the final destination is a CD or DVD. It could be an interactive form, or an animated cartoon. It's even possible that your goals for this project involve more than one destination.

Called Multi-purposing, Flash will help you design a project version that is small enough to run efficiently, as well as a higher-quality version, intended to run directly off the hard drive. It really doesn't matter where the project is headed, because Flash's advanced publishing options will effortlessly guide you through the process.

Before you ever open Flash, create your first graphic, or write your first piece of text, always remember to plan the project. In other words, begin the project with the end in mind. That's not new, but it bears remembering. If you plan for the end of a project, you will create a road map that will accurately guide you to your final destination.

When you are ready to publish a Flash movie, you can use Flash publishing settings and tools in this chapter to make the job easier. You can also use the Adobe Flash deployment kit to post Flash Player SWF files to your Web site and control the experience of visitors who do not have the Flash Player installed in their browser. Flash standardizes the method used for detection of the plug-in on the client-side, reducing the amount of code that must be written to implement the detection option. If you're interested in working with the Flash Development Kit, simply point your browser to *http://www.adobe.com/devnet/devices/development_kits.html*. Since Flash is always creating new ways for us to design great Flash documents, this site is constantly changing to reflect the latest technologies.

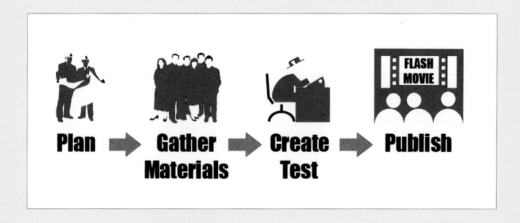

Modifying Publish Settings

Once you've determined how your project will be published, it's time to let Flash assist you with all the details of getting your project from conception to an output file suited to your needs. Flash's publishing settings go far beyond converting a Flash source file FLA into a published movie SWF; they give you the ability to adjust the output to a specific version of the Flash player, incorporate specific Flash compression features, and even save screen shots of the source file's frames in several different formats. And, if a Flash movie is not what you're after, you can even publish a Flash source file in other formats, including GIF, JPEG, PNG, and Windows or Macintosh Projector. In addition, you can also export a Flash source file in a variety of file formats, including a QuickTime movie MOV.

Modify Publish Settings

1. Open a Flash source document.

   Generic publish settings are initially linked to a specific Flash file.

2. Click the **File** menu, and then click **Publish Settings**.

3. Select or clear the option check boxes to enable or disable the Publish Settings.

4. Enter a name for the individual options in the File name input box.

5. To revert the names to default, click the **Use Default Names** button.

   The default name refers to the name of the source document.

6. Click **OK** to save the changes.

   IMPORTANT *When you publish a Flash movie, the changes only affect the published .swf document, never the .fla source document. If you delete or misplace the .fla source document, you will never be able to re-edit, or republish the movie.*

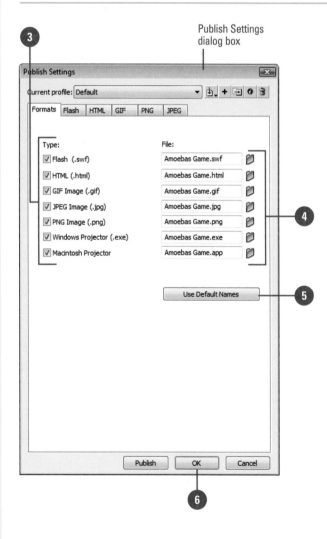

Publish Settings dialog box

Specifying Flash Options

A Flash document is like a fingerprint: no two Flash movies are the same. So it stands to reason that different Flash documents would require different publish settings. Flash gives you the ability to conform a Flash document using specific output settings. Everything from the version of the Flash player plug-in and ActionScript to the movie compression and quality of embedded JPEG images are available options in the Publish Setting dialog box.

Specify Flash Options

1. Click the **File** menu, and then click **Publish Settings**.

2. Select the **Flash** check box, and then click the **Flash** tab.

3. Click the **Player** list arrow, and then select the version of the player to publish the Flash document.

4. Click the **Script** list arrow, and then select the version to publish the Flash document.

5. Drag the **JPEG Quality** slider to increase or decrease the amount of compression applied to the image. The lower the value, the more information is removed from the image.

6. Select the **Enable JPEG deblocking** check box to reduce the appearance of common artifacts found in highly compressed JPEG files.

7. Select from the following options:

   - Click **Set** to modify the Audio Stream settings for the active Flash document.

   - Click **Set** to modify the Audio Event settings for the active Flash document.

   - Select the **Override Sound Settings** check box to override any sound settings applied to the individual sound files within the active Flash document.

8 Select from the following options:

- **Compress Movie.** Compresses the movie (only for movies played with Flash 7 player).

- **Include Hidden Layers.** Includes hidden layers in the Flash document.

- **Include XMP metadata.** Includes XMP data. Click File Info to view the data.

- **Export SWC.** Exports a .swc file, which is used for distributing components made up of ActionScript code.

- **Generate Size Report.** Creates a frame-by-frame size report for the active document.

- **Protect From Import.** Prevents the published Flash document from being reopened in the Flash application.

- **Omit Trace Actions.** Prevents trace actions from being carried over to the published document.

- **Permit Debugging.** Permits debugging of the Flash movie.

9 Enter a password for the Flash document (2.0).

This option is available if Protect From Import or Permit Debugging are selected in step 10.

10 Click the **Local Playback Security** list arrow, and then select the local only or network only option.

11 Click the **Hardware Acceleration** list arrow, and then select an option to take advantage of available hardware for better playback performance.

12 Click **OK** to save the settings.

For Your Information

Security Options

The Flash Player 8 and later incorporates a security option that allows you to determine the local and network playback security for published SWF files. SWF files have read access to local files and networks by default, but they cannot communicate with the network. In the Flash tab on the Publish Settings dialog box, you can select a Local Playback Security option to access network resources, which allows the SWF file to send and receive information. If you select the option to access network resources, local access is disabled for security reasons. Flash also provides buffer overrun protection, which prevents misuse of external files, such as a virus. The player also provides stricter security; SWF files with nonsecure protocols (HTTP) cannot access content loaded using secure protocols (HTTPS).

Specifying Adobe AIR Options

Adobe AIR is a cross-operating system runtime that allows you to leverage your existing web development skills in Flash to build and deliver Rich Internet Applications (RIAs) to more devices, including the web, mobile, and desktop. You can create a new Flash file for AIR from the Welcome page or the New dialog box by clicking Adobe AIR 2 (**New!**), or use an existing Flash file (ActionScript 3.0), and then convert it to an Adobe AIR file through the Publish Settings dialog box (**New!**). Before you can publish a file to Adobe AIR, you need to have a digital certificate that represents the application publisher's identify. After you publish an AIR application, you can install it by using the Installer Package with the AIR extension and start the program like any other program on your system. When you no longer want to use it, you can remove it like a normal program too.

Publish to Adobe AIR

1. Click the **File** menu, and then click **Publish Settings**.

   ◆ You can also access AIR Settings by clicking the **Edit** button in the Property Inspector or click the **File** menu, and then click **AIR Settings**.

2. Select the **Flash** check box, and then click the **Flash** tab.

3. Click the **Player** list arrow, and then click **Adobe AIR 2**.

4. Click **Settings**.

5. Click the **General** tab.

6. Select from the following General settings:

   ◆ **Output File.** Specifies where to save the AIR file.

   ◆ **File Information.** Enter the following file information: File name, Name, Version, ID (a unique identifier, no spaces or special characters), Description, Copyright, and Window style.

   ◆ **Profiles.** Select profiles for the application types you want to create (**New!**).

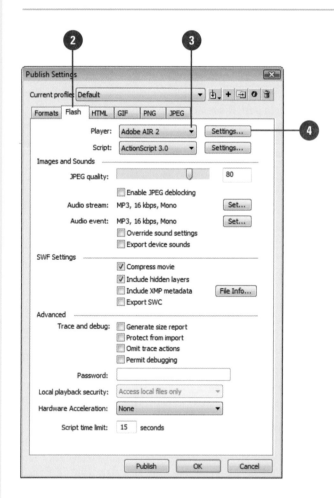

- ◆ **Included files.** Specifies which additional files and folders to include in the AIR file.

7 Click the **Signature** tab.

All Adobe Air applications must be signed to be installed on another system.

8 Click an option to select or create a digital certificate or use AIR Intermediate (AIRI) for temporary use that will be signed later.

- ◆ **Create Digital Signature.** Click **Create**, specify publisher and organization information, password, type (use default), click **Browse** to select the folder with the FLA file, and then click **OK**. Enter the password from the certificate, and select the related options as desired.

9 Click the **Icons** tab, select an application icon size, and then select an application icon.

10 Click the **Advanced** tab, specify any associated file types, initial window settings, install and program menu folders.

11 Click **Publish** to publish it, and then click **OK**, or click **OK**, and then click **OK** to save settings.

Did You Know?

You can use certain versions of Adobe AIR with certain versions of Flash. Flash CS5 only supports and publishes to AIR 2.0, Flash CS4 only supports and publishes to AIR 1.1, and Flash CS3 only supports and publishes to AIR 1.0.

Create certificate

Inserting File Information

When you save a document, you have the ability to save more than just Flash information. You can save copyright, camera, and even image category information. This data is saved with the file as metadata in the XMP format (Extensible Metadata Platform) in SWF files, and can be recognized and accessed by any application, such as Adobe Bridge, that reads XMP metadata. In addition, if an image is a photograph, you can save data specifying the type of image, where it was shot, or the camera used. You can even get information on shutter speed and f-stop. You can do the same with video and audio data too. That information will not only protect your intellectual property, but will supply you with vital statistics on exactly how you created that one-of-a-kind image.

Insert File Information into a Flash Document

1. Open a document.

2. Click the **File** menu, and then click **File Info**.

3. Click the **Description** tab, and then enter information concerning the author and any copyright information.

4. Click the **IPTC** tab to enter information concerning the image's creator, description and keywords, location where photograph was taken, date created, copyright, and usage terms.

5. Click the **Camera Data** tab, which reveals information about the camera that took the image.

6. Click the **Video Data** tab or **Audio Data** tab to reveal information about video and audio data, and then enter your video and audio data.

7. Click the **Mobile SWF** tab or **Audio Data** tab, and then enter file information for a mobile SWF.

8. Click the **Categories** tab, and then enter category keywords for search purposes.

9. Click the **Origin** tab, and then enter data pertaining to the origin of the image.

10. Click the **DICOM** tab, and then enter data pertaining to the Digital Imaging and Communications in Medicine.

11. Click the **History** tab to view historical information about the active document, such as dates last opened and saved, and a list of image adjustments.

12. Click the **Advanced** tab to view additional information on the active document, such as EXIF, and PDF document properties.

13. Click the **Raw Data** tab to view raw RDF/XML information.

14. Click **OK**.

Did You Know?

You can add metadata to files saved in the PSD, PDF, EPS, PNG, GIF, JPEG, and TIFF formats. The information is embedded in the file using XMP (eXtensible Metadata Platform). This allows metadata to be exchanged between Adobe applications and across operating systems.

You can use the XMP Software Development Kit to customize the creation, processing, and interchange of metadata. You can also use the XMP kit to add fields to the File Info dialog box. For information on XMP and the XMP SDK, check the Adobe Solutions Network.

Specifying HTML Options

The most common way to display a Flash movie is on the Internet, using an HTML document as the movie container. HTML creates tags that embed the Flash movie in an HTML document for viewing on the Web. Flash publish settings give you the ability to create an HTML document specifically tailored to the active Flash document; including options to use an HTML template, and control the playback and quality of the final published document. You can also set options to specify the scale and alignment of the movie as well as the way it opens.

Specify HTML Options

1. Click the **File** menu, and then click **Publish Settings**.

2. Select the **HTML** check box, and then click the **HTML** tab.

3. Click the **Template** list arrow, and then select a Flash container template (including templates for PocketPC devices).

4. Click the **Dimensions** list arrow, and then click **Match Movie**, **Pixels**, or **Percent**. If Pixels or Percent, enter width and height.

   The Match Movie option matches the size of the Flash movie. The Pixels option sets the exact size. The Percent option allows for scaling within a browser.

5. Select from the following Playback options:

   ◆ **Paused At Start.** Select this option to pause the Flash movie, when loaded.

   ◆ **Loop.** Select this option to cause the Flash movie to loop, when loaded.

   ◆ **Display Menu.** Select this option to have the HTML document display a control menu for the Flash document.

   ◆ **Device Font.** Select this option to use device fonts in the Flash document.

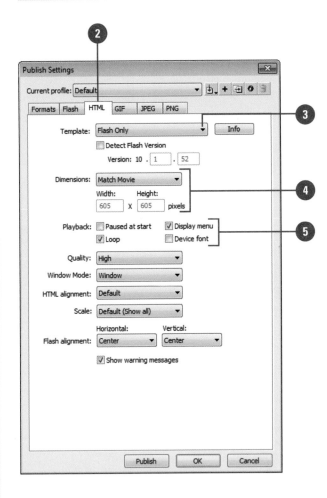

6 Click the **Quality** list arrow to select a quality level for the document.

   ◆ **Low** No anti-alias.

   ◆ **Auto Low.** Starts with no anti-alias, but changes as needed.

   ◆ **High.** Allows anti-alias.

   ◆ **Auto High.** Starts with anti-alias, but changes down as needed.

   ◆ **Medium.** Anti-aliases most items, but does not smooth bitmaps.

   ◆ **Best.** Anti-aliases everything.

7 Click the **Window Mode** list arrow, and then select a mode (Window, Opaque Windowless, or Transparent Windowless) for opening the Flash document.

8 Click the **HTML Alignment** list arrow to select the alignment of the HTML page.

9 Click the **Scale** list arrow to select how to scale the Flash document, when loaded into the HTML page.

   ◆ **Default.** Shows entire document; keeps proportions.

   ◆ **No Border.** Fills area to the border; keeps proportions.

   ◆ **Exact Fit.** Fills entire SWF movie; doesn't keep proportions.

   ◆ **No Scale.** SWF remains the same size if Player window is resized.

10 Click the **Horizontal** and **Vertical** list arrows to select how the Flash document is aligned with in the HTML page.

11 Click **OK** to save HTML settings.

For Your Information

Using Version Detection

Version Detection checks what version of the Flash Player is running on your viewer's computer. If the Flash Player is missing or the version number is not high enough to display the movie, you can have Flash display a message, link to Adobe's Web site to download the correct version, display an alternative image file, or display a different site. To detect a viewer's Flash Player version, click the File menu, click Publish Settings, click the Flash tab, click the Version list arrow, click Flash version 4 or higher, click the HTML tab, select the Detect Flash Version check box, click Settings, and then specify file names (.html) for Detection (detects Flash Player version), Content (displays the .swf file), and Alternate (displays a warning and link to download the Flash Player). To let Flash create its standard Detection and Alternate files, click the Generate Default option, or click Use Defaults. This uses SWFObject2 for Flash Player detection (**New!**). To use your own alternate file, click the Use Existing option, and then click Browse to select the file.

Specifying GIF Options

When you publish a Flash document, you're not limited to just the creation of the Flash movie, you can instruct Flash to create a GIF image of the Flash movie, based on the currently selected frame. The GIF file format (Graphics Interchange Format) is used primarily for clipart, text, and line art, or for images that contain areas of solid color. Once the image is created, you can open and use it in any application that supports the GIF file format.

Specify GIF Options

1. Select a specific frame on the Timeline.

2. Click the **File** menu, and then click **Publish Settings**.

3. Select the **GIF** check box, and then click the **GIF** tab.

4. Enter a **Width** and **Height** (in pixels) for the JPEG image, or select the **Match Movie** check box to create a JPEG image that matches the size of the Flash movie.

5. Select from the following Playback options:

   ◆ **Static.** Prevents the GIF animation from playing.

   ◆ **Animated.** Animates the GIF document.

   ◆ **Loop Continuously.** Forces the animation into a continuous loop.

   ◆ **Repeat.** Enter a value representing the number of times the file loops.

6 Select from the following Options:

- ◆ **Optimize Colors.** Creates an optimized (smaller) set of colors for the active document.

- ◆ **Interlace.** Creates an interlaced image where the file, when displayed on a Web page, loads in three passes.

- ◆ **Smooth.** Uses a color dithering scheme to create visually smoother color transitions.

- ◆ **Dither Solids.** Dithers (mixes) solid colors if they fall outside of the viewable color gamut.

- ◆ **Remove Gradients.** Removes gradients from the active image.

7 Click the **Transparent** list arrow, and then click **Opaque**, **Transparent**, or **Alpha**.

The Alpha transparency mask generates transparent areas within the GIF image.

8 Click the **Dither** list arrow, and then click **None**, **Ordered**, or **Diffusion**.

9 Click the **Palette Type** list arrow, and then click **Web 216**, **Adaptive**, **Web Snap Adaptive**, or **Custom**.

10 Enter a number for the Maximum Colors.

This is available for Adaptive and Web Snap Adaptive. Flash lets you select how many colors are available for the image's color table.

11 Click to select a color table file for the Custom Palette Type.

12 Click **OK** to save the GIF settings.

Palette Type Options

Option	Use
Web 216	Creates an image with only Web Safe colors.
Adaptive	Creates an image where the color table (CLUT) adapts to the image colors.
Web Snap Adaptive	Creates a color table that adheres closely to the Web Safe Color palette.
Custom	Creates a customized color palette.

Specifying PNG Options

When you publish a Flash document, you're not limited to just the creation of the Flash movie. You can instruct Flash to create a PNG image of the Flash movie, based on the currently selected frame. The PNG file format (Portable Network Graphic) is a hybrid format designed to save clip art, photographic images, text, and line art. Once the image is created, you can open and use it in any application that supports the PNG file format.

Specify PNG Options

1. Select a specific Frame on the Timeline.

2. Click the **File** menu, and then click **Publish Settings**.

3. Select the **PNG** check box, and then click the **PNG** tab.

4. Enter a **Width** and **Height** (in pixels) for the PNG image, or select the **Match Movie** check box to create a PNG image that matches the size of the Flash movie.

5. Click the **Bit Depth** list arrow, and then select **8-bit**, **24-bit**, or **24-bit With Alpha**.

6. Select from the following Options:

   - **Optimize Colors.** Creates an optimized (smaller) set of colors for the active document.

   - **Interlace.** Creates an interlaced image where the file, when displayed on a Web page, loads in three passes.

   - **Smooth.** Uses a color dithering scheme to create visually smoother color transitions.

   - **Dither Solids.** Dithers (mixes) solid colors, if the colors fall outside of the viewable color gamut.

   - **Remove Gradients.** Remove any gradients from the active image.

Bit Depth Choices

Option	Selection
8-bit	Maximum of 256 colors
24-bit	Maximum of 16.7 million colors
24-bit with Alpha	Maximum of 16.7 colors and supports the alpha transparency

Click the **Dither** list arrow, and then click **None**, **Ordered**, or **Diffusion** to dither (mix) colors that fall outside the viewable color gamut.

Click the **Palette Type** list arrow, and then click **Web 216**, **Adaptive**, **Web Snap Adaptive**, or **Custom** to select a specific palette type.

Enter a number for the Maximum Colors.

This is available for Adaptive and Web Snap Adaptive. Flash lets you select how many colors are available for the image's color table.

Click to select a color table file for the Custom Palette Type.

Click the **Filter Options** list arrow, and then select from the available filter options to control the filtering of the colors in the active image.

Click **OK** to save the PNG settings.

Specifying JPEG Options

When you publish a Flash document, you're not limited to just the creation of the Flash movie, you can instruct Flash to create a JPEG image of the Flash movie, based on the currently selected frame. The JPEG file format (Joint Photographic Experts Group), is used primarily to reduce the size of photographic images. Once the image is created, you can open and use it in any application that supports the JPEG file format. You can select a quality option to compress the file size, which reduces download time over the Internet. You can specify a quality value between 1 and 100. A higher value preserves image quality, but retains a higher file size.

Specify JPEG Options

1 Select a specific frame on the Timeline.

2 Click the **File** menu, and then click **Publish Settings**.

3 Select the **JPEG** check box, and then click the **JPEG** tab.

4 Enter a **Width** and **Height** (in pixels) for the JPEG image, or select the **Match Movie** check box to create a JPEG image that matches the size of the Flash movie.

5 Drag the **Quality** slider to increase or decrease the amount of compression applied to the image.

The lower the value, the more information (quality) is removed from the image.

6 Select the **Progressive** check box to create a progressive JPEG image. The file, when displayed on a Web page, loads in three passes.

7 Click **OK** to save the JPEG settings.

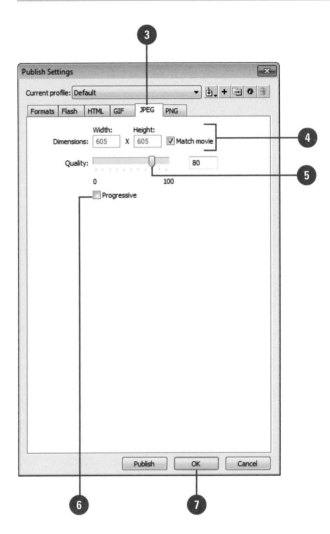

Creating a Windows or Macintosh Projector

The Flash publish settings gives you the ability to create a self-contained player document for the Macintosh or Windows operating system. When you publish a document using the projector options, Flash creates a Flash movie according to your setting, and embeds the player application into the file. Creating a projector document increases the size of the final document by almost 1MB, so this option would not be used to create Internet documents, but for movies destined for playing on a hard drive, or burned onto a CD or DVD. When you publish using the Projector options, there are no additional options.

Create a Windows or Macintosh Projector

1. Click the **File** menu, and then click **Publish Settings**.

2. Select the **Windows Projector (.exe)**, and/or **Macintosh Projector** check boxes.

3. Click **Publish**.

   Flash generates the Macintosh or Windows Projectors documents, and saves them in the same location as the original source document.

Did You Know?

You can play Flash SWF files different ways. Besides playing SWF files in a stand-alone projector, you can also play Flash content in an Internet browser, such as Internet Explorer or Firefox; in Director, Microsoft Office and other ActiveX applications with the Flash ActiveX; and as part of a QuickTime video.

Creating a Publishing Profile

Flash lets you generate profiles for often-used publish settings within a Flash source file. For example, you're creating a multi-purpose Flash document and you need specific settings to create a fast-loading Internet version, as well as a version designed to run on a CD or DVD. You could create a publishing profile to fit both needs, and save them with the source document. The benefits of this are obvious: Not only can you quickly publish a Flash document using different profiles; you're assured the settings will be accurate every time. Fast and accurate are two words which describe Flash publishing.

Create a Publishing Profile

1. Click the **File** menu, and then click **Publish Settings**.

2. Click the **Current Profile** list arrow to select the profile.

3. Make the necessary changes in the Publish Settings dialog box.

4. Click **OK**.

5. Click the **Create New Profile** button.

6. Enter a unique name in the Profile Name box.

7. Click **OK**.

   IMPORTANT *When you save a Flash profile, it's only available to that specific document.*

Editing Profile Properties

Once you create a unique profile settings file, it's available for use with the click of the Current Profile list arrow in the Publish Settings dialog box. Unfortunately, not everything is perfect the first time you do it, and it's possible that after you create a profile, you discover a mistake in the settings. The good news is that you don't have to begin again. All you have to do is edit the profile.

Edit Profile Properties

1. Click the **File** menu, and then click **Publish Settings**.

2. Click the **Current Profile** list arrow, and then select the profile you want to change.

3. Make the necessary changes in the Publish Settings dialog box.

4. Click **OK**.

5. Select the **File** menu, and then click **Save**.

   Flash profiles are saved when you save the Flash source document.

   IMPORTANT *Profile properties are recorded as you change them, and then saved when you save the file. If you change your mind after modifying the profile, your choices include manually changing the profile back to its original settings, or closing the file without saving. However, if you've also made changes to the Flash document, closing without saving will also cause you to lose those changes.*

Exporting and Importing a Profile

Saving Flash profiles is a great way to cut down on repetitive publish settings. However, the disadvantage is the user-defined settings only relate to the original source document. If you open a new file, you're starting from scratch. It would be great to be able to create a series of setting files, and then use them over and over again on a new Flash document. Flash understood this need and gave Flash users the ability to create settings files, and then export them as a separate file. Then, if you need to use the settings in a new Flash document, all you have to do is import the settings file. Exporting Dreamweaver profiles gives you the ability to import and use the profile on multiple Flash projects. In addition, you can send copies of exported profiles to other Flash users, so they can benefit from your efforts. When you export a Flash profile, you have the ability to reuse it, via the Import option. It's a good idea to save (export) all of your profiles into a single location. That way, when you go to import a specific profile, you will know exactly where to point your finder.

Export a Profile

1. Click the **File** menu, and then click **Publish Settings**.

2. Click the **Current Profile** list arrow, and then select the profile you want to export.

3. Click the **Import/Export Profile** button, and then click **Export**.

4. Navigate to the drive or folder location where you want to save the exported profile.

5. Click **Save**.

Import a Profile

1. Click the **File** menu, and then click **Publish Settings**.

2. Click the **Current Profile** list arrow, and then select the profile you want to import.

3. Click the **Import/Export Profile** button, and then click **Import**.

4. Navigate to the drive or folder where the profile is located.

5. Select the file name of the exported profile.

6. Click **Open**.

> **IMPORTANT** *Once a profile is imported into a Flash document, it becomes a copy of the original item. You can use it in the active document, or make some minor adjustments, and export it out as a new profile.*

Duplicating a Profile

When you work with a profile, you're creating a time-saving file that lets you use the same settings over and over again. Not only does Flash make the creation of a profile easy; it will let you create a duplicate of the file. In truth, a duplicate file would not serve much of a purpose: Why would you want an exact copy of something that already exists? Actually, creating a duplicate can be a very smart thing to do. For example, say you create a profile for a specific job that involved several changes to the default settings, and you name it: Output_A. Then, two weeks later you need another profile that's almost exactly the same as Output_A, with one or two minor changes. Rather than start from scratch, you create a duplicate of Output_A, make the minor changes, and Export it using the name: Output_B. It's fast and easy, and it means you're working smart.

Duplicate a Profile

1. Click the **File** menu, and then click **Publish Settings**.

2. Click the **Current Profile** list arrow, and then select the profile you want to duplicate.

3. Click the **Duplicate Profile** button.

4. Give the duplicate a new name.

5. Click **OK**.

See Also

See "Exporting and Importing a Profile" on page 496 for more information on how to export a Flash publishing profile.

Previewing a Movie

Previewing a Flash movie is an important part of the design process. As you work, you should periodically stop and preview the movie. It's also a good idea to periodically save your document. In fact, you should always save the Flash document before previewing. That way, if there happen to be any problems, it's an easy matter of restoring the file from the last-saved version. To preview your Flash SWF file with the publishing format and settings you've selected, you can use the Publish Preview command. This command exports the file and opens the preview within the default browser.

Preview a Movie

1. Click the **File** menu, point to **Publish Preview**, and then select from the following options:

   ◆ **Default (HTML).** Select this option to display the Flash document within an HTML document.

   ◆ **Flash.** Select this option to create and play a Flash .swf file.

   ◆ **HTML.** Same as Default (HTML).

   ◆ **GIF.** Select this option to create a GIF version of the currently selected frame in the Timeline.

   ◆ **JPEG.** Select this option to create a JPEG version of the currently selected frame in the Timeline.

   ◆ **PNG.** Select this option to create a PNG version of the currently selected frame in the Timeline.

   ◆ **Projector.** Select this option to display the Flash document in a self-contained projector file.

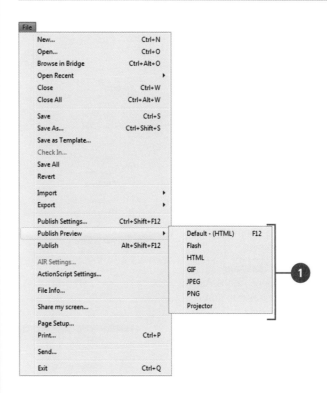

For Your Information

Changing Magnification in Flash Player

In the Flash Player, you can increase or decrease the magnification of the current Flash movie (SWF), as well as play, rewind, step forward, or step back. To zoom in or out in a browser, press Control+click (Mac) or right-click (Win) anywhere in the movie window, and then click Zoom In or Zoom Out. Click Show All to see the entire Flash movie.

Testing a Movie

As you work, you should periodically stop and test your movie as a Flash SWF. The Test command allows you to quickly see your movie on different devices and players—Flash Professional, Device Central (**New!**) or Air Debug Launcher (Desktop or Mobile) (**New!**)—without leaving the program. The Test command tests the movie based on the current test option. Flash uses the document type the default until you change it. Each time you test your movie as an SWF, Flash creates a log entry in the SWF History in the Property Inspector (**New!**). The SWF History shows you the difference in file size between the different tests. If there is over a 50% increase in size, a warning icon appears next to the log entry. In the SWF History, you can view or clear the log entries.

Test a Movie and View a SWF History

1 Click the **Control** menu, and then point to **Test Movie**.

2 Select the option where you want to test your movie:

- **in Flash Professional.** Plays the movie in a separate window in Flash Professional.

- **in Device Central.** Opens Adobe Device Central CS5 and displays the movie.

- **in Air Debug Launcher (Desktop).** Opens Adobe Air Player for the desktop and displays the movie.

- **in Air Debug Launcher (Mobile).** Opens Adobe Air Player for mobile devices and displays the movie.

- **Test.** Performs a test with the currently selected test option.

TIMESAVER *Press Ctrl+Enter (Win) or ⌘+Return (Mac).*

3 To view and work with the SWF History log, click the **Window** menu, and then click **Properties** to open the Property Inspector.

- **Clear the SWF History.** Click the **Clear** button.

- **View the SWF History Log.** Click the **Log** button.

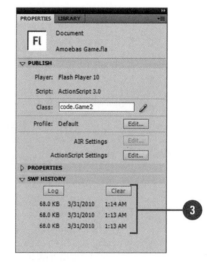

Using the Bandwidth Profiler

To view the performance of a Flash document using a graph, use the Bandwidth Profiler. The Bandwidth Profiler displays how much data is sent for each frame in the active Flash document, according to the speed you specify. The Bandwidth Profiler has two windows. The left window shows information about the active document and the current download settings, and the right window displays information about each frame in the document. In addition, the Bandwidth Profiler lets you view how the page loads, based on a specific bandwidth. For example, you could specify to load the Flash document using a speed of 28.8Kbps. To maintain an accurate download test, the Bandwidth Profiler compensates for added compression support applied to SWF files, which reduces the file size and improves streaming performance.

Use the Bandwidth Profiler

1. Click the **Control** menu, point to **Test Movie**, and then click **Test**.

2. Click the **View** menu, and then click **Bandwidth Profiler**.

3. Click the **View** menu, point to **Download Settings**, and then select from the available bandwidth options, or click **Customize**, and then create a user-defined setting.

4. Click the **View** menu, and then click **Simulate Download**.

    This tests the load of the Flash movie against the current settings.

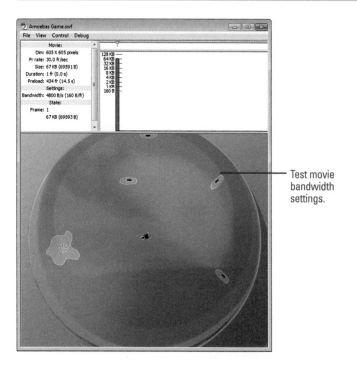

Test movie bandwidth settings.

Exporting a Movie to Different Formats

Flash can export an entire movie or frame to several different formats that are not included in the Publish Settings dialog box. These formats include Adobe FXG, Bitmap, JPEG Image or Sequence, GIF Image or Sequence, PNG Image or Sequence, Quick Time (MOV), Animated GIF, Windows AVI, and WAV (for Windows only). When you export a movie or image (frame), some file formats require you to select additional format specific options, such as resolution (dots per inch) and number of colors or color bit depth, to complete the operation. To set the resolution to match your monitor, select Match Screen.

Export a Movie Frame to Different Formats

1. Open a document.

2. Select a frame you want to export in the Timeline.

3. Click the **File** menu, point to **Export**, and then click **Export Image**.

4. Navigate to the location where you want to save the file.

5. Enter a name in the Save As (Mac) or File Name (Win) box.

6. Click the **Format** popup (Mac) or the **Save As Type** list arrow (Win), and then select a file format.

7. Click **Save**.

   Some file formats require you to select additional format specific options to complete the operation.

8. If a dialog box appears, select the options you want, and then click **OK**.

Available file formats

Options vary depending on export format

Export a Movie to Different Formats

1. Open a document.

2. Click the **File** menu, point to **Export**, and then click **Export Movie**.

   TIMESAVER *Press Option+Shift+⌥⌘+S (Mac) or Ctrl+Alt+Shift+S (Win) to export a movie.*

3. Navigate to the location where you want to save the file.

4. Enter a name in the Save As (Mac) or File Name (Win) box.

5. Click the **Format** popup (Mac) or the **Save As Type** list arrow (Win), and then select a file format.

6. Click **Save**.

   Some file formats require you to select additional format specific options to complete the operation.

7. If a dialog box appears, select the options you want.

8. Click **OK** or **Export**.

   When you export a movie, Flash creates a separate file for each frame of the movie and numbers them in sequential order.

Printing from the Flash Player

In your browser, you can press Control+click (Mac) or right-click (Win) a Flash movie in a Flash Player to display a contextual, or shortcut, menu. The menu contains Flash Player related commands, such as Print. You can give viewers the option to print some, or all of your movie. By default, the Print command prints every frame in the movie unless you restrict printing to specific frames by labeling them as printable in the Flash document before you publish it. You label frames as printable by typing #p in the Frame box of the Property Inspector. By default, the movie's Stage size determines the print area.

Label Frames as Printable and Print from the Flash Player

① Open a document.

② Select the frames or keyframes in the Timeline you want to label as printable.

③ Type **#p** in the Frame box in the Property Inspector.

④ Repeat steps 2 and 3 for each keyframe you want to label as printable.

⑤ Publish your movie using the Publish command on the File menu, and then view it in your browser using the Flash Player.

⑥ Press Control+click (Mac) or right-click (Win) anywhere in the movie window, and then click **Print**.

#p appears in the selected frames.

Did You Know?

You can disable printing from the Flash Player. Open the Flash document, select a frame in the Timeline, open the Frame Property Inspector, and then type **!#p** in the Label box.

You can disable the contextual menu in the Flash Player. Click the File menu, click Publish Settings, click the HTML tab, clear the Display Menu check box, and then click OK.

For Your Information

Printing with ActionScript

You can also print with ActionScript using the following commands: print (target, bounding box), printasBitmap (target, bounding box), or Printjob class. The target is the Movie Clip Timeline (or specific frames) and bounding box is bmovie (frame with a #b used as print area), bframe (each frame used as print area), or bmax (one big print area).

Working with Projects and Other Programs

Introduction

Adobe programs are designed to work together so you can focus on what you need to do, rather than on how to do it. In fact, the Adobe programs share tools and features for your most common tasks so you can work uninterrupted and move seamlessly from one program to another.

If you need more advanced scripting features, you can use Adobe Flash Builder to work with ActionScript 3.0, yet still quickly switch back to Flash Professional as needed. As a designer, you can use the Adobe FXG file format to exchange graphic content between programs with high fidelity, which includes Fireworks, Photoshop CS5, Illustrator, Flash Catalyst, and Flash Builder. If you want to create a stand-alone application from a Flash document, you can publish it as an Adobe AIR application, which you can install or remove like any other program. In addition to developing content for computers, you can also use Flash to develop content for mobile devices using Adobe Device Central CS5 to test it.

In Flash, you can manage multiple document files within a Flash Project. A Flash Projects lets you group multiple, and related files together to help you keep track of complex applications. Flash lets you apply version-control to ensure that the correct file versions are used during editing and to prevent accidental overwriting.

If you want to access additional resources from Adobe, you can use the Adobe CS Live menu. Adobe CS Live is an online service that allows you to set up or manage (sign in and out) an Adobe account, access the Acrobat.com subscription-based Web site or the Adobe ConnectNow Web site (Share my screen command) where you can collaborate with others, display CS news and resources, and access an Adobe Web site with information about CS Live Services.

What You'll Do

Work with Adobe Flash Builder

Exchange Content with Adobe FXG

Create an Adobe AIR Application

Create Content for a Mobile Device

Map MIDI Sounds on a Mobile Device

Create and Manage a Project

Manage Project Files

Test a Project

Send a Document Using E-Mail

Explore CS Live Services

Share My Screen

Use Adobe Extension Manager

Working with Adobe Flash Builder

Adobe Flash Builder 4 (formerly Adobe Flex Builder) is a stand-alone program or plug-in that allows you to develop cross-platform Web applications using the Flex framework, which includes compilers, component library, and debuggers. You can use Flash Builder to work with UI layouts and behaviors, and ActionScript 3.0. With Flash Builder 4 and Flash Professional CS5 installed, you can open Flash FLA files and edit ActionScript 3.0 in Flash Builder (**New!**) and test, debug, or publish in Flash Professional. You can also create or open ActionScript 3.0 AS files (either class or interface) (**New!**) from Flash Professional for edit in Flash Builder.

Create an ActionScript File and Open in Flash Builder

1. Click the **File** menu, and then click **New**.

   TIMESAVER *Click Action-Script 3.0 Class or ActionScript 3.0 Interface on the Welcome screen to create a new AS document.*

2. Click the **General** tab.

3. Click **ActionScript 3.0 Class** or **ActionScript 3.0 Interface**.

4. Click **OK**.

5. Click the **Flash Professional** or **Flash Builder** option.

6. Enter a class or interface name.

7. Click **OK**.

   If you selected Flash Builder, the program opens, asking you to create a new Flash project.

8. Click **Browse**, select the target FLA or XFL file, and then click **Open**.

9. Click **Finish**.

10. Edit the code in Flash Builder.

11. To publish, test, or debug back in Flash Professional, click the **Publish**, **Test Movie**, or **Debug Movie** button on the toolbar.

12. When you're done, exit Flash Builder.

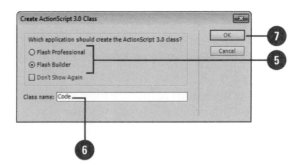

Open Flash or ActionScript Files in Flash Builder

1. In Flash, open the Flash FLA or ActionScript AS document.

2. Do the following to open a Flash or ActionScript file:

   ◆ **Flash FLA.** Open the Property Inspector, enter a document class name in the Property Inspector if blank, and then click the **Edit Class Definition** button.

   ◆ **ActionScript AS.** Control+click (Mac) or right-click (Win) a symbol associated with the class interface, click **Properties**, or click the **Edit Class Definition** button in the Symbols Properties dialog box.

3. If prompted, click the **Flash Professional** or **Flash Builder** option, if prompted, and then click **OK**.

4. If prompted, click **Browse** to select the target FLA or XFL file (as needed), and then click **Finish**.

5. Edit the code in Flash Builder.

6. To publish, test, or debug back in Flash Professional, click the **Publish**, **Test Movie**, or **Debug Movie** button on the toolbar.

   When you close the tested or debugged movie window in Flash, it switches back to Flash Builder.

7. When you're done, exit Flash Builder.

Exchanging Content with Adobe FXG

Adobe FXG (Flash XML Graphics) is a file format based on a subset of MXML, the XML-based programming language used by the Flex framework, which you can use to build rich Internet applications. The FXG file format allows designers to exchange graphic content between programs with full fidelity. Flash allows you to import and export your individual objects or the entire Stage in the Adobe FXG file format (version 2.0) (**New!**). You can use the FXG file format in other Adobe programs for export (Fireworks, Photoshop CS5, and Illustrator) or for import and export (Flash Catalyst and Flash Builder). When you export vector and bitmap graphics, a separate folder is created to store the images along with the FXG file. Elements without a recognizable tag (such as some blends, gradients, masks, and 3D) are exported as bitmap graphics.

Import Content From an Adobe FXG File

1. Open a document.

2. Click the **File** menu, point to **Import**, and then click **Import to Stage** or **Import to Library**.

3. To open a specific type of Flash file, click the **File as type** list arrow (Win), or the **File type** popup (Mac), and then click **Adobe FXG (*.fxg)**.

4. Navigate to the drive or folder where the file is located.

5. Click the Adobe FXG graphic file you want to open.

6. Click **Open**.

Export Content as an Adobe FXG File

1 Open a Flash document.

2 To export objects on the Stage, select them on the Stage.

3 Click the **File** menu, point to **Export**, and then click **Export Image** (for entire Stage) or **Export Selection** (for selected objects on the Stage).

4 Navigate to the location where you want to export the file.

5 Enter a name in the Save As (Mac) or File Name (Win) box.

6 Click the **Format** popup (Mac) or **Save as Type** list arrow (Win), and then click **Adobe FXG (*.FXG)**.

7 Click **Save**.

The following constrains apply to exporting to the FXG file format:

◆ **Scale-9 Grids.** Exported, however only readable by Adobe Illustrator.

◆ **Sound and Video.** Not exported.

◆ **Components.** Not exported.

◆ **Tweens and Animation with Multiple Frame.** Not exported; however a selected frame can be exported as an object.

◆ **Embedded Fonts.** Not exported.

◆ **Button Symbols.** Exports only the Up state of buttons.

◆ **3D Properties.** Not exported.

◆ **Inverse Kinematics (IK) Properties.** Not exported.

◆ **Text Attributes.** Some attributes not exported.

For Your Information

Using Adobe Flash Catalyst

Adobe Flash Catalyst CS5 (**New!**) is a stand-alone professional interaction design tool for rapidly creating expressive interfaces and interactive content without writing code. Create interactive proto-types, portfolios, product guides, microsites, site navigation, and interfaces. You can transform artwork created in Adobe Illustrator, Photoshop, and Fireworks into interactive designs. For example, you can create screen designs or graphics in Illustrator, open the art-work in Flash Catalyst, and add interactive components to it, yet still maintain the ability to make changes back in Illustrator without affecting the Flash Catalyst content. For more information about Flash Catalyst and where to get it, go to *http://labs.adobe.com/technologies/flashcatalyst*.

Creating an Adobe AIR Application

Adobe AIR is a cross-operating system runtime that allows you to leverage your existing web development skills in Flash to build and deliver Rich Internet Applications (RIAs) to more devices, including the web, mobile, and desktop. You can create a new Flash file for AIR from the Welcome page or the New dialog box by clicking Adobe AIR 2 (**New!**), or use an existing Flash file (ActionScript 3.0), and then convert it to an Adobe AIR file through the Publish Settings dialog box (**New!**). Before you can publish a file to Adobe AIR, you need to have a digital certificate that represents the application publisher's identify. After you publish an AIR application, you can install it by using the Installer Package with the AIR extension and start the program like any other program on your system. When you no longer want to use it, you can remove it like a normal program too.

Create a New Adobe AIR Document

1. Click the **File** menu, and then click **New**.

   TIMESAVER *Click Adobe AIR 2 on the Welcome screen to create a new blank document.*

2. Click the **General** tab.

3. Click **Adobe AIR 2**.

4. Click **OK**.

5. Create your application in Flash.

6. Click the **File** menu, and then click **Adobe AIR 2 Settings**.

7. Click the **General, Signature, Icons**, and **Advanced** tabs to select or create a digital certificate and other AIR publishing settings.

8. Click **Publish**, and then click **OK**.

See Also

See "Specifying Adobe AIR Options" on page 482 for more information on specific publishing settings.

Install and Start an Adobe AIR Application

1. In Windows Explorer (Win) or Finder (Mac), navigate to the folder with the published AIR application.

2. Double-click the installer program for the AIR application (.air), and then follow the installer instructions.

3. Use the Start menu or Windows Explorer (Win) or Finder (Mac) to start the AIR application.

4. To remove the AIR application, use the Uninstall a program link in the Control panel (Win) or drag the application folder to the Trash can (Mac).

Did You Know?

You can access gesture events in ActionScript. Adobe's AIR 2.0, built on the same technology framework as Flash, introduces a new set of events that detect when you touch the screen called gestures. Gestures can also be used in the new Flash iPhone Packager.

Digital certificate file

Creating Content for a Mobile Device

Flash content deployment is expanding from the Web to other mediums, such as cell phones, PDAs, and other mobile devices. In conjunction with Adobe Device Central CS5, Flash allows you to create and test content for mobile devices. You can use the New Document dialog box to create a blank Flash document for mobile devices using Adobe Device Central. Flash uses the right settings from Device Central to create the content you want. To display content on mobile devices, Flash uses Flash Lite, a specialized player for mobile devices. After you create your mobile content, you can test it using Adobe Device Central and Flash Lite.

Create a Document for a Mobile Device

1. Click the **File** menu, and then click **New**.

2. Click the **General** tab

3. Click **Adobe Device Central**.

4. Click **OK**.

   Adobe Device Central CS5 opens, where you can select the device and any options you want.

5 Select the device you want and check the device profile for support and compatibility issues.

6 Click **Create**.

The new document appears in Flash, where you can develop your content.

Device Library tab with device information

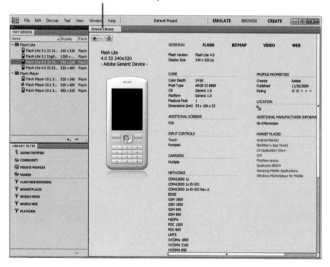

Mapping MIDI Sounds on a Mobile Device

Every day the world is getting smaller, and mobile devices are getting smaller, and smarter. Using Flash, you can include event sounds when creating documents for playback on mobile devices. Flash does not support sound file formats used for mobile devices (such as MIDI and others); when authoring for mobile devices, you must temporarily place a proxy sound in a supported format such as MP3 or WAV in the Flash document. The proxy sound in the document is then mapped to an external mobile device sound, such as a MIDI file. During the document publishing process, the proxy sound is replaced with the linked external sound. The SWF file generated contains the external sound and uses it for playback with Flash Lite on a mobile device. Flash Lite is the Flash Player for mobile devices.

Map MIDI Sounds on a Mobile Device

1. Click the **File** menu, point to **Import**, click **Import to Library**, and then import one or more sounds into the Flash Library.

2. Control+click (Mac) or right-click (Win) the sound you want to work with, and then click **Properties**.

3. Enter a path to the location where the mobile device sound is located.

4. Click **OK**.

5. Add a button instance to the Stage.

   IMPORTANT *You can use a pre-made Flash button. Click the Window menu, point to Common Libraries, and then click Buttons.*

6. Open the button in the Library, and then add the linked sound to the Hit frame of the button.

7. Click the **File** menu, and then click **Publish Settings**.

8 Click the **Flash** tab.

9 Click the **Player** list arrow, click **Flash Lite 1.x** thru **3.x** (ActionScript 1.0 or 2.0) or **Flash Lite 4.x** (ActionScript 3.0), and then select the ActionScript version you want, if necessary.

The Export device sounds option is automatically selected.

Flash Lite is a player for mobile devices.

10 Click **OK**.

The SWF file now contains the linked mobile device sound.

11 Click the **Control** menu, point to **Test Movie**, and then click **in Device Central**.

When you execute a Flash document using Flash Lite, Flash opens Adobe Device Central CS5 to emulate the display with the currently selected mobile device.

When Adobe Device Central CS5 opens, its displays an emulator of the currently selected mobile device, or asks you to select one.

12 If necessary, select the device you want and check the device profile for support and compatibility issues.

13 Use the Device Central controls to test out your Flash document on the mobile device.

The mobile device sound has been modified to emulate the Flash .swf file sound.

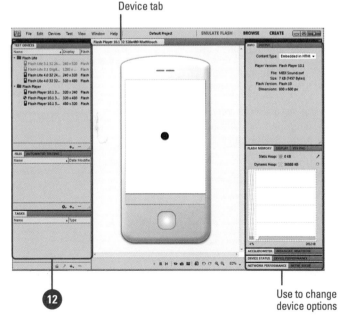

Device tab

Use to change device options

Creating and Managing a Project

In Flash, you can manage multiple document files within a Flash Project. A Flash Projects lets you group multiple, and related files together to help you keep track of complex applications. Flash lets you apply version-control to ensure that the correct file versions are used during editing and to prevent accidental overwriting. A Flash Project is essentially a collection of any Flash or other file types, including Flash SWF and FLA files and even other Flash projects. When you open an existing project, the Project panel gives you instant access to all the various parts of the project. The Flash Project panel is used to create and manage projects. The Project panel displays the contents of a Flash Project using a collapsible tree structure. Flash limits you to opening or creating one project at a time. Any changes made to the project are automatically saved to the project file, so it's not necessary to perform a Save operation.

Create and Manage a Project

1. Click the **Window** menu, point to **Other Panels**, and then click **Project** to open the Project panel.

   ◆ **Quick Project.** You can create a quick project. A quick project is based on the currently open FLA file. Click the **Projects** list arrow in the Project panel, and then click **Quick Project**.

2. Click the **Projects** list arrow, and then click **New Project**.

3. Name the new project, locate and select a root folder location for the project file, and then click **OK**.

   Any folders in the selected root folder appear in the Project panel.

4. Click the **ActionScript version** list arrow, and then click **ActionScript 3.0** or **ActionScript 2.0**.

5. Click **Create Project**.

Did You Know?

You can open a project. Click the Projects list arrow in the Project panel, and then click Open Project, browse to the project folder, and then click OK.

6 Manage a project using any of the following options:

- ◆ **Add Folder.** Click the **New Folder** button, type the folder name, and then click **Create Folder**.

- ◆ **Delete Folder.** Select the folder, click the **Delete** button to delete a selected project asset.

- ◆ **Close Project.** Click the **Options** menu, and then click **Close Project**.

- ◆ **Delete Project.** Open the project, click the **Options** menu, and then click **Delete Project**. Select a delete content option, and then click **Yes**.

- ◆ **Rename Project.** Click the **Options** menu, click **Rename Project**, type a name, and then click **OK**.

- ◆ **Switch Open Projects.** Click the **Project** list arrow, and then click the open project name.

- ◆ **Project Properties.** Click the **Options** menu, click **Project Properties**, specify options on the different tabs (Classes, Locations, and Paths), and then click **OK**.

7 Click the **Close** button on the Project panel.

Did You Know?

You can convert previous projects to the new project format. In previous versions of Flash, projects used an XML file with a .FLP extension. To convert it, simply open it in Flash CS4. Open the Project panel, click the Project list arrow, click Open Project, navigate to the folder with the project, and then click OK.

Project name

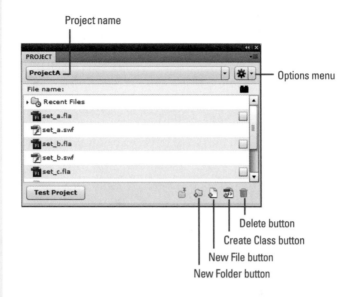

Options menu

Delete button
Create Class button
New File button
New Folder button

Create a new folder

New folder   **7**

Project files

Managing Project Files

A project is a collection of files that you can manage directly from Flash. The Project panel displays files by filename extension. By default, the Project panel only shows Flash documents type (FLA, SWF, SWC, AS, JSFL, ASC, MXML). If you want to display other types, you can change settings in Panel Preferences. You can also hide files or folder by preceding the file or folder name with a special character, such as an underscore, and enabling the option in Panel Preferences. When you work with the same project, the Project Panel shows all recently opened files in the Recent Files folder for easy access. You can create files, including Flash and ActionScript, from the Project panel.

Manage Project Files

1. Click the **Window** menu, point to **Other Panels**, and then click **Project** to open the Project panel.

2. Manage files using any of the following options:

   ◆ Create File. Select the folder where you want the file (no selection is the root), click the **New File** button, enter a name, select a file type, and then click **Create File**.

   ◆ Open File. Double-click the file in the Project panel.

   ◆ Delete File. Select the file, click the **Delete** button, and then click **Yes** to delete a selected project asset.

   ◆ Publish. Select or clear the file check box on the right to add or remove the file to/from the publishing list.

   ◆ Pin a Directory. Select a folder, and then click the **Pin Directory** button; click again to unpin.

3. Click the **Close** button on the Project panel.

Options menu

Delete button

New File button

Options menu

Panel Preferences

Did You Know?

You can clear the Recent Files list. In the Project panel, click the Options menu, and then click Clear Recent Files.

Change Project Properties

1. In the Project panel, click the **Options** menu, and then click **Project Properties**.

2. Click any of the following tabs:

   ◆ **Classes.** Specify the ActionScript version, and class file folder locations.

   ◆ **Locations.** Specify additional source folder locations.

   ◆ **Paths.** Specify the location Flex SDK files for use in Flash to create skins and other visual elements in Flex.

3. Click **OK**.

Change Panel Preferences

1. In the Project panel, click the **Options** menu, and then click **Panel Preferences**.

2. Click any of the following tabs:

   ◆ **Classes.** Specify the ActionScript version, and class file folder locations.

   ◆ **Settings.** Change defaults filters, hide files or folders based on the name, and show or hide classes folder, hidden files, or recent files.

   ◆ **Locations.** Specify additional source folder locations.

3. Click **OK**.

Testing a Project

A project is a collection of files that constitute a complex project. For example, you can create a Flash project that contains 5 Flash documents, with interactive buttons on the pages to call the other pages. If all of the FLA files are located within the same project, it's an easy matter to test the entire project. You must first select one of the files as the main file, and then simply click the Test Project button. Flash will automatically publish all of the Flash documents in the project, display the main file, and then allow you to test its operation. It's that simple.

Test a Project

1. Click the **Window** menu, point to **Other Panels**, and then click **Project** to open the Project panel.

2. If the project you want to test is not open, click the **Project** list arrow, click **Open Project** in the Project panel, and then select the appropriate file.

3. Click **Open**.

   IMPORTANT *Since testing a project involves moving among different Flash movies, your published documents will have to have interactive buttons linked to all the other pages within the project, or the test will not work.*

4. Right-click (Win) or Control-click (Mac) one of the FLA or HTML files in the project.

5. Click **Make Default Document** from the available options.

6. Click **Test Project**.

See Also

See Chapter 17, "Debugging a Movie" on page 409 for more information on how to perform debugging operations on a running Flash movie.

Project comes up to test.

Sending a Document Using E-Mail

After you finish making changes to a document, you can quickly send it to another person for review using e-mail. Flash allows you to send documents out for review as an attachment using e-mail from within the program so that you do not have to open your e-mail program. An e-mail program needs to be installed on your computer before you begin. When you send your document out for review, reviewers can add comments and then send it back to you.

Send an Office Document Using E-Mail

1. Click the **File** menu, and then click **Send**.

   ◆ If prompted, click **Yes** to save your Flash document.

   IMPORTANT *To complete the following steps, you need to have an e-mail program installed on your computer and an e-mail account set-up.*

   Your default e-mail program opens with your document attached.

2. Enter your recipients and subject (appears with document name by default).

3. Enter a message for your reviewer with instructions.

4. Click the **Send** button.

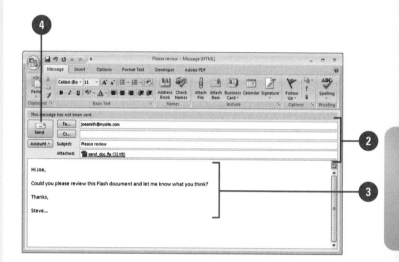

Exploring CS Live Services

Adobe CS Live (**New!**) is an online service that allows you to set up or manage (sign in and out) an Adobe account, review CS5 documents (Illustrator, InDesign, and Photoshop) online, access the Acrobat.com subscription-based Web site or the Adobe ConnectNow Web site where you can collaborate with others, display CS news and resources in a panel within CS5 programs, and access an Adobe Web site with information about CS Live Services. You can access these options directly from the CS Live menu on the right side of the menu bar next to the Search bar. When the CS Live menu icon includes a bulls eye, you are signed in to the online services.

Explore CS Live Services

1. Click the **CS Live** menu (**New!**), and then select any of the following commands:

   - **Set Up Your Access To Adobe CS Live Online Services, Sign In**, or **Sign Out.** Select to set up, sign in, or sign out of the CS Live online service.

   - **Create New Review** or **Learn More.** Creates a CS5 document review in Illustrator, InDesign, or Photoshop.

   - **Acrobat.com Home.** Opens the Acrobat.com subscription-based Web site that allows you to work and collaborate with others.

   - **Share My Screen.** Opens the Adobe ConnectNow Web site where you can start an online meeting and collaborate on any design project across platforms and programs.

   - **CS News and Resources.** Opens the CS News and Resources panel with news and resources from Adobe.

   - **Manage My Account.** Opens a secure Web site with your Adobe account information after you sign in.

   - **Explore CS Live Services.** Opens an Adobe Web site that describes CS Live Services.

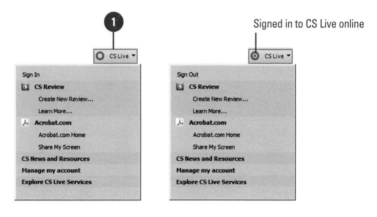

Signed in to CS Live online

Sign In to Adobe CS Live

Sharing My Screen

The Share My Screen command on the File or CS Live (**New!**) menu allows you to connect to Adobe ConnectNow, which is a secure Web site where you can start an online meeting and collaborate on any design project across platforms and programs. You can share and annotate your computer screen or take control of an attendee's computer. During the meeting, you can communicate by sending chat messages, using live audio, or broadcasting live video. In addition, you can take meeting notes, and share files.

Share My Screen

1. Click the **File** or **CS Live** menu, and then click **Share my screen**.

2. Enter your Adobe ID and password.

   ◆ If you don't have an Adobe ID and password, click the Create a Free Adobe ID link, and then follow the online instructions.

3. Click **Sign In**.

   ◆ If prompted, sign in to ConnectNow.

4. To share your computer screen, click the **Share My Computer Screen** button.

5. Use the ConnectNow toolbar to do any of the following:

   ◆ **Meeting.** Use to invite participants, share my computer screen, upload a file, share my webcam, set preferences, end a meeting, and exit Adobe ConnectNow.

   ◆ **PODS.** Use to show and hide pod panels.

   ◆ **Help.** Use to get help, troubleshoot problems, and set account and Flash Player settings.

6. Click the participant buttons at the bottom to specify roles, remove a user, or request control of a user's computer.

Using Adobe Extension Manager

The Adobe Extension Manager is a program you can use to install and delete added program functionality, known as extensions, to many Adobe programs. The Extension Manager is automatically installed when you install Flash, Dreamweaver, InDesign, or Fireworks. You can use the Extension Manager to access the Adobe Exchange site, where you can locate, research, and download many different types of extensions. Some are free and some are not. After you download an extension, you can use Extension Manager to install it. Extension Manager only displays extensions installed using the Extension Manager; other extensions installed using a third-party installer might not appear. After you install an extension, you can find and display information about it.

Download and Install an Extension

1. Start Adobe Extension Manager from the Start menu (Win) or the Applications folder (Mac).

   TIMESAVER *In Flash, Dreamweaver, InDesign, or Fireworks, click the Help menu, and then click Manage Extensions.*

2. Click the **Exchange** button on the toolbar.

3. Select the extension you want to download, and then save it to your computer.

4. In Extension Manager, click the **Install** button on the toolbar.

5. Locate and select the extension (.mxp) you want to install, and then click **Install**.

6. You can perform any of the following:

   ◆ **Sort.** Click a column heading.

   ◆ **Enable or Disable.** Select or clear the check in the **Enabled** check box next to the extension.

   ◆ **Remove.** Select the extension, and then click **Remove.**

7. When you're done, click the **Close** button in the Extension Manager window.

Extensions for the selected CS program

Adobe CS programs

Downloaded extension

New! Features

Adobe Flash Professional CS5

Adobe Flash Professional CS5 means superior results faster, with new features and enhancements that help you create and manage your images more easily and efficiently. The indispensable new and improved features help graphic web designers, photographers, and video professionals create the highest quality images, with the control, flexibility, and capabilities that you expect from the professional standards in desktop digital imaging.

Each new release of Flash brings with it new features, improvements, and added sophistication. This edition is aimed at the Web designer, interactive media professional, or subject matter expert developing multimedia content, and the application developer.

Only New Features

If you're already familiar with Flash CS4, you can access and download all the tasks in this book with Adobe Flash CS5 New Features to help make your transition to the new version simple and smooth. The Flash CS5 New Features as well as other Flash CS4 to Flash CS5 transition helpers are available on the Web at *www.perspection.com*.

What's New

If you're searching for what's new in Flash CS5, just look for the icon: New!. The new icon appears in the table of contents and throughout this book, so you can quickly and easily identify a new or improved feature in Flash CS5. The following is a brief description of each new feature and its location in this book.

Flash Professional CS5

◆ **Adobe CS Live (p. 4, 522)** Adobe CS Live is an online service that allows you to set up or manage an Adobe account, and access an Adobe Web site with CS Live online services. You can access these options directly from the CS Live menu on the right side of the menu bar next to the Search bar.

◆ **Welcome Screen (p. 5)** You can work in other programs as Flash starts up. When you start Flash, the Welcome screen no longer stays in front, so you can work in other programs

- **Packaging Applications for the iPhone (p. 12, 385-408)** Flash includes a packager for iPhone that allows Flash files to be deployed as iPhone applications.

- **Templates (p. 13)** Flash includes a range of new templates that make it easier to create common types of projects in Flash. The templates appear in the Welcome screen and the New Document dialog.

- **XFL File Format (p. 14, 20-21)** Flash FLA files now contain a new internal format called XFL (eXtensible Form Language). This new format is based on XML. The new format enables better exchange of data with other Adobe applications, and allows you to optionally work in uncompressed XFL format.

- **Uncompressed XFL File Format (p. 20-21)** The uncompressed XFL file format allows you to see each of the separate parts, or sub-files, that make up a Flash file. This enables working in team environments with source control systems.

- **Adobe Community Help (p. 24-25)** When you start Flash Help, the Adobe Community Help window opens, displaying help categories and topics. You can search product help from Local Help, Community Help, or Adobe.com by using keywords or phrases or browsing through a list of categories and topics.

- **Adobe Updater (p. 26-27)** The Adobe Updater Preferences dialog box allows you to set update options for Flash and other installed Adobe products, such as Bridge. You can also set an option to have Adobe notify you of updates in the menu bar.

- **Text Layout Framework (TLF) (p. 62, 163, 165-179, 182, 184)** The TLF text engine provides significantly improved control over text properties and flow. You can create columns, rotate text, indent text, change text direction and orientation, change text case, adjust the text baseline, and apply text blending and color effects in the Property Inspector.

- **SWF Size History (p. 65, 500)** The Document Property inspector now displays the size of all SWF files generated during Test Movie, Publish, a Debug Movie operations.

- **Font Embedding (p. 65, 184-185)** Font embedding is FLA file based instead of text object based. The Font Embedding dialog box provides quick access to all font embedding functions.

- **Info Panel (p. 88)** The Info panel displays live values while you draw, move, or resize an object.

- **Color Panel (p. 98, 105)** The Color panel displays HSB values and changes gradient flow options.

- **Decorative Drawing Tool Effects (p. 109)** Several new effects have been added to the Decorative Drawing tool. You can use brushes to draw buildings, flames, lightning, trees, and other animations.

- **Edit with Photoshop CS5 (p. 208)** You can perform round-trip editing of bitmap graphics in Photoshop CS5.

- **Spring Properties for IK Bones (p. 292-293)** Strength and Damping properties enable IK bones to display realistic physical effects in bone animation.

◆ **Skins (p. 327)** The The Video Import Wizard includes additional skins for the FLVPlayback component.

◆ **FLVPlayback Live Preview on Stage (p. 328-329)** When you import a video, Flash places the video on the Stage with the first frame and playback controls at the bottom. You can use the playback controls on the Stage to play and work with the video.

◆ **Components Inspector Panel (p. 328-329, 428-431)** Component parameters are no longer available in the Parameters tab of the Components Inspector panel. The parameter options are available in the Property Inspector.

◆ **Video Cue Points (p. 332-333)** With Flash video, you can create and manage ActionScript cue points in the Properties panel. A cue point is a marked moment in time within a video clip.

◆ **Auto Close-Bracket Insertion (p. 348-349, 371)** When you type an open bracket { in the Actions panel or Script window, Flash automatically adds the corresponding close bracket } to save you time writing code and debugging.

◆ **Code Snippets Panel (p. 349, 372-373, 412)** The Code Snippets panel allows non-programmers to apply ActionScript 3.0 code for common interactions without learning ActionScript.

◆ **Flash Builder Workflows (p. 349, 506-507)** Flash Professional CS5 and Flash Builder 4 work together to make it easier to work with ActionScript code.

◆ **Flash Player Detection (p. 368, 487)** Flash uses SWObject2 for version detection and embedding SWF into Web pages.

◆ **Code Hinting for Custom Classes (p. 370-371)** Code hinting is enabled for custom ActionScript 3.0 classes in addition to the built-in classes. Flash also automatically imports custom classes you use.

◆ **Compiler Errors Panel (p. 418-419)** When a problem is encountered, Flash displays the location and description of the warnings and errors in the Compiler Errors panel, where you can show or hide warnings or errors, scroll through each one, and display/highlight them in the code.

◆ **Reorganized AIR Publishing Settings (p. 482-483, 510-511)** The AIR Application & Installer Settings dialog box has been reorganized for simpler, easier access to the many settings required when publishing for Adobe AIR.

◆ **Test Movie (p. 500)** The Test command allows you to quickly see your movie on different devices and players—Flash Professional, Device Central or Air Debug Launcher (Desktop or Mobile)—without leaving the program.

◆ **FXG File Format (p. 508-509)** The FXG file format allows Flash to exchange graphics with other Adobe applications with full fidelity.

◆ **Motion Objects JSAPIs** Several new JavaScript APIs have been added for manipulating motion tweens in the Flash Professional CS5 authoring environment.

What Happen To ...

◆ **Screen-based Flash Documents**   Flash CS5 can no longer open or create Screen-based Flash documents. All JavaScript API related to screens have been removed.

◆ **Version Cue**   Version Cue is not available in Flash CS5. If you want to work with a common set of files in a collaborative environment, please use a 3rd party source control solution.

◆ **Data Binding Components**   The ActionScript 2.0 Data components are no longer available in the Components panel.

◆ **Some File Formats**   Flash CS5 can no longer import FreeHand, PICT, PNTG, SGI and TGA files, and export EMF files, WMF files, WFM image sequences, BMP sequences, or TGA sequences.

◆ **Save and Compact Command**   Since the new default FLA file format contains XFL formatted data, the Save and Compact command is no longer necessary.

Adobe Certified Expert

About the Adobe Certified Expert (ACE) Program

The Adobe Certified Expert (ACE) program is for graphic designers, Web designers, systems integrators, value-added resellers, developers, and business professionals seeking official recognition of their expertise on Adobe products.

What Is an ACE?

An Adobe Certified Expert is an individual who has passed an Adobe Product Proficiency Exam for a specific Adobe software product. Adobe Certified Experts are eligible to promote themselves to clients or employers as highly skilled, expert-level users of Adobe software. ACE certification is a recognized worldwide standard for excellence in Adobe software knowledge. There are three levels of ACE certification: Single product certification, Specialist certification, and Master certification. To become an ACE, you must pass one or more product-specific proficiency exams and sign the ACE program agreement. When you become an ACE, you enjoy these special benefits:

- ◆ Professional recognition
- ◆ An ACE program certificate
- ◆ Use of the Adobe Certified Expert program logo

What Does This Logo Mean?

It means this book will prepare you fully for the Adobe Certified Expert exam for Adobe Flash Professional CS5. The certification exam has a set of objectives, which are organized into broader skill sets. The Adobe Certified Expert objectives and the specific pages throughout this book that cover the objectives are available on the Web at *www.perspection.com*.

 FL 3.1

Choosing a Certification Level

There are three levels of certification to become an Adobe Certified Expert.

◆ **Single product certification.** Recognizes your proficiency in a single Adobe product. To qualify as an ACE, you must pass one product-specific exam.

◆ **Specialist certification.** Recognizes your proficiency in multiple Adobe products with a specific medium: print, Web, or video. To become certified as a Specialist, you must pass the exams on the required products. To review the requirements, go online to *http://www.adobe.com/support/certification/ace_certify.html*.

◆ **Master certification.** Recognizes your skills in terms of how they align with the Adobe product suites. To become certified as a Master, you must pass the exam for each of the products in the suite.

Preparing for an Adobe Certified Expert Exam

Every Adobe Certified Expert Exam is developed from a list of objectives, which are based on studies of how an Adobe program is actually used in the workplace. The list of objectives determine the scope of each exam, so they provide you with the information you need to prepare for ACE certification. Follow these steps to complete the ACE Exam requirement:

1 Review and perform each task identified with a Adobe Certified Expert objective to confirm that you can meet the requirements for the exam.

2 Identify the topic areas and objectives you need to study, and then prepare for the exam.

3 Review the Adobe Certified Expert Program Agreement. To review it, go online to *http://www.adobe.com/support/certification/ace_certify.html*.

You will be required to accept the ACE agreement when you take the Adobe Certified Exam at an authorized testing center.

4 Register for the Adobe Certified Expert Exam.

ACE testing is offered at more than a thousand authorized Pearson VUE and Thomson Prometric testing centers in many countries. To find the testing center nearest you, go online to *www.pearsonvue.com/adobe* (for Pearson VUE) or *www.2test.com* (for Prometric). The ACE exam fee is US$150 worldwide. When contacting an authorized training center, provide them with the Adobe Product Proficiency exam name and number you want to take, which is available online in the Exam Bulletin at *http://www.adobe.com/support/certification/ ace_certify.html*.

5 Take the ACE exam.

Getting Recertified

For those with an ACE certification for a specific Adobe product, recertification is required of each ACE within 90 days of a designated ACE Exam release date. There are no restrictions on the number of times you may take the exam within a given period.

To get recertified, call Pearson VUE or Thomson Prometric. You will need to verify your previous certification for that product. If you are getting recertified, check with the authorized testing center for discounts.

Taking an Adobe Certified Expert Exam

The Adobe Certified Expert exams are computer-delivered, closed-book tests consisting of 60 to 90 multiple-choice questions. Each exam is approximately one to two hours long. A 15-minute tutorial will precede the test to familiarize you with the function of the Windows-based driver. The exams are currently available worldwide in English only. They are administered by Pearson VUE and Thomson Prometric, independent third-party testing companies.

Exam Results

At the end of the exam, a score report appears indicating whether you passed or failed the exam. Diagnostic information is included in your exam report. When you pass the exam, your score is electronically reported to Adobe. You will then be sent an ACE Welcome Kit and access to the ACE program logo in four to six weeks. You are also placed on the Adobe certification mailing list to receive special Adobe announcements and information about promotions and events that take place throughout the year.

When you pass the exam, you can get program information, check and update your profile, or download ACE program logos for your promotional materials online at:

http://www.adobe.com/support/certification/community.html

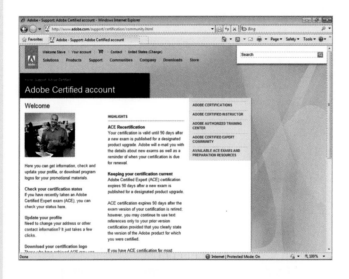

Getting More Information

To learn more about the Adobe Certified Expert program, read a list of frequently asked questions, and locate the nearest testing center, go online to:

http://www.adobe.com/support/certification/ace.html

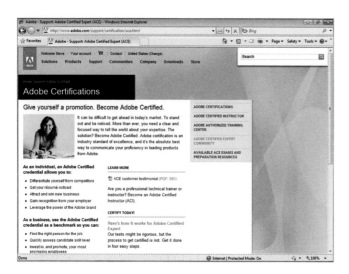

To learn more about other Adobe certification programs, go online to:

http://www.adobe.com/support/certification

Index